The Eastern Enlargement of the European Union

In May 2004, eight former Communist states in Central and Eastern Europe acceded to the European Union. The negotiation process took fifteen years and was arguably the most contentious in EU history.

This comprehensive volume examines the eastern expansion of the EU through a tripartite structure, developing an empirical, conceptual and institutional analysis to provide a rounded and substantive account of the largest and most challenging enlargement in EU history. Beginning with a foreword written by Pat Cox, who was President of the European Parliament during the final enlargement negotiations of 2002, John O'Brennan's new book explores and analyses:

- why the EU decided to expand its membership and the factors that drove this process forward;
- the key roles played by individual EU institutions, such as the Council, Commission and European Parliament, in the enlargement process;
- the relative importance of geopolitical, economic and normative factors in the EU's enlargement decisions.

This important volume will be of great interest to students and scholars of European politics and European Union studies.

John O'Brennan is IRCHSS Postdoctoral Research Fellow at the University of Limerick, Ireland.

Routledge Advances in European Politics

The Eastern Enlargement of the European Union

John O'Brennan

NEW YORK AND LONDON

First published 2006 by
Routledge
2 Park Square, Milton Park, Abingdon, Oxon OX14 4RN

Simultaneously published in the USA and Canada
by Routledge
270 Madison Avenue, New York, NY 10016

Routledge is an imprint of the Taylor & Francis Group, an informa business

© 2006 John O'Brennan

Typeset in by Baskerville by Bookcraft Ltd, Stroud, Gloucestershire
Printed and bound in Great Britain by Biddles Digital Ltd, King's Lynn

British Library Cataloguing in Publication Data
A catalogue record for this book is available from the British Library

Library of Congress Cataloging in Publication Data
A catalog record for this book has been requested

ISBN10: 0-415-36126-5 (hbk)
ISBN10: 0-203-00870-7 (ebk)

ISBN13: 978-0-415-36126-2 (hbk)
ISBN13: 978-0-203-00870-6 (ebk)

Contents

Tables

Foreword

Ours is an old continent but for the first time in history we have come together on a truly continental scale, not at the point of a sword nor through the barrel of an imperial nor ideological gun but by the free will of free and sovereign governments and peoples. Europe has reinvented itself successfully since the dark days of the Second World War. It has equipped itself with institutions and capacities that have proved enduring yet capable of change. Successive enlargements and Treaties, testament to the vitality of the idea and ideals of Europe, have widened and deepened the territorial and policy remit of the Union. Last year, 2004, was a highwater mark with the accession to full membership of ten new member states – Poland, Hungary, the Czech Republic, Slovakia, Slovenia, Estonia, Latvia, Lithuania, Cyprus and Malta – and the signing of the Constitutional Treaty in Rome.

I firmly believe that our continent, divided for decades by the Cold War, the Iron Curtain and the Berlin Wall, and faced by the Soviet threat, has taken a dramatic turn for the better. Whatever challenges the new order poses they are as nothing compared to the cost in human, economic and political terms of what went before. This coming together is not, however, simply an event but is, rather, a complex process of transformation, already long since engaged and set to continue. It is a story that deserves to be told, to be analysed, and to be understood. This text fulfils an important part of that mission and I congratulate its author Dr John O'Brennan and the publishers for their endeavours.

Particularly pleasing for someone like myself who has served as a Member of the European Parliament is the recognition in this book of the role played by the Parliament in the enlargement process. Too often, both in the academic and, more particularly, in the media communities this is the Cinderella of the European institutions. Its role, functions and influence have changed dramatically in recent years. First directly elected in 1979 it had a mandate but was in search of a mission.

The Parliament has become today a significant European legislator. During the last five years – 1999–2004 – 403 co-decision procedures have been concluded, establishing the European Parliament as a mature and reliable legislative partner with the Council of Ministers and the Commission on behalf of European citizens. This is an increase of 250 per cent over the previous five-year mandate and reflects the impact of successive treaty changes.

A respected MEP can lead Parliament in the adoption of amendments to continental-scale legislation that in their ultimate effect equal the sum of amendments of all the member states. Yet extraordinarily one still frequently hears and reads, during elections and at other times, dated and ignorant commentaries that it has no legislative powers and it is just a talking shop. Informed academic discourse can contribute to reversing this prejudice.

The Parliament is an important arm of the budgetary authority of the European Union. It is also an authorizing environment for executive action. I can think of no national parliament in recent years on the issue of budgetary accountability of the Executive that comes close to the decisive role played in 1999 by the European Parliament in the unprecedented resignation of an entire European Commission.

As a tribune of the people, the Parliament and its members have increasingly fulfilled a role as a focal point for the expression of concerns held by ordinary citizens across a wide range of policy areas including the environment, consumer protection, transport, financial and other services, not to mention wider issues of war and peace such as Iraq or the Middle East.

It is the Parliament's power of assent, a vote by a qualified majority to accept or reject agreements with third countries such as the accession of new member states, which introduces its role in the current text. Correctly the author has chosen to look beyond the formal to the informal in appraising Parliament's influence on the enlargement process. Preparing for EU membership is an arduous task for candidate states. They must adopt their legal base to accommodate the *acquis communautaire*, the entire body of EU law.

In engaging at all levels with national parliaments and parliamentarians in the candidate states the European Parliament animated this grinding but indispensable process. We were a voice talking a common parliamentary and political language, talking about a Europe of values and not just an arid Europe of directives to be transposed. We were a bridge offering two-way advocacy for the EU and for our interlocutors. We showed that when the Commission and the Parliament act together in common European cause that the synergies can be powerful and influential. We pre-integrated nominated observer MPs from the accession states in the work of the Parliament after the signature of the Accession Treaty, as earnest of our determination to underpin the irreversibility of the process.

Before the vital Copenhagen Summit in December 2002 to decide the outstanding terms of settlement for the candidate states, together with the Commission and the Council, led respectively by President Romano Prodi and Prime Minister Anders Fogh Rasmussen of Denmark, we hosted an unprecedented plenary debate on the future of an enlarged Europe involving speakers from the European Parliament and the parliaments of the candidate states. Our message to Europe's holdouts on budgetary matters could not have been clearer, that this was not the time nor the occasion for backsliding.

Inside the European Parliament we drove our systems to prepare for this new dawn. As the only directly elected European institution we had a special responsibility to prepare for and to respect Europe's cultural and linguistic diversity. This was not simply the discharge of a duty to new MEPs but more fundamentally the discharge of a duty to the citizens of new member states on whose behalf we would act as their European legislature.

And we learned about each other, sharing not just a journey but developing a narrative. Let me share one such story. I made a new Lithuanian friend, Vytenis Andriukaitis. He served as the Chairman of the European Affairs Committee of the Seimas (parliament) in Lithuania. I last met him in Greece on 16 April 2003, on the day of signing of the Accession Treaty by the ten new member states of the European Union. We were in the ancient Agora at the foot of the hill of the Acropolis in the shadow of the Parthenon but it was new and not ancient history which touched me on that day. He was overcome with emotion. 'What's wrong?' I asked. 'I have just been talking with my 95-year-old mother on my mobile phone,' he answered, 'about my journey to Athens.'

In 1940 the Soviet Union brutally cast aside the young independence of the three Baltic States under a dirty and self-serving deal between Hitler and Stalin. Mr Andriukaitis Sr was a young married man, an engineer and a part-time municipal councillor in his home city of Kaunas. For this he was suspect in the eyes of their new masters and so he and his young bride were sent to the Gulag. They were placed on a godforsaken island in the Arctic circle that alternated between constant nights and constant days but never altered in terms of its oppressive isolation. My friend Vytenis was born on that prison island. Years later they were allowed to return to Kaunas. He was speaking to his mother about his family's journey from the Gulag to freedom.

As a Member of the European Parliament from the collapse of the Berlin Wall through to the reunification, perhaps the first unification, of our continent based on common values and the exercise of free and sovereign engagement, I had a privileged view from the inside of this special moment and process. I am pleased that scholarship too, through this text, is staking its claim.

Pat Cox, Cork

Acknowledgements

This book was a long time in preparation and I would like to express my appreciation to a large number of people for their assistance and support.

In the first place thanks are due to Professor Eddie Moxon-Browne who supervised my PhD thesis and offered me consistent support over the years. Thanks also to Professor Mike Smith of Loughborough University, the external examiner of my PhD thesis, who has been unfailingly generous in providing references since. I owe a great deal of thanks to my colleague Brid Quinn and her husband John, for dinners in Kilfinane and the odd racing tip (which did not help me pay the fees at any level of university!). Many thanks also to my colleagues in the Department of Politics and Public Administration at the University of Limerick, Maura Adshead, Luke Ashworth, Bernadette Connaughton, Tracey Gleeson, Lucia Quaglia, Mary Murphy, Nick Rees, John Stapleton, Alex Warleigh, and Owen Worth. Neil Robinson has been a tremendously supportive head of department and at all times enthusiastic about the book. Thank you to University of Limerick colleagues in different departments: Liam Chambers, Patricia Conlan, Eoin Devereux, Marie Dineen, Sean Donlan, Breda Grey, Vicky Kelly, Carmen Kuhling, Padraig Lenihan, Alistair Malcolm, Orla McDonnell, Anthony McElligott, Angus Mitchell, Caolfhionn Ní Bheachain, Eugene O'Brien, William O'Brien, Pat O'Connor and Bernadette Whelan.

I owe a great debt of gratitude to John Logan, who read the text and provided the most concise and valuable advice on textual changes. He has helped an enormous number of young scholars find their feet in the academic world and I am enormously grateful for the steadfast support he offered as head of department and friend. Pat Cox wrote the foreword to the book at relatively short notice and between trips to the United States. As a key participant in the enlargement negotiations and witness to the historic events his contribution to the book is of immense value and very much appreciated.

A special word of thanks to Catherine Lawless and Ruán O'Donnell, who have been exemplary colleagues and stellar friends. They variously becalmed, cajoled, and encouraged me with sound advice and constant reassurance that my methods would eventually deliver the finished product. The weekly curry may have proved a short-term hindrance to the completion of academic work but undoubtedly also represented a most valuable forum for the exchange of ideas, so long as a measure of sobriety was maintained! Dolores Taaffe has long been a source of inspiration as she manages uncooperative cows, needy children and grandchildren, an irascible husband, and less than engaged students. I am indebted to her for encouragement and steadfast support.

Trish and Dave provided a bed and many a diverting night out in London. Hillary Pierdt also offered me a bed (and a car) whilst completing the PhD when I really was disconnected from the real world. Thank you also to Jack Anderson, Hugh Atkinson, Brendan Bolger, Antoeneta Dimitrova, Mark Downes, Milka Gancheva, Aidan Hehir, Kristana Ivanova, Jordan Jordanov, Rory Keane, Fidelma Kilbride, Ian King, Sean Molloy, Anna Murphy, Cait ni Ceallaigh, Christopher Lasch, John O'Connor, Liam Rimmer, Tapio Raunio, Maria Tzankova Ros Wade and Dara Waldron.

The Irish Research Council for the Humanities and Social Sciences (IRCHSS) supported both my doctoral and postdoctoral research. That support enabled me to conduct research work away from Limerick and a vital period in writing-up in 2004–5. I would thus like to express my thanks to Dr Marc Caball and his staff. It would have been much more difficult to get the book published without their help. In 2005 I was a Visiting Fellow at the EU Institute for Security Studies (EUISS) in Paris, where I completed the manuscript and made many good friends. Thanks to Judy Batt, Dov Lynch, Antonio Missiroli, Walter Posch and to the other Visiting Fellows. Thanks also to the University of Limerick Foundation and the College of Humanities, both of which provided funding for parts of this research over the last few years. At Routledge I want to thank Heidi Bagtazo and Harriet Brinton for help in preparing the manuscript.

Finally, I owe the greatest debt to my parents, Mary and John, for years of unstinting support.

Abbreviations

AP	Association Partnership
BDI	Bundesverband der Deutschen Industrie
CAP	Common Agricultural Policy
CBI	Confederation of British Industry
CDU	Christian Democratic Union
CEE	Central and Eastern Europe
CEFTA	Central European Free Trade Area
CFSP	Common Foreign and Security Policy
CIS	Commonwealth of Independent States
CMEA	Council for Mutual Economic Assistance
CoE	Council of Europe
Coreper	Committee of Permanent Representatives
COSAC	Conference of Standing Committees of National Parliaments
DG	Directorate General
EA	Europe Agreement
EBRD	European Bank for Reconstruction and Development
EC	European Community
ECSC	European Coal and Steel Community
ECU	European Currency Unit
EEC	European Economic Community
EFTA	European Free Trade Area
EIB	European Investment Bank
ELDR	European Liberal Party (European Parliament)
EMU	European Monetary Union
EP	European Parliament
EPP-PD	European People's Party (European Parliament)
ERT	European Roundtable of Industrialists
ESDP	European Security and Defence Policy
EU	European Union
EUI	European University Institute
EUISS	EU Institute for Security Studies
FDI	Foreign Direct Investment
FRG	Federal Republic of Germany

GAERC	General Affairs and External Relations Council
GDP	Gross Domestic Product
GDR	German Democratic Republic
GNI	Gross National Income
GNP	Gross National Product
IFI	International Financial Institution
IGC	Intergovernmental Conference
IIA	Inter-Institutional Agreement
IMF	International Monetary Fund
IPE	International Political Economy
IR	International Relations
ISPA	Instrument for Structural Policies for Pre-Accession
JHA	Justice and Home Affairs
JPC	Joint Parliamentary Committee
LI	Liberal Intergovernmentalist
MEP	Member of the European Parliament
NATO	North Atlantic Treaty Organization
NGO	Non-Governmental Organization
NPAA	National Programme for the Adoption of the *Acquis*
OECD	Organization for Economic Cooperation and Development
OSCE	Organization for Security and Cooperation in Europe
PES	Party of European Socialists (European Parliament)
PHARE	Poland and Hungary: Assistance for Restructuring Economies
SAA	Stabilization and Association Agreement
SAP	Stabilization and Association Process
SAPARD	Special Accession Programme for Agriculture and Rural Development
SEA	Single European Act
SEM	Single European Market
TEU	Treaty on European Union
USSR	Union of Soviet Socialist Republics
WTO	World Trade Organization

1   Introduction

On 1 May 2004 at a historic, if understated, signing ceremony in Dublin the European Union (EU) formally recognized the accession to the Union of ten new states.[1] These were Cyprus, Malta, and eight Central and Eastern European (CEE) states – the Czech Republic, Estonia, Hungary, Latvia, Lithuania, Poland, Slovakia, and Slovenia – which, for more than forty years, had been cut off from the European integration process by virtue of their geopolitical imprisonment behind the Iron Curtain. The history of European integration had been one of successive and successful enlargement rounds. Indeed, there is some evidence that there existed among the founding fathers an ambition to enlarge to continental scale. For more than three decades after World War Two, the Cold War stood in the way of the realization of that ambition. But with the demise of the Soviet Union and the loosening of its post-war grip on its Central and Eastern European satellite states in the wake of 1989's so-called 'geopolitical earthquake', Jean Monnet's ambition of a European construction stretching from the Atlantic to the Urals suddenly seemed possible. Thereafter, enlargement to Central and Eastern Europe gradually made its way to the top of the European Union's political agenda. On 1 May 2004 the ambition was finally realized.

Although most commentators describe the eastern enlargement as the fifth EU enlargement, it would be more correct to describe it as the fourth such expansion. In the process of expanding eastwards the EU has completed a geographic sweep that first embraced western Europe, then the south and north in succession. The first (western) enlargement came in 1973 with the accessions of Denmark, Ireland and the United Kingdom. This was followed by the second (southern or Mediterranean) expansion that saw the accessions of Greece in 1981 and Spain and Portugal in 1986. Although most commentators treat these as separate it is more correct to consider them as part of a single process underpinned by the same structural dynamics. The third (northern or EFTA) enlargement occurred in 1995, with the accessions of Austria, Finland and Sweden. Thus eastern enlargement should be considered the fourth such round of EU expansion and not the fifth.[2]

The eastern enlargement has frequently been depicted as the culmination of a series of processes that has reunified Europe. This judgement is one that derives from an understanding of Cold War Europe as one of artificial geopolitical division of a previously indivisible civilizational unit, imposed by the strategic competition of the Cold War. It overlooks the fact that previous to the Second World War there existed many different 'Europes'. At no time could one identify a genuine collective governed by common rules and legal norms. Where particular forms of political unity had emerged that was usually as a result of coercion and territorial aggression and acquisition. In addition, as William Wallace attests, one of the defining characteristics of earlier 'European projects' was that, although most started in Western Europe, they usually spread only some way eastwards. This was as true of Immanuel Kant's perpetual peace plan as it was of the Duc de Sully's proposals for a European federation in the early sixteenth century. In the nineteenth century Prince Metternich famously proclaimed that 'Asia begins at the Landstrasse'.[3] The idea of a European collectivity binding together western and eastern Europe was not taken seriously, partly because of the divisive structural environment emanating from Great Power rivalries but also because of western perceptions of the east as exotic, inferior and 'oriental'.

The 2004 accessions are much better understood as part of an ongoing contemporary process, which has created the foundations of a genuinely trans-European political community, built on shared values, reciprocal obligation and institutionalized rule-following. In that sense eastern enlargement constitutes one of the key building blocks of the post-Cold War European integration process. But if in time eastern enlargement is viewed as a critical advance in moving the EU towards genuine political unity, the emerging Europe is a very different entity to those which emerged from previous efforts of European unification. There are four reasons for this.

First, the decisions made by sovereign governments to accede to the EU were voluntary and not coerced. These governments made their decisions on the basis of national interests and perceptions of common or European values, which linked them solidly to each other and to the collective. The decisions of those sovereign governments were then given formal popular sanction through the accession referendums held in each accession state in 2003. Second, the European Union which the CEE states joined is a political community with defined supranational, national, and regional competences and autonomous institutions, which are delegated responsibility by the member states in a range of policy areas deemed to be of common interest. For all of the focus on the putative loss of sovereignty that accompanies entry into the club, member states retain a formidable capacity for independent action.[4] Third, the EU is also supported by a loose but nevertheless identifiable socioeconomic system, which is highly regulated through supranational legislation and the Union-wide writ of the European Court of Justice (ECJ). Finally, the enlarged EU is developing a collective approach to foreign and security policy that increasingly seeks to give expression to the values that underpin the European integration process. Thus the Europe of the early twenty-first century can manifestly be understood as the first voluntarily enacted transnational political community in the history of international politics. And eastern enlargement, facilitating as it has the transfer of EU norms on everything from human rights to environmental legislation, has contributed as much to that process of European unification as any constitutional or political project that preceded it. If a further enlargement to the Balkans helps to embed democracy in modern Europe's most conflict-prone region then the process of enlargement will in the future stand as the most significant contribution to the pacification and transformation of Europe.

Perhaps the most striking feature of the eastern enlargement was its scale and magnitude, and the transformative effect it has had on the shape of the European Union. From a membership of six countries and 185 million people in the late 1950s, the EU expanded gradually to 15 member states and a population of 375 million people after the 1995 EFTA enlargement. With eastern enlargement the Union expands to 25 member states with a combined population of 450 million.[5] Nor does this represent the culmination of even the eastern enlargement process. In the latter part of 2004 Bulgaria and Romania completed negotiations for membership and are expected to become members of the EU on 1 January 2007. Croatia is expected to be next to open negotiations with the EU and, although in the course of 2005 there arose significant difficulties that temporarily postponed the opening of negotiations, that country is still widely expected to accede with Bulgaria and Romania in 2007 or soon after.[6] EU strategy on southeastern Europe has been closely modelled on eastern enlargement and seeks to gradually integrate all of the states of former Yugoslavia including Serbia, for long Europe's pariah state. The Brussels European Council of December 2004 formally committed the EU to the opening of accession negotiations with Turkey. And with the 'roses revolution' in Georgia in 2003 and the 'orange revolution' in Ukraine in 2004, the prospect of those countries moving closer to and seeking membership of the EU appeared much closer. So it is clear that the 2004 enlargement, although of great significance for both the EU and the accession states, may end up constituting but the first important part of a much larger process of expansion to eastern and southeastern Europe.

In developing arguments about the nature and content of the eastern enlargement process the book draws upon a variegated literature that expanded in tandem with the political process it sought to depict. In the first place there are the general texts that describe and analyse the main features of and important challenges thrown up by eastern enlargement. Two types of approach in particular stand out. The first includes empirical work that sought to describe the evolution of the enlargement process and the development of EU relations with the CEE states. This literature also includes the contributions of EU insiders such as Graham Avery, Fraser Cameron, and Peter Ludlow.[7] These books contain valuable accounts of the internal EU deliberation on enlargement and especially the inter-institutional context in which enlargement politics were played out. A second type of general text presented comprehensive studies of important parts of the EU policy process and the likely impact which eastern enlargement would have in specific policy domains.[8] The number and diversity of these studies increased steadily as the negotiations on eastern enlargement moved toward conclusion.

A second stream of literature analysed eastern enlargement from the perspective of country studies, especially of the candidate states in Central and Eastern Europe. These included consideration of negotiation strategies, domestic enlargement debates, the impact of 'Europe' on domestic institutions and institutional choice, and studies of public opinion.[9] Where some of these studies provided important information and analysis of developments in the candidate countries, increasingly also they sought to engage with ongoing debates in EU studies in different subdisciplines of political science, cultural studies, sociology and economics. On the EU side there were a smaller number of studies, which analysed the implications of enlargement for specific member states, some of a general nature, others focused on specific areas of public policy, élite contestation and public attitudes to enlargement. The question of domestic institutional adaptation and policy choice featured strongly in these studies, especially in those countries where enlargement threatened the privileges of important interest groups.[10]

A third important stream of analysis flowed from scholars of economic integration. These studies included a range of macroeconomic analyses of the different ways in which eastern enlargement would impact on key EU policies such as agriculture and structural funding, and others which analysed such issues as investment flows into Central and Eastern Europe and the transnational restructuring of European industry which developed in parallel with the enlargement process. Perhaps the most influential of these contributions was that of Alan Mayhew, whose *Recreating Europe* analysed the political economy of eastern enlargement and bridged the divide between academic analysis and policy-making.[11]

A fourth stream of literature examined the constituent elements of EU enlargement policy, highlighting the importance of various capacity-building programmes and compliance strategies employed by the EU in its efforts to transfer its policy-making apparatus and institutional culture to the candidate states. As the enlargement process developed, and measurement of EU 'successes' and 'failures' became possible, a growing number of scholars sought to analyse the use of various types of conditionality, and especially political conditionality, by the EU. In this respect studies of the application of the Copenhagen criteria within the enlargement process were increasingly foregrounded as scholars sought to determine the extent to which Central and Eastern Europe was becoming (alternatively) 'Europeanized', 'modernized', and 'democratized' through the enlargement process.[12]

Finally, somewhat belatedly a theoretical literature began to develop, which drew on two juxtaposed bodies of thought from the subdiscipline of International Relations (IR), and conceptualized eastern enlargement from those perspectives. In the first place, a rationalist literature grew up around the study of the constitutional and institutional dimensions of the enlargement process. The study of national decision-making and supranational bargaining that accompanied specific aspects of the eastern enlargement framework drew attention to a part of the process which was at least as important as the inside–outside bargaining between the EU and the candidate states.[13] In addition, scholars sought to determine the likely impact of enlargement on EU decision-making by focusing on changes to the rules governing the use of Qualified Majority Voting (QMV) within the Council and the general costs of institutional adaptation. Perhaps the most important theoretical template for analysing enlargement from a rationalist perspective was Andrew Moravcsik's *The Choice for Europe*, which offered a view of the European integration process as one characterized by intergovernmental bargaining and dominated by the powerful economic interests of the larger member states. *The Choice for Europe* had very little to say about eastern enlargement (or indeed any previous enlargement of the EU), but in other contributions Moravcsik applied his liberal intergovernmentalist framework to argue that enlargement did not fundamentally re-order any of the important features of the integration process and that the EU bargaining which accompanied the enlargement process resulted in typical compromises which protected the structural interests of the larger member states whilst buying off potential losers with compensatory 'side payments'.[14]

The second strand of theoretical literature developed around the importance of identity, norms, and social interaction within the eastern enlargement process. This literature, although itself increasingly diverse, sought to highlight the normative importance of different features of the process, and especially the transposition of EU values and identity on to Central and Eastern Europe. One school of thought focused on EU motivations deriving from a sense of historical obligation, such as 'uniting Europe', or 'undoing the historical injury wrought on the CEE states at Yalta'.[15] Another approach analysed eastern enlargement from different identity perspectives.[16] A final stream focused on the content and role of norms and normative transposition within the enlargement process.[17] Where rationalist scholars highlighted so-called 'logics of consequentiality' which allegedly governed enlargement decision-making, sociologically-grounded scholars instead argued for 'logics of appropriateness' as the key cognitive templates which informed and guided the behaviour of decision-makers. This disciplinary clash was both a product of and contributed significantly to the rationalist/constructivist divide which had come to define a large part of the academic conversation on EU public policy-making.

This book contributes to that debate in a number of ways. First it embeds the evolution of the eastern enlargement process in both conceptual and institutional analysis. The focus is exclusively on the internal EU dimension, on the deliberation and decision-making process, and how enlargement unfolded from the new dawn of 1989 through to accession day on 1 May 2004. Second, the narrative that runs through the book is a normative one. Its main claim is that normative and ideational factors rooted in issues of identity, norms and values drove the eastern enlargement process forward and proved decisive in determining its content and form. The EU used the eastern enlargement process as the main instrument supporting its efforts to 'democratize' and 'Europeanize' Central and Eastern Europe and transform the geopolitics of Europe. Notwithstanding the criticisms of those who point to the flawed fabric of democratic practice in many of the existing member states, and those on the CEE side who rightly point out that the democratic revolutions in CEE were local and spontaneous, it is clear that a successful transition to EU democratic norms, involving the entire reconstitution of political life in the candidate states, was the major objective of EU policy. This is of a pattern in that democracy promotion has 'gone mainstream' not just in EU practice but on a global level, over the past two decades, with the UN, the OSCE, innumerable NGOs and even the World Bank and IMF vigorously promoting best democratic practice in their activities.[18] It is in and through the EU, however, that the most explicit forms of democracy promotion are pursued. And nowhere more than in the eastern enlargement process has that desire to effect positive and society-enhancing democratization been as vigorously championed as by the European Union.

The norms which the book focuses on as decisive in shaping the eastern enlargement are not all exclusive to the European Union. Indeed, many are universal in their scope. But the European integration process has encouraged the development of a specific norm set that has seen the salience of these norms increase in the member states over time. The norms of reciprocity, multilateralism, respect for fundamental freedoms and minority rights, and transparency of administrative, judicial, and political institutions are now firmly rooted in both the domestic legal systems of the member states and the cognitive templates that guide decision-makers. In fact these norms are so deeply embedded that they have a 'taken for granted' quality about them. And although one of the most important debates occupying scholars of EU studies in the current period is that which focuses on the diffusion, interpretation, penetration and resonance of these norms within individual member states, it seems clear that the EU sought to use as many and as varied a range of instruments as possible within the framework of its eastern enlargement process so as to ensure the successful transposition of these norms in the new democracies of Central and Eastern Europe.

The EU's attachment to its political norms was highlighted again and again in the course of the eastern enlargement process. Indeed it seems clear now that while the Union was prepared to overlook deficiencies in the economic preparedness of candidate states it would not do so with respect to the political criteria for membership. This was especially evident in the case of negotiations with Bulgaria and Romania and even more so in the decision to open negotiations with Turkey. The norms of transparency of democratic institutions and fundamental freedoms for all took precedence over those of market capitalism in every case. That is because these norms most cogently represent what the European Union *is* in the international political system – a transnational pluralistic security community, founded on the principles of peaceable interstate relations, and dedicated to institutionalizing both market relations and political problem-solving among its member states.

In outlining how the eastern enlargement came on to the EU agenda, and thereafter how the contours of EU policy developed, the book does three things. First, it examines the evolution and unfolding of the eastern enlargement process, beginning with the heady days of peaceful revolution in 1989 and ending with the historic signing ceremony at Áras an Uachtaraan in Dublin on 1 May 2004. In future years historians will no doubt provide a large range of narratives, which will, of course, much more fully and satisfactorily explain the events, people and processes at the heart of the enlargement story. The political scientist, at too close a juncture to actual events, can only hope to produce a narrative that captures the essential elements of the picture. That is what part I of the book seeks to do. It describes how the EU relationship with the countries of Central and Eastern Europe developed after the dramatic events of the *annus mirabilis* of 1989, the important features of the early EU approach to enlargement, and the crucial foundations of the enlargement process which were gradually introduced as EU relations with Central and Eastern Europe deepened. It examines both the important intergovernmental summit meetings from which important enlargement decisions emerged and the supranational institutional processes that helped shape those European Council gatherings. It analyses the strengths and weaknesses of the various capacity-building instruments employed by the EU in Central and Eastern Europe and how these linked to the macro-objectives of EU policy. Finally, part I also traces the complex and contentious accession negotiations, which were officially instituted in early 1998 and completed in late 2002.

Part II of the book presents an analysis of the intra-EU institutional politics which accompanied and in many senses shaped the eastern enlargement process. This has been perhaps the most neglected area of academic analysis of enlargement and thus where the book's main contribution to our understanding of enlargement lies. The enlargement of such a complex and multifaceted international entity as the EU entails an important institutional dimension. Enlargement both arises out of specific forms of institutionalized cooperation and subsequently produces a reconfiguration of the norms and practices which structure that cooperation. Thus any substantive analysis of an enlargement process necessitates an understanding of the institutional dimension of the process. The three chapters in part II analyse the different roles played by the three principal institutions of the EU – the Council, Commission and Parliament – in the accession process, focusing on both the formal treaty-based division of labour which governs enlargement decision-making and the informal practices which have grown up around the enlargement process over the years. The chapters are concerned principally with the following questions: What were the formal treaty-based responsibilities of each of the three EU institutions with respect to enlargement decisions, and how did each institution seek to assert its influence on the process? How and through what instruments did each of the institutions engage with the candidate states during the enlargement process? To what extent did each institution act as a unified actor vis-à-vis the candidate states? Where there existed fragmentation within an individual institution how did this manifest itself and with what effect on the enlargement process? To what extent did each of the institutions act as European 'institution builders' and/or 'identity builders' within the structures of the enlargement process? And, finally, which of the institutions proved most important to enlargement decisions?

Although the *formal* decision rules laid down in Article 49 TEU suggest that it is the Council, and thus the member states, which makes the key decisions on enlargement, a more substantive contextual analysis of Article 49, informed also by knowledge of how the EU system operates in practice, reveals a more complicated picture of the decision-making process. Indeed enlargement can now only be understood as a process governed both by the formal/legal rules laid down in the treaties and the customary enlargement practice which has developed over the years.[19] The very absence of formal institutional instructions regarding the management of enlargement encouraged the development of a set of informal practices which eastern enlargement further developed and entrenched. The

European Commission, for example, although legally mandated only to deliver its opinion on membership applications to the Council, effectively acts as principal conduit with the candidate states and has an important influence on both the content and shape of the process as it develops. The treaty articles also bestow an important role on the European Parliament. No accession decision can be taken without the Parliament's assent. And, in the final instance, the outcome of the process rests on the ratification procedures in both the acceding states and the member states. All of this suggests that it is quite wrong to identify the Council as the *only* EU actor that counts in the process. The chapters on the Commission and Parliament thus outline the important ways those institutions contribute to enlargement decision-making.

Part III of the book contributes to the developing literature on the conceptualization of EU enlargement by analysing eastern enlargement from different conceptual standpoints. The chapter on geopolitical perspectives analyses enlargement, and particularly EU motivations for enlargement, from the standpoint of security, statecraft and international diplomacy. It utilizes realist theory to conceptualize important geopolitical issues such as the EU relationship with Russia, interstate relations in Central and Eastern Europe, and the location and ubiquity of power within the enlargement process. Although the central arguments of the book are those which highlight the normative importance of eastern enlargement for the EU, geopolitical issues also matter, and no serious examination of the subject can avoid engaging with the geopolitics of the new Europe. The chapter on economic perspectives focuses on EU economic motivations for enlargement and the main economic issues which enlargement brought to the fore. It employs Andrew Moravcsik's Liberal Intergovernmental framework in analysing the input into enlargement decisions by important EU producer groups and the preferences of transnational capital. In so doing it also highlights the extent to which domestically-generated enlargement preferences, especially in the larger, more powerful member states impacted on the enlargement process. The nature of both internal EU bargaining and the EU-candidate state negotiating relationship is also examined against Moravcsik's explicit and parsimonious framework. The final chapter in this section examines the normative dimension to eastern enlargement and employs social constructivist approaches to international relations to assess the importance of identity and norms within the enlargement process. It tests the proposition that the eastern enlargement process was governed in the main by 'logics of appropriateness', which helped define both member state preferences and EU modes of action. It argues that although the enlargement process was contested to different degrees and by a range of different actors within the EU, the logic which won out was the normative one which stressed the centrality of EU values and the importance of securing those values in Central and Eastern Europe. The norms that the EU sought to transpose through the enlargement process were exactly those that gave meaning to the existing process of European integration and rendered legitimate the structures of institutionalized cooperation and decision-making that supported that process.

The arguments presented in the book are constructed around a recognizable methodological approach. Although the political scientist is constrained in some important respects by his or her proximity to events, especially by the absence of memoirs, biographies and official documentation that are crucial to the process of historical reconstruction, there is nevertheless a greater range and diversity of sources relating to the European integration process available now than ever before. The EU institutions publish most of their documentation quickly and this is disseminated widely via the worldwide web. These documents constitute the crucial primary sources for this book. National documentation, although much more scarce, is also increasingly accessible to scholars and makes a contribution here throughout. The speeches and wider public discourse of national and EU representatives are also a vital source of information and frequently go beyond official papers in presenting public policy and the ideas that inform it. Secondary material consisting of traditional sources such as monographs and peer reviewed journal articles also constitute an important resource, especially in the effort to interpret EU motivations for eastern enlargement. In addition the worldwide web has facilitated the development of another type of secondary source – analysis and opinion provided by dedicated think-tanks such as the Centre for European Policy Studies (CEPS), the Centre for European Reform (CER), the European Policy Centre (EPC), and many others which focus on more specific parts of the integration process. The analysis of these groups features prominently throughout the book. In addition newspapers and magazines with established reputations in covering EU politics such as *The Economist*, the *Financial Times* and others are utilized throughout. Finally, interviews with policy-makers contribute to the analysis, especially in part II of the book, which focuses on the internal EU management of eastern enlargement.

Enlargement, as Desmond Dinan reminds us 'has been a central and quasi-permanent element in the EU's history'.[20] The first set of new members (the UK, Denmark and Ireland) had hardly been assimilated when the second set (Greece, Spain and Portugal) applied to join. Similarly, the Community was still assimilating the second set when the third set of ultimately successful applicants (Austria, Finland, and Sweden) requested accession. There followed the absorption of the old GDR, and, in the aftermath of the 1989 revolutions, the tabling of accession requests by the CEE states, Turkey, Cyprus and Malta. So from the beginning of the process of integration, enlargement has always hovered over internal and external EU activity. EU Intergovernmental Conferences (IGCs), as well as day-to-day activity, have, over the years, been influenced in important ways by enlargement issues.[21] The main reason for the convening of an IGC in 1996 was to revisit the Treaty on European Union (TEU). But, as Sedelmeier and Wallace point out, the link was made early on between the constitutional conclave and eastern enlargement. Both the Reflection Group – representatives of heads of government, charged with preparing for the IGC – and the Commission presented eastern enlargement as the main rationale for the IGC. Similarly, the IGC that concluded with the Nice Treaty in December 2000 was very much an enlargement IGC, with the treaty changes eventually agreed considered at least a minimum step toward ensuring the continued functioning of an enlarged Union.[22] The Convention on the Future of Europe and the negotiations on the Constitutional Treaty that followed it also took place against the shadow of eastern enlargement. In fact one of the most important justifications for the Constitutional Treaty was that which stressed the need to streamline decision-making in the EU of 25. Thus even if the eastern enlargement differed significantly from previous rounds in terms of scale and diversity, academic literature and political commentary continued to focus on the established preoccupation with widening and deepening.[23] The questions related to the *'finalité'* of integration are of course intimately connected with the EU's ambitions for further widening. This is because, as Jan Zielonka suggests, one cannot study the question of enlargement without reference to that of more or less integration, or at least the impact of enlargement on the process of integration.[24] The relationship between the two phenomena therefore will also be a factor throughout the book. This, however, will not impinge on the main task at hand, which is the analysis of the *eastern enlargement* process and its significance for the European Union.

Part I

The unfolding of eastern enlargement 1989–2004

2 1989 and beyond

The New Europe takes shape

Introduction

In the spring of 1994, the first formal applications for membership of the European Union by the Central and East European (CEE) states were made. Almost five years had passed since the dramatic days of peaceful revolution of 1989. In that period, many of the old certainties of the Cold War had disappeared. The Soviet Union's implosion had rendered the CEE states free to pursue their own external policies for the first time since the 1930s. Across Europe the entire framework of economic, political, security, and cultural relationships seemed to be in flux as the EU struggled to put in place a concrete process that would govern its relationship with the new democracies. Although it was cautious about making any categorical promises of membership, it became clear that enlargement of the Union to include those countries in CEE that had expressed an interest in joining represented the only viable policy option for the Union. This chapter serves a dual purpose. First, it seeks to describe the evolution of the EU's relations with the CEE states in the years after the 'new beginning' of 1989; second, it will outline the main elements of EU enlargement strategy towards CEE and how the EU became progressively committed to a wide enlargement round. It begins by describing the events of 1989–90 and their significance for the European Union.

The EU response to the 1989 revolutions

The dramatic but largely peaceful revolutions that transformed Central and Eastern Europe in 1989 are often described in grandiloquent terms. Phrases such as 'velvet revolutions', 'geopolitical earthquake' and 'acceleration of history' quickly entered political discourse as scholars and public figures struggled to come to terms with the magnitude of the events. Within a short time it became clear that the demise of Communism held profound implications for the future of Europe – both east and west. As the old certainties of the Cold War era gave way to a somewhat amorphous geopolitical framework, the EU found itself confronted with a drastically altered European configuration. The Europe of the Twelve would now have to address the question of how it might relate to *and* possibly assimilate its neighbours to the East.

In Central and Eastern Europe, the Gorbachev reforms had effectively embold-ened reformers and encouraged dissent. In short, internal Soviet disarray provided Warsaw-Pact dissident opportunity. Prior to the era of *glasnost* and *perestroika*, rela-tions between the EU and the CEE states were practically non-existent.[1] EU activity was mainly confined to a few narrowly concentrated areas of trade, ensuring the protection of key economic sectors from unfair competition from the Eastern Bloc.[2] At a political level, Cold War geopolitical thinking hindered the development of closer relations.

For the Central and East European states emerging from the shadow of the Soviet monolith, the aspiration was clear: a 'Return to Europe' – the Europe from which, it was frequently asserted, these states had been forcibly separated for over four decades.[3] The new CEE governments from the beginning framed their endeavours and aspirations with explicit reference to the core values of European integration.[4] They sought freedom, prosperity, and a secure place in the interna-tional community of nations, especially within European organizations. Opinion polls pointed to massive support for 'joining Europe'.[5] For the European Union, however, the aftermath to the peaceful revolutions would produce a period of intensive questioning: first, what was actually meant by 'European'; second, and more pragmatically, how should the Community respond to the CEE states' stated desire for membership of the club. For the first time, Article 237 of the Treaty of Rome, which simply stated that 'any European State can apply' for membership of the Community, began to be scrutinized.[6]

Even at this early stage, however, a division between EC/EU 'drivers' (advo-cates) and 'brakemen' (obstructionists) was in evidence. On one side British Prime Minister Margaret Thatcher unashamedly made the case for an EC commitment to enlarge. The question of what motivated her advocacy is usually answered with the assertion that she saw a wider Europe as a tool for slowing down the integration process and forestalling, if not derailing, any moves to embrace federalism. It was undoubtedly the case, however, that she also admired the CEE states for over-throwing communism and embracing the dual freedom of the market and the ballot box. At the Aspen Institute in Colorado on 5 August 1990 she called for a pan-European 'Magna Carta'.[7] Her foreign minister Douglas Hurd was equally supportive, as was John Major once he became Prime Minister.[8] For some Euro-pean leaders, however, the idea of a speedy enlargement was just too big a leap of the imagination. French President Francois Mitterand, for example, declared in Prague that it would be several decades before the CEE states could become members of the Community.[9] The Commission for its part took a middle path at this time, urging closer links but seeking to deflect the question of membership.[10]

In November 1989 the enthusiasm and readiness of the West to help was clearly expressed.[11] Altruism could indeed be detected, not just in the rhetoric but also in the actual nature of the response.[12] The heady atmosphere was captured in the European Council's declarations at the Strasbourg summit in December 1989 where it specifically acknowledged a 'special responsibility' for Central and Eastern Europe and suggested that the Community was the only point of reference of significance for the CEE states.[13] This was despite the fact that the revolutions had caught the Community off guard. For the EU this was as much a question of adjusting the cognitive, as well as the physical, map of Europe. EU policy, according to Sedelmeier and Wallace, was characterized at this time by, among other things, hyperactivity, enthusiastic pledges of support, and consensus that the EU should play a leading role in the transformation process in CEE, even if it was unclear what this might involve.[14]

Initially, talk of a Marshall-type Plan for Eastern Europe was commonplace, with the EU appearing to acknowledge the existence of a moral imperative for large-scale aid transfers to the eastern countries.[15] The Luxembourg accord of June 1988, billed as the Joint Declaration on the Establishment of Official Relations, led to the initiation of bilateral trade deals with the CMEA member states, and can be seen as ushering in a new phase of more normal relations.[16] The Community removed long-standing import quotas on a number of products and extended the General System of Preferences (GSP) to the CEE countries. The Commission began a major assessment of the progress of economic and political reform in the region.[17] The resulting Trade and Cooperation Agreements (TCAs) would, by October 1990, be signed by all of the former Warsaw Pact states in Central and Eastern Europe.[18] A Central European Free Trade Association (CEFTA), formed from former Comecon members, was also instituted in 1993 as an additional mechanism for freeing up trade.[19] This was in addition to a Central European initiative – the so-called Visegrad declaration – which sought to turn the three countries Hungary, Poland, Czechoslovakia into a single economic zone.[20] Further encouragement was garnered from the decisions made at the G24 summit of July 1989 (actually the G7 summit but recognized retrospectively as the wider G24 grouping), which provided substantive help to the reforming Eastern countries by means of rescheduling of debt, provision of aid to tackle fiscal problems, and, most significantly, commitments on aid for economic development. With respect to pledges of financial aid, it is estimated that the G24 block together committed approximately $45 billion over a three-year period.[21] Further commitments were made in the months that followed.[22] Alan Mayhew's calculations show that the actual grant assistance delivered to the recipient countries amounted to only 15 per cent of the headline figure promised.[23]

Despite the EU's rhetorical support for the process of transition, however, the reality was that doubt and vacillation soon replaced Western enthusiasm. Consequently, a tremendous gap developed between, for example, the amount of aid promised and that which was actually disbursed. Iver T. Berend showed that had the Marshall Plan been emulated for Central and Eastern Europe, even on a limited basis, with, for example, a Western contribution of only one half of one per cent of GDP, this would have yielded up to $100 billion annually for reconstruction and transition in Central and Eastern Europe.[24] Nothing on this scale was realized.[25] If one shifts the focus to EU aid alone, and employs Berend's model the outcome reflects very poorly on the EU15. In 2004 the combined EU15 GDP amounted to over €9 trillion. A Marshall-style financial aid programme would have delivered approximately €90 billion per year to CEE. Even a contribution of one half of one per cent of EU GDP would have yielded a figure of €45 billion annually for a limited period. The financial package agreed for the acceding states at the Copenhagen summit in 2002 amounted to a total of €40.8 billion for the period 2004–2006.[26] At first glance the headline figure seems quite generous. But it equates only to approximately 0.15 per cent of EU15 GDP for each year 2004–2006. Further probing, however, reveals a significant dilution of that headline amount. It does not include contributions made to the EU budget by the incoming states for 2004, 2005 and 2006. If that is factored in the net financial aid accorded the CEE states in the period amounts to a sum of only €10.3 billion for 2004–2006. That amounts to no more than one thousandth of EU GDP.[27] As Table 2.1 demonstrates this is a very long way short of Marshall-era support and even significantly less than the support the EU15 provide on a bilateral basis to developing countries. The aggregate EU15 financial aid to developing countries amounts to

Table 2.1 EU GDP and potential financial aid to Central and Eastern Europe 2004–6

Country	2001 GDP (billion euros)
Austria	210
Belgium	257
Denmark	180
Finland	135
France	1446
Germany	2063
Greece	130
Ireland	116
Italy	1217
Luxembourg	22
Netherlands	427
Portugal	123
Spain	650
Sweden	234
United Kingdom	1591
EU15 Total GDP	**8811**
1% of EU15 GDP	**88**
0.5% of EU15 GDP	**44**
0.1% of EU GDP	**8.8**

Source: author's calculations

0.3 per cent of EU GDP, in other words about three times the amount the CEE states will receive between 2004–2006.[28]

Further evidence of this apparent failure of response is provided by comparative analysis of actual EC/EU aid to CEE and transfers to its own poorer member states. In 1992, the peripheral EU countries (Ireland, Spain, Greece and Portugal) received fifteen times more per capita than did the CEE countries.[29] Ten years later the gap had narrowed but was still very significant. Poland would receive €67 per capita, Hungary €49, Slovenia €41, and the Czech Republic €29 in the period up to the end of the 2006 financial framework. By contrast, in 2000, Greece received €437 per capita, while Ireland got €418, Spain €216 and Portugal €211. Further, it was stipulated that aid to individual CEE states was not to exceed the imposed 'absorption capacity' figure of 4 per cent of GDP. This threshold was set much lower than had been the case in previous enlargement rounds. It is little wonder that the CEE states look wistfully at the Cohesion states and their very generous levels of subvention.[30] The point is further put in perspective when one considers that Ireland, although already by 2000 one of the richest states in the Union, was still in receipt of almost six times more aid than was envisaged for Poland.[31] To further emphasize the lack of support offered CEE a comparison with German transfers to its eastern Länder can be evinced: in 1993, these amounted to a staggering $5900 per capita.[32] In the decade after unification, net fiscal transfers from the German Federal Government to the former East Germany amounted to some 1.2 trillion DM. This figure amounts to ten times what the EU has allocated in aid to all the CEE candidate countries in the financial framework to 2006.[33] The impression of the CEE countries remaining the poor relations is difficult to refute and is reflected in the opinion of some that the Oder-Neisse line quickly transmuted into a new and lasting economic divide, separating Europe's haves and have-nots.[34]

PHARE

Notwithstanding the gap between EU commitments and disbursements, there did emerge a more coherent collective approach to financial aid and economic restructuring in the transitioning states. The G24 conference of July 1989 committed its members to aiding the economic reconstruction of Central and Eastern Europe. Out of this would evolve a practical operational device to assist with financial aid and technical matters. This became known as PHARE;[35] it would eventually encompass all of the CEE states.[36] The European Commission at the time identified the prime missions of PHARE as supporting the process of economic transformation, with a focus on core areas such as industry, agriculture and energy, and providing financial support for CEE efforts to reform and rebuild.[37] In addition, the programme included food and humanitarian aid, balance of payments help and access to European Investment Bank (EIB) loans.[38] PHARE soon became the biggest assistance programme in CEE with funding increasing from an initial amount of €500 million in 1990 to €1600 million in 1995. In total, the PHARE programme allocated €4.2 billion for the period 1990–94; this increased to €6.693

billion for the period 1995–99, with another €4.7 billion provided between 1999 and 2002. The focus of PHARE would change in time from demand-driven support for transition-related restructuring, developing in parallel with the pre-accession strategy, into an entirely accession-driven instrument.[39]

If PHARE was intended as a crucial instrument for the support of restructuring it quickly became apparent that inherent problems compromised its effectiveness.[40] Firstly, the financial support was very modest given the scale of ambitions for PHARE. Second, analysts railed against the perceived inadequacies of the PHARE distribution system and in particular against the preponderance of western management consultants employed in implementation. Pflueger demonstrated that only ten per cent of PHARE funds were channeled into investment in the early 1990s, whereas management consultants, frequently from the west, pocketed vast amounts.[41] Official concern was publicly expressed and this contributed to a demonstrable loss of confidence in the programme on the CEE side.[42] The EU itself acknowledged the legitimacy of the complaints. In 1993, the EC Court of Auditors brought into sharp focus the mismanagement of specific components of the aid budget concluding that 'almost none of the leading personnel in the management units are nationals of the recipient countries. Thus, the claimed recipient control over implementation seems specious.'[43] The question of serious fraud undermining the new aid programmes was also a recurring one. There did not seem to be sufficiently rigorous scrutiny of EC aid.[44] Further criticism of PHARE was based on the employment of a mixture of bilateral and multilateral aid, which at times compounded the problems of implementation and conspired against the overall goals of the programme. A Belgian government memo expressed the general frustration: it called for more consistency between the policies of member states and that of the Community.[45] The overall picture was one of good intentions, compromised by administrative deficiencies and a lack of coordination.[46] Acknowledgement of the inadequacies of the PHARE programme came at the Copenhagen European Council summit meeting in June 1993. Consequently PHARE took on a new and explicitly political orientation; it was redesigned to keep pace with political developments, in particular with regard to a more concrete accession scenario. After 1994 the programme was characterized by support for the legislative framework and administrative structures, as well as for projects promoting democratization and civil society, and for investment in infrastructure, involving cross-border cooperation.[47] The move to substantive capacity-building had begun, even if it was somewhat tentative.

In addition to PHARE the EU also put in place two new financial institutions intended to provide finance and advice to governments in Central and Eastern Europe. These were the European Investment Bank (EIB) and the European Bank for Reconstruction and Development (EBRD). The EIB was guaranteed by the EU and made project-based loans, targeted at productive or infrastructure investment available at competitive interest rates. EIB loans were hugely important for the transitioning countries in the early 1990s when their access to investment capital was negligible. Later investment would be focused on trans-European infrastructure projects such as the upgrading of train and motorway routes.[48] The

EBRD, a French government initiative, was designed to provide support for balance of payments problems, currency convertibility, and aid in instituting programmes in technology, training and development.[49] There was an enormous amount of publicity attached to its launch on 15 April 1991.[50] An amount of disquiet, however, centred on both the choice of London as the headquarters for the bank and on the activities of its larger-than-life president, Jacques Attali.[51] As early as 1991 there were suggestions that the bank was failing in its remit.[52] At its second annual meeting in London on 1 April 1993 there was uproar amid claims of great extravagance.[53] When Attali decided to resign there was little surprise.[54] Even after his departure, however, the Bank was dogged by negative publicity with suggestions that management consistently favoured French companies and Gallic interests.[55] Nevertheless change was effected and the bank began to have an impact.[56]

The Europe agreements

The third arm of early EU policy developed out of the existing template of association and association agreements, which had been used to manage relations with third countries since the inception of the EC.[57] It became apparent that a deeper form of association agreement would be required in managing relations with CEE. Following on from the initial trade and cooperation agreements of 1989 and 1990, the EU saw the need for a more effective institutional framework in which the new relationships, both political and economic, might be consolidated. The Association Agreements (or Europe Agreements as they were more commonly referred to) were described as 'second-generation' agreements, symbolic of a second stage of relations between the EU and the CEE countries. The first such Agreements, with Poland, Hungary and Czechoslovakia, were signed on 18 December 1991 and came into operation on 1 March 1992.[58] The European Commission defined the Agreements as 'a legal, political and economic framework for the relationship of the signatory CEE countries with the EU'.[59] They provided the framework for bilateral relations between the EU and its member states with the partner countries. Described as representing 'far-reaching liberalization' with respect to trade and economic ties, the Agreements were viewed by the EU as a positive contribution to the CEE efforts to reduce the economic disparities with the EU member states. They covered trade, political dialogue, legal approximation and other areas of cooperation, including industry, environment, transport and customs. They aimed progressively to establish a free trade area between the EU and the associated countries over a given period, on the basis of reciprocity, but applied in an asymmetrical manner. According to the Commission, the Agreements were 'based on shared understanding and values' and prepared the way for economic and political convergence.[60]

For all of the normative rhetoric that framed the new EU–CEE relations, the tectonic plates of economic reality continually impinged upon efforts at deeper engagement. Testimony to the protectionist nature of the Europe Agreements abounds.[61] In this respect, they were frequently portrayed as being one-sided in defending EU interests, and hardly representative of a mechanism designed to lead to membership of the associated countries.[62] CEE leaders were quick to point to the incongruity of the EC position.[63] Indeed, the delays and tensions which would characterize much of the enlargement process to follow were very evident in the negotiation of the Europe Agreements.[64] Although the EC had made concessions during the final negotiations, the Agreements nevertheless protected the so-called 'sensitive' sectors of key EU industries such as agricultural products, textiles and coal and steel.[65] These were the sectors where CEE producers wielded significant comparative advantage relative to their EU competitors. Although the EU provided greater market access, the restrictive features of the Agreements effectively limited CEE market penetration. These sectors accounted for approximately 40 per cent of total CEE exports. The impact of these restrictions on CEE trade may be gauged by focusing on one important component of CEE trade: agricultural goods. The clear trend is of a highly advantageous swing to the European Union in the terms of trade. The EU, which in 1989 had a trade deficit in agricultural goods of some 960 million ECU, had by 1993 turned this into a surplus of 433 million ECU.[66] Although CEE trade with the EU certainly increased, EU trade performance improved much more significantly. Between 1995 and 2000, for example, while EU total exports grew by 63 per cent, exports to CEE grew by 112 per cent. Between 1995 and 2000, the EU's global trade surplus amounted to some €45 billion. Its trade surplus with CEE, however, reached €100 billion, or more than twice the global figure.[67]

The protectionist instincts of the EU were already evident during the negotiation of the association agreements, as some member states sought to block generous terms for the CEE countries.[68] Mayhew identified three important results of such use of instruments of commercial defence by the EU: it caused damage to the economies of the associated countries at a critical stage in their transition to market economies, caused many in these countries to doubt the wisdom of trade liberalization and had a negative impact on public opinion.[69] Indeed, concern grew to such an extent that Jacques Delors was forced to comment thus: 'You cannot shed tears of joy for the people of Eastern Europe one day and the next tell them that you will not buy their products.'[70] His view was shared across Europe.[71] A second criticism of the Europe Agreements was that they did not establish a clear link between association and membership.[72] The Commission had attempted to pre-empt the argument by denying any clear relationship and stating that there was 'no link either explicit or implicit' between association and accession with membership constituting a 'totally separate question'.[73] A formula in the preambles to the Agreements recognized membership as a final objective of the CEE states. But this was very different from endorsing in any way the prospect of CEE accessions.[74]

This hesitant and rather ungenerous response to CEE on the EU's part was predicated on a number of factors. First, the Union's self-absorption in the early 1990s stands out. Paradoxically, the demise of Communism acted to the disadvantage of the CEE-associated countries because it triggered an intensification of Western European integration efforts.[75] Indeed, Maastricht is singularly identified as the *quid pro quo* for German Unification; the assurance of a united Germany's renewed commitment to its EU partners. Suspicion of German hegemonic or aggrandizing intent was not slow in materializing. Eastward enlargement, it was widely thought, would benefit Germany economically and geopolitically much more than any other EU member state. Thus, fear of the putative German giant caused some of the present member states to steer enlargement along the 'slow lane'. For the CEE states this meant that, at precisely the moment of their return to the mainstream European interstate arena, they were effectively locked out of the central political process that would shape the future Europe. Their absence from the Maastricht negotiations, for example, was striking.[76] Exclusively the incumbent members would determine the shape of the new European compact without any input from the Central and Eastern European States. CEE leaders thus watched Maastricht unfold with a great degree of concern.

Second, the impact of the 1990s Europe-wide recession on the member states, and, later, the deflationary policies employed in many countries in order to conform to the EMU convergence criteria, also had a measurable negative influence on the Union's early approach to eastward enlargement. Budget deficits, increased unemployment and attendant social strain resulted in the subordination of enlargement to domestic policy issues in many member states in the early to mid 1990s. Third, the logistical problems encountered by the Commission in its efforts to coordinate aid programmes for the CEE states were significant; it had never before in its history been presented with a challenge on this scale. Dependent on outside experts brought in on contract and with a lack of resources devoted to the management of programmes in DG I, the Commission soon ran into implementation difficulties and lots of criticism. Sedelmeier and Wallace assert that the EU found it easier to devise ad hoc policy than to design a more rounded approach. This was a common charge, though mostly levelled with the benefit of hindsight and with little regard to the problems relating to speed, timing, and staff and expertise shortages.[77] In addition, rivalries within the Commission – principally between DG I and DGs III (industry) and VI (agriculture) – and within national administrations – typically foreign ministries against sectoral ministries – contributed to the problems in the early stages. Sedelmeier and Wallace present this as a 'macro/meso' divide among policy makers, with 'macro' policy-makers (usually located within the foreign ministries of national administrations) typically taking the long-term view and being more sympathetic to the CEE concerns, while 'meso' policy-makers (usually to be found in sectoral ministries) engaged in short-termism and were very susceptible to the claims of special interests. Even within DG I there was significant division along similar lines.[78]

Finally, the gradual realization, on the part of EU leaders, of the daunting institutional and policy implications of enlargement also encouraged caution and inertia. Analysis of the micro-implications of enlargement was provided by a wide range of commentators and by the European Commission and European Parliament.[79] The shadow of enlargement thus hovered over every major internal EU debate from the early 1990s onwards. Throughout that period growing concern about the direction of EU policy towards Central and Eastern Europe manifested itself on a regular basis. Indeed, a European Commission official was quoted as saying: 'The level of seriousness about enlargement is not minimal, it simply does not exist.'[80] The initial euphoria of 1989 then soon gave way to muted resignation as the EU found that its response to the emerging democracies became increasingly affected by the economic and political vicissitudes of both EU and global politics. For their part the CEE states continued to press for membership at the earliest opportunity.[81]

Toward a new phase in relations: the Copenhagen summit

If the peaceful revolutions of 1989 constituted a starting point for the EU's efforts to integrate Central and Eastern Europe into EU structures, then the decisions taken by the European Council at Copenhagen in June 1993 represented no less significant a milestone. Copenhagen provided real momentum, according to Peter Ludlow, by transforming the enlargement question 'from a theoretical possibility to an agreed goal', and by articulating substantial if vague criteria by which progress could be measured.[82] In the run-up to the summit meeting the Commission produced a new report on enlargement strategy.[83] This proposed specific measures for deepening the relationship with the associated countries, including accelerated market access for the CEE states, increased economic and technical assistance, and an intensification of political dialogue.[84] Crucially also, it recommended that the associated countries become eligible for accession once they met certain economic and political conditions. EC foreign ministers, meeting in the General Affairs Council (GAC) at Luxembourg on 8 June 1993, agreed in principle on measures to accelerate the political and economic integration of CEE into the Community.

The European Council endorsed the Commission's view, announcing that it 'agreed that the associated countries in Central and Eastern Europe shall become members of the European Union'. As Graham Avery points out this was the first time such a promise of membership had been extended to third countries even before they had officially applied for it.[85] Further, it was decreed that accession would take place 'as soon as the associated country is able to assume the obligations of membership by satisfying the economic and political conditions required'. These conditions included the achievement of stable institutions that guaranteed democracy, the rule of law, human rights, and respect for and protection of minority rights, the existence of a functioning market economy as well as the capacity to cope with competitive pressure and market forces within the Union.[86] The European Council also introduced another important criterion – the ability of the Union to absorb new members 'whilst maintaining momentum' and without compromising the deepening of the Union. Thus there was formed an explicit linkage between further deepening and widening of the EU. Enlargement could take place, as long as it did not impair the integrity of the integration process. The European Council also agreed that 'future cooperation with the associated countries shall be geared to the objective of membership', thus establishing an explicit link between cooperation and accession that did not exist in the Europe Agreements. To this end, the European Council proposed the creation of a new 'structured relationship' with the CEE states, which it defined as a 'multilateral framework for strengthened dialogue and consultation on matters of common interest'.[87] The structured relationship would consist of meetings between the Council and its counterparts (government ministers) from the CEE states on policy matters falling under each of the three pillars of EU activity: EC areas (single market), CFSP, and JHA (immigration, asylum, combating organized crime including the traffic of human beings). Separate procedures were also established for meetings of foreign ministers under CFSP. The European Council also proposed regular high-level meetings of the Commission President and EU Presidency with their counterparts from the applicant states, and joint meetings of the heads of state and government when appropriate.[88]

The Copenhagen summit also further elaborated measures to accelerate efforts to open EC markets to CEE products, moving faster in this regard than was originally envisioned in the Europe Agreements.[89] Important changes to the PHARE programme came about as a response to the concerns about its efficacy.[90] The reorientation of PHARE included a new emphasis on infrastructural development. The EC also committed itself to more financial assistance and help in the approximation of laws by providing training in EC law and procedure.[91] As PHARE's objectives changed it became much more oriented towards the preparation of the associated (later candidate) countries for accession.

In retrospect the Copenhagen Process was also notable for the activism displayed by a range of different political actors. Most commentators now concede the importance of the European Commission's advocacy in pressing for the accommodation of CEE preferences in respect of trade. Also of significance was the approach adopted by CEE state representatives, much of which consisted of reminding the EU leaders of the 'historical obligation' and 'practical necessity' which enlargement represented. In a key memorandum presented to the Commission in October 1992, the three Visegrad governments declared that:

> Our three countries are convinced that stable democracy, respect for human rights and continued policy of economic reforms will make accession possible. We call upon the Communities and the member states to respond to our efforts by clearly stating the integration of our economies and societies, leading to membership of the Communities is the aim of the Communities themselves. This simple, but historic statement would provide the anchor which we need.[92]

The pressure from the CEE states was important in particular for highlighting the gap between EU rhetoric about welcoming the post-Communist democracies into the democratic and market capitalist fold, and the substance of actual EU policy, which was much less accommodating of CEE interests. Through such pressure, the CEE states exploited the feelings of moral obligation toward Central and Eastern Europe held by many within the EU.[93] To this we must add the pressure exerted by the academic community and the governments of key member states. The German government, in particular consistently argued that the post-Communist countries must be given a firm prospect of membership. During a visit to

Warsaw in February 1992, the then German Foreign Minister Hans Dietrich Genscher declared that Poland, Hungary and Czechoslovakia should become full EC members 'as soon as possible'.[94] The following month, he declared that these countries should be admitted to the EC by the end of the decade.[95] Even among the member states that were less enthusiastic about enlargement, there was a growing acceptance of the need to better integrate the CEE states. After Copenhagen the enlargement process took on a more identifiable and discernible shape as new modes of cooperation, adaptation and preparations for membership evolved.

3 Beyond Copenhagen

The deepening of EU–CEE relations

Introduction

For all of the positive developments that emerged from Copenhagen, progress was difficult as ever in the months after the summit. At times it looked to the CEE states as if the gap between the rhetorical commitments and EU action was alarming. What was needed, it was frequently asserted, was a concrete timetable and a road map for accession. This chapter examines the second stage in EU–CEE relations, traces developments through the deepening of institutional relationships, and the move to a firm pre-accession process. It concludes with an analysis of the 1999 Helsinki summit where enlargement was declared an 'irreversible' process by the European Council.

In the aftermath of Copenhagen two particular problems presented themselves. The first lay in the EU's continued absorption with internal problems. With a succession of exchange rate crises and attendant threats to the plans to launch EMU, along with the problematic ratification of the TEU, enlargement seemed to recede in importance.[1] To this was added the distraction presented by the ongoing accession negotiations with the EFTA states – Austria, Sweden, Finland and Norway.[2] A wide-ranging Commission policy review was followed by further reform of PHARE and declarations stressing the need for the CEE states to harmonize their competition and state-aid policies with EU regulation in these areas.[3] The Commission's strategy came together in a wide-ranging policy document published in September.[4] Perhaps less obvious, but nonetheless significant, was the fact that with the arrival of the Santer Commission at the beginning of 1995, 'there was a major shift in priorities and commitment'. Jacques Santer and his Chef de Cabinet Jim Cloos approached enlargement in reactive rather than proactive terms. Where Delors and his team had taken a lead and acted as persuaders for unity, Santer and his team were much more cautious in their approach; their essential view of enlargement was, according to one informed insider, one of 'disbelief in the feasibility of the enterprise'. They held to a 'firm conviction that the EU would do damage to itself, if it tried to go too far too fast'.[5]

Notwithstanding the inertia produced by this cautious approach, a deepening of relations in the economic sphere continued apace.[6] The integration of political and security structures also came on to the agenda, if at a slower pace and fashioned through more minimalist clothes. In early March 1994, plans for greater foreign policy cooperation were aired which included plans for yearly meetings among the EU Presidency, the Commission and the heads of state or government of the associated countries as well as special Council meetings involving the foreign ministers of the associated countries. The Council's plan also provided for formal cooperation between the EU and associated countries at international conferences. Significantly, it provided them with the opportunity to associate with EU statements on individual foreign policy questions and created the possibility of joint foreign policy actions by the EU and the associated countries. Thus the extension of the nascent CFSP began to take shape.

In the spring of 1994 the first formal applications for membership by the CEE states were made.[7] These formal applications only increased the pressure on the EU to develop a strategy to prepare the associated states for membership and added to existing tensions within the EU on the direction of policy. Especially evident at this time was the divide between northern and southern member states. This was partially resolved with a compromise that saw the southern member states, led by France and Spain, accept the need for eastern enlargement, while the German government endorsed the idea of a new Mediterranean policy (which would become the Barcelona Process). With this agreement in place, the way was clear for the institution of a comprehensive pre-accession strategy. At the Corfu summit on 24–5 June 1994, the European Council asked the Commission to make specific proposals to advance the process. Specifically, it called for a clear pre-accession strategy to follow up on the Copenhagen decisions.

The Commission's response to the Council request emerged within weeks. The communication, entitled *The Europe Agreements and Beyond*, outlined the major components of the pre-accession strategy:

> The goal for the period before accession should be the progressive integration of the political and economic systems as well as the foreign and security policies of the associated countries and the Union, together with increased cooperation in the fields of justice and home affairs, so as to create an increasingly unified area.[8]

The conscious effort to link pillars two and three to the most integrated area of activity (pillar one) was most striking. This was backed up by the insistence that all acceding states would have to accept not only the *acquis communautaire* but also the *acquis politique* and the *finalité politique* of the Union. In this sense, the EU approach was markedly different to that of previous enlargement rounds. The CEE states were effectively set a much higher threshold than had ever been set for prospective members. The Commission claimed that the existing 'structured relationship' held out the dual benefit of promoting a closer working relationship between the EU and the CEE states, while encouraging cooperation in resolving collective (or trans-European) problems.[9] However, the Commission called for expansion of the structured relationship beyond joint meetings with the Council to include other EU institutions, especially the European Parliament. It also argued that CFSP and

JHA issues should be included in the EU's multilateral dialogue with the associated states.[10] The main focus of the Commission's proposed strategy, however, was integrating the CEE states into the Community's internal market. Thus the greatest importance was attached to the transposition of EU law into the domestic legislation of the CEE states. In a more detailed follow-up, the Commission proposed specific measures for promoting its pre-accession strategy. These included recommendations regarding critical policy areas, from state aid and competition policy to further changes to the PHARE programme, and suggestions on the further adaptation of the corpus of EU law and new financial aid instruments.[11]

While the Commission spearheaded EU strategy, it was also greatly promoted by the German government, which held the EU presidency in the second half of 1994. Upon assuming the presidency, the Kohl government declared that progress on enlargement was a key goal of its term in office.[12] Germany encouraged an 'enhanced structured relationship' that would be multilateral in nature and would complement existing bilateral meetings held under the Europe Agreements. Such an arrangement would allow representatives of the associated states to participate in extended meetings of the Council of Ministers and European Council.[13] Not all member states favoured this arrangement, however, and in securing this agreement the German presidency, as Baun shows, had to overcome the fears of some member state governments that Bonn was trying to give the CEE states EU membership 'through the backdoor'.[14] With the invitation to CEE leaders to attend the Essen summit, scheduled for 9–10 December 1994, the German feeling was that this represented an important symbolic gesture, because it would send the CEE states an unequivocal message that the EU was 'not a closed shop'. As Helmut Kohl put it: 'we want to show that these countries will be welcome if they want to join'.[15] Exactly five years after the Berlin Wall had come down, however, ideas about how to best realize enlargement were far from clear.[16]

If, in retrospect, the 1993 Copenhagen summit is identified as the summit which laid out the macro-basis for a successful eastern enlargement, then the Essen summit should be viewed as no less important in terms of outlining the micro-agenda of economic reform necessary to prepare the associated countries for membership. In Essen, EU leaders formally approved a comprehensive pre-accession strategy. Following the Commission's original proposals, this strategy had two key parts: first, an enhanced structured relationship, and second, a White Paper drawn up by the Commission that would provide a 'route plan' for progressively integrating the CEE states into the Single Market.[17] The enhanced structured relationship was aimed at integrating the associated countries politically and at promoting cooperation between the EU and the associated countries in addressing common problems. It also aimed at socializing them into the complex process of EU policy formation and decision-making.[18] Again, the emphasis was cross-pillar in nature. Although the primary focus of the Essen framework was economic, there was also a symbolic and normative importance attached to having the CEE leaders present.[19] Just as important was the inclusion of an insistence on 'good neighbourly relations', effectively a new pre-condition for membership, which in time would evolve into the Pact on Stability in Europe. Based on a French plan,[20] the Pact was designed to help 'resolve the problems of minorities and strengthen the inviolability of frontiers'. In addition, it was supposed to be a 'staple component of a joint action to promote stability and peace in Europe' and help 'reinforce the democratic process and regional cooperation in CEE'.[21] In the end, the Pact was a success for the fledgling CFSP and a positive step in the EU's efforts to become an effective external actor. By helping to resolve potentially dangerous bilateral disputes, the pact promoted stability and security in CEE.[22] It also helped to create the political and security preconditions for enlargement by minimizing the security risks of taking in new member states.

The main element of the pre-accession strategy set out at Essen was, however, the outline of a detailed road map for integrating the CEE economies into the Single Market. The European Council requested the Commission to prepare and deliver this White Paper in time for its next regularly scheduled meeting at Cannes in June 1995. Despite a number of problems, the Commission delivered on the request and approved the final version of the White Paper in early May.[23] The stated purpose of the White Paper was to provide guidance to assist the associated countries in preparing themselves for operating under the requirements of the European Union's internal market.[24]

Baun suggests that the White Paper did three things. First, it identified the key legislation (or elements of the *acquis communautaire*), to be adopted by the associated countries in domestic law; second, it stressed that the simple transposition of EU legislation by the associated countries would not be enough. Each country was required to put in place a comprehensive legal and administrative infrastructure capable of supporting the legislation. Many felt that this represented the greatest challenge facing the candidate states. Finally, the White Paper also outlined the various forms of financial and technical assistance the EU would provide the CEE states to help in the reform process.[25] Although there were many complaints from the associated countries, the EU insisted that the measures were non-negotiable. Commissioner van den Bröek pointed out that the White Paper was not an obstacle but rather an essential mechanism which would facilitate economic adaptation in the CEE states.[26] The European Council at its Cannes summit formally approved the White Paper. In stressing the importance of not just the transposition but actual implementation of key legislative instruments, the White Paper presented the process of adaptation as both technical and horizontal, in every sense a rational policy process. This meant that it reduced the opportunities for veto groups on the EU side to intervene and block progress. There were both practical and tactical reasons for using this sort of approach. Seen in this light the White Paper stands out as a proactive measure by the Commission to draw out opponents of deeper engagement with CEE.[27]

Given the impetus provided by successive summits, it seemed that the essential building blocks were now successfully in place. Not surprisingly attention increasingly turned to the issue of a timetable for accession. During a visit to Warsaw, Chancellor Kohl promised that Poland, and by implication Hungary and the Czech Republic, would enter the EU by 2000. He thus became the first EU leader to advance a prospective date for enlargement. According to Baun, Kohl's statement surprised 'almost everyone' and Bonn officials were soon backtracking, suggesting that the date should only be regarded as an assurance of future entry: it need not actually happen prior to or on the date.[28] However, German government officials also acknowledged that Kohl was setting out a strategy that Germany intended to pursue.[29]

In advance of the Madrid summit (15–16 December 1995) the European Council asked the Commission to prepare official Opinions on all ten CEE countries and to forward these to the Council as soon as possible after the conclusion of the intergovernmental conference, due to begin in early 1996 under the Italian Presidency. It also asked the Commission to prepare a 'composite paper' on enlargement and to pursue further its analysis of the impact of enlargement on EU policies, especially the CAP and structural funds.[30] These various reports and analyses would form the basis of the Commission's document, *Agenda 2000*, which would be published in July 1997. Given the large number of countries to be assessed and the short timeframe in which to produce the Opinions the exercise represented a considerable test of the Commission's organizational capacity.[31] By the end of 1995, the focus of policy had thus switched firmly from pre-accession to an accession scenario, though there were still many contingent factors, not least, the upcoming IGC.[32]

The Luxembourg and Helsinki summits

The impression that the enlargement process was one where each step forward was followed by the proverbial two steps back was yet again reinforced when in 1996 the EU's agenda shifted once more to domestic issues, namely the IGC scheduled to be formally launched in Florence in March 1996, and the continuing difficulties faced by many countries in meeting the Maastricht criteria for monetary union. Although advances in the structured dialogue were noted, it was clear that further decisions on enlargement could be taken only when the Commission had completed its various analyses.[33] These were due to be delivered prior to the June 1997 Amsterdam summit, which would conclude the IGC process. The Commission began work on the Opinions in early 1996.[34]

The Opinions were primarily technical assessments of the capacity of each applicant to assume the obligations of membership. The Commission took into account information provided by each candidate country, assessments made by the member states of the Union, European Parliament reports and resolutions, the analysis of other international organisations such as the Council of Europe (CoE), the Organisation for Security and Cooperation in Europe (OSCE), and International Financial Institutions (IFIs).[35] They were intended as an aid to the European Council, which would make the final political decisions about the opening of accession negotiations with individual candidate countries.[36] The Commission's work involved an assessment of the compatibility of the laws, regulations and policies of the applicant countries with the *acquis communautaire*, as well as their ability to transpose EU legislation.[37] The Commission also had to take account of the prevailing political and economic conditions in the associated countries in accordance with the Copenhagen criteria. On 16 July the Commission formally presented the Opinions (*avis* in French) as part of the *Agenda 2000* report.[38] The Opinions differed from previous enlargement rounds in some crucial respects. Most importantly, they did not evaluate the applicants' preparedness for membership at the time of assessment, but rather in the medium term.

The Commission identified problems in each applicant country with establishing the rule of law and ensuring fundamental freedoms. However, only Slovakia was given an overall negative evaluation in the form of explicit references to, among other things, the treatment of the parliamentary opposition and the lack of independence of the judiciary. Consequently, the Commission recommended that Slovakia be excluded from the group of applicants with which the EU should open accession negotiations, even though it met the economic criteria for beginning accession. The treatment of Slovakia demonstrated clearly that the Union's political criteria were non-negotiable. Whilst there was some latitude in relation to economic issues such as market access and agricultural reform, no such approach could be adopted on the fundamental value system upon which the Union was founded.

In addition to the Opinions and a report on enlargement strategy, *Agenda 2000* also contained the Commission's analysis of key EU policies and their future development. In particular, it focused on the CAP and the Structural and Cohesion funds, two policy sectors that together consumed a great majority (approximately 80 per cent) of the EU budget.[39] The third part contained the Commission's proposed financial framework for the 2000–6 period. In this section the Commission argued that enlargement could be accomplished without any increased budgetary contributions from the member states. Instead, EU spending would be kept within the 1.27 per cent budget ceiling agreed at the Edinburgh summit in December 1992. The Commission's financial perspective included spending on agricultural and structural assistance for new members and pre-accession aid for the applicant states not included in the first wave. The proposals would be the subject of intensive debate and intergovernmental negotiations over the next two years, before a final agreement was reached at the Berlin summit in March 1999.[40] The Commission recommended in effect that enlargement should take place in a series of 'waves', and that a policy of differentiation (among the applicants) should be adopted. Although this led to charges of favouritism, the Commission retorted that its strategy was not based on exclusion of any associated country but rather 'it is a process of inclusion, which will be pursued permanently'.[41] Reaction to the package, needless to say varied according to cost–benefit calculations of both insiders and outsiders.[42]

Agenda 2000 helped shift the enlargement debate to new ground, according to Sedelmeier and Wallace. In effect, the EU had moved to consider the practical policy and institutional implications of enlargement and away from purely external matters such as trade liberalization and political dialogue. The external was now rapidly becoming the internal.[43] *Agenda 2000* also allowed for a much more transparent analysis of progress made by individual candidate states. Each state could now compare its own performance in specific areas to that of other

candidate states and engage in thinking about the type of policy changes necessary to sustain progress. The availability of much more information on the differential rates of progress being made by the candidate states also arguably helped
provide a template for EU policy-makers to move the enlargement game forward
in a more substantive way. It could equally be argued, however, that *Agenda 2000*
further muddied the enlargement waters. The Commission's insistence on balanced
and uniform language, designed to bolster reforms whilst underlining the importance of better and more substantive progress left candidate states none the wiser
as to the desired pathways of reform in given policy areas. This was especially the
case with CFSP and JHA.[44] Neither did the new approach betray any clue as to
the eventual date of accessions.

The main instrument that would underpin the Commission's 'reinforced pre-
accession strategy' would be the bilateral 'Accession Partnerships' (APs). These
would identify specific priorities for reform in each country; each applicant would
make precise commitments and outline the ways in which the PHARE programme
would support such commitments.[45] These Partnerships provided, *inter alia*, for a
single framework covering the priorities in and preparations for accession in each
candidate country.[46] Each candidate country would receive its own specific set of
accession-related goals and objectives. Future aid would then be conditional upon
the achievement of specified objectives and the general direction of reforms. The
Commission also recommended increased participation by the applicant countries
in various EU educational, cultural, and technological programmes as part of the
enhanced pre-accession strategy. Toward the end of March 1998 the EU finalized
and approved its Accession Partnerships for each of the CEE candidate states.[47]
These included National Programs for the Adoption of the *Acquis* (NPAAs) within a
precise timetable, focusing on the priority areas outlined by the Commission in its
Opinions. In this sense, each NPAA complemented the Association Partnership: it
contained a timetable for achieving the priorities and objectives and, where
possible, indicated the human and financial resources to be allocated. The Accession Partnerships would also provide a single framework for EU financial aid and
constitute the basis for the Commission's annual reports on the progress of the
candidate states.

Each of the Accession Partnerships followed a similar format, setting out both
short- and medium-term objectives. These reflected the various chapters of the
acquis communautaire and covered areas such as the political criteria for membership,
economic reform, reinforcement of institutional and administrative capacity, preparation for membership of the internal market, justice and home affairs, agriculture, environment, transport, employment and social affairs, regional policy, and
cohesion.[48] The Partnerships would contain precise commitments on the part of
the candidate countries relating in particular to democratic norms, macroeconomic stabilization, industrial restructuring, nuclear safety, and the adoption of the
acquis, focusing on the priority areas identified in each of the Commission Opinions. The programming of accession priorities, as set out in the Opinions, broke
down into short-, medium- and long-term priorities to be adjusted in subsequent
revisions of the Association Partnerships. The progress made by each applicant

country would be recorded in a screening process and thereafter in individual annual reports.[49]

Although welcomed by CEE governmental leaders, the Accession Partnerships also came in for some criticism, not least for the strictly defined conditionality that accompanied many of the constituent elements of the process. The asymmetry of positions between insiders and outsiders was obvious.[50] Not unnaturally, CEE governments were upset at the explicit linkage within the framework of the Partnerships between future aid and the progress of reforms. Sedelmeier and Wallace thus concluded that 'the language of partnership disguises rather thinly the imposition of EU priorities'.[51] Notwithstanding these criticisms, however, it seems clear that the Accession Partnerships provided an important institutional step toward immersing and integrating the candidate states in Community structures. Familiarity with EU best practice, with respect to issues such as the certification and standardization of professional bodies, or the norms pertaining to structural and cohesion funding would prove important as the process developed. The Partnerships thus represented a further step toward substantive institutionalization of relations short of membership.

In accordance with the priorities of the Association Partnerships, PHARE's role changed again. Two clear priorities emerged. First, because the capacity of the candidate countries to implement the *acquis* was deemed paramount, PHARE would help national and regional administrations – as well as regulatory, supervisory and other bodies – in the candidate countries to familiarize themselves with Community law and procedures. Second, PHARE would continue to help the candidate countries bring their industries and economic infrastructure up to EU standards by helping mobilize the investment required to drive forward technological change and sectoral competitiveness. Particular emphasis was to be accorded to areas such as environment, transport, industrial plant, and quality standards in products, all areas where EU norms were becoming increasingly demanding. PHARE was also allotted a key role in helping with institution-building in the candidate countries. This work centred on adapting and strengthening democratic institutions, public administration, and organizations that had a responsibility in implementing and enforcing Community legislation. It included the development of relevant structures, human resources and management skills and training for a wide range of civil servants, public officials, professionals and relevant private sector actors: from judges and financial controllers to environmental inspectors and statisticians, to name but a few. After the Luxembourg summit PHARE funds were channelled specifically toward these institution-building needs. Later PHARE would be used as a learning vehicle of sorts for the administrative underpinning of the structural funding regimes for the new member states.[52] A review of PHARE commissioned by Gunter Verheugen in 1999 showed that the reforms introduced in 1997 had begun to show positive results even if still quite uneven in terms of outcomes.[53]

Capacity-building instruments

The EU's support for pre-accession reforms in CEE also took on a more goal-oriented form with the introduction of three new instruments of support. The Commission saw these instruments as the most important pillars of the re-structuring programmes underway in the candidate states. The Instrument for Structural Policies for Pre-Accession (ISPA) was launched in 1998. It provided support for the emerging regional entities in CEE and closely paralleled the existing EU structures supporting structural and cohesion funding.[54] The Special Accession Programme for Agriculture and Rural Development (SAPARD) would become the second plank of administrative capacity building. SAPARD foresaw the delegation of substantial responsibility to the candidate states themselves regarding the management of EU funds for rural development.[55] The Commission also showed some innovation by encouraging meaningful local participation including social partners, NGOs and local representatives.[56] The third and final pre-accession instrument, the Twinning project, was launched in March 1998. Twinning aimed to help the candidate countries in their development of modern and efficient public administrations, with the structures, human resources, and management skills needed to implement the *acquis communautaire*. Twinning provided the framework for administrations and semi-public organizations in the candidate countries to work with their counterparts in specific member states. The main feature of the Twinning mechanism was that it set out to deliver specific and guaranteed results and not to foster general cooperation. The parties agreed in advance on detailed programmes designed to meet objectives concerning priority areas of the *acquis*. The key input from the member state administration came in the form of a core team made up of at least one pre-accession adviser seconded to work full time for a minimum of a year in the corresponding ministry of the candidate country, and a senior project leader responsible for the overall thrust and coordination of the project. They were supplemented by carefully planned and timed missions of other specialists, training events, and awareness-raising activities.

The assessment of such capacity-building efforts by the EU yields mixed results. In May 2003 the Court of Auditors reported on environmental aid programmes (effectively an audit of PHARE/ISPA) and on Twinning. It was clear that the acceding states still had a lot of work to do to build their administrative capacity for implementation. Certain EU projects designed to assist institution-building could be seen, at best, as only partially successful.[57] The finding on Twinning was that it had not lived up to initial expectations. Significant progress was made, according to the Auditors, in adopting Community law, but much less on implementation and enforcement. It admitted that it was 'too optimistic' to expect that 'fully-functioning, efficient and sustainable' candidate country organization could be established within a framework of a single project – eighteen months on average. In addition the Court described the Twinning project as excessively bureaucratic, with lengthy periods between needs-assessment and project-realisation, as well as having complicated payment systems. The old PHARE problem of deficiencies in consultant performance was again in evidence. Management shortcomings on both the candidate state and Commission sides were noted. The low level of take-up of ISPA projects in some candidate countries was telling.[58]

The PHARE annual report for 2002 and the interim evaluation produced in March 2004 (covering the period 1999 through to November 2003) highlighted the strengths and weaknesses of the different forms of capacity-building. The reports revealed an increased emphasis on support for national programmes (NPAAs) designed to address specific weaknesses identified in the annual Commission reports. The 2002 report detailed spending of €1700 million for the year was achieved including some 191 Twinning projects.[59] Some of the internal judgements on PHARE were extremely critical however. The 2004 report stressed that as many as one-third of programmes proved unsatisfactory with substantial weaknesses in needs analysis and design.[60] The most effective of the various programmes were those in the sphere of civil society, where there seemed convincing evidence of successful capacity-building among NGOs.[61] Despite the negative assessment of the programmes most candidate countries could point to some successes in achieving macro policy objectives by the time accession came around. Poland, despite difficulties with ISPA, succeeded in meeting most of its environmental targets. Similarly the Czech Republic could cite improved air quality partly as a result of PHARE-funded monitoring instruments and expert help.[62]

The Luxembourg summit

After *Agenda 2000* the sequencing of both intra-EU decisions and accession negotiations started to take a much clearer shape. The issue of enlargement strategy, however, continued to be the subject of considerable debate within the Commission. This came to a head in early July 1998. By this point, there was general agreement that differentiation among the CEE applicants was necessary, and that an 'enlargement in waves' strategy was preferable to a common start or so-called 'big bang'. Disagreement remained, however, on the number of countries to be included in the first wave.[63] The main proponents of a broader first wave were Commissioner van den Bröek and the Nordic Commissioners. President Santer was among those who favoured limiting the first wave to a smaller number of countries. On 10 July, after an intense week of discussion, the full Commission met to endorse van den Bröek's proposal for opening negotiations with five CEE states plus Cyprus. Thereafter, this would become known as the five-plus-one strategy. Michael Baun argues that the intervention of two important Commissioners, the United Kingdom's Leon Brittan (trade) and Germany's Martin Bangemann (industry), was critical. Each argued that the two countries which were the main subject of debate, Estonia and Slovakia, were prepared for accession negotiations based on an objective assessment of economic performance and that to exclude them would amount to political discrimination.[64] In recommending that the EU begin negotiations with five CEE countries, the Commission claimed that its decision was based on objective performance and adherence to specified economic and political criteria by the applicant states.[65]

The European Council, meeting in Luxembourg on 12–13 December 1997, formally decided to begin the accession process for the ten CEE states plus Cyprus. In the Presidency Conclusions the European Council underlined the historic significance of this decision, declaring that 'with the launch of the enlargement process we see the dawn of a new era, finally putting an end to the divisions of the past'.[66] To provide an inclusive framework for enlargement, the Council decided to set up a European Conference 'which will bring together the member states of the European Union and the European States aspiring to accede to it and sharing its values and internal and external objectives'.[67] The European Council also decided that formal accession negotiations would be launched in March 1998. The decisions were generally welcomed by the applicant countries, including those not in the first wave of negotiations.

The first phase of the accession process for all applicants was the analytical examination or 'screening' of the 31 chapters of the *acquis communautaire*. The Commission, with the help of the applicant countries, carried out this exercise. By early summer 1998 the screening process was well under way and the EU was contemplating the next step, the launching of substantive negotiations with the first-wave countries.[68] Those negotiations actually began on 29 October, with a deputy-level meeting in Brussels between EU permanent representatives and the chief negotiator of each of the six applicant states. The European Council followed the Commission's recommendation of a two-tier approach, even if this was to be subsumed within a 'single framework' that would treat the second-wave candidate countries as equals and give them the chance to catch up. From this point attention focused on the Commission, which was expected to issue the first of its 'Regular Reports' on candidate countries' progress in meeting the criteria in late 1998. The lobbying efforts of the second-wave countries were quite intense in the run-up to the publication of the Commission's second set of Regular Reports in December, as government leaders from these countries visited Brussels.[69] The hopes of the second-wave countries were disappointed, however. Whilst the Commission praised the reform efforts made by the second-wave countries, it nevertheless restated its view that none was ready to begin accession negotiations.[70]

In the aftermath of the Kosovo War in 1999, the Commission proposed that accession negotiations should be opened with all remaining candidate countries.[71] This was despite doubts about whether some had made enough progress in their preparations.[72] Clearly the deterioration of the situation in Kosovo propelled much more serious thought on enlargement strategy.[73] Momentum was in evidence from early in the year. Even the resignation crisis that destabilized the Santer Commission failed to have a serious impact on the process.[74] This strategy rethink reflected the shift in focus to Southeastern Europe and support grew for the idea of including Bulgaria and Romania in the accession negotiations. Many felt that to continue to exclude them would send the wrong message, thus undermining their efforts at political and economic reform with potentially disastrous consequences for stability and security in Southeastern Europe.[75] It was also felt that Bulgaria and Romania should be rewarded for their (domestically unpopular) support for NATO's bombing campaign against their neighbour Serbia, a fellow Orthodox country. The EU also recognized the economic hardship these countries faced in the wake of the Kosovo conflict and agreed that this deserved special consideration in the EU's decisions on enlargement strategy. The UK and Germany were especially active in promoting the change of strategy, with Prime Minister Tony Blair visiting Bulgaria and Romania in May 1999 and promising to work for their inclusion in negotiations.[76]

The Commission took the view that Slovakia alone did not satisfy the Copenhagen political criteria, but stressed the importance of institution-building in the candidate countries, especially reform of the judiciary and public administration.[77] In justifying the Commission's new 'regatta' approach for accession negotiations, President Prodi declared that it was necessary to 'take a bold step forward'. Thus, the Commission recommended to the Council that it open accession negotiations in 2000 with all applicants that had met the Copenhagen political criteria, and that 'have proved ready to take the necessary measures to comply with the economic criteria'. Commenting on the decision, Commissioner Verheugen argued:

> This strategy will help strike the right balance between two potentially conflicting objectives in the enlargement process: speed and quality. Speed is of the essence because there is a window of opportunity for enhanced momentum in the preparations for enlargement, in accordance with the expectations of the candidate countries. Quality is vital because the EU does not want partial membership, but new members exercising full rights and responsibilities.[78]

The element of conditionality was strong once more with the Commission insisting that the opening of negotiations with Bulgaria should be conditional on a decision by the Bulgarian authorities before the end of 1999 on acceptable closure dates for the Kozludy nuclear power plant. In the case of Romania, the opening of negotiations would depend on progress in reform of childcare institutions. At an extraordinary meeting in Tampere, Finland, several days after the Commission issued its report, the European Council largely endorsed the Commission's new strategy. A broad consensus among the member states in favour of the Commission's plan to expand the accession negotiations was reported, thus paving the way for a formal decision at Helsinki.[79]

At the Helsinki European Council on 10–11 December 1999 the decision was taken to formally invite the second-wave candidates – Romania, Bulgaria, Slovakia, Latvia, and Lithuania – to open accession negotiations in early 2000. It was also announced that, in the accession negotiations, 'each candidate will be judged on its own merits'.[80] With these decisions the EU formally abandoned the strategy of 'enlargement in waves' that had been adopted at Luxembourg and guided the process in the interim period. In explaining the change Commissioner Verheugen argued that the political situation had changed completely, making it necessary to adopt a more inclusive strategy, in particular with respect to Southeastern Europe.[81] Verheugen described the summit's decision as an historic step towards the unification of Europe, declaring 'the iron curtain has been definitively removed'.[82] The Helsinki summit also represented a major turning point in EU relations with Turkey, and specifically, Turkey's place within the accession framework.[83] Turkey would now be considered as a candidate country although there was no question of opening negotiations at that stage. Whilst it is clear that Helsinki represented a major step forward in the process there was still an amount of work to be done to 'seal the deal'.[84] The next two and a half years would involve complex and protracted negotiations, periods of regression, and eventually a triumphal end to negotiations at the Copenhagen summit in December 2002.

4 Closing the deal

Helsinki to Copenhagen

Introduction

If Helsinki had produced a commitment from the EU that enlargement was now 'irreversible' then the millennium began with the now familiar shadow-boxing that had characterized the process over the previous six years. The EU desired more tangible evidence of successful transposition and implementation in the candidate states, while on the candidate state side the by now regular expressions of frustration were never far from the surface. The momentum gained at Helsinki was not totally lost, however. Some member states pressed the initiative using the language of the timetable outlined at Helsinki to make the case for a concrete date.[1]

In the Commission's third series of Regular Reports in November 2000, the same basic procedure was followed as in 1998 and 1999.[2] The Commission's attention was focused on whether the reforms announced or recommended had actually been implemented since 1998. It also assessed each candidate country's progress in terms of ability to implement the *acquis*. The Commission's chief concern was the 'revitalization' of the negotiations, to 'take them into a more substantial phase', and point the way toward a conclusion. The need to reinforce administrative and judicial reform was again a major concern.[3] As to the specific requirements embodied in the *acquis* the picture was generally positive. Many of the legislative changes that the enlargement process required either had been made or were in the process of being introduced. There was also a marked improvement in implementation capacity.

The Regular Reports were accompanied by an Enlargement Strategy Paper, which contained a new accession 'road map'.[4] The 'road map' effectively revolved around the negotiation of the 31 'negotiating chapters' of the *acquis* and was understood as a timetable for completing the negotiations, chapter by chapter, by the end of 2002.[5] Negotiations on each chapter could only begin when both parties – the EU and the candidate countries – were in a position to communicate their respective starting positions. This process alone required a considerable amount of effort, not least on the EU side, where every draft 'common position' submitted by the Commission had to be approved by the Council. In nine cases out of ten, this meant agreement within the Council Working Group on Enlargement composed of middle-ranking officials in the member states' permanent representations.[6]

The French Presidency

With substantive negotiations under way France took over the Presidency of the EU in July 2000. Although many were disappointed by the results the EU did at least manage agreement on the institutional reforms necessary to underpin the enlarged Union. The European Council also endorsed the Commission's road map and made important gestures towards non-EU states, particularly those of the Western Balkans.[7] Most commentators, however, took a very negative view of the French Presidency's impact on the course of negotiations. At both the Biarritz summit in October and the Nice summit in December, Jacques Chirac, the French President, tried to force unilaterally formulated decisions on France's EU partners.[8] Matters were not helped by the complications of French domestic politics, with growing 'cohabitation' rivalry evident between Prime Minister Jospin and President Chirac in the weeks leading up to the Nice summit. In fact, the French EU Presidency frequently put forward draft texts that were then opposed by the French government delegation sitting at the same table. Diplomats from other EU states also found that points apparently agreed during negotiations in Brussels acquired a different spin after having been sent back to Paris to be formulated as texts for further negotiation.[9]

The shabby bargaining surrounding institutional recalibration was perhaps best symbolized by President Chirac, who 'like a late medieval Pope doling out indulgences to prop up an impossible cause, ended up distributing parliamentary seats to anybody who looked likely to cause trouble'.[10] All of this contributed to an atmosphere in which everybody looked for trophies rather than consensus'.[11] This would not be the last time that French politicians wrought controversy and uncertainty upon the enlargement negotiations. In late 2001 foreign minister Hubert Védrine caused consternation in Brussels by suggesting that Bulgaria and Romania should both be fast-tracked to join the other eight CEE states in an even larger 'big bang' enlargement. Citing the need for fairness and the risk of leaving the two countries behind, Védrine argued that there wasn't much difference between adding ten or twelve countries. Many commentators interpreted his suggestion as one designed to derail rather than accelerate enlargement and based on a view that the French government in fact was terrified at the implications of enlargement and the prospect of the EU's centre of gravity moving eastwards.[12] All of this contributed to the existing impression that enlargement negotiations were bogged down and not likely to make much progress.[13] Public opinion polls also tended to reflect the negative mood – in both the EU and in the candidate countries.[14]

The Swedish Presidency

Sweden took on the EU Presidency for the first time on 1 January 2001. Declaring definitive progress on enlargement the central priority of the presidency from the outset, the government of Göran Persson won many plaudits for its handling of the negotiations.[15] Ludlow asserts that although the Swedish Presidency was far from unblemished, the management of the accession negotiations was an unqualified success, and that no Presidency could have done a better job. Although public opinion surveys showed Sweden to be among the EU's least enthusiastic members, paradoxically the Swedes were the most enthusiastic about enlargement. This prompted Persson to remark 'the Swedes want other countries to join the EU and our own to leave'.[16] At the European Council summit meeting at Gothenburg on 15–16 June 2001 the EU 'confirmed the breakthrough in negotiations and agreed the framework for the successful completion of the enlargement'. Attesting to the fact that the candidate countries had made 'impressive progress' in meeting the accession criteria, the European Council made two other historic statements. The first declared the enlargement process 'irreversible'. The second provided the long-awaited 'road map' or timetable for the first accessions by suggesting 'the road map should make it possible to complete negotiations by the end of 2002 for those candidate countries that are ready. The objective is that they should participate in the European Parliament elections of 2004 as members'.[17] Ludlow asserts that the language used in the Gothenburg conclusions was indicative 'of how much the process had moved on'. First, rather than (Nice) 'welcome new member states which are ready as from the end of 2002', it talked about 'complete negotiations by the end of 2002'. Second, it emphasized that the aim was to enable the new member states to take part in the European Parliament elections of 2004 'as members'.[18] Another significant development was the upgrading of some of the later negotiating entrants to the top tier of negotiations. These included Slovakia, Latvia, and Lithuania. This meant 'the principle of catch-up in the negotiations has been fully realized', according to Gunnar Lund, the Swedish ambassador to the EU.[19]

The breakthrough had come in the final session when Germany, which had resisted the idea of setting the end of 2002 as the date for completing negotiations, bowed to the will of a strong majority of EU states. German hesitation had been based partly on a fear that the provision of a deadline would undermine the EU's negotiating hand, and more importantly, by fears that Poland simply would not be ready in time.[20] The Swedish Presidency managed 'not just to resist but to sweep away most of the objections to enlargement' according to one commentator. By putting the timetable in place it was clear that outstanding differences among EU member states in areas such as agriculture and regional aid would now have to be seriously addressed.[21] Reaction to the breakthrough was uniformly positive with speculation rising that the 'big bang' was not such an unlikely scenario after all.[22] Many people had been sceptical that the big bang could be achieved. The number of such people decreased after Gothenburg.[23] For many observers the political entrepreneurship of Göran Persson was crucial.[24] The Swedish strategy could only succeed, however, because of the substantive attachment on the part of EU political élites to a normative understanding of the enlargement process. The sense of drama was captured in Prime Minister Persson's assertion that 'I was overwhelmed, almost every one of them [leaders of the candidate states] took the floor and expressed their gratitude for what we have done during the last six months'.[25]

The November 2001 annual reports, the fourth, recorded steady progress towards accession by the candidate countries.[26] The reports also clearly indicated that the 'enlargement in waves' strategy had bitten the dust and that all candidates were being assessed on merit. This was neatly summed up in the definition of a so-called 'Laeken group' of ten countries, which signalled the end of the distinction between the 'Luxembourg' and 'Helsinki' groups.[27]

The Danish Presidency

With momentum building in the early part of 2002, Denmark took over the Presidency of the Union in July. The Danish game plan for concluding negotiations revolved around three interrelated aims: movement toward substantive agreement on Council reform; a holding operation on agriculture; and a timetable which prioritized the October European Council summit meeting. Danish Prime Minister Anders Fogh Rasmussen brought to the presidency energy, commitment and evident communication skills. As importantly, he was supported by a solid administrative and diplomatic foundation. At every level, the Danes were solidly equipped to broker the upcoming talks at the most critical stage in the process. Along with Rasmussen Danish Permanent Representative Poul Christoffersen played a crucial role in anchoring the accession talks.[28] There were still considerable problems to be faced, however, not least the uncertainty surrounding the German elections in September and the second referendum on the Nice Treaty in Ireland, which was due to be held in October and the outcome of which was far from certain.[29]

Financial issues

Financial and budgetary issues, although they had dominated debate on the 'how' and 'when' of the eastern enlargement debate since *Agenda 2000*'s publication in 1997, were left to the very latter stages of the accession negotiations. The Danes assumed the EU Presidency facing the prospect of a total disagreement among the EU15 about how to proceed with the financial and agriculture chapters.[30]

The Berlin agreement of 1999 assumed an entry of six countries in 2002, not ten in 2004. Some form of re-adjustment would thus have to take place in the calculations. And this was reflected in a Commission memorandum in January 2002.[31] The memorandum proposed significant changes in the negotiating position of the Union but without breaking the commitment ceiling entered into at Berlin.[32] The essence of the Commission proposal lay in a phasing-in of both agricultural and regional aid to the candidate states, and the requirement that they pay contributions to the EU budget in full from the moment of accession. The package made a significant concession to the candidates by accepting the principle of direct aid to CEE farmers, even if only on a gradual basis. It also provided the member states with estimates of what each country would contribute to the EU budget in the first years after accession. Commission calculations showed that in addition to Cyprus and Malta, the Czech Republic, Hungary and Slovenia would be losers in net terms. The budgetary imbalances to be redressed were not insignificant.[33] In the end it was decided that no new member state should end up in a worse budgetary state after accession than before.

The Berlin agreement had not provided for any direct payments to farmers in the new member states. The level of uncertainty regarding the future form and nature of the CAP made it possible for a Commission fudge to be utilized. It argued that the newcomers should be given credible assurances that they would be 'fully integrated into the CAP, *whatever its nature may be*'. This at least went some way to meeting the charge of second-class membership and outright discrimination.[34] The Commission thus went on to propose the introduction of direct payments from 2004, but on only a limited basis, beginning at 25 per cent of the EU15 level in 2004, and progressing to parity by 2013.[35] The Commission judgement was informed in large part by the existence of large numbers of semi-subsistence farms in Central and Eastern Europe.[36] The Commission thus argued that introducing direct aid too quickly could slow down the restructuring process. This could create a vicious circle of low productivity, low standards and high hidden unemployment.[37] The Commission's paper was widely criticized both inside the EU and amongst the candidates.[38] In the immediate aftermath the member states 'gave an impressive display of their disunity. The confrontation was as always three-cornered, with the net contributors in one corner, the partisans of the CAP in another and the Cohesion countries in yet another. All of them expressed their concerns but none more so than the French and the Germans.'[39]

The German view that CAP reform was a precondition for enlargement to take place was accepted neither by the French nor the candidate states. The impasse suggested nothing of significance could be resolved until after the French and German elections. The deterioration in the German domestic budgetary situation was clearly an important factor behind Chancellor Schröder's position, notwithstanding consistent German pressure for CAP reform. Schröder put it like this in the *Frankfurter Allgemeine Sonntagszeitung* on 16 June 2002:

> Even if many find it difficult to believe, Germany is at the limits of its capacity to pay. If I were in these circumstances to countenance the application of the direct payments system to the candidate countries, Commissioner Solbes might as well start immediately to draft a series of blue letters.[40]

To the Germans and their allies on CAP such as the UK the prospect of a midterm review was to be welcomed. It opened up the possibility of using CAP reform (necessary as an end in itself) as an instrument for alleviating the financial pain of enlargement provision. It was clear also that Germany's concerns were widely shared. Gerrit Zalm, the Dutch finance minister, and his Austrian counterpart, Karl Heinz Grasser, both publicly voiced opposition to the extension of the direct aid programme to candidate states.[41]

The EU began the final lap of the accession negotiations on 19 April 2002. As anticipated the talks would cover the most difficult matters relating to finances and voting powers. The draft common positions drawn up by the Commission came in for extensive review and discussion in the Council working group on enlargement whilst bilateral talks between the Commission and the candidates accompanied this process.[42] The Germans, the Dutch, and other net contributors clung firmly to their objections and refused to sign blank cheques before they knew what was in the Fischler CAP reform paper. In an effort to calm fears of a delay in enlargement ministers pledged to reach an agreement on direct payments at the EU summit in Brussels in October. Commissioner Verheugen aptly summed up the sense of drift in his address to the European Parliament on 12 June when he admitted: 'there are winds of resistance growing. The climate has become more brutal, more sceptical … all based on a lack of knowledge and fear'. Chancellor Schröder in a newspaper interview again re-iterated that Germany could not and would not bear the cost of extending the CAP eastward.[43]

On 10 July 2002, Franz Fischler presented his long-expected mid-term review of the CAP.[44] Its main proposals included first, and most importantly, a decoupling of the link between production and direct payments. The Commission recommended that the whole payments system should be replaced by a single payment per farm, the level and character of which would no longer be linked to production. Second, the Commission argued for a reinforcement of environmental, food safety, animal welfare and occupational safety standards. The new payments would be conditional on the recipients' respect for these enhanced standards, thereby increasing the pressure on farmers to follow 'good farming practices'. In addition new schemes in quality assurance and food certification were proposed. Third, there was increased support for rural development particularly by small farmers. This would be achieved by a new system of 'dynamic modulation', which would reduce direct payments by 3 per cent per annum to farmers.[45] The reforms were much more ambitious than most had expected and, according to Ludlow the 'thrust was unpalatable'.[46] Rasmussen, as incoming President of the EU, sought consistently to decouple the enlargement negotiations from debates about CAP reform. But agriculture would continue to complicate the enlargement negotiations to the end.

The 2002 Regular Reports

The next important milestone in the process would be the (earlier than usual) publication of the Commission's annual reports prior to the October Brussels European Council. The reports divided into two parts. The first consisted of a series of so-called regular reports on progress made by the candidates in specific areas (more or less conforming to the negotiating chapters of the *acquis*). The second – the Strategy paper – represented a macro-political analysis of overall progress.[47] Given that the political desire for enlargement had been ratcheted up, however, by the Gothenburg timetable, it was clear that these reports would not simply consist of a functional reporting of progress but indicate also a definite political determination to complete the process. The Commission's determination to conclude the process successfully was manifested in a change in the language employed in the Strategy Report. From an early version, which stated that candidates 'should' be ready to assume the obligations of membership in 2004, the final version inserted 'will' over 'should', thus signaling the Commission's desire to bring finality to the process.[48] The Commission also endorsed what was already accepted, namely that once the Accession Treaty had been signed, the new member states in waiting should become active observers in all Community institutions and activities. In addition, the Commission also proposed detailed monitoring of the application of Community law in the acceding member states. Six months before the accession date a comprehensive monitoring report, not dissimilar to the regular reports, would be produced. This was unprecedented in previous enlargement rounds and more than anything else reflected the serious gap in legislative implementation still in evidence.

The task of improving the administrative and judicial capacity of the acceding states was also central and had been prioritized in the pre-accession agreements and the NPAAs.[49] Although the Commission had worked with each candidate country on an Action Plan to reinforce their administrative and judicial systems there still existed serious gaps not only in legislation, but in necessary complimentary measures, such as setting up management structures and authorities, establishing coordination and arbitration systems, the training of judges and upgrading of IT systems.[50] Acknowledging the ongoing difficulties in capacity-building the Commission proposed a special, three-year transitional facility for institution-building after accession. In a sense this was an acknowledgement of failure to build up capacity over the past number of years, or at least to do enough, but more importantly it represented a commitment to substantive help in respect of ongoing reform efforts.[51]

Administrative capacity became an even more prominent issue in the run-up to the accession date in 2004 with revelations that the acceding member states were having great difficulty in finding suitable projects to match spending appropriations. The Commission warned that there was a great risk that the new member states would not be able to use the €22 billion allocated to them under the structural and cohesion funds in the programming period 2004–6. Most concern was centred on the apparent failure to fully transpose and implement the necessary statutory legislation.[52] Corruption continued to be a serious impediment to progress. An Open Society Institute publication, *Corruption and Anti-Corruption Policy*, suggested the EU had 'missed or neglected' a number of key areas in examining corruption – 'state capture, public procurement, and public administration in particular'. Collusion between public procurement bidders 'appears to be widespread'.[53]

Although the negotiations continued to deliver results, there remained some troubling issues, which had the capacity to wreck the timetable if not the negotiations themselves. Three in particular stood out in the early autumn of 2002 in the run-up to the crucial Brussels European Council summit. The first was the second referendum on the Nice Treaty in Ireland, which the Irish government went some way toward turning into a referendum on enlargement.[54] The second issue was how the net contributors would deal with the financial implications of enlargement. Finally, there was the destabilizing impact of the Dutch government's political problems to contend with. In particular, one of the three coalition parties, the Dutch Liberal Party (VVD), sought to whip up fears about enlargement. As early as 1 October, the VVD minister for European affairs, Atzo Nikolai told the *Financial Times Deutschland* that his government would not sanction direct payments to candidate country farmers unless there was at the same time a clear commitment by present member states of the EU to reform the CAP: 'No phasing in without phasing out'. The Dutch, he declared, were bigger net contributors to the EU budget than even the Germans. At a time when the new coalition was pledged to austerity at home, it could not countenance additional burdens abroad.[55] Gerrit Zalm, the influential VVD leader and former finance minister, argued that the entry of most candidate states as planned by the Commission was premature. In an interview on 13 October Zalm claimed that Poland in particular and also Slovakia and Latvia were not ready to take up the obligations of membership. Other members of the VVD expressed strong doubts about Latvia's membership. Sources close to the Dutch government asserted publicly that the decision to be taken in December should not be irrevocable and that, until eventual accession in 2004, it should always be possible to say no to a candidate country that does not meet the criteria.[56] Eventually the caretaker government of Jean Peter Balkenende agreed that it would not exercise a veto over enlargement but insisted on some greater guarantees on monitoring especially of frontier controls. The amount of time given over by Rasmussen and the Danish Presidency to ameliorating Dutch concerns was considerable in the run up to Brussels.

The Brussels European Council

In advance of the Brussels European Council in October 2002 there was considerable pessimism that the meeting would fail to resolve important issues such as CAP reform, the financing of enlargement, and outstanding institutional issues.[57] The proposals of the Commission remained simply proposals.[58] Disagreements on direct payments to candidate state farmers continued to generate tension and also entangled the enlargement negotiations in the debate on the future of the CAP. As Mayhew points out this meant that as the negotiations proceeded the countries most in favour of enlargement, Germany, Sweden, the UK and the Netherlands were those against conceding direct income subsidies to the new member states because this would impede the reform of the CAP, while countries traditionally less positive about enlargement, such as France, Portugal and Ireland, were in favour of accommodating CEE preferences.[59] More positively Coreper and the GAERC managed to resolve a lot of outstanding difficulties before the actual European Council meeting took place.[60]

At the summit meeting itself the European Council agreed to the Commission's proposal on direct income subsidies, whilst simultaneously agreeing that budgetary expenditure on market support and direct income subsidies in the period 2007–13 could not rise by more than 1 per cent per year over the level reached in 2006.[61] The dispute about CAP, however, produced 'an open clash between Prime Minister Blair and President Chirac at the table, and, it is said, an even sharper one in the margins of the meeting'.[62] Chirac's suggestion of tying CAP reform to renegotiation of the UK budget rebate, which had been in place since 1984, was rebuffed not just by the British but also by Rasmussen who argued: 'if we raise all of those questions, we will never finish'.[63] Many saw France as the undisputable winner in the deliberations over agriculture.[64] This was not least because the agreement delayed any lowering of expenditure on the CAP. There was significant resentment at the 'private deal' on agriculture thrashed out between Chirac and Schröder at a pre-summit meeting at the Hotel Conrad in Brussels. Despite constant protestations from Germany about the need to ensure that the cost of enlargement would not be excessive, it looked to many as if the outcome of the Chirac–Schröder Conrad meeting indicated that Schröder was prepared to accept continuing to shoulder the expense of CAP and extending it to new member states as the price to be paid for a successful enlargement.[65]

The Brussels European Council cleared the way for the negotiations to move to a conclusion. But the intra-EU bargaining was far from concluded. There remained significant hurdles and time was running out quickly. Poul Christoffersen, the Danish Permanent Representative believed, however, that an intra-EU negotiation would endanger the Presidency's timetable. He therefore decided to dispense with it. On that basis the Presidency and the Commission proceeded to prepare a 'final offer' that Ludlow argues went well beyond the 'absolute limits' laid down at the Brussels Council. Subsequently there was 'consternation' when Christoffersen announced his plan to Coreper on 25 November.[66] It represented a 'calculated risk' that Copenhagen would present an opportunity to iron out difficulties. What the Commission and the Presidency dubbed 'the final position' in the final week of November was thus their final position and not that of the EU15. It is highly unusual for the Presidency to operate without a mandate from the member states, yet it was, Denmark believed, the only way to progress the negotiations to a conclusion in the short time left.[67]

The joint Presidency–Commission paper went some way toward tackling the considerable difficulties of the candidate countries.[68] This meant, inevitably, increasing the costs of enlargement to the existing member states. The proposal raised considerably, for example, the payments for the decommissioning of nuclear facilities in the acceding states.[69] Cumulatively they implied a significant increase in EU spending over the three-year period, compared with the Brussels European Council figures. According to estimates attached to the 8 November document, total commitments would be just over €1 billion higher than the heads of state and government had agreed to at the Brussels meeting, even though, by moving the accession date forwards from January to May 2004, the Union should in principle have been saving a significant amount of money. It was inevitable that such proposed increases would be contested, perhaps vigorously, by some of the member states.[70]

On 24 November Christoffersen presented, as part of the final negotiating package, a revised budget proposal. Although coming in at about €1 billion less than that of the Commission in January 2002, it was nevertheless significantly more (about €2.5 billion) than that proposed at Brussels in October.[71] The budget included €900 million for a so-called 'Schengen facility', to reimburse candidates for the expenditure, and to accelerate their preparations on border control; €600 million for decommissioning nuclear power plants; and €1 billion as a lump sum for budgetary compensation, to be distributed among the new member states on the basis of their GNI.[72] Although some of the permanent representatives expressed concern about and even opposition to the package, Christoffersen was not for changing course. His out was that governments would have ample room to negotiate with the Presidency in the weeks ahead. In both Germany and the Nethelands the proposals generated considerable unease, being seen as far too generous and having been conceded far too early in the final negotiating process. The Commission and Presidency were thus presented as 'allies' of the candidates rather than negotiators on behalf of the EU15. Both Chancellor Schröder and foreign minister Joschka Fischer argued that the Brussels figures had to be respected, as did President Chirac on another bilateral visit to Germany.

The package, of course, was not read routinely in all the candidate countries. In fact adjusted for population size there seemed to be some remarkable differences. The Baltic States emerged well over the period 2004–6, Poland and the Czech Republic significantly less so.[73] Thus the likelihood of very difficult negotiations with the latter group of candidate states now presented itself. For many states the prospect of referendums on membership to follow the conclusion of negotiations meant that securing a generous financial package was of the utmost importance if the accession deal was to be sold domestically. Not surprisingly the Polish government was proving particularly difficult. A formal statement from the ten heads of government after a meeting in Warsaw highlighted many of the difficulties the candidate countries had with the package. The statement called for greater budgetary relief, a faster phasing-in of farm subsidies, and a 'fair balance of the rights and obligations of membership'.[74] Less pressing issues related to the problems of individual countries continued to be worked on if not solved. The candidate states seemed to be moving in private toward greater realism in their negotiating positions and it was striking that their most contentious demand – on full and immediate access to direct payments – was not even mentioned in the formal exchanges at the meeting.[75] The Danish Presidency presented its draft 'final package' to each of the ten leading candidate states on 26 November – but without any certainty it would be accepted by the candidates or by the EU member states.[76]

The Copenhagen European Council summit

For many observers it was fitting that the endgame of the eastern enlargement negotiations would be played out at Copenhagen. After all it was at Copenhagen in 1993 that the EU had taken the first important steps toward accepting the former Communist states into its ranks. Going in to the summit meeting the rhetoric of the main players demonstrated no more than a cautious optimism. One early indicator of the negotiating difficulties was the cancellation of the reception and dinner at the Christianborg Palace.[77] The sense of occasion and nervousness was captured in a letter to the *Gazeta Wyborzca* from many of the leading figures in the communist dissident movements who feared the collapse of the negotiations and the opportunity to re-unite the continent: 'We urge that the original idea of solidarity in a united and democratic Europe should not be buried under the negotiations and group and local lobby interests.'[78]

The most important question to be addressed remained the size and shape of the final financial package for enlargement. In effect the Danish Presidency 'took a punt', to use a gambling expression, on the Copenhagen summit delivering the right result, on the member states not being able to countenance disappointing the candidate states again with another delay. Given the problems experienced at Nice and protracted arguments on the cost of enlargement this was a considerable risk to run. As far as the financial package was concerned the Presidency made clear that this was a matter for the heads of state and government at the summit meeting. Gerhard Schröder, before leaving Berlin, told journalists that a fifth enlargement without Poland was simply inconceivable. The Danish Presidency took this as a signal of Schröder's willingness to go that extra mile for a fair accord. This hopefulness was not as obvious in Warsaw, where after a whole day's meeting of the Polish Council of Ministers it was still less than clear what the Polish bottom lines might be.[79] The Polish position was extraordinary in negotiating terms. Prime Minister Miller was supported by his coalition partner and deputy prime minister Jaroslav Kolinowski, of the Polish Peasants' Party, who over the previous few months had repeatedly threatened to quit the government if Poland failed to get a good enough deal. Miller was being far from disingenuous when claiming that if the deal for Poland was not improved his government would implode. And this was of the utmost importance as the negotiations at Copenhagen were largely centred on the bilateral negotiation between Poland and the EU.[80]

The 'final offer' made by Rasmussen was the revised version of the lengthy paper on the financial package which had been represented to Coreper on 25 November and reflected developments in the last pre-Copenhagen round of negotiations with the candidates on 9 December and the GAERC meeting of 10 December. The total package of financial aid amounted to €40.8 billion (to 2006). But given that the new member states would also contribute to the budget something approaching €15 billion, the net figure was reduced to about €25 billion. The Commission thus suggested a net cost for ten countries over three years of just €10.3 billion per annum, which amounted to just one-thousandth of EU GDP.[81]

The Polish delegation continued to express disquiet. What was to be done? It seems clear that Verheugen was quite heavily involved with the German government in coming up with the idea for a transfer of some money earmarked for future structural operations into a special cashflow facility, which Christoffersen had created after Coreper on 25 November. For the Poles the merit of this was first and foremost that it involved the delivery of cash up front rather than commitments into the future.[82] A figure of about €1 billion 'extra' could thus be procured for the Poles. This was because German Chancellor Schröder agreed to another €1 billion being found for Poland but only by a process of re-classifying money earmarked later for regional aid as a straight and immediate cash transfer.[83] This certainly constituted a negotiating success for the Poles. They clearly envisaged difficulties in finding enough viable projects for regional aid. But the 'cashflow facility' instead represented a lump sum paid into the national treasury with few strings attached.[84]

Once this measure was agreed the success of the negotiations was guaranteed. The successful conclusion of the eastern enlargement process was then announced to the world press in suitably colourful language. The outcome was one which 'testifies to the common determination of the peoples of Europe to come together in a Union that has become the driving force for peace, democracy, stability and prosperity on our continent'.[85] Whatever the nature of the descriptives, the deal had been successfully concluded.

Reaction to the summit focused on the historic nature of the outcome as well as the outstanding contribution of the Danish Presidency. Others took the historical view that this meant, finally, the closing of the darkest chapters in Europe's history. Poland's daily *RzecPospolita* summed up the acceding states mood: 'Good morning, Europe.' The Czech daily *Lidove noviny* asserted: 'A new Europe is born.' The Hungarian broadsheet *Magyar Hirlap* announced: 'The end of divided Europe.'[86] Not surprisingly British Prime Minister Tony Blair felt the hand of history once more upon all present! Not all commentators were as dewy-eyed. In the Eurosceptic London *Times* Roger Boynes castigated the EU for 'behaving disgracefully … bullying and bludgeoning Central Europe' and cautioned the newcomers on dampening their entrepreneurial spirit within a stagnant EU economy. Conservative leader Ian Duncan Smith attacked the EU for delaying enlargement for so long.[87] The overriding feeling, however, both in the EU and the accession states, was one of relief that the negotiations, which had seemed to teeter on the brink of collapse at regular intervals, had been brought to a successful conclusion.

Completing the formalities and tying the knot

The interregnum between the Copenhagen summit meeting and the signing ceremony in Dublin on 1 May 2004 was not without its moments of excitement. The American-led invasion of Iraq brought to the fore important differences in respect of attitudes to European foreign policy. President Jacques Chirac succeeded in alienating a great number of the new member states in castigating them as 'infantile' and 'reckless' because of their support for the United States in the Iraq war.[88] There was discontent also in some of the acceding states as the accession terms were studied closely. In Poland small farmers were the most vocal in their criticism of the Copenhagen package. Religious groups also complained when it became clear that Poland's accession treaty was not going to include a measure to ban same-sex marriages. All of this boded ill for the referendum.[89]

The finalized text of each accession treaty was the outcome of intensive discussion during January 2003 between the Commission and the acceding states, and was not significantly different from that which was negotiated at Copenhagen. The treaty itself consisted of two parts; the first listed the acceding countries and their dates of accession as well as the official languages in which the treaty was drawn up. The second part was much more complex and voluminous, being composed of five parts, nine protocols, 44 declarations, the Final Act, and 18 annexes. The complete set of documents, drawn up in 21 languages, each occupying 1,000 pages in the

Official Journal or up to 6,000 pages in normal text, was then deposited officially in the archives of the Italian government.[90] The sheer complexity of the treaties threw open different interpretations. The EU stance was simple: any changes were merely the consequences of detailed clarifications.[91] The Accession Treaty itself was signed at the foot of the Parthenon in Athens on 16 April 2003.[92] The Athens daily *Apoyevmatini* referred to the accession treaty as a 'contract of hope'. The EU's expansion not only guaranteed a peaceful future, but would increase solidarity among the member states. German Chancellor Gerhard Schröder declared: 'With this step, the Union is finally overcoming the division of Europe into east and west … just like the Berlin Wall [in 1989] today it is a reason for shared joy – joy that we are creating a united and peaceful Europe.'[93] The Declaration which accompanied the Accession Treaty and was signed by all 25 signatory heads of state or government was explicit in setting out the fundamental basis not only for the enlargement being realized but the European integration process itself:

> Our achievement is unique. The Union represents our common determina-
> tion to put an end to centuries of conflict and to transcend former divisions on
> our continent. The Union represents our will to embark on a new future based
> on co-operation, respect for diversity and mutual understanding. Our Union
> represents a collective project: A project to share our future as a community of
> values.[94]

The *sui generis* nature of the European Union and the determination to further transpose its value system on to neighbouring states and regions was also clearly emphasized:

> Accession is a new contract between our citizens and not merely a treaty
> between states. As citizens of this new enlarged Union we proclaim our
> commitment to the citizens of the candidate countries. We are also committed
> to developing ever deeper ties and bridges of cooperation with our neighbours
> and to share the future of this community of values with others beyond our
> shores.

The accession referendums

In the aftermath of Copenhagen attention turned toward the accession referendums that were planned for each acceding state. Recent experience of the referendum process in Denmark and Ireland had demonstrated that voters simply could not be taken for granted. And although 'Yes' votes were expected in most states there arose concern about unfavourable opinion polls in Poland, Hungary and Estonia especially. A more likely scenario was that turnout figures would fail to reach the required threshold levels in a number of states. If that happened the accession referendums would fail, at least in those states where reaching the threshold level was a constitutional requirement.[95] The first state to vote on the Accession Treaty was Malta on 9 March. The result there – a 'Yes' vote of 53 per

Table 4.1 Results of EU accession referendums in Central and Eastern Europe

Country	Ref. Date	Yes (%)	No (%)	Turnout (%)
Slovenia	23 March 2003	89.66	10.34	55
Hungary	12 April 2003	83.76	16.24	46
Lithuania	10–11 May 2003	89.92	10.08	64
Slovakia	16–17 May 2003	92.46	7.54	52
Poland	7–8 June 2003	77.45	22.55	58.85
Czech Republic	13–14 June 2003	77.33	22.67	55.21
Estonia	14 September 2003	66.92	33.08	63.4
Latvia	20 September 2003	67	32.3	72.53

cent – undoubtedly emboldened pro-Europeans in Central and Eastern Europe. This was followed by a comfortable majority in Slovenia, despite public opposition to the war in Iraq, which had complicated the government's case for a 'Yes' vote.[96] The Slovak referendum on 16 and 17 May resulted in a resounding vote for accession, although again on a less than overwhelming turnout. The Polish referendum held over two days on 7 and 8 June resulted in a strong 'Yes' vote once again and was achieved on a relatively high turnout of almost 60 per cent.[97] In the Czech Republic on 13 and 14 June a turnout of 77.3 per cent saw a winning majority of 55.2 per cent of votes cast. Estonia voted to join the EU by a decisive 67 per cent to 33 per cent in its vote on 14 September 2003 on a turnout of 66 per cent. Latvia completed the set on 21 September with a similar 67 per cent 'Yes' vote.[98] There was widespread relief after the latter result as Latvia had been seen as the most Eurosceptic of the candidate states.[99] With the referendum process complete national ratification procedures were fully realized.

At the Salonika summit attention turned naturally enough to the Balkans and the prospect of further enlargement. EU leaders effectively promised the political direction necessary to guide the region toward and possibly into the EU. As Romano Prodi put it: 'Europe's unification will not be complete until the Balkan countries are members of the Union.'[100] The task of maintaining momentum toward the accession date was, as ever, that of the Commission. In its so-called 'comprehensive monitoring reports' of 5 November, a post-negotiation continuation of the screening reports of previous years, the Commission made it clear that although there were no serious obstacles now in the way of accession, the problems still being experienced in implementing EU legislation in the acceding states might mean the imposition of safeguard clauses which had been outlined in the Accession Treaty.[101]

For all of the caution on the EU side, however, there was also a palpable sense of relief that the most difficult and protracted enlargement negotiation in its history had been successfully concluded. The fact that the honour of hosting the accession ceremony fell to Ireland during its 2004 Presidency of the EU was highly symbolic in that Ireland had joined the Community as a poor peripheral state, beset by economic underperformance and high emigration, and made membership of the Union work for it by transforming and modernizing its economy. Ireland indeed was an exemplar of what EU membership offered for the new member states.

Part II

The institutional dimension of eastern enlargement

5   The Council of Ministers and eastern enlargement

Introduction

It has become a truism in politics that institutions matter. In recent years much of the literature on international relations has sought to locate institutional power and analyse its significance within local, national and global politics. For some, political decisions are largely a function of embedded institutional power or the product of specific patterns of institutional interaction and delegation. Others, while less accepting of the claims for institutional efficacy, acknowledge the increasing number of international institutions and their impact on at least some forms of interstate relations. Perhaps unsurprisingly, the European Union has attracted most attention from scholars of international institutions in recent years. For it is within the EU's variegated structure that the most advanced patterns may be found in global politics of interstate institutionalization of economic, political and, increasingly, security relations.[1] The enlargement of such a complex and multifaceted international entity necessarily entails an important institutional dimension. Enlargement both arises out of specific forms of institutionalized cooperation and subsequently produces a reconfiguration of those institutionalized norms, practices and structures. Thus any substantive analysis of an enlargement process necessitates an appreciation of the institutional dynamics that influence and underpin decision-making.

The three chapters of part II of this book focus on the internal EU decision-making process on eastern enlargement. As such they analyse the different roles played by the three principal EU institutions – the Council, Commission and Parliament – in the accession process. The timeframe under review includes the various periods encompassing association, pre-accession and actual negotiations with the focus on a number of key questions. What were the formal treaty-based responsibilities of each of the three EU institutions with respect to enlargement decisions, and how did each institution seek to assert its influence on the process? How and through what instruments did each of the institutions engage with the candidate states during the enlargement process? Where there existed fragmentation within an individual institution how did this manifest itself and with what effect on the enlargement process? To what extent did each of the institutions act as European 'institution-builders' and/or 'identity-builders' within the structures of the enlargement process? Before proceeding to examine the role played by the Council of Ministers it seems useful to briefly outline the formal treaty-based provisions which govern EU enlargement decisions.

Enlargement decisions

Enlargement is a policy domain which involves each of the main EU institutions in a distinctive way. This is clearly reflected in the institutional division of labour laid down in the treaties, with respect to accession decisions:

> Any European state which respects the principles set out in Article 6(1) may apply to become a member of the Union. It shall address its application to the Council, which shall act unanimously after consulting the Commission and after receiving the assent of the European Parliament, which shall act by an absolute majority of its component members.
>
> The conditions of admission and the adjustment to the treaties on which the Union is founded, which such admission entails, shall be the subject of an agreement between the Member States and the applicant State. This agreement shall be submitted for ratification by all the contracting States in accordance with their respective constitutional requirements.[2]

Thus the *formal* hierarchy of power with respect to an enlargement decision appears very clear: the Council, consisting of representatives of the member state governments, takes the decision, having consulted the Commission. The decision seems then to be purely a matter for the member states. But a more substantive contextual analysis of Article 49, informed by an understanding of how the EU system works in practice, reveals a more complicated picture of the decision-making process. The European Commission effectively acts as principal interlocutor with the candidate states and has an important influence on both the content and shape of the process as it develops. The treaty articles also bestow an important role on the European Parliament in that no accession decision can be taken without the Parliament's assent. And, in the final instance, the outcome of the process rests on the ratification procedures in both the acceding states and the member states. All of this suggests that it is quite wrong to identify the Council as the *only* EU actor that counts in the process.[3]

In this respect four points substantiate the argument. First, the requirement that the Council makes a unanimous decision makes it more difficult to reach agreement on acceptance of specific candidates. Member states may have different preferences as to which countries to invite in. On the other hand, the unanimity requirement makes it less likely that disagreement will spill over into the post-enlargement Union and undermine the cohesiveness of the organization. In addition, the history of enlargement shows that member states use the enlargement negotiations to re-open so-called 'package deals', either with respect to institutional arrangements or important EU policies such as agriculture or regional funding. In this sense the veto offers the opportunity to protect vital national interests. Accession negotiations thus can, and do, become entangled with different elements of the existing integration process. Or, in EU jargon, 'widening' is extremely difficult to disentangle from 'deepening'.

Second, the Commission, which, in its key normative role is the custodian of the Community interest, is a much more uniform actor throughout the accession negotiations than the Council. This is because commissioners, under the treaty, are enjoined not to 'seek nor take instructions from any government or from any other body'.[4] Although it is usually accepted that the link between commissioners and their national governments is, in practice, much closer than the treaties allow, this has not normally translated into partisan approaches being adopted on enlargement-related issues. There is a sense in which all parties respect the fact that enlargement supersedes the normal 'low' politics of integration; it is thus deemed inappropriate for commissioners to make representation on behalf of their particular state interests. This principle of non-interference tends to make the Commission a more consistent and credible actor within the process, especially for the candidate states. The Council, because of its attachment to national prerogatives, has historically tended to produce much more division on key enlargement issues.

Third, Article 49 makes it clear that the Council can only act on the basis of engagement and consultation with the Commission. This poses the question of the degree to which the Commission's general oversight and day-to-day management of the enlargement process privileges it in terms of access to candidate states, information and expertise. The Council may in fact be reliant on the Commission at critical stages in the process of decision-making. It is the Commission after all that shapes the substantive enlargement agenda through its right of initiative, that issues Opinions on the candidate states' ability to meet the membership criteria, and that, during the eastern enlargement round, issued Regular Reports, largely consisting of measurements of compliance by candidate states with the Copenhagen criteria and *acquis communautaire*. Similarly, the European Parliament by virtue of its right of assent, enjoys a degree of formal power within the decision-making process. It will be argued, however, that this formal power also bestowed upon the Parliament a degree of informal power throughout the process in the sense that neither the Commission nor Council were willing to disregard the Parliament's views and risk that body's eventually withholding consent. In addition, accession decisions are governed not only by the primary law of the EU, but also by a much less developed but nevertheless important set of quasi-legal means, including the Copenhagen criteria and a vast body of documentation produced by the Commission and adopted by the Council regarding the transposition and implementation of particular rules and normative practices. As Kochenov has pointed out, the scope, meaning and legal effect of these instruments are far from clear. Within that context then the scope for *interpretation of rules* by the Commission and Parliament acts to deprive the Council of full authority in decision-making. It was precisely because the Copenhagen criteria were rather vague and imprecise as to implementation that the Commission was able to exert great influence on the eastern enlargement process at different stages.[5]

Finally, the accession treaties can only be implemented after ratification has taken place in each and every member state of the Union and in the candidate states, in accordance with each state's constitutional requirements. This means that even if a consensus emerges in the Council on specific issues, it may be subject to, or qualified by, the particularistic demands of any member state or candidate state in the final negotiations. Council deliberations and EU-candidate state negotiations thus take place with one eye on prospective ratification prospects. Less likely but also possible is the chance of negative public opinion in the acceding state resulting in a rejection of the accession treaty. The Norwegian rejection of EU membership on two occasions (1972 and 1994) is one such example. Should, for example, the terms of entry prove unsatisfactory to public opinion in the candidate state then a referendum could well result in a rejection of the accession treaty. This was a real concern in the case of the Polish referendum on accession, although, in the event this concern was misplaced, as Poles voted by a strong majority to accept the accession treaty. Nevertheless the rejection of EU Treaties by both the Danish and Irish electorates in recent years (and more recently the French and Dutch rejections of the Constitutional Treaty) suggests that where referendums are required for ratification, the EU cannot simply rely on the mechanism of permissive consensus – nothing can be taken for granted where European issues are subject to popular control.

All of this suggests that the institutional politics of enlargement are a lot more complex than a simple reading of the treaty articles suggests. It is clear that it is not simply a matter of the Commission proposing and the Council disposing. Although the European Council is the ultimate arbiter of any accession decision, there are a number of reasons for suggesting that such power is limited. Subsequent chapters will argue for prominent and proactive institutional roles played by both the Commission and the Parliament. In the case of both institutions the case can be made for a much more significant role in this enlargement process than previous rounds. Notwithstanding that, it is the Council of the European Union that sits at the apex of the decision-making structure of the EU. Institutional analyses of EU politics and, in our case, of eastern enlargement, must begin by examining the role, influence and organizational input of the Council.

Differentiated responsibility and fragmentation within the Council

A starting point for consideration of the role of the Council within the enlargement process, or indeed the integration process in general, is recognition of the multiplicity of institutional entities, each occupying a different institutional space, which it embodies. Implicitly one includes the Council of Ministers and Coreper (Committee of Permanent Representatives) and the technical or working groups, which report to Coreper.[6] In addition, the European Council, consisting of heads of state and government, and meeting up to four times annually, has carved out an important role for itself within the EU system.[7] Finally, the Presidency of the EU is also part of the Council machinery, and one, which, in some ways, now plays the most influential role in the final stages of an enlargement negotiation. The Presidency, as Jonas Tallberg points out, 'can play a crucial role in unlocking incompatible negotiating positions and securing agreement, thus preventing negotiation failure from emerging'.[8] These different parts of the machinery combine to form a Council which is complex and multifaceted and which has responsibility across a wide range of policy domains, with negotiations going on concurrently. This differentiated sharing of responsibility, however, can, and in the case of eastern enlargement manifestly did, contribute to a fragmentation of EU policy, to the detriment of the goals set for the process. The fragmentation in the Council undermined the coherence of the EU position and alienated the candidate states, sometimes leaving them quite unsure as to the modes of action to be pursued. In addition, such fragmentation offered the opportunity to enlargement obstructionists within the EU15 to slow down the process at certain junctures. Fragmentation manifested itself in a number of different ways.

In the first instance there arose a problem of *territorial fragmentation*. The Council, as the 'ultimate guardian of the territorial dimension in EU decision-making',[9] was in a markedly different position to the Commission and EP within enlargement decision-making. As Conrad points out, though fragmented across sectors, the individuals working together in the Council are there exclusively as representatives of their respective member states, and as such, they represent relatively clearly defined and fixed national policy objectives, communicated to them regularly by their national administrations. Hence the Council's ability to develop its own distinctive 'enlargement perspective' or 'enlargement identity' within the process was somewhat circumscribed by this form of fragmentation.[10] Not surprisingly fifteen different national perspectives on eastern enlargement produced frequent clashes on such issues as the selection of candidate states, the content of specific EU pre-accession programmes, the nature of support offered the candidates, and the timescale for accession.

The second identifiable form of fragmentation was that of *sectoral fragmentation*. This arose from the fact that the Council is something of a 'hydra-headed conglomerate' of more than fifteen functional Councils, each comprising the ministers in a given sectoral area such as environment, agriculture or transport.[11] Although the General Affairs and External Relations Council (GAERC) is tasked with the coordination of other Councils, this is not always an easy task, especially given the power of key ministries such as finance and agriculture within domestic political settings. As Sedelmeier attests internal EU policy debates are characterized as much by functional cleavages as by national cleavages. This means that the policy process is frequently disrupted by a transgovernmental cleavage, which pits foreign policy-makers against different coalitions of sectoral policy-makers from across the EU.[12]

In the case of enlargement decisions there were consistent efforts by the GAERC to coordinate and move the process along, but these were frequently impeded by difficulties of coordination. Finance ministers, particularly those from the net contributor states such as Germany and the Netherlands, feared the budgetary consequences of enlargement. Powerful agriculture ministries (such as those of

France) undermined their governments' espousal of enlargement by staking out recalcitrant positions on specific elements of the negotiations, and clashed with other important ministries, principally the 'high politics'-oriented foreign ministries, which were on the whole much more enthusiastic about enlargement.[13] The sectoral fragmentation this produced frequently undermined the Council's ability to carve out a consistent enlargement policy. Sedelmeier demonstrates that meso or sectoral policy-makers tended to support the status quo and oppose accommodation of CEE preferences in enlargement negotiations. When macro policy-makers took the lead, as, for example, at Copenhagen in 1993, the access of sectoral veto players was much more restricted and the Council decisions were generally much more accommodating of CEE interests.[14]

A third problem was *intra-institutional fragmentation*. This arose principally out of the relations between the sectoral Councils, Coreper, the GAERC, and the Presidency. Coreper is responsible for preparing Council meetings but in practice the bulk of day-to-day Council work takes place at the expert working group level. It is within Coreper, however, that the substance of all legislative proposals is first discussed.[15] With respect to enlargement three parts of the Council machinery carried principal responsibility: the Enlargement Working Group, supported by a group of experts on financial issues; Coreper 2; and the GAERC. The inter-relationship of all three with the Presidency was also of some importance throughout and very significant toward the end of the negotiations. Where the Enlargement Working Group provided the important functional expertise, Coreper 2 and the GAERC added bureaucratic problem-solving and political nous. The Council Secretariat, particularly in liaising with and supporting the Presidency, acted as a vital information channel, which assisted the Presidency in negotiations.

So how did this complex intra-institutional mosaic of political and bureaucratic decision-making actually function? It seems clear that in the early stages of the enlargement process (1989–93) the Council machinery was much less important than that of the Commission. This was because European political leaders, although publicly supportive of the CEE states' desire for membership, were quite unclear as to the modalities and content of any potential membership negotiation. The Commission was effectively delegated the task of managing the EU's relations with the former Communist states; input from the Council began to increase only after the EU decided to seriously embrace the idea of enlargement after the Copenhagen summit in 1993. Thereafter, as the relationship with CEE deepened, the Council machinery took on more responsibility, sometimes duplicating the work of the Commission bureaucracy, but gradually assuming more and more importance. Ludlow's insider account of the final stages of negotiations in 2002 presents a convincing picture of how the structure worked. The Enlargement Working Group, composed of middle-ranking officials in the permanent representations, chaired by Lars Bjørn Holbøll, took a leading role. Coreper 2 was led by Poul Christoffersen, the Danish Permanent Representative, while Per Stig Moller, the Danish foreign minister, chaired the GAERC.[16] Ludlow's account, however, presents evidence of the intra-institutional competition for influence. He points out that Coreper was effectively neutralized by the forcefulness of Poul Christoffersen and his colleagues, working in tandem with Eneko Landaburu and his Commission staff. Similarly, the Swedish Permanent Representation had performed very effectively during the Swedish Presidency in 2002.[17] There was also remarkable harmony between Christoffersen and Prime Minister Rasmussen in Copenhagen, which it is alleged, angered the Danish foreign minister and his officials.[18] The picture that emerges from this account is confirmed by others, which show that policy debates within the Council were often impeded by bureaucratic clashes over territory and policy choices. In addition the fact that the coordination of Council work was supported by both the Council bureaucracy described here and the Presidency's own national civil service made for another form of bureaucratic fragmentation. A key factor underlying the successful conclusion of the enlargement negotiations, however, was the coordination and political commitment of the Danish Presidency. As Ludlow argues, it may have been the exception rather than the rule.[19]

The final form of fragmentation arose out of the tendency to leave key enlargement decisions to gatherings of the European Council at summit meetings. We may term this a problem of the '*theatre of summitry*'. Intergovernmentalists would argue that these summit meetings produced important political guidelines, which facilitated, even guided, the development of the enlargement process. Part I of this book demonstrated how the European Council meetings at Copenhagen (June 1993), Essen (December 1994), Luxembourg (December 1997), Helsinki (December 1999), Gothenburg (June 2001) and, finally, Brussels and Copenhagen (October and December 2002) contributed very effectively to the shape of enlargement policy by providing explicit directions to the Commission and candidate states regarding practical steps towards accession. Even if the proceedings were sometimes characterized more by declaratory diplomacy than by hard decisions, the summit meetings still encouraged an ever deeper and more explicit commitment to CEE membership.

However, it is also true that the organizational dynamics of European Council summitry frequently undermined the political decisions that emerged from the high-octane gatherings. One important structural feature of the system that has grown over the years is the tendency of heads of state and government to come away from summit meetings claiming 'victory' on issues of national importance, of having successfully defended their 'red lines', no matter how trivial the issues at stake. The national media and domestic opinion must be presented with a 'win'. In the case of eastern enlargement this did not occur as obviously or as often as it did with more mainstream integration issues. However, on sensitive issues, such as agriculture, migration, institutional representation, and the EU budget, there was a marked tendency toward the defence of putative national red lines at the expense of collective problem-solving and accommodation of candidate state preferences. The cumulative effect of this was threefold. First, it frequently left candidate states exasperated and reduced the level of trust between insiders and outsiders. Second, it reinforced the impression that instead of providing political direction, the European Council was more apt to descend into petty squabbling when faced with important decisions. This was demonstrated most obviously in the debacle that was

Nice in December 2000. Finally, the 'theatre of summitry' encouraged a kind of negotiating stasis, which meant that the negotiations on eastern enlargement dragged on for longer than any others in EU history.

Presidencies

One of the most remarkable changes in the politics of EU enlargement in recent years relates to the development of the role of the EU Presidency. The Presidency of the EU Council of Ministers is one of the key institutional actors in the EU negotiating arena. The Presidency is expected to take a leadership role, act as a broker in situations of institutional or policy disputes, and generally guides the integration process forward in its period in office. In recent years, the Council Presidency has received increasing attention in EU studies.[20] Few of these works, however, have sought to analyse the agenda-shaping powers of the Presidency in any great detail.[21] The role of the Presidency in enlargement negotiations, however, presents a good opportunity to study its modes of agenda-setting and agenda-shaping. The ability to set and shape the enlargement agenda mattered for two crucial reasons. In the first place, where a large number of member states had no fixed preferences on given issues the Presidency was in a good position to impose its agenda, if what it proposed seemed reasoned and neutral. More importantly, where there existed profound disagreement between the member states on some issues, the Presidency was able to use its brokerage role to argue for sometimes innovative solutions that it could design and pursue. The Presidency's role has evolved over time as part of what Kochenov terms 'customary enlargement practice'. Article 49 does not specify any role for the Presidency in the enlargement process, nor indeed for the European Council, yet both parts of the Council machinery proved decisive in shaping enlargement decisions.[22]

Following Tallberg's conception of agenda-shaping three distinct forms of Presidency input into enlargement policy may be identified: agenda-setting, agenda-structuring and agenda-exclusion.[23] *Agenda-setting* refers to the Presidency's ability to introduce its own initiatives and policy preferences in the process. *Agenda-structuring* refers to the ability to shape the substantive form of those enlargement issues already on the Council agenda. Third, *agenda-exclusion*, in the shape of the non-selection of specific issues, was just as evident in Presidency enlargement activities. Analysis of the agenda-shaping efforts by the Presidency offers the opportunity to compare and contrast Presidencies, their different priorities and emphases, and the balance they struck between national agendas and the collective EU interest. As with the Commission, the Presidency was able to use both formal and informal institutional and political instruments for advancing its own enlargement agenda. In addition, this analysis assumes, as does Tallberg elsewhere, that the Presidency can play a crucial role in unlocking what may at first, and for long periods, seem like incompatible negotiating positions, thus preventing total negotiation failure which would effectively derail accession.[24] In particular, four aspects of Presidency agenda-shaping may be identified in the eastern enlargement process. First, Presidencies developed concrete proposals for action, sometimes on request from the member states, sometimes on their own initiative, in response to recognized macro- and micro-problems within the process. Second, some Presidencies brought entirely new issue areas and sometimes neglected ones to the forefront of enlargement policy debates. Third, Presidencies engaged in acts of both institutional and political entrepreneurship aimed at decisively influencing specific parts of the policy process. Finally, all Presidencies sought to use their powers of mediation and brokerage to advance the collective decision-making process and move the enlargement process forward.

In the first instance Presidencies developed concrete proposals for action in response to recognized problems within the enlargement process. Sometimes these related to problematic policy areas such as agriculture or budgetary matters. More often they related to macro-questions such as the timing and sequencing of accession and the parameters of negotiations. Frequently this activity helped to change the way particular problems were framed and perceived. Here the complex relationship with the Commission became particularly important.[25] In general Presidencies that enjoyed good working relations with the Commission were better able to achieve consensus within the Council and bring about solutions to existing problems. Where the agenda-shaping activity was a joint Presidency–Commission effort it was difficult for member states to oppose the proposed policy solutions.

The Swedish Presidency of 2001 serves as a good example. More chapters were closed during the Swedish Presidency than expected.[26] In part this was because of a successful alliance forged with the Commission. But it was also a function of the Swedish government's commitment to the normative goal of enlargement and a penchant for framing enlargement issues in collectivist terms. Sweden found creative solutions in areas such as environment, freedom of movement for capital and labour, and other enlargement issues. Bjurulf argues that the most important outcome authored by the Swedes, however, was a shift in the framing of enlargement from one dominated by negative issues such as migration, budgetary problems and welfare provision, to one centred on security and prosperity for the collective Europe. Sweden's guiding logic can be seen as a normative power logic and rooted in Swedish commitment to internationalism and the global spread of democratic norms. From a Swedish perspective the Presidency was clearly of some importance. After all, it was the first time Sweden had held the Presidency of the EU since it acceded in 1995. Some even suggested that it was the most important responsibility and contribution of Sweden to international affairs since the Congress of Vienna in 1815.[27] Thus the Swedish EU Presidency was driven by notions among Swedish decision-makers about how a 'good European' should behave and by their visions of European governance. Even with a strongly intergovernmental preference for decision-making, officials firmly held to the democratic peace model of international relations and framed their enlargement policy and EU Presidency in those terms.[28] The Swedish preference for framing enlargement in these liberal internationalist macro terms (rather than instrumentalist micro terms) effectively shaped the enlargement agenda of the EU at a crucial period and made it much more difficult for enlargement obstructionists within the EU to make a convincing case.

A similar argument may be made for the Danish Presidency's proactive stance on the financial package available to the candidate states during the final stage of negotiations in late 2002. It represented an outstanding example of a Presidency's proactive engagement with a specific problem leading to a change in the macro framing of enlargement. After a meeting between the foreign ministers of the applicant countries and their EU counterparts on 18 November 2002, the Danish Presidency went on to launch a compromise package which increased the amount available to incoming states for 2004–06 by €1.3 billion and allowed them to 'top up' the direct payments in agriculture by switching some budgetary resources from rural development. A second proposal to delay the date of accession until 1 May 2004 (rather than 1 January) meant that the incoming states would pay significantly less into the EU budget for that year, thereby helping to solve the 'cashflow' problem which they were facing.[29] The Danes, like the Swedes, effectively framed the problem in collectivist and normative terms and achieved an outcome, at once accommodating of candidate state preferences, and neutral in respect of the EU budget, which many had imagined unattainable.

A second feature was the extent to which Presidencies shaped the policy agenda by raising the awareness of problems hitherto neglected within the enlargement process or brought entirely new issues to attention. It seems clear that whilst both intensely supportive of the macro goal of enlargement, both Finland and Sweden sought to change the framing of the eastern enlargement process by developing a more distinct 'Northern' dimension to the enlargement process. Whilst some saw this as a counter to the EU's Mediterranean focus (centred on the Barcelona Process), it was also about re-positioning EU enlargement policy around Russia and the Baltic region, ensuring a more balanced geopolitical underpinning of the process, and improving the overall coherence of policy. In particular both Presidencies sought to prioritize the resolution of the Kaliningrad issue in advance of the final stages of negotiations.[30] In much the same way a number of Presidencies sought to foreground the importance of decommissioning aged nuclear power stations in Bulgaria, Lithuania and Slovakia. Indeed a considerable sum was set aside for this in the financial package which accompanied the final deal on accession. And while some of these initiatives were undoubtedly motivated by instrumentalist concerns of individual Presidencies, it is also true that the prioritizing of these issues helped foreground problems which had hitherto been quite marginal within the enlargement process.

A third form of agenda-shaping by the Presidency can be demonstrated by reference to specific practices of institutional and political entrepreneurship. In the first instance institutional entrepreneurship can be evinced in the development of new or innovative institutional practices that structure future cooperation and influence the future shape of decision-making. This is in addition to the fact that the Presidency 'enjoys asymmetrical control of the negotiating process, on the basis of a broad repertoire of procedural instruments'.[31] The fact that the Presidency has relatively few formal responsibilities has (ironically) meant that Presidencies have had ample room for institutional and administrative manoeuvring within the Council structures.[32] Tallberg's analysis of the procedural instruments open to the

Presidency can as usefully be applied to enlargement as the general integration framework. In the first place, the Presidency holds the formal prerogative to decide the format of negotiating sessions. These may take the form of a formal ministerial meeting at the Council's headquarters in Brussels, a more restricted session where only a few officials participate and ministers have more room for manoeuvre, or a meeting in the home country where the more collegial atmosphere can 'soften up' opponents of particular Presidency initiatives.[33] Second, the Presidency enjoys a degree of flexibility and control in determining the pace of the negotiations. It is the Presidency that fixes the meeting schedule and decides the number and frequency of formal and informal negotiating sessions. Should the Presidency decide so, further meetings can be scheduled on specific issues, meeting agendas can be altered to allow greater room for negotiation, and formal time restrictions placed on the length of particular deliberations.[34]

The evidence from the eastern enlargement process suggests that different Presidencies relied to different degrees on particular forms of procedural control. Some Presidencies introduced innovative institutional practices and sought to shape the enlargement agenda with them. The German Presidency of 1998, for example, made full use of the various instruments of control and mediation available to it to steer the negotiations on *Agenda 2000* toward a successful conclusion. Its strategy was to exploit its powers of procedure, intensifying the formal meeting schedule, and moving *Agenda 2000* to the top of specific meeting agendas. Where Sweden and Denmark also demonstrated a willingness to test the boundaries of the formal powers of innovation of the Presidency in the cause of accommodating CEE preferences, France, however, made active use of the procedural and informational advantages of the chair in 2000 to advance its own national interests. As Tallberg observes: 'the French government scrupulously used the position of the chair to advance proposals that essentially constituted national position papers framed as Presidency compromises'.[35]

If different Presidencies used different types of formal and informal resources to engage in institutional entrepreneurship then they also employed different forms of political entrepreneurship to advance their goals. Political entrepreneurship, loosely defined as the willingness and ability to frame and publicize key enlargement issues in specific ways, manifested itself in two distinct forms. The first was the utilization and deployment of distinct strands of public discourse in which the Presidency's enlargement agenda was made clear. The second was the frequent resort to shaming tactics by different Presidencies as they sought to move the enlargement game along. In many instances such shaming tactics took on both a private and public dimension with quiet diplomacy being matched by a public discourse designed to achieve the desired outcome.

Such political entrepreneurship, whether in the form of an official Presidency position on a specific issue or a discursive intervention from a prominent state leader, was sometimes ineffective but never less than interesting as a reflection of the different attitudes to eastern enlargement on the part of member states. And where some Presidencies deployed a utilitarian enlargement discourse, which highlighted economic or security externalities, it was more common to find enlargement presented in normative terms. This normative discourse usually framed eastern enlargement as (variously) a moral imperative for the European Union, an outgrowth of EU institutional norms and practices, and/or the key instrument for the successful transposition of EU values in Central and Eastern Europe. This was often accompanied by willingness on the part of some Presidencies to name and shame those member states more attached to a more instrumentalist or narrow enlargement perspective. In publicly deploying such a normative discourse some Presidencies went much further than others. What such cases demonstrate is the importance of such discursive interventions as acts of political entrepreneurship.

The combination of normative discourse and a willingness to name and shame recalcitrant member states was perhaps most evident in the leadership of Göran Persson, during the Swedish Presidency. In particular his activism and strategy before and during the Gothenburg summit in June 2001 was designed to frame enlargement in normative and collectivist terms and 'smoke out' the obstructionists within EU ranks. Ludlow puts it thus:

> Persson engaged in an energetic campaign to discredit his opponents. Led by the *Financial Times*, many newspapers that appeared on the Saturday of the Gothenburg summit gave the impression that German Chancellor Schröder in particular was 'turning sour on enlargement'. The German Chancellor made no secret of the fact that he deeply resented his Swedish colleague's tactics.[36]

Two other aspects of Persson's activity also emphasize the point. His insistence that Gothenburg should produce an 'irrevocable' commitment to enlargement was an act of significant political leadership at a time when that commitment was only surface-deep in many member states. Another key Presidency aim of the Swedes was to bring the second-track countries up to the speed of the fast-track candidates. To this end negotiations on important chapters were opened with Latvia, Lithuania and Slovakia.[37] Swedish representatives, were from the outset strongly attached to a 'regatta' model, based on equality of treatment of candidates, as opposed to a model of political differentiation, which would have slowed down the process and, most certainly, have left some of the candidates isolated. Ludlow argues that the single most important achievement of the Swedish Presidency was the decision to open up the process and go for a so-called 'big bang' enlargement: 'Lots of people had been sceptical that the big bang could be achieved. The number of such people decreased after Gothenburg.'[38]

A fourth important role performed by the Presidency in the enlargement process was that of mediator. Within the enlargement framework this meant three different foci. The first was *inside–outside mediator*, with the Presidency acting as principal EU interlocutor with the applicant states. This was important at all stages of the process but arguably critical toward the end of negotiations. The second was *internal mediator* between member states who disagreed about aspects of policy or the general course of negotiations. And finally, the Presidency acted as an *inter-institutional mediator* between the Council and Commission (and less often the Parliament) in the inter-institutional setting. The role of mediation played by the Presidency within the EU is facilitated by the perception of it as a neutral arbiter or 'honest broker'. Elgström argues that the norm that the Presidency should be neutral and impartial is almost uncontested within the EU, thereby providing a substantial instrument which works against biased behaviour by Presidencies. The norm is highly institutionalized and permeates both academic and practitioner thinking to a substantive degree. It might be expected that the norm has even greater salience in the enlargement domain, as member states tend to view enlargement as a non-partisan issue area. Therefore all parties, and especially the Presidency, are expected to make that further effort to accommodate the Union interest. To persistently challenge progress, or to obstruct negotiations, is seen not only as unacceptable but almost as a negation of membership and of the value system upon which the EU rests. That necessarily means sublimating national interests to those of the Union as a whole.

That of course represents a problem in enlargement decision-making, as the Presidency is manifestly the collective representative of the insiders in the negotiations with outsiders, and sometimes it will hold specific and intense attachments to existing policies, which may need to be reconfigured in anticipation of or as a consequence of enlargement. Thus the conflict presented to Presidencies in seeking to base their activities on neutrality and impartiality is not insignificant. Member states holding the Presidency cannot simply be expected to change their own positions in the desire to achieve a collective outcome which can then be presented to outsiders. The French resistance to CAP reform, for example, did not disappear on the assumption of the French Presidency in 2000. It did, however, make it more difficult for the Presidency to gain the trust of both outsiders and insiders in progressing the agriculture dimension of the enlargement process. Similarly it affected the general search for consensus in a markedly negative way. Thus the evidence from the enlargement process contradicts, to some extent, this widespread assumption about the behaviour of the Presidency. This accords with Ole Elgström's view that Council Presidencies are, despite the deep institutionalization of the norm, 'seldom neutral and not always impartial'.[39] But the reaction to French behaviour in 2000, perceived as strongly corrosive of the European integration ideal (and of Presidency practice), also suggests Elgström is correct in arguing that the norm of impartiality is so embedded in the organizational culture of the EU that contradictory actions are seen as 'immoral and aberrant'.[40]

The French Presidency and the negative reactions to it also highlight the differences of approach to eastern enlargement taken by large-state and small-state Presidencies. French interventions during Nice, especially on issues such as the future institutional balance of power and the distribution of votes in Council, were reflective of a view that large-state interests had to be protected no matter the collective wish to advance the enlargement negotiations to a successful conclusion. This view was also very evident in President Chirac's now infamous suggestion that in offering support to the American-led coalition against Iraq in 2003 the Central and East European states were 'behaving like infants'. Of course large member states tend to have national interests which sometimes bring them into conflict with the consensus opinion in any given issue area. That will be the case during a Presidency as in any other situation. Smaller states may incline more toward compromise out of a recognition of asymmetry in terms of distribution of power or simply because they do not have important interests at stake, or at least not nearly as many as larger states. Thus conducting negotiations and mediating between the different internal and external players in enlargement is more difficult for larger member states than for smaller states. Another issue is that larger member states prefer to manage their Presidencies from their own national capitals thus tending to negate the supranational or Union influence on process. Smaller states tend to be much more reliant on their own permanent representations in Brussels and on cooperation with the Commission to operate effectively.[41] That was certainly the case for the Finnish Presidency of 1999, the Swedish Presidency of 2001, and the Danish Presidency of 2002. A smaller and more confined set of national interests and a positive relationship with the Commission, combined with attachment to the normative appeal of enlargement, made for more engaged and neutral Presidencies, which each produced significant advances in the process.[42]

Advocacy and obstructionism within the Council

Notwithstanding the important institutional and political resources deployed by different Presidencies, internal EU divisions on enlargement remained significant. Neither peer pressure nor the normative claims of the candidate states caused them to completely disappear. From beginning to the end of the process, deliberation and bargaining within the Council structures was characterized by clashes between enlargement advocates and enlargement obstructionists. Disagreements arose initially on the substantive question of whether to enlarge at all and later on questions of which countries to include, the terms under which accession could be agreed, and the timetable. Although open opposition to eastern enlargement rarely manifested itself, there were nevertheless suggestions of alternative frameworks such as 'privileged partnership' or 'associated membership', which more often than not were intended as a substitute for, not a stepping stone to, membership.

The support for enlargement within the Council needs to be viewed within the parameters of what Sedelmeier and Wallace term a wide-ranging 'advocacy alliance', which included key actors within the European Commission and important figures in the domestic politics of leading member states. This loose and rather ad-hoc grouping helped ensure that there was movement in the EU's enlargement policy, crucially between the Europe Agreements and the Copenhagen summit and then again towards a more coherent pre-accession strategy.[43] It made effective use of agenda-setting powers and successfully carved out transgovernmental and inter-institutional alliances. In a policy area where there was no concerted lead role played by any national actors (with the possible exception of Germany), it was the Commission, at crucial periods, which kept enlargement on the agenda and acted as persuader in the EU context. But the Commission's influence, even if significant throughout, also needed to be buttressed by the advocacy and public rhetoric of representatives of member states and their governments. This advocacy alliance also included leading academics or public intellectuals such as Timothy Garton Ash and Jürgen Habermas, and former political leaders such as the long-serving German foreign minister, Hans-Dietrich Genscher.[44] Finally, Central and Eastern European politicians, academics, intellectuals and writers made the public case for membership forcefully and frequently.[45] The prestige and intellectual standing of Vaclav Havel and other former dissidents such as Adam Michnik and Milan Kundera, who were not slow to remind EU leaders of the promises made during the Cold War period, was also deployed to some effect. The editorial and opinion pages of major publications such as *The Economist*, *El Pais*, the *Financial Times*, the *Guardian*, the *Independent*, the *Irish Times*, and *Libération* also frequently made the case for early and wide enlargement.[46] Such advocacy discourse consisted of different elements depending on the advocate, location, the intended audience, and the situational context. Nevertheless it would be true to say that it usually included a reference to the following: the idea of an EU 'special responsibility' for Central and Eastern Europe; enlargement as a moral imperative influenced crucially by the guilt induced by the Cold War division of Europe; and enlargement as integral to the transposition of EU democracy and human rights norms on a pan-European scale.

Notions of affiliation and a EU 'special responsibility' for CEE were evident from the earliest days of the process, where the EU issued a public pledge of full support for the transformation process in Central and Eastern Europe at the Strasbourg European Council in December 1989:

> The Community and its member states are fully conscious of the common responsibility which devolves on them in this decisive phase in the history of Europe ... They are prepared to develop ... closer and more substantive relations in all areas ... The Community is at the present time the European identity which serves as the point of reference for the countries of Central and Eastern Europe.[47]

The Strasbourg statement, although it stopped short of an outright offer of membership, laid down the basis for the Community's relationship with Central and Eastern Europe as one rooted in a common identity with the prospect of anchoring CEE on existing structures. The emphasis on the Community's special responsibility for integrating the transitioning countries was consistently prominent in the speeches of EU leaders in the early 1990s and was justified by a variety of references to historical connectedness, cultural indivisibility, and the achievements of the integration process. The latter in particular emphasized the inclusivity of the European project, its civic-secular basis, and that enlargement was not just a prize in the gift of the existing Community but a community-enhancing process to be nurtured and brought to a successful conclusion. The leadership role ascribed to the EU became all the more important and anxieties about it the more acute as Yugoslavia descended into bitter sectarian warfare. The Community remained on the sidelines and manifestly failed to demonstrate the leadership qualities implicitly referred to in the Strasbourg statement. In the now infamous phrase of then

Luxembourg Foreign Minister Jacques Poos, 'the hour of Europe' had struck, and Europe had patently failed the test. Paradoxically, however, that failure made it all the more imperative that the EU succeed in Central and Eastern Europe. And thus European leaders' sense of responsibility for the process of transition and integration in CEE only increased with the failure of EU policy in Yugoslavia. Full membership of the EU for the candidate states became the only real alternative to the chaos in the Balkans.

The second discursive theme of enlargement advocates was that of expansion as a moral imperative for the EU. It is clear that many within the EU (individual citizens, individual policy-makers, governments) felt a strong sense of moral obligation toward the former Communist states, believing that the West's freedom and prosperity was somehow paid for by Eastern Europe's subjugation during the Cold War.[48] Now that the Iron Curtain was down, they felt an obligation to assist their eastern neighbours by integrating them with the EU and the Western zone of peace and prosperity. By doing so, some Westerners clearly hoped to assuage the feelings of guilt for the abandonment of the Central and Eastern European states at Yalta and the Cold War division of Europe. Enlargement provided a moral instrument for 'undoing the wrongs of half a century', as Leon Brittan put it.[49]

Foremost among those making such arguments were senior German politicians and policy-makers. Now that conditions permitted, former Chancellor Helmut Kohl argued in 1996, the EU 'should not ... disappoint the trust that these countries have put in us'. Further, Kohl argued, by failing to enlarge, the EU would lose moral and political credibility and this 'would be a terrible loss that Europe would not quickly recover from'.[50] Notwithstanding Kohl's penchant for framing his European arguments in dramatic 'Europe or war' tones, the feeling was widely shared in Germany. Many felt a moral obligation to the people of Poland, Hungary and the former Czechoslovakia whose actions in 1989 brought about the end of Communism and so rendered German unification possible. Many were also motivated by the desire to atone for past aggression and atrocities committed against Germany's Eastern neighbours by the Nazi regime. Because of such feelings of moral obligation, the German government repeatedly proclaimed itself the primary advocate (*Anwalt*) of the CEE states on behalf of their efforts to join the EU. Joschka Fischer, in his important and expansive Humboldt University speech of 12 May 2000, spoke of enlargement not just as a 'supreme national interest' of Germany but also as a 'moral duty' of the EU.[51] The representation of enlargement as moral obligation was not confined to the discourse of German politicians. It permeated the discourse of government representatives throughout the European Union. Belgian Prime Minister Guy Verhofstadt similarly displayed the West European 'guilt complex' in many of his speeches:

> For me, enlarging Europe is a question of fairness. Peoples and nations in this part of Europe have suffered most of the greatest enemies of European progress in the twentieth century, Nazism and Communism. They deserve our greatest efforts to heal the wounds of the twentieth century.[52]

The framing of eastern enlargement in such moral terms was not exclusive to northern Europeans. The discourse of Spanish, Greek and Portuguese leaders also demonstrated a clear attachment to the idea of EU membership as a natural right of the transitioning states, and one rooted in a moral interpretation of the recent European past. Former Spanish Prime Minister José Maria Aznar, for example, argued before the *Cortés* in 1994 that the CEE states 'have acquired an indisputable right to become members that nobody has the moral authority to deny'. Spain's consolidation of democratic institutions and practices was routinely presented as underwritten by the EU and appeared as a moral script for interpreting eastern enlargement. As Aznar's foreign minister, Josep Piqué, put it in 2000: 'a country with this perspective cannot deny the same perspective to the current candidates'.[53]

Enlargement advocates consistently argued the importance of the process as a vehicle for the transfer of EU democratic norms and practices to a potentially volatile and unstable region. The violent break-up of Yugoslavia made clear just how high were the stakes in the geopolitical reconstitution of Europe. From early in the process the EU thus sought to prioritize the domestic adoption of EU democracy norms and EU shared values as an integral part of the enlargement process. The reshaping of everything from electoral systems to minority rights legislation, judicial appointments and public administration could be used to ensure the successful transposition of EU best practice in the candidate states in advance of accession. Guy Verhofstadt put it succinctly in denying the importance of materialist considerations in the enlargement process, arguing that it was 'hardly a question of figures and arithmetic. We are witnessing a peaceful revolution without any precedent in the past'. He went on to underline the importance of the values of the integration project:

> We uphold both the ancient values of liberty and equality but also the newer values of growth, progress and opportunity for all and not only for the happy few. And we want an open, a tolerant and a humanist Europe, taking up its unique responsibility for European and non-European nations alike. I have come here to make clear that no European nation willing to join us shall be refused. For Europe is an inclusive, not an exclusive idea. Indeed, that is what enlargement is about. It is about restoring through peaceful means the historic, philosophical and geographical unity of Europe.[54]

More recently other examples of such discourse have served to emphasize the normative importance of enlargement. Launching the idea of a Stability Pact for Southeast Europe, German Foreign Minister Joschka Fischer urged an opening of the door to 'a long term political and economic stabilisation process'. This would aim to prevent ethnic conflict, create stable conditions for democracy and 'anchor the countries of South East Europe firmly in the values of and institutional structures of the Euro-Atlantic community'.[55] Fischer's ideas undoubtedly drew on the experience of eastern enlargement. The process made possible the democratization of CEE, including the remaking of political institutions and civil society. Enlargement structures were used and justified as centres of social learning and policy transfer from the EU to the candidate states. The deepening of those structures over time would ensure the successful transposition of EU practice and further support the case for the EU model as the only frame of reference for states in pan-Europe. Enlargement advocates continually reminded their audiences. both private and public, of the benefits which this would deliver over time. The combined impact of these diverse discursive strands used by the enlargement advocates produced a cumulative effect which helped frame enlargement cognitively in a specific and decisive fashion and which made it difficult for obstructionists or outright oppositionists to make their case.

Conclusions

This chapter examined the internal EU decision-making process which governed the eastern enlargement and, specifically, the role played by the different parts of the EU Council of Ministers. The Council's role is a complex and multifaceted one, not least because of the lack of specification of institutional responsibilities in Article 49. The Council was disadvantaged by various forms of fragmentation which hampered its ability to act in a unified way throughout the enlargement process. Nevertheless the Council mattered to enlargement outcomes in three crucial ways. First, the member states, through the Council of Ministers, Coreper, and the working groups, sought to maintain a high degree of control over the process from the outset. This was important because the Commission succeeded early on in establishing authority in key parts of the EU's enlargement framework. The member states thus sought to use the Council structures to scrutinize the Commission's activities and ensure that their national interests were articulated and defended as the process developed. Second, the European Council provided political direction to the enlargement process, by negotiating agreements at crucial summit meetings at regular intervals and instructing the Commission to follow up with analysis and recommendations regarding key parts of the policy process. And although summit meetings such as Copenhagen in 1993, Luxembourg in 1997 and Gothenburg in 2001 certainly provided momentum where it was lacking, the structural dynamics of intergovernmental bargaining were as often inclined to produce non-decisions, which set back progress and in equal measure disappointed and frustrated the applicant states. Where summit meetings did produce EU agreement, that was more often than not because of the informal day-to-day supranational process which increasingly characterized EU enlargement practice and provided the problem-solving capacity in advance of intergovernmental gatherings. Finally, the Presidency played perhaps the most crucial role within the Council structures in facilitating agreement and maintaining momentum in the process. Whilst the analysis presented here demonstrates significant differences of emphasis, enthusiasm and activity by different Presidencies, it also shows that where the political will existed Presidencies could and indeed did prove crucial to outcomes. The Swedish and Danish Presidencies emerge from the analysis of eastern enlargement with particular credit, facilitating as they did the important internal EU and EU-candidate state deals that accelerated and eventually concluded the negotiations. What both Presidencies demonstrated was a willingness and ability to structure and shape the negotiating agenda, to bring into focus new or neglected issues within the enlargement process, engage in different forms of institutional and political entrepreneurship, and mediate between the different parties in both the internal and external negotiations. The complex nature of the EU's evolving enlargement practice is demonstrated, however, in the fact that the institutional activity of the Presidency was much more likely to succeed where it forged a good working relationship with the Commission and combined with the latter to frame the parameters of EU policy. In particular the horizontal fragmentation of the Council left member states vulnerable to pressure emanating from a Presidency–Commission alliance. Thus evidence from the eastern enlargement process demonstrates that the formal institutional division of labour laid out in Article 49 no longer reflects what actually happens in practice. In effect the formal/legal structure of responsibilities has been overtaken by a new and quite amorphous decision-making structure which is both intergovernmental and supranational and provides opportunity structures within the enlargement process for institutional and policy entrepreneurship. As the next chapter will show it is no longer the case (if indeed it ever was) that the Commission 'proposes' and the Council 'disposes'.

6 The European Commission and eastern enlargement

Introduction

Although of immense political significance for the EU, the eastern enlargement was characterized principally by modes of technocratic and functional policy adaptation by the candidate states and policy transfer by the EU. The requirement that candidate states in Central and Eastern Europe adopt in its entirety the EU's *acquis communautaire* meant that oversight and monitoring of the process of adaptation gradually became the primary concern of EU policy. And it is in this respect that the role of the European Commission becomes central to the institutional politics of eastern enlargement. Arguments about the role of the Commission are especially important in the context of integration perspectives, as they go to the heart of the traditional academic divide between realists and intergovernmentalists on the one hand, and neofunctionalists and constructivists on the other.[1] Intergovernmentalists view the Commission as little more than the bureaucratic agent of the Council of Ministers whereas neofunctionalists, and more recently, many constructivist scholars, posit the Commission as a strategically important and sophisticated institutional actor, possessed of the resources and scope to crucially influence the direction of EU policy-making.

Given the formal responsibilities each institution is assigned under Article 49 of the treaties, it might be expected that state actors would dominate an enlargement process, with the critical decisions made in intergovernmental forums. After all, the Commission acts only in an advisory capacity; the Council as a collective body takes the important political decisions. Undoubtedly this is why the role played by the Commission in enlargement policy-making has been so neglected by scholars of enlargement over the years. If that neglect was somewhat justified in the analysis of previous enlargement rounds, it cannot be justified in the case of the eastern enlargement. From the institution of relations with the former Communist bloc in 1989, the Commission carved out for itself a much more significant role in the eastern enlargement process than any formal reading of Article 49 might have suggested. This chapter analyses the different dimensions of the Commission role and argues that, *inter alia*, its formal right of initiative under the treaties, its direct engagement with a range of internal EU and candidate state actors, its extensive network of technical expertise and its ability and willingness to act as a political entrepreneur all combined to ensure that the Commission played a crucial role (at times *the* crucial role) in the important decisions that marked the eastern enlargement process. Its role was thus *both* functional-bureaucratic *and* normative-political.

Eastern enlargement: a different type of challenge for the Commission

In seeking to explain the complex role played by the Commission in the eastern enlargement process, it seems useful to embed this analysis in something of a historical context. This enables us to determine how and in what ways the Commission's role differed with previous rounds. Three reasons can be advanced for the more visible and 'hands-on' role played by the Commission in this enlargement.

In the first place, the sheer scale of the eastern enlargement dwarfed all previous expansions. Specifically, it would mean parallel negotiations with up to ten candidate states (including Cyprus and Malta), each defined by its own cultural and historical experiences and each with different sets of demands that would require EU attention. The EU had only ever negotiated simultaneously with a maximum of four states, each of which was much closer to the Union in respect of economic development and political maturity and so presented a fairly straightforward negotiating challenge. Recognition of the scale of the challenge led some influential insiders from the outset to argue that the process would be best served by investing management authority in a single EU institutional actor. Support for this position was further encouraged after the confusion caused by the duplication of functions, and mix of bilateral and collective initiatives, which characterized early EU policy toward Central and Eastern Europe. It quickly became evident that only the Commission, with its strategic organizational know-how and informational reach, could properly coordinate the integration of the CEE states into EU processes.

The Commission's role had also changed because of the extension, especially after the Single European Act, in the nature and reach of the *acquis communautaire*. For aspiring members this meant a significant 'moving of the goalposts', a vast increase in the quantity of EU-generated legislation to be absorbed into domestic law. For the EU significant difficulties potentially arose in measuring the progress of applicant states without a far-reaching and deeply institutionalized scrutiny of the process of transposition and implementation. The Commission, which was already responsible for compliance monitoring within the EU, was thought to be the best-placed institutional actor to advise on and interpret the *acquis*.

The expansion of the *acquis* continued apace as the EU deepened in anticipation of widening and as it put in place the elements of a new economic and political relationship with Central and Eastern Europe. But the sheer vagueness of Article 237 – 'any European state may apply' – meant that by the early 1990s, as more demands for membership were received, a new 'quasi-legal' set of enlargement instruments had to be adopted. Whilst some of these measures were introduced with the Mediterranean enlargements it was really only with the prospect of eastern enlargement that a new set of priorities for applicant states became informally introduced into the process.[2] Over time this meant a vast body of new rules being imposed on the applicant states, including some such as state protection for minority rights, which had no legal basis in the treaties, and which had been completely absent from previous enlargement rounds. Thus the Commission's role in compliance monitoring was much more extensive (and intrusive) than ever before.

A third significant change to the Commission's role is evident in the fact that it became a significant actor in the domestic politics of the CEE applicant states to an extent not previously imagined let alone experienced. Indeed Commissioners van den Bröek, Verheugen, Fischler, Patten and Wallström became so well known and influential within applicant state politics that they sometimes carried more clout than domestic cabinet ministers. The depth of their influence can clearly be discerned from the scale of media coverage of their visits to the applicant states, which frequently eclipsed coverage of domestic political issues. While this is certainly reflective of the asymmetry of power between the EU and the candidate states, it also suggests a much more significant role for the Commission in the external governance of the Union than intergovernmentalists and realists would allow.

Thus the combined effect of the changes in the legal regulation of enlargement, the development of new informal accession norms, and the sheer scale of the challenge before the Union, meant that the Commission gradually assumed a very different role within the eastern enlargement process than in previous rounds. Whilst the member states were free to disregard the Commission's views they chose consistently to support the recommendations that it put forward.

The Commission as agenda-setter

Within the structures of EU policy-making the Commission's agenda-shaping and agenda-setting ability derive principally from its formal treaty-based power – the sole right of initiative it enjoys for nearly all 'first-pillar' legislation – meaning that any legislative measure can only proceed through the EU system on the basis of a proposal from the Commission. In conceptualizing EU public policy-making formal agenda-setting refers to the 'ability of an actor to set the *procedural* agenda of a legislature by placing before it legislative proposals that can be adopted more easily than amended, thus structuring and constraining the choices faced by a group of legislators'.[3] Even Moravcsik, who regards the Commission as little more than an agent of the member states' will, concedes that 'the ability to select among viable proposals grants the Commission considerable formal agenda-setting power'.[4] It is with respect to this formal role that Pierson has stressed the importance of the Commission as 'process manager' of large parts of EU public policy-making, which is heavily tilted toward regulation. The development of complex social regulation requires the assembly and coordination in particular of dense networks of experts.[5] This power, of course, is far from uniform and, as Pollack points out, varies across the dozens of distinct legal bases and complex voting rules that have been developed through the treaties and subsequent amendments. Further, this influence is also contingent upon a number of key factors, including the sensitivity of the particular issue, the institutional rules governing which actor may propose an initiative, the distribution of actor preferences, and prospective deadlines for securing agreement.[6] Notwithstanding such caveats it is clear that within the formal rules and procedures that govern the integration process the Commission wields considerable influence on policy-making.[7]

In tandem with its formal powers of initiative the Commission also utilizes a range of informal agenda-setting instruments. This broader concept of institutional power refers to the ability of a policy entrepreneur to 'set the substantive agenda of an organization, not through its formal powers, but through its ability to define issues and present proposals that *can rally consensus* among the final decision-makers'.[8] This power, as Marlene Wind suggests, derives from the norm-constituting and informal practices that have developed through the years at EU level.[9] Similarly, for Friis, an important component of the Commission's power derives from its ability to frame the policy agenda in certain ways. Specifically, the exact *social and political construction of* the issues before the EU proves crucial to policy outcomes. The argument here is that in an environment characterized by uncertainty, imperfect information and limited timeframes for decision-making, supranational agents such as the Commission can progress negotiations by constructing *focal points* for deliberation and negotiation, around which discussion can be structured and state preferences teased out.[10] Framing is an activity of selection, aggregation (of options) and interpretation of a complex reality, so as to provide a cognitive road map for analysis and coordinated response to perceived common problems.[11] Thus where the Commission finds that its formal treaty-based powers are insufficient to shape policy it readily resorts to such informal methods of agenda-shaping.

Like any self-interested political actor the Commission has an *institutional interest* in having its initiatives adopted; it will take the pulse of the different institutional actors within the decision-making system and only produce policy proposals it feels can be successfully adopted. In addition, the Commission, as guardian of the treaties, holds a *systemic interest* in the adoption of successful policy proposals. The integrity of the EU public policy process is predicated upon the production of a sufficient number of policy proposals to drive the integration project forward and make it work for the member states. Prior to submitting a proposal the Commission will have been lobbied by interest groups, engaged with national officials in Coreper, and taken soundings on the views of Parliament. It may well modify a proposal in anticipation of difficulties that might be encountered at different stages of the policy process. Thus the complex nature of the bargaining process within the EU makes it difficult to identify 'ownership' of specific policy proposals with precision, even if they emerge from the Commission. The difficulties of attributing 'success' to individual institutional actors are as evident in the enlargement process as in any other area of EU public policy.

The Commission's formal responsibility under Article 49 of the treaty is to prepare and present an Opinion (*avis*) on an applicant state's suitability for membership and on the likely impact of enlargement on the Union. The Commission at this stage is supposed to consult and reflect and make recommendations (to the

Council).[12] The Commission submits compromise solutions that usually become the basis for joint positions of the existing member states and then for an agreement between them and the candidate states.[13] But the Commission also has a key role in the formulation and implementation of policies; within the enlargement process this applies to the association and pre-accession strategies as well as in the accession negotiations.[14] At all stages of the process, therefore, the Commission is well positioned to contribute to enlargement policy-making.

In the case of selecting and proposing policy initiatives on eastern enlargement, the Commission, from the beginning, sought to use its formal powers to the fullest extent. Undoubtedly it won success in finding acceptance for many of its own policy initiatives because they were tailored to fit with the policy interests of key member states. In other cases the Commission was able to forge alliances with shifting coalitions of member states on specific issues. Undoubtedly also, the normative appeal of proposals which the Commission routinely presented as 'Community-enhancing' made for acceptance over rejection of many proposals. A key reason, however, for the Commission's success in enlargement agenda-setting, was the fact that, from the beginning of the process in 1989, the member states were *unclear* about how to embrace the Warsaw Pact states (despite the rhetorical offerings of wholehearted support), *fearful* of the institutional and policy implications of a potential large-scale enlargement, and thus *reluctant* to embrace any radical policy proposals. The sheer uncertainty surrounding the transition process in Central and Eastern Europe also meant that the member states were reluctant to take control of a process that was not necessarily going to lead to membership for the CEE aspirants. Thus, almost by default, the Commission found itself playing the principal EU role in the eastern enlargement process from the earliest stage.

There were some striking early examples of the Commission's willingness and ability to use its formal agenda-setting powers on important issues. Sedelmeier and Wallace, for example, demonstrate that during the negotiations on the initial Europe Agreements with Poland, Hungary and Czechoslovakia, the Commission successfully persuaded the Council to amend the negotiation directives in order to take better account of CEE demands.[15] With respect to the groundbreaking Copenhagen summit of June 1993, which effectively reshaped EU policy toward Central and Eastern Europe, the services of DG I and Franz Andriessen's *cabinet* proved particularly important. The Commission succeeded in forging a coalition with Denmark, Germany and the UK, thus succeeding to a large extent in circumventing the more hesitant and protectionist member states and vested interests. One result (discussed in chapter 2) was a significant increase in CEE access to the EU market. EU producers in the steel sector were particularly opposed to the Commission's liberal strategy of opening markets to CEE producers. In the end the Commission's adept management of alliances and advocacy neutralized their opposition.[16] Again, in the run-up to the Corfu summit in 1994, there is evidence of effective Commission agenda-setting. In cooperation with the German government (due to take up the Presidency in the second half of the year), the Commission secured a mandate to produce what in effect would amount to a pre-accession strategy for the applicant states. This mandate secured for those enlargement advocates within the Commission a much more secure platform from which to continue their work.[17] As importantly, the Commission's 1995 White Paper on CEE adoption of internal market measures accommodated the preferences of CEE producers to a degree that suggests that the Commission's ability to author and frame the content of policy proposals significantly reduced the veto opportunities open to EU producer interests and their state sponsors.

One of the best examples of the Commission's ability to frame the EU's eastern enlargement agenda is provided by Friis in relation to the Luxembourg summit of 1997, where many member states entered the negotiation with loosely defined preferences. In this situation the Commission was able to 'move the game along' by framing the agenda in a specific way (typically invoking the normative importance of enlargement to the EU) and forging alliances with key member states (Denmark, Germany and Sweden) on important issues. Luxembourg produced the commitment that the applicant states had desired – the opening of negotiations early in 1998, which a number of member states opposed. The Commission had objected to a mooted minimalist accession and succeeded in particular in the inclusion of Estonia and Slovakia in the first wave of negotiations. Such an outcome suggests, as Frank Schimmelfennig argues, that the Commission's extensive use of its powers of proposal along with its ability to construct alliances within the Council helped 'lock' the EU into an enlargement commitment.[18] As the relationship with the candidate states deepened the Commission continued to force the pace, but, conscious also of the sensitivity of many issues in the negotiating process, relied also on its relationship with the Presidency and forging successful alliances in order to achieve its objectives.

Commission advocacy and the framing of eastern enlargement

Outside of its formal treaty-based powers the Commission also sought to shape the contours of the internal EU debate on eastern enlargement through a sustained public discourse, designed to neutralize the opponents of enlargement and create a EU-wide consensus on the normative character of the process. Far from being content with the disinterested provision of policy advice on enlargement issues, parts of the Commission were often the most vocal and enthusiastic proponents of early and inclusive CEE membership of the EU. The Commission was just one arm of a highly visible and vocal advocacy coalition which also included key decision-makers within member state governments, important interest groups and epistemic communities, academics, media commentators and public intellectuals, all of whom consistently made the case (publicly and privately) for the inclusion of the candidate states and a generous accommodation of their preferences. The Commission's pivotal position within the EU as guardian of the treaties and independent arbiter of policy proposals, as well as its mastery of the detail of enlargement issues, left it uniquely placed to inform, harangue, cajole and persuade both the applicant states and the member states of the merits of its strategy. The methods by which it sought to frame enlargement are thus deserving of attention.

Jeffrey Checkel's work on agency is a reminder that well-placed and influential actors with entrepreneurial skills can often turn their individual beliefs into broader, shared understandings. In effect, these individuals have the ability to transpose their beliefs and values on to other actors in a given policy environment. In this situation, as agents engage in cognitive information searches and alignment of preferences, seemingly fixed preferences often dissolve. Processes of social learning are crucial for furthering the norm-creating potential first begun by individual agents. Checkel identifies two distinct diffusion pathways through which norms are transmitted: a 'bottom-up' approach, whereby non-state actors and policy networks are most influential, and, second, a 'top-down' approach where social learning among élites is the vital mechanism for norm diffusion.[19] Although elements of both tendencies may be identified within different aspects of the eastern enlargement framework, the Commission's discursive framing activities may only properly be understood as part of an élite-centred social learning process. In addition, it must be acknowledged that some officials and policy-makers were more important than others. This might be because of their relative seniority and records in public life or their handling of policy issues where they gained special understanding of the issues involved. It is clear that the diffusion of norms through processes of socialization and social learning was given a high priority by the Commission as institutional relations with the candidate states deepened.

Identifying the most important public advocates of eastern enlargement within the Commission is not difficult. From an early stage the EU's external policy representatives took the lead in both private and public discussion of enlargement. Commission officials, especially those located around the *cabinets* of Commissioners Franz Andriessen and Leon Brittan, 'promoted an accommodation of the CEEC's interests not only because of far-sighted self-interest, but also for its own sake'. This group of policy-makers was most frequently the source of statements acknowledging and asserting a special role for the EU with respect to CEE, and frequently justified policy preferences with reference to norms of accommodation and EU responsibility.[20] In many instances the exertion of such discursive pressure left them at odds with state representatives who were less inclined to cast aside their partisan preferences. Both Andriessen and Brittan in their public advocacy of enlargement went far beyond what might have been expected of a supposedly neutral bureaucratic arm of the EU. Their rhetorical support for the applicant states underscores the deeply political role played by the Commission throughout the eastern enlargement process.[21]

Commission presidents also played their part. Jacques Delors, Jacques Santer and Romano Prodi all acted as advocates of eastern enlargement, even if they exhibited significant differences of tone and emphasis. During the negotiation of the Europe Agreements, for example, Jacques Delors excoriated member states for their continued protectionist instincts vis-à-vis CEE.[22] Like other enlargement supporters the father of the Single Market programme also frequently framed his speeches in normative terms: 'Building an area of peace brings us back to the basic foundations of the initial European project. Europe was built to say no to conflict, no to the wars that repeatedly tore the continent apart.' Enlargement thus constituted the most important security-enhancing project which the EU had attempted.[23] In contrast, as Peter Ludlow shows, the Santer Commission was much more reactive than proactive: 'they acquiesced in demands placed upon the Commission by successive European Councils. They did not, as the Commission had done at Copenhagen in June 1993, help to provoke these demands.' In large part this was because Santer's Commission worked from a 'bleak and unimaginative political strategy' with 'the earliest advice emanating from Hans van den Bröek and his officials brutal. None of the CEECs were anywhere near the required standards.'[24] Santer himself was known to favour only a small enlargement intake of Hungary, Poland and the Czech Republic. It was little wonder then that the period in office of the Santer Commission saw enlargement recede as a political priority for the European Union.

The Prodi Commission, in contrast, was not just more committed to enlargement but was both privately and publicly enthusiastic and proactive. From the beginning of his term Prodi signalled that eastern enlargement represented an absolute political priority and he subsequently lost no opportunity to publicly commit the Union to the cause of speedy accession whilst emphasizing the need for CEE adaptation and substantive reform. A key contribution to the EU's more sure-footed enlargement strategy under Prodi was the administrative reorganization of the Commission machinery that he effected.[25] The newly created Enlargement DG acquired a new director in Eneko Landaburu, one of the most senior officials in the Commission, with a proven success record as an administrator and connections at the highest levels.[26] His remoulding of the Enlargement Task Force was particularly important in providing a credible organizational structure from which the move to final negotiations could proceed. Neither was he afraid to venture into sensitive political territory by publicly discussing the opportunity costs of non-enlargement.[27] The most significant innovation was the establishment of an entirely new administrative tier within the Enlargement DG, consisting of five directors, who together with Landaburu shaped and agreed almost all the most important elements in the Commission's new enlargement strategy. Three of the directors, Francoise Gaudenzi, Pierre Mirel and Michael Leigh, were each responsible for a group of candidate countries, while the other two, Matthias Ruete and Augosto Bonucci, were in charge respectively of the coordination of pre-accession policies, including the appropriate financial instruments, and resources and finance. Graham Avery, one of the Commission's most experienced enlargement experts, was also party to the most important decisions.[28]

Günter Verheugen

If administrative support helped underpin the Commission's strategy, the political lead given by commissioners was of the utmost importance. In this respect the outstanding figure was Günter Verheugen, who succeeded Hans van den Bröek as Commissioner for enlargement in 1999. In office, Verheugen demonstrated from the outset remarkable energy and enthusiasm, and had 'political clout and imagination well above the average in any Commission'.[29] Verheugen, in effect, became a classic 'norm entrepreneur', engaging in public discourse across the membership–non-membership nexus and consistently deploying ideas about appropriate and non-appropriate behaviour for both insiders and outsiders. He was more trusted in the candidate states than his predecessor and enjoyed close working relations with a large number of senior EU leaders.

The record demonstrates Verheugen's aptitude for enlargement entrepreneurship. In the aftermath of the election of Jörg Haider's Freedom Party as part of the Austrian coalition government, Verheugen insisted that this could not and would not slow down the enlargement negotiations. This was in a context where Haider was making veiled threats about Austria vetoing eastern enlargement, in a country where there existed greater fears about the implications of enlargement than any other.[30] Verheugen was also adamant that the ongoing deepening of the EU should not interfere with the timetable or negotiations on enlargement. At Salzburg in June 2000 Verheugen insisted that enlargement should not be delayed by IGC-related disagreements on major constitutional reform in the EU. The two processes had to be kept apart.[31] More controversially, Verheugen also supported the right of applicant states to delay the sale of land to wealthy EU15 nationals for periods after accession, at a time when this was a difficult issue in the negotiations with some candidate states.[32] His visits to candidate state countries were characterized by speeches seeking to enthuse and encourage further reform whilst expressing confidence that negotiations could be concluded speedily.[33] He was also not averse to directly interfering in the domestic debate on EU membership in candidate states. In Poland, for example, in a wide-ranging speech on 11 July 2002, he warned Poles against falling for lies about what EU accession would mean for them.[34] He openly attacked Polish Eurosceptics, and assertively set out the advantages of EU membership.

Such strident advocacy of enlargement made Verheugen seem at times to member states as a traitor in the ranks, recalling the old pun by a German diplomat that he was known in Bonn not as the *ständiger Vertreter* (permanent representative) but as the *ständiger Verräter* (permanent traitor). The mirror image of this negative persona could be found in his depiction in the candidate states, where Verheugen was sometimes presented as the representative of an ever-demanding and unreasonable EU.[35] Unlike Commission President Prodi, Verheugen's tenure was relatively free of controversy and gaffes.[36] Although it was the Danish Presidency that took the principal negotiating role on behalf of the Union in the final stages, Verheugen and Eneko Landaburu both acted as interlocutors with candidate state governments. Verheugen was by then so trusted in CEE capitals that ministers and officials confided in him, consulted him, and continually lobbied him. His importance as a key broker in the negotiations was demonstrated in the part he played liaising with and between Chancellor Schröder and Polish Prime Minister Leszek Miller in the weeks immediately before the final Copenhagen summit.[37]

The Commission, however, was far from a uniform actor in the eastern enlargement process. The Delors, Santer and Prodi Commissions contained commissioners who were sceptical about the benefits of enlargement and sought to highlight the inadequacy of CEE preparations. In retrospect, Hans van den Bröek, for example, seems much more an enlargement 'realist' than 'idealist'. Internal Market Commissioner Fritz Bolkstein was at times the scourge of the candidate states or certainly the most consistently trenchant critic of Commission policy. He had in 1996, for example, while still in Dutch politics, fought hard to block Poland's entry into NATO. He had also expressed scepticism about the Commission's analysis of candidate state preparation in some of the annual reports. In particular he was far from convinced that the candidate states could meet the internal market competition they would face. He was not the only doubtful commissioner. Loyola de Palacio, Viviane Reding and David Byrne are also mentioned as reluctant enlargers in Ludlow's account.[38] Thus, for Verheugen and Prodi, where enlargement proposals were concerned, the internal battle within the Commission was sometimes as charged as any battle with the Council or candidate states. But for all that the Commission was still the most unified institutional body within the enlargement process throughout and more often than not succeeded in turning its own positions into collective EU positions.

The Commission's discursive framing of enlargement

If individual Commissioners and parts of the Commission bureaucracy contributed significantly to EU support for eastern enlargement, a crucial part of their strategic armoury may be located in the discursive deployment of strategic rhetoric. There were two dimensions to this, an *internal EU dimension* aimed at mobilizing member states and EU citizens, and an *external dimension* involving key commissioners and their staff in selling enlargement to candidate state representatives and their citizens. In this respect, policy speeches and statements, along with official communications to the Council, are revealing of a body that framed its arguments with respect to EU values, norms and obligations rather than instrumental benefits. In effect, the Commission usually sought to appeal to the member states in terms of the medium- to long-term potential of enlargement to secure peace and prosperity for a wider Europe, rather than a short-term perspective based on economic and utilitarian concerns. On some occasions, depending on circumstance and the commissioner in question, enlargement was also framed as a 'win–win' economic prospect. But the dominant discourse was that of a liberal international peace community seeking to export its value system to its eastern neighbours, in the greater interest of securing, on a wider basis, the very values from which it derived its legitimacy.[39]

In arguing for an important discursive dimension to the Commission's role the importance of language and discourse in the social construction of reality is foregrounded. Indeed the material fact of eastern enlargement can only properly be understood as socially constructed by language, representation and symbolism. And it was the Commission that played a lead role in discursively constructing enlargement. It is possible to dissect the Commission's normative framing of enlargement more precisely. In doing so one can identify three distinct pillars of the Commission's discursive strategy. The first presented enlargement as a vehicle for the expansion of the EU value system and legal and democratic norms to Eastern Europe. The second sought to present enlargement to Central and Eastern Europe as a 'special responsibility' and moral imperative for the EU. This pillar also sought to link this moral dimension to the 'Return to Europe' narrative that was the main discursive foundation of CEE claims to membership. Finally, a materialist discourse, which posited enlargement as a 'win–win' scenario for both member states and candidates, was also deployed to support the primary normative discourse.

In the first instance Commission representatives routinely presented enlargement as an effort to extend the EU model of interstate reconciliation eastwards and, as such, as the vehicle for reshaping the emerging Europe in the image of the EU. In his controversial book *Paradise and Power* American neo-conservative Robert Kagan, although fundamentally underestimating the normative underpinnings of the EU, does capture an essential part of the post-Second World War European compact. The European states embraced a Kantian concept of interstate relations, what Kagan terms a 'postmodern paradise', and thereafter embraced a genuinely pacific perspective on the role of power in international relations. The modern European strategic culture represents 'a conscious rejection of the European past, a rejection of the evils of European *Machtpolitik*. It is a reflection of Europeans' ardent and understandable desire never to return to that past.'[40]

The EU value system and its model of interstate reconciliation and reciprocity evolved only slowly over the years but with the prospect of eastern enlargement assumed a new importance in EU thinking. At every point during the eastern enlargement process the Commission stressed the importance of EU values as the underlying basis for membership. And while those values assumed a central importance in the framing of the Copenhagen criteria for membership the Commission also suggested several additional criteria, which had not been in evidence in earlier rounds. Applicants now had to accept the entire Community system, the *acquis communautaire* and the *acquis politique* as well as the *finalité politique* of the Union.[41] The core of the Commission's enlargement strategy thus lay in the effort to successfully export the EU norms and practices at the heart of the *acquis*. This is surely what Commission President Romano Prodi meant when he said that 'our enlargement strategy ensures that these values are enshrined in the candidate countries before they can join the EU. Democracy, the rule of law and respect for human rights will become the norm throughout the expanding Union.'[42]

Reflecting on the eastern enlargement and musing on its significance as a template for future enlargement, Olli Rehn, the Finn who succeeded Günter Verheugen as enlargement commissioner in the Barroso Commission, makes the point succinctly: 'Geography sets the frame, but fundamentally it is values that make the borders of Europe. Enlargement is a matter of extending the zone of European values, the most fundamental of which are liberty and solidarity, tolerance and human rights, democracy and the rule of law.'[43] Of equal importance was the fact that enlargement is based on the fundamental post-war European compact referred to by Kagan. As Rehn asserts: 'equally important is that countries relinquish power politics and spheres of influence as their modes of operation inside the EU. The greatest achievement of post-war Europe is that its governing principle is no longer "might is right".'[44] Extending that principle to Eastern Europe became a central part of EU strategy and this found a prominent place in Commission discourse.

The second strand of the Commission's enlargement discourse centred on the notion of the EU's 'special responsibility' for Central and Eastern Europe and the moral approach to enlargement that this impelled. Sedelmeier argues that EU–CEE relations were, to a great extent, shaped by this EU desire to act appropriately. This approach was fundamentally based on different types of identity linkage and was present throughout the enlargement process.[45] In the previous chapter this discursive strand was also identified in the public framing of enlargement by key state representatives and public intellectuals across the EU. The European Commission regularly stressed the notion of a EU special responsibility, not as some latter-day 'White Man's Burden' but as something located in a shared historical experience, a common cultural repertoire, and the sense of kinship duty that linked Western to Central and Eastern Europe. This strand of Commission discursive support manifested itself especially in buttressing the 'Return to Europe' discourse regularly deployed by candidate state representatives. European Commission officials were in fact explicit in outlining the moral claims of the applicant states. Commissioner Verheugen, for example, in a speech to the European Parliament in 2000, suggested:

> Enlargement is the only adequate response to two great historical changes that have occurred in our lifetimes: the end of the Cold War and the collapse of the Communist camp. How could we say to the nations of Europe who have so recently won through to freedom and self-determination, sorry, the benefits of European integration are reserved for those who happened to be on the 'right' side of the Iron Curtain in 1945?[46]

In its policy documents and public pronouncements the Commission frequently resorted to the moral argument in its efforts to accelerate the negotiation process.[47] The Regular Reports, for example, just as they stressed the importance of enlargement as a vehicle for securing EU values across Europe also presented eastern enlargement as one with 'an unprecedented moral dimension'.[48] The speeches of Romano Prodi and Günter Verheugen in particular were studded with references to Hungary, the Czech Republic and Poland as 'an integral part of Europe', or part of the 'extended family of European nations'.[49] Jacques Delors too in retrospect presented enlargement as an act of historical and moral justice:

> Active peace is not the 'peace of cemeteries' we experienced during the Cold War. We must not forget that we west Europeans found ourselves on the right side of the line drawn by the Yalta agreement and that our East European relatives were less fortunate. I consider we have a debt toward them from a

historical point of view. Not in terms of negotiating the body of Community law, but in terms of history. At the same time, we are overjoyed at seeing the whole family brought together.[50]

This notion of indivisibility of the European family of nations recurs frequently as a predominant and systematic pattern, underlying the idea of East and West in Europe as two parts of the same entity. The aim of policies toward CEE is 'to overcome the division'. Thus 'we will not let Europe be divided again'.[51] The underlying argument is that CEE is a part of 'us' that must be returned. This emphasis on indivisibility foregrounded the element of justice inherent in the 'Return to Europe' claims, and further helped frame eastern enlargement as not just a moral good but a moral imperative for the EU.

The final thematic strand of Commission discourse was an interest-based one, stressing the economic benefits to be derived from enlargement, of expansion as a 'win–win' scenario for both the EU and the candidate states. The expansion of democracy and consolidation of democratic institutions would be underpinned by a market system which brought solid benefits to both the EU and candidate states. Even if the gains were more on the candidate state side and, within the EU, distributed somewhat unequally, enlargement would provide the basis for a dynamic medium-term reconstitution of market relations. This type of argument was a subsidiary one, however, and more usually deployed in support of the normative discourse outlined above. It rarely featured as a stand-alone logic for expansion.

How important was this discourse as an argument based on first principles? If we accept the notion that discourse matters in international politics the case for the 'Return to Europe' looks much more convincing than rationalists would allow. Neumann would suggest that this is a concrete example not only of the unfolding of identity politics but also of how specific carriers of discourse – artists, intellectuals, policy-making groups, epistemic communities – have the ability to change the frame of reference of a particular debate in what they consider an advantageous direction.[52] If we consider this in tandem with the EU's own self-consciousness about its image and credibility, then it is quite tenable. The Commission, as guardian of the treaties, honest broker, and moral conscience of the enlargement process, acted principally from a cognitive template that stressed legitimacy, justice, responsibility, and the normative desire to secure the core values of the European integration process on the widest scale possible.

In employing such a 'logic of appropriateness' it sought to guide the candidate states toward membership, whilst exerting pressure, privately and publicly, on those states within the EU which were cautious or reluctant about enlargement. The articulation by Commission officials of a certain vision of Europe (inclusive, indivisible, whole) consistently represented Central and Eastern Europe as integral to the process of European integration and the candidate states as equal partners. Unquestionably this bolstered their claims to membership of the Union. In effect, the Commission, where it made distinctions in its public pronouncements, did so not on the basis of insider and outsider but rather on the basis of the 'us' and the 'future us', as Commission advisor Graham Avery put it so succinctly.[53] And whilst private solicitation and institutional innovation were the Commission's preferred instruments for securing its policy preferences, we should not ignore the cumulative impact that the Commission's normative discourse produced within the enlargement process.

The Commission as an agent of socialization

If its ability to shape the EU agenda on eastern enlargement was boosted by its ability to frame enlargement in specific ways and build alliances to fight internal battles, then the Commission's direct engagement with the candidate states also helped it influence the nature and direction of EU policy. One route to understanding the Commission's ability to influence outcomes in the candidate states is to employ the typology developed by Tanja Börzel with respect to its role in monitoring compliance with EU legislation within the EU. Börzel identifies four strategies that the Commission uses either singly or in combination with each other within the integration process: *capacity-building* (positive incentives), *persuasion* (learning), *sanctioning* (negative incentives), and *legal internalization* (litigation).[54] Given that the candidates were not yet members of the club, the last strategy was not available within the pre-accession process. But the inside–outside nature of the negotiations gave the Commission extraordinary room for manoeuvre with respect to the other modes of compliance. In particular two important dimensions of the Commission's ability to act as inside–outside mediator and agent of socialization of the applicant states into EU normative practice may be identified. In the first place a range of capacity-building instruments was deployed to boost the candidate states' ability to transpose the *acquis*. In tandem with this the Commission employed an intensive strategy of political conditionality and compliance monitoring in overseeing the transposition and implementation of EU norms in CEE. Whereas the former rendered the Commission a positive agent of change within the domestic politics of candidate states, the latter frequently left it at odds with candidate state governments.

The extent of the Commission's involvement in such activities effectively allowed it to act in what Brigid Laffan terms an *identity-building capacity* in the process of eastern enlargement. Laffan argues that the identity-building capacity of the formal EU institutions depends on their place in the institutional landscape, the roles that are associated with the institutions, the proactive identity-building policies that institutions foster, and the attitudes of the individual social agents that occupy these roles.[55] Institutionalized cooperation does indeed have the identity-shaping effects that normative and constructivist approaches suggest. Such approaches stress the importance of institutionalized communicative practices, social learning and deliberation.[56] The Commission, in managing the functional socialization of the applicant states into EU normative practice, acted as both institution-builder and identity-builder within the process. Such a perspective has a starting point in the acknowledgement that the Commission exists at the centre of a web of functional networks in Brussels. But those functional relationships are endowed with substantive meaning only by the complex social relationships that underpin them and shape their content. This is the context for understanding the journey of enlargement policy proposals and the macro-politics of EU engagement with the candidate countries. The Commission's pre-eminent role in the enlargement process, stemming from its position as chief interlocutor of the CEE states, translated into layer after layer of social and institutional interaction, which enabled it to contribute decisively to policy and institutional innovation in the candidate states. In effect the Commission became the central agent for what is now known as the 'Europeanization' of large parts of the policy process in the candidate countries.[57]

Socialization through capacity-building

Two specific modes of capacity-building may be discerned from the Commission's enlargement activities. The first was the institutional management of structural aid programmes in the candidate states. The second focused on building human capital particularly through reform of public administration systems. And through that process of building institutional capacity the Commission implicitly also sought to build a European consciousness, first in the minds of CEE political élites, and, it was hoped, through the demonstrated success of the programmes, in the hearts and minds of candidate state citizens. And whereas at élite level there seems little doubt that the process succeeded in engendering an EU identity, citizens of the new member states seem as remote from and unconnected with 'Brussels' as their counterparts in EU15 member states.

The clearest early indication of the Commission's eagerness to forge a leadership role in institutional innovation was reflected in its assumption of responsibility for coordinating the early financial and technical aid programmes for Central and Eastern Europe in the wake of the 1989 revolutions. At the G24 conference in Paris in 1989, as outlined in chapter 2, the Commission took on responsibility for coordinating financial aid to the CEE states through what would evolve into the PHARE programme. For some observers this responsibility was of only secondary importance, revolving as it did around classic modes of functional institutional delegation. The evidence, however, suggests that the Commission used its resources and autonomy to shape the content of the aid programmes, from the initial proposals through to management and implementation. Its direct oversight of such programmes rendered it the best-placed EU actor in formally engaging the candidate state representatives in EU policy-making procedures and practices. PHARE became the umbrella programme for the distribution of large amounts of EU aid. So from the beginning the Commission was the EU actor most directly associated with the positive programmes supporting CEE transition, which, over time, would deliver more and more direct aid to the candidate states. And although the early PHARE programme experienced considerable management difficulties, the delivery of large tranches of subvention undoubtedly helped to counter the image of the EU as imperialist and over-demanding.[58]

The Commission also learnt an enormous amount about candidate state economies and systems of public administration through the management of PHARE programmes, which undoubtedly helped it to make more precise judgements about the wider policy mix needed in CEE. The informational advantages it enjoyed meant that over time its arguments carried more weight than any others within EU deliberations. Early on the Commission decided to establish official representation in all the candidate states. The Commission Delegations were responsible for collecting information, administering programmes and advising on key parts of legislative programmes designed to assist the candidate states in effectively transposing the *acquis*. As important was their role in liaising with government ministers, members of national parliaments, and civil society groups in explaining EU policy. The case for the socialization mechanism described by normative scholars can certainly be made in these factors and the highly institutionalized relations established by the Commission in the candidate countries.

The capacity-building measures introduced by the Commission expanded from the early relatively straightforward and narrow PHARE regime to much more specific and targeted institution-building instruments such as ISPA, aimed at structural policy support, and SAPARD, designed to provide aid to CEE agricultural regimes. But the need for far-going change in systems of public administration meant that other capacity-building instruments had to be developed in tandem with the main pillars of PHARE. Two main vehicles, the Technical Assistance Information Exchange Office (TAIEX), and the Twinning model, were designed to facilitate the transfer of knowledge from member states to candidate states and to help build technical capacity in selected sectoral areas.[59] Papadimitriou and Phinnemore argue that the Commission in a sense developed policy in an ad hoc manner. This was because of the absence of a specific 'European model' of public administration. Therefore the Twinning model as an instrument for capacity building was unusual if not peculiar.[60]

The Commission's role in designing and moulding Twinning arrangements was crucial. In large part this was because it was determined to avoid the type of errors of implementation and control which plagued the early PHARE programme. With this in mind the Commission insisted on its officials having a high degree of control over implementation.[61] With each new programme the Commission effectively colonized important parts of the enlargement process, using its resources, informational expertise and epistemic networks to impose specific concepts and templates of transposition and policy adaptation. In addition, the Commission also negotiated transition measures with the candidate states, which were negotiated with the Council and then built into the bilateral accession agreements. This of course allowed for more flexibility in the implementation of European law and allowed crucial 'breathing space' for catch-up by the accession states. Some aspects of the Twinning programme also yielded unexpected but welcome effects. Commissioner Verheugen points out that the long-term exchange of senior administrative officials further increased interest in and knowledge of enlargement in the member states, by producing a 'trickle-down' effect from the government level to the working level in the various branches of the national administrations. There was also a benefit in that the process of socialization increased the member states' expertise in the problems of transition and adaptation, which in turn made it easier for solutions to be found for specific problems in the final accession negotiations. The various modes of capacity-building also succeeded in integrating candidate state officials into the political as well as administrative decision-making processes in the EU in advance of membership thus making for a smoother transition after accession.[62] The capacity-building instruments used by the Commission thus emerge from the enlargement process as a high value, low-cost mode of administrative and institutional knowledge transfer. These instruments developed from the ad hoc and catch-all type of the early PHARE years to increasingly sophisticated models of institution-building that became important elements of EU enlargement policy.

Socialization through compliance

The Commission's socialization of candidate states was not confined to positive capacity-building measures. It also extended to a much more intrusive programme of monitoring and compliance of candidate state commitments. Milada Ana Vachudova uses the term 'active leverage' to describe the use of conditionality and compliance monitoring by the Commission within the enlargement process.[63] She argues that up to 1994 the EU had minimum impact on domestic political change in Central and Eastern Europe. That changed with the development of a more concrete membership perspective and EU efforts to explicate membership conditions. It was the Commission that was at the forefront of these efforts. The principle concern, of course, in pursuing compliance, lies in the need to ensure credible commitments by all partner states in the process of integration. Contractual reciprocity necessarily requires the utilization by member states of an independent monitoring body. Given its experience in monitoring compliance within the EU it was not surprising to find the Commission asked to perform a similar role as the *acquis communautaire* was extended to candidate states.

Phedon Nicolaides points out that the issues of effective implementation and compliance only came to the forefront of enlargement debates and practice in a gradual way. The conclusions of the Copenhagen European Council meeting in June 1993 made no mention of transposition or implementation capacity. The first reference to these came at the Madrid European Council in December 1995, which merely alluded to the need for adjustment in candidate state administrative structures. This new focus followed the White Paper on the internal market introduced at Cannes earlier in June. Implementation capacity only really came into focus, or was at least tentatively defined, after the Luxembourg summit in December 1997, and the launch of the pre-accession process and specific and tailored Accession Partnerships (APs) and National Programmes for the Adoption of the *Acquis* (NPAAs) for the candidate states. The Luxembourg communiqué stated: 'incorporation of the *acquis* into legislation is necessary, but not in itself sufficient; it will also be necessary to ensure that it is actually applied'. At Helsinki in December 1999 the European Council restated: 'progress in negotiations must go hand in hand with progress in incorporating the *acquis* into legislation and actually implementing and enforcing it'. However, it was only at Feira in June 2000 that the most explicit statement regarding capacity to implement was made: 'in addition to finding solutions to negotiating issues, progress in the negotiations depends on incorporation by candidate states of the *acquis* in national legislation and especially on their capacity to effectively implement and enforce it'.[64] The Regular Reports thereafter increasingly stressed the centrality of transposition and implementation capacity.[65]

Although the EU has no formal mechanisms for monitoring member state compliance and does not, for example, pass judgements on the quality of their public administration systems, it does use 'informal' channels to evaluate and encourage compliance. In order to detect violations, the Commission uses a number of different approaches, including the assembly and analysis of legal data from the member states and, where necessary, targeted local checks.[66] However, as with monitoring of EU legislation in the EU15, the Commission's ability to assess CEE adaptation was weakened by resource incapacity and thus it had to rely to a significant extent on contacts with national implementation authorities, non-governmental organizations, academic bodies and private corporations in the candidate states, all of which provided information on national records on transposition of directives, the publication of surveys of business opinion about continued barriers to trade within the internal market, and individual citizen and company court actions against national administrations.[67] But, given the lack of resources the Commission had for effective monitoring, why did the candidate states not take advantage and cheat more? A number of reasons might be cited. These consisted of a mix of cost–benefit calculations regarding compliance and non-compliance and the familiar logics of appropriateness which governed candidate state behaviour.

First and foremost, candidate states had to factor in the risk of non-compliance interfering with and *hampering progress* in the drive for membership. Therefore it had to be considered whether the short-term benefit of non-compliance superseded the long-term goal of membership of the EU. Second, the potential *economic cost* of non-compliance was much higher for candidate states than for EU15 states that failed to implement collective policy. The threat of the withdrawal of pre-accession aid especially was a potent weapon in the armoury of the Commission. Just as the Commission was able to use the threat of ECJ-sanctioned fines for persistent non-compliance and infringement against EU15 states, it was in a much better position to use the credible threat of financial sanctions against candidate states. Third, the candidate states ran the risk of significant *reputational* costs if non-compliance persisted. Being perceived as 'awkward' in advance of membership would not help in the final negotiations for accession. All candidates sought to present themselves as 'good Europeans'. Non-compliance threatened such positive images and was thus avoided wherever possible.

The Commission was reluctant to impose direct sanctions for non-compliance but did so when it found overt opposition or unwillingness to implement the *acquis* effectively. In this respect it was more disposed to using economic sanctions for infringements of clauses of the Europe Agreements, and content merely to wield the political weapon of potentially consigning candidate states to a delayed accession as the only form of sanction for failure to meet the Copenhagen political criteria. This reluctance to embrace direct and substantive political sanctions prompted Kochenov to argue that the Commission consistently failed to be critical enough in its oversight of key political requirements such as transparency of political institutions, the development of judicial systems, and corruption.[68] Maresceau is similarly critical of the Commission's approach to minority rights.[69] In the Commission's defence, however, it must be pointed out that those criteria were so vaguely defined by the EU that compliance assessments would always be perceived as highly subjective. Candidate states could also readily point to deficiencies in the 'quality' of democracy in many of the EU15 states. In addition commentators often forget that the Commission's strategy was one of effecting long-term change rather than short-term direct adaptation. Neither was the Commission unwilling to issue vocal condemnation of candidate states for non-compliance or ongoing problems of implementation.

Whilst the Commission's preferred option was for private representation leading to voluntary enforcement, it did also opt for more forceful measures where they were deemed necessary. In May 1998 the Commission did not hesitate to withhold PHARE projects worth a combined €34 million from Poland in response to poor preparation and domestic political wrangling.[70] During the same period, agriculture commissioner Franz Fischler, accounting for the delay in the introduction of SAPARD in Poland, suggested the delay in the establishment of paying agencies in the candidate states was the main problem and that subvention would not be supplied until proper procedures were in place.[71] In 2001 the EU suspended aid to Slovakia because of irregularities in its internal disbursement of monies. Earlier, during the Mečiar era, EU policy was much less effective, but Vachudova argues that the Commission's increased institutional capacity to follow domestic politics in the candidate states at least enabled it to provide detailed criticisms of the Mečiar government policies, which then had a significant domestic impact.[72]

Neither should the importance of the Commission's annual Regular Reports as assessments of compliance and templates for further change be underestimated. The publication of the Regular Reports created an 'atmosphere of permanent follow-up' which gradually deepened the institutional capacity to implement.[73] The Reports contained assessments of the efforts made to meet the Copenhagen criteria and the quality of reforms enacted in each individual candidate state. The great media attention generated by the publication of the Reports was one asset that the Commission used effectively. More important was the presentation of the Reports as a sort of administrative beauty contest, with each state examining its progress against that of the other candidates, and seeking above all to maintain momentum toward accession by securing public approval by the Commission of its efforts. This generally favoured a 'compliance push' in advance of the publication of the Reports in order to avoid reputational damage.

The Commission's vigilance regarding compliance monitoring persisted even after the successful completion of accession negotiations in late 2002. Its mantra of continued application to effective implementation of the *acquis* may be seen in many of its communications to the candidate countries. Even after the signing of the accession treaty in Athens in May 2003 it was urging the acceding member states to progress rapidly with reform. Keeping the pressure on meant offering advice and exerting informal coercion in many forms. In May 2003, for example, the Commission sent a letter to Poland urging it to make efforts to improve food safety standards in the run-up to accession.[74] The seriousness of the measures was set out by Eneko Landaburu when he told an EU–Poland Joint Parliamentary Committee in Warsaw at the end of April 2003 that Poland might face EU safeguard mechanisms if it did not accelerate its preparations for accession – particularly on freedom of movement of services, agriculture and food safety.[75] This followed on from a Commission initiative which saw nine acceding countries issued with so-called 'early warning' letters on specific areas where they were deemed to be behind schedule in their efforts to transpose and implement the *acquis*. All these points were underlined in the comprehensive monitoring reports of 5 November 2003.[76] The Commission again stressed that 'immediate and decisive' action should be taken by acceding member states in specific areas. Poland, with nine issues to tackle, had the largest number and Slovenia, with one, the smallest.[77] Clearly the pressure would be kept up all the way to the finishing post on 1 May 2004.[78] The monitoring reports were intended to be a crucial link in the chain of ensuring that EU enlargement imposed no undue strains – and offered protection where needed through a series of safeguard clauses. These were set out in the Accession Treaty and were phrased in a way that aimed at being even-handed, protecting new member states as well as existing members.[79] A seemingly even more invasive monitoring stance was adopted by both the Commission and the European Parliament with respect to Bulgarian and Romanian preparations for membership after they had signed accession treaties in April 2005.

Not unnaturally, the candidate states felt that there was an element of unfairness and arbitrary judgement by the Commission in the assessment of their preparedness. As Nicolaides points out the EU does not have explicit criteria for judging whether its member states have capacity for effective implementation of EU rules and it does not subject its own members to the same sort of scrutiny of their domestic implementation mechanisms and procedures. This point underscores the fact that this enlargement has seen very different treatment of the candidate states on this issue. Nicolaides points out, for example, that a recent publication on Finland's entry into the EU in 1995 contained no details at all about transposition and implementation. He argues that the EU was not at all concerned about the capacity of the EFTA entrants to transpose, 'it even accepted vague commitments from them to establish the requisite implementing procedures to enforce EU rules after they had entered the EU'.[80] The Commission's compliance monitoring, however intrusive it may have seemed to the candidate states, was part of a concerted effort to socialize CEE public officials into the variegated patterns of EU public policy-making.

Conclusions

The chapter set out to demonstrate the extraordinary challenge which confronted the European Commission when it took on the task of managing EU relations with the new democracies of Central and Eastern Europe in the early 1990s. The challenge was quite unlike anything the Commission had previously faced in EU enlargement history. Although at many levels the Commission acted throughout the enlargement process in conformity with Article 49, and thus as a classic bureaucratic agent of the member states of the EU, the claims advanced in this chapter suggest that the Commission also managed to carve out for itself a very significant role in the eastern enlargement. In the first place it was responsible for most of the important formal policy proposals that shaped the deepening of relations with the CEE states. The Commission was both able and willing to act as an agenda-setter and so frame the parameters of EU policy toward the applicant states. And although more often than not its choice was to operate through coalitions within the Council, and where possible with the Presidency, it also frequently drove the EU agenda on key parts of the process. Where formal prerogatives were absent the Commission used customary enlargement practice to carve out an informal agenda-setting role, framing problems and urging consensus where difficulties arose. Individual commissioners such as Günter Verheugen emerged from the enlargement story as political entrepreneurs, forceful and proactive and integral to the eventual success of the negotiations in late 2002. And the Commission itself, through its capacity-building and compliance functions within the process, was the EU institutional actor closest to the candidate states throughout the process, providing advice, urging broader and deeper transposition of EU norms, and actively socializing CEE public representatives into EU practice. Viewed by the candidate states as ever-demanding and frequently unreasonable in its insistence on full and unconditional implementation of the *acquis*, viewed by the member states as too accommodating of candidate state preferences, the Commission often trod a thin line between process manager and political entrepreneur. More often than not, however, it was the only actor within the process to look beyond narrow partisanship and focus on the Community-building logic which eastern enlargement rested upon. If that sometimes meant being perceived as a bully that was a price well worth paying given the greater prize which enlargement facilitated. If it meant being watched suspiciously by the member states as it engaged with the candidate states then that too was simply a function of the tensions inherent in the EU's unique governance structure. And although it might seem decidedly unfashionable to describe what is sometimes misidentified as the 'Brussels Bureaucracy' as the unsung hero of the eastern enlargement process, much of the evidence suggests that this is exactly how the Commission emerges from the process. In its engagement with the candidate states, imaginative framing of policy proposals within the EU, and not inconsiderable diplomatic skill in pushing the sometimes reluctant member states toward completion of the negotiations, the Commission performed the type of role which, if indeed unglamorous and hidden from the European public, was integral to the success story that was eastern enlargement.

7 The European Parliament in the enlargement process

Introduction

If the Council and Commission maintained their traditional dominance of the institutional politics of enlargement throughout the eastern expansion, there was also another dimension to the drama that was often neglected by political actors, media commentators and academics. That was the parliamentary dimension. More than any previous enlargement in the EU's history the eastern enlargement was conceptualized and understood as an expansion of democratic ideals, norms and practices. Where previous enlargements focused almost exclusively on economic issues and market integration, eastern enlargement highlighted the importance of human rights, fundamental freedoms, representative political institutions and good governance in the emerging Europe. This was hardly surprising given that the 1989 revolutions had been forged out of a yearning for freedom and political choice whilst the central legacy of Communism was one of moribund and dysfunctional political systems. It was clear from the outset that EU efforts to integrate Central and Eastern Europe into the structures of the European integration process would be focused as much on shaping political institutions as on market relations. Thus no analysis of the institutional politics of enlargement can be attempted without extensive reference to the role played by the EU's most important representative institution – the European Parliament (EP) – in the process. The Parliament was involved in the process from the beginning and sought to assert its influence in specific ways and through a range of political instruments.

A literal reading of Article 49 of the treaty would suggest that the European Parliament's contribution to enlargement decision-making occurs only at the end of the process when it is required to decide whether or not to accept each candidate state. This power constitutes a veto power but is seen as a negative type of power in that the EP has no options other than to say 'yes' or 'no'. But it seems clear now that the eastern enlargement saw the European Parliament come of age within the institutional politics of enlargement and play a significant role at all stages in the process. Its formal power of assent translated also into other forms of informal influence on the process, not least on the shape of new democratic thinking and representative politics in the candidate states. The chapter examines the input of the EP into the enlargement process and the various instruments through which it sought to influence the outcome of events. And whilst less influential than the Council and Commission, neither the candidate states nor the other EU institutions were prepared to disregard the Parliament's views on critical issues such as human rights, minority protections, and administrative preparedness.

Previous enlargements

The European Parliament's role in EU enlargement has evolved over time. Prior to the introduction of direct elections in 1979, the Parliament had a role in accession procedures, and whilst this was formally quite limited, its views on accession and association were nevertheless 'clearly influential', as David Phinnemore points out.[1] The Birkelbach Report of 1961, drawn up by the European Parliament's Political Committee, emphasized the inclusivity of the integration process by arguing that the norm for European states should be EEC membership and not just association. It pointed to the dangers of being formally associated with countries deemed unable or unwilling to become members, most importantly the danger that the Community would undermine its own long-term development prospects. In a crucial sense, the Birkelbach Report demonstrated a willingness on the part of the Parliament to take the lead in formulating guidelines for a policy of outside states establishing closer links with the Community beyond mere trade agreements. It claimed that Association should not be in a category of its own but should be considered with a view to membership; basically, it should be reserved for those countries that did not yet fulfil the economic conditions for full membership but which were politically willing to do so.[2] These guidelines became quite important, since they were followed by the Commission in subsequent opinions on membership or association, and had two immediate effects: they opened the way for transitional association agreements for both Greece and Turkey.[3]

In the aftermath of the so-called Colonels' coup in Greece in 1967, the Parliament also played an important role in calling for the abolition of the existing association agreement. This was not followed, either by the Commission or by the member states, which claimed that the text of the agreement did not allow for such one-sided action. The Parliament then claimed that Greece prevented the institutions of the association agreement from functioning because it had put an end to the existence of the Greek Parliament, and thus the joining committee was not operational. This argument succeeded in at least having the association agreement frozen. After the restoration of democracy in Greece in 1974 the EP became one of the most ardent advocates of early Greek membership, arguing that membership was the best instrument for strengthening Greek democracy.[4]

Long before eastern enlargement of the EU became even imaginable, the European Parliament had also, since the 1970s, dealt in different resolutions and reports with the Community's relations with the Warsaw Pact countries and expressed its positions on human rights issues and on the general developments in these countries. After 1988 interparliamentary delegations for relations with the respective countries in Central and Eastern Europe were established as new forms of political dialogue began to emerge in the region. That was a key date in the forging of constructive relations as it opened the way for new perspectives on a wide range of issues. In 1989, however, the political situation in Europe radically changed. And thus inter-parliamentary relations would face a radical reconstitution also as new democracies emerged from the shadow of Soviet domination and the politics of EU–CEE relations began to take shape.

Formal role: the assent procedure

Like the Commission, the Parliament is involved in the enlargement process partly in a formal capacity, partly in an informal capacity. Prior to the Single European Act (SEA), it was only required that the Parliament be consulted; the SEA in 1987 introduced the 'assent' procedure, whereby the European Parliament effectively obtained a veto over any accession decisions made by the Council. This advance in institutional power was a precursor for more important gains by the Parliament in the 1990s. The Maastricht Treaty and, later, the Amsterdam Treaty both significantly advanced parliamentary influence in deciding EU legislation. During the Convention and IGC of 2003–4 the Parliament again played a very significant part and achieved many of its objectives.[5]

In general terms the assent procedure provides that, in a restricted number of issue areas, the Council may act only after receiving the assent of the European Parliament, which is required to vote on the proposed measure. Originally confined by the SEA to the approval of EC association and accession agreements with third countries, the procedure has subsequently been extended to six additional areas including, importantly, the right under Article 7 TEU to recommend sanctions in the event of a significant and persistent breach of human rights by a member state.[6] It is one of the many curiosities of the Parliament's role within the EU structure of decision-making that the power of assent which the Parliament enjoys on accession agreements has not been extended to other important international agreements to which the EU is party such as those in international trade. It is similarly excluded from, and, by implication, marginal to, processes of constitutional revision. But enlargement is viewed differently from other international agreements. In a sense it represents more a domestic European affair than an international one.

In formal terms, the European Parliament has one very clear role in the enlargement process – it has to vote by an absolute majority at the end of the accession negotiations, in order to permit the ratification of each individual accession treaty.[7] A similar ratification procedure has to take place in the national parliaments of the member states of the European Union and, indeed, in the parliaments of the candidate countries (or ratification according to the constitutional requirements of each state).[8] The assent procedure is also governed by a 'logic of appropriateness' in that member state governments, in granting the EP a veto power over the accession of outside states, do so on the normative understanding that the assent of a directly elected representative assembly bestows an important layer of democratic legitimacy on an élite-negotiated process. Clearly the view is that the EP's assent adds to the democratic mandate garnered from the assent of the member states through their governments and various national ratification procedures.[9]

Rationalist scholars would argue that member states were aware, in granting the power of assent to the EP, that this constituted a so-called 'nuclear option', that it was something which, in practice, the Parliament could not and would not resort to using. Bailer and Schneider, for example, argue that because the Parliament tends to be more integrationist than other EU actors, the threat of a future veto is not credible since the legislature will typically perceive the admission of new member states as an improvement on the status quo.[10] For other scholars assent represents a 'cruder form of codecision', in that there is no scope for amendments to be put forward in the case of disagreement with the Council.[11] Thus, in this view, the power garnered by the EP through the assent procedure was quite illusory. The EP would rubber-stamp the Council's decisions in all conceivable circumstances. In addition, whereas the Parliament has demonstrated a clear and consistent willing-ness to confront both the Council and the Commission in an adversarial fashion over such issues as budgetary matters, the nature and scope of inter-institutional agreements, and the selection and performance of the Commission, there has always been a sense that enlargement, because of the magnitude of the issues, somehow transcended the normal political boundaries and lay outside the terrain of 'politics'. However, the chapter will show that in quite a number of ways the Parliament did manage to impose its perspective on Council, Commission and candidate countries at various stages of the enlargement process. At the very least the Parliament had to be taken seriously by all actors. The different mechanisms used by the EP to assert its influence are examined in the context of the general framework of agenda-shaping examined in the previous two chapters. Thus, it will be argued, the formal power to withhold consent actually facilitated an *informal parliamentary power* within different stages of the process, which ensured that deci-sions went some way toward satisfying the Parliament on its key concerns. The Parliament was also highly successful in socializing candidate state representatives into its own modes of operation and practice. The chapter now goes on to examine the various mechanisms used by the EP to assert its influence on the process and the concerns it sought to uphold throughout.

The European Parliament as norm entrepreneur

The European Parliament, throughout the eastern enlargement process, main-tained strongly held views on the nature and direction of the process. It may genuinely be viewed as an important *norm entrepreneur* on the EU side, using a carrot-and-stick approach to induce candidate states into accepting EU norms, and actively socializing candidate state parliamentarians into EP practices. Parlia-mentary activism produced important constituent effects, not least in inducing candidate states to more effective transposition of EU norms, and more satisfac-tory implementation of agreements concluded with the EU. It also encouraged a transnationalization of party groupings within and outside the structures of the enlargement process. In particular three aspects of the Parliament's norm entrepreneurship can be demonstrated. First, it insisted on placing the EU's democracy norms at the core of the eastern enlargement process and was willing to defend those norms in its engagement with the candidate states and within the EU's institutional structure. Where other parts of the EU institutional machinery may have been more concerned with candidate state adjustment to the EU's market regime, the Parliament provided a significant counterweight in its emphasis on substantive commitment to representative democracy. Second, the Parliament insisted throughout the enlargement process on the equality of treatment of all candidate states. It thus sought from an early stage to establish this as a core norm for the EU in its selection and monitoring of candidate states. A third aspect of the Parliament's approach was its eagerness to protect the integrity of enlargement-related inter-institutional prerogatives. Where the Council in particular sought to dominate EU policy the Parliament countered by invoking the norms governing the institutional division of labour on enlargement policy-making. In these three areas of Parliamentary activism we find both the willingness and the capacity to act in a consistently forceful and entrepreneurial manner.

Embedding EU democracy norms

The EP's role as a norm entrepreneur and defender of the EU value system stressed as a first principle the importance of the Parliament's attachment to and insistence on upholding the EU's value system. Thus from the beginning of the enlargement process, the Parliament, in an explicit and forthright way, staked out positions on human rights, fundamental freedoms, and protection of individual and minority rights within the association and pre-accession frameworks and the actual accession negotiations. Candidate state preparation, in the Parliament's view, had to focus as strongly and substantively on strengthening the fragile institutions of the new democracies, as on the market reforms which were boldly being enacted. It was the Parliament in 1992 that effectively introduced political conditionality into the enlargement process by insisting on the insertion of a democracy clause into the general budget for 1992, 'in order to focus more attention on politics and civil society' within the process.[12] Clearly, the principles enunciated earlier in the Birkelbach Report served as a template for the emerging parliamentary perspective on relations with the transitioning states. Human rights groups had for long been utilizing the EP as an arena for generating precisely the sort of normative pressure one might expect from a representative parliamentary body. Such pressure meant that the Parliament kept a watchful eye over the unfolding and development of the democratic process throughout Central and Eastern Europe as the enlargement process took shape. In its communications on the process the Parliament lost no opportunity to highlight the importance of the different components of the EU's democratic framework.

If the Parliament sought to ensure that the Commission and Council protected the fabric of EU democracy in negotiating with the former Communist states, then it was equally insistent in its contacts with candidate state representatives. Indeed a significant component of the EP's enlargement strategy focused on deep institutional engagement with and socialization of CEE representatives into EP norms and practices. From the outset the European Parliament was the most outspoken EU actor on civil society issues, whether it be the commitment to parliamentary democracy in Slovakia, media freedom and diversity in Bulgaria, homosexual rights in Romania, or the rights of Russian-speakers in Estonia or Latvia.[13] The Parliament's country monitoring reports consistently highlighted such issues as police brutality, disenfranchisement of voters because of artificial language barriers and discrimination against certain sections of the population. EP Committees pressed for full implementation of the EU's non-discrimination legislation and the ending of all forms of discrimination related to ethnic origins, cultural and religious difference or sexual orientation.[14] The Parliament considered these to be issues of fundamental concern and not matters for negotiation. In many instances strategic use of domestic CEE media outlets, especially in the run-up to important EU decisions (such as the Commission's publication of Regular Reports), created enough pressure that changes to domestic legislation or on-the-ground policy followed.[15] And although the role of the EP constituted just one arm of the EU machinery, the Parliament's democratic legitimacy often left it better placed to argue for the substantive changes sought by the EU in specific candidate countries than any other EU body.

The Parliament's willingness to deploy the 'democratic stick' reminded all parties of the widespread attachment within the assembly, irrespective of ideological bent, to the Copenhagen political criteria, and other quasi-formal membership criteria. The transposition of clear and transparent democratic norms was not only necessary for the adoption of good governance practice in the candidate states, it also represented a clear and unequivocal commitment to the normative integrationist ideals built into the treaties that the Parliament had always championed. The record of parliamentary activism was particularly evident in respect of human rights issues. Attending the EP's Foreign Affairs Committee on 20 February 2002, for example, Hungarian Prime Minister Viktor Orban was accused by Green party MEP Daniel Cohn-Bendit of flirting with anti-Semitism. In a newspaper interview the day before, Orban had refused to rule out a post-election coalition with the far right Justice and Life Party. Orban was also criticized for his government's handling of the Roma minority with MEPs arguing that Hungary had made insufficient progress in meeting the Parliament's concerns. In addressing another of the EP's committees, Commissioner Verheugen was pressed consistently on the Roma issue, particularly on what MEPs perceived as the wide gap between candidate state commitments on their Roma minorities and the actual situation confronting the Roma.[16] The Commission was urged to press for a deeper commitment to the implementation of reforms. This was part of a pattern in that the EP asked candidate states to develop and implement policies, strategies and action programmes to improve the living conditions of their Roma minorities and their integration into society, and used every opportunity to emphasize the direct link between this issue and overall progress in each state's enlargement prospects. The Parliament's determination to effect change was underlined by its decision to make progress on Roma issues a *precondition* for garnering its assent.[17]

For some the attachment to and employment of different variants of political conditionality by the Parliament suggested a body attempting to place further obstacles in the way of the candidate states. But most observers would rather concur with the view that Parliamentary vigilance on the transposition of EU democratic norms and practices was simply a reflection of the deep attachment to those norms upon which the very legitimacy of the EU was founded. The fact that member states of the EU tended to promote their own national interests in the enlargement process, even if these sometimes conflicted with declared EU commitment to democratic norms, made it all the more important, the Parliament argued, that their institution take the lead on embedding democratic practice within the candidate states.[18]

Direct socialization of candidate states

As the enlargement process unfolded it encouraged a cumulative institutionalization of individual, state, and bureaucratic contacts, and the Parliament, no less than the other EU actors in the process, sought to imprint its own integration perspective on the candidate states. Conrad points out that the EP provides the most intriguing and/or promising arena for testing claims for institutional socialization within the EU. This has to do primarily with organizational factors such as the trans-territorial composition of the Parliament and the fact that ideological or party cleavages take precedence over national cleavages.[19] Viewed from a rationalist or self-interested perspective the Parliament's socialization efforts seem perfectly logical. The institution's desire to function optimally in a Union of 25 states encouraged the adoption of its own rules and structures by the political representatives of the candidate states in advance of accession. Therefore from an early stage, the EP sought to communicate with national parliaments in the candidate countries (and prospective MEPs) a sense of best parliamentary practice. The two principal channels for such communicative exchange were the transnational party groupings in the EP and the Joint Parliamentary Committees (JPCs). Both channels also allowed for a significant degree of individual interparliamentary contact and socialization.[20]

One interesting study that provides a template for understanding the socializing role played by the EP examines the NATO Parliamentary Assembly and its efforts to inculcate a sense of 'we-ness' amongst European and North American parliamentarians since 1989.[21] Flockhart argues that social learning has been much in evidence and facilitated through the participation of parliamentarians and their parliamentary support staff in programmes aimed at teaching, intensive networking and building personal and institutional relationships.[22] The comparison with eastern enlargement of the EU holds especially for the important social learning process located in the committee system. These represented a forum for both familiarizing delegates with specific areas of policy and fostering strong interpersonal ties. It is clear that many parliamentarians, on both the EU and candidate state sides, developed a sense of attachment to the idea of being a part of a transnational liberal democratic family of parliamentarians. On the candidate state side individuals wanted to be seen as upholding EU and EP norms to the highest degree. MEPs saw their role as educational and one of collective responsibility.[23] Such socialization activity represented another important feature of the EP's efforts to 'export' its norms and practices and was buttressed by intensive forms of inter-parliamentary dialogue, both EU–CEE and intra-EU. The latter centred in particular on advice and briefings to EU member state parliaments on the parliamentary dimension to enlargement.[24] Ludlow points out that some of the leading figures on both sides acquired real expertise, and, in the case of the MEPs, a significant profile in the countries with which they dealt. As a result, the EP was able to get its messages across to the candidates in a striking way.[25]

Transnational party groupings

The EP's successful transfer of normative practice can be demonstrated firstly in the *transnational and pan-European party linkages* established in advance of accession. These left the 2004–9 European Parliament organizationally (and ideologically) indistinct from its predecessor, with new member state parliamentarians being readily absorbed into existing groups. Thus the EP and its party groupings used the eastern enlargement process as a transnational learning framework, successfully instituting a genuinely trans-European and familiar (if indeed embryonic) 'European party system'. The importance of the transnational structure of the Parliament mattered in two crucial ways with respect to enlargement. First, the transnational socialization culture within the Parliament meant that its members were more receptive to the European interest than member states, and indeed sometimes the Commission, when faced with difficult enlargement decisions.[26] Second, as Raunio and others have demonstrated, party group cohesion within the Parliament is strong.[27] Since the political groupings have a vested institutional interest in arriving at common positions, in combination with the fact that the Parliament itself has a clear systemic interest in achieving consensus in order to have its preferences taken seriously by the Council, there is a *dual impetus* toward overcoming interest-based and nationally oriented positions on enlargement. Thus during the past decade, as Day and Shaw have pointed out, the Euro-parties have been engaged in their own independent enlargement exercise.[28]

   The European Parliament, not unnaturally, encouraged this and provided functional help toward the realization of the ambition of the enlargement of party groupings. This, however, is not to argue that party groups were in complete agreement about the objectives of the EU's enlargement strategy at all times, nor indeed that there did not exist significant divisions *within* the different party groupings at all times also.[29] It does suggest, however, that party group pressure towards establishing and maintaining a unified parliamentary position helped, first, to legitimate the EP in the eyes of both the candidate states and the other EU institutional actors, and, second, to override some of the less integrationist national positions on enlargement.[30] MEPs and their umbrella groups were also not unaware of the medium-term institutional benefit to be garnered from being viewed as more positively disposed toward CEE preferences. Making friends in Hungary, Poland and Lithuania in advance of accession would undoubtedly increase the prestige and legitimacy of the Parliament in the eyes of élites in those countries and potentially advantage the EP in the enlarged EU's inter-institutional battles.[31]

Joint Parliamentary Committees

Originally the Joint Parliamentary Committees (JPCs) provided a forum for discussing political and economic aspects of the associated countries' integration into the EU, as well as problems encountered in the functioning of the Association Agreements and EU assistance programmes. With the evolution of the reinforced pre-accession strategy and the start of the formal accession negotiations in 1998, their role became more important than the limited tasks assigned to them by the Association Agreements. Primarily, the JPCs provided an opportunity for the members of each parliament to share information and deliberate on methods of joint parliamentary oversight of the enlargement process. The JPC, it has been argued, also represented the one forum within the enlargement process where, prior to accession, both incumbent and candidate were equal.[32] The presence at the JPC meetings of representatives of the governments concerned, the European Commission and the Presidency gave the members a chance to question key decision-makers directly and in unison. For the Commission and the Presidency, the JPC framework provided a convenient opportunity to convey EU perspectives directly into the heart of the political system of a candidate country.

Perhaps the most striking feature of this forum was the willingness of MEPs to speak frankly, sometimes on matters that were extremely sensitive. This was particularly notable in the JPCs with Romania and Slovakia, where fundamental questions about the nature of democracy in those countries were consistently raised. Meetings with the Czech Republic were sometimes dominated by trade disputes and lingering tensions associated with the Beneš Decrees; meetings with Poland often highlighted the Parliament's dissatisfaction with the rate of progress in transposing the *acquis*.[33] The JPCs had a very high public profile in the CEE countries throughout the enlargement process. This is reflected by the political importance of some of the leading figures involved. For example, before becoming Prime Minister of Hungary in 1998, Viktor Orban was the chairman of his Parliament's European Affairs Committee. Similarly the former Polish Prime Minister Tadeusz Masowiecki was chairman of the Polish delegation to the EU–Poland JPC for a period. Other candidate state leaders to address the JPCs included the Latvian President Vaira Vike-Freiberga, Romanian Prime Minister Adrian Nastase, and Slovak Prime Minister Mikulas Dzurinda. Harris asserts that the JPCs significantly tested the commitment to parliamentary democracy in the candidate countries. The criticism offered by MEPs of particular countries on specific issues was often misinterpreted as hostility. On the candidate state side, if opposition MPs asked questions of their own government's performance in meeting EU criteria this was often presented back home as a form of national betrayal.[34] For all the contestation, however, the JPCs added significant value to the Parliament's efforts to integrate candidate state representatives into existing EP structures, norms and practices.

If the JPCs offered the opportunity for MEPs to press the importance of full and effective transposition of EU democracy norms, they also evolved over time into unmistakable enlargement advocacy fora. It became difficult in fact to distinguish the EP position on enlargement issues from candidate state positions. Thus the socialization process also worked in reverse to a significant degree. The JPCs were less impartial than the EP as a whole and to many observers too uncritically in favour of enlargement.[35] The establishment of close contacts and the deeply political nature of the work made it difficult for MEPs to stay on the fence. Rapporteurs in particular were likely to adopt positions closer to the candidate state position than the EU position and rapporteurs usually took the lead in formulating EP positions.[36] Two examples of the close-knit positions emerging out of the JPC process can be cited here. In the heat of the final negotiations on enlargement in late 2002 a joint declaration issued by MEPs and Estonian parliamentarians largely supported Estonia's position on key negotiating chapters. The declaration of the EU–Estonia JPC on 28 May 2002 urged that 'the introduction of full direct payments' from the CAP for Estonian farmers following accession 'should be open to discussion concerning the length of the transition period'. Further, the JPC declaration recommended 'that every effort be made to introduce full direct payments as soon as possible'. The JPC position was clearly one which was much closer to the candidate state than to the Commission or the Council and which held as a central concern complaints about second-class membership from the candidate state.[37]

The second example involves Bulgaria. As the enlargement process unfolded the decommissioning of the Kozludy nuclear power plant became a real thorn in the side of EU–Bulgarian relations. The EP–Bulgarian JPC in 2002 came out strongly in favour of Bulgaria's position on Kozludy. In its official declaration, the JPC said it was 'aware of the strength of feeling in Bulgaria, and of expert opinion, in favour of prolonging the life of units three and four' of the plant. The European Commission had insisted on the closure of these units before 2006. The JPC supported Bulgarian arguments that it had invested in enhanced safety measures for reactor three and four and warned of 'the impact closure would have on local employment, foreign currency earnings and overall energy capacity'. The Commission position was very different in insisting on outright closure of the units as soon as possible.[38] The JPC's work did not go unnoticed outside the Parliament.[39] To summarize, the JPCs represented a vast 'getting to know you exercise', given that the members of the European Parliament and the members of the parliaments of the candidate countries did not know much about each other. They also provided a democratic forum where the citizens of both the EU and the applicant countries were represented in what for many was a process dominated by executive bodies. This made them the main framework for ensuring that the enlargement process was subject to a measure of democratic oversight and control.

Alongside these bilateral meetings, the European Parliament also encouraged the development of a multilateral Parliamentary dialogue. This dialogue conducted with the presidents of the parliaments of the participating candidate countries was broad in nature and intended to buttress the more micro-oriented work at JPC level. Starting with Enrique Baron Crespo in 1989, the Presidents of the European Parliament made an increasing number of visits to the countries concerned. The purpose of these visits was at first to initiate relations between the EP and the parliaments of the new democracies, later to strengthen dialogue with and amongst those states aspiring to join the EU. To further strengthen cooperation, a programme of administrative fusion was launched. This consisted of a staff exchange programme, training sessions, information visits, and the transmission of documents and seminars. In addition national parliamentarians from the EU member states and candidate states met regularly in the Conference of Standing Committees of National Parliaments dealing with EU Affairs (COSAC). Although too large and unwieldy to be utilized in any formal way within the enlargement process, COSAC provided an extra parliamentary forum within which views could be exchanged. The combined impact of these different forms of parliamentary consultation, engagement and deliberation certainly helped the European Parliament achieve a key aim of helping the candidate states internalize EU democratic norms and rules.

EP enlargement advocacy

If the Parliament's socialization of candidate states proved critical to the inside–outside dimension of the enlargement process, then as noteworthy within the internal EU debate was its consistent willingness to champion the macro goal of enlargement, whilst urging the accommodation of CEE preferences to the greatest extent possible within the process. Although this was apparent throughout the different periods of association and pre-accession it was perhaps most evident (and important) in the difficult negotiations of 2002. The Parliament's position was made clear in May 2002 with the publication of two key reports that were strongly supportive of the completion of negotiations. Reimer Böge's report on the financial implications of enlargement urged a realistic effort by member states to find workable compromises with the candidates, as did that of Elmar Brok on progress in the negotiations that carried a similar message.[40] Both reports were debated at the Parliament's plenary session in June in Strasbourg when the Parliament again enjoined the member states to take a more generous view of the funding arrangements. Many speakers made expressions of support for the Böge and Brok reports.[41]

An even more striking indication of the Parliament's willingness to go much further than the Council was apparent in its opening the chamber to candidate state representatives before their accessions had been successfully negotiated. On the initiative of its President Pat Cox, it did so for the first time for the debate of 20 November 2002, when almost 200 deputies participated in the special debate on 'The Future of an Enlarged Europe' in a plenary session in Strasbourg.[42] The EP President described the gathering as 'unprecedented' and 'an early investment in cultural diversity'.[43] Its significance lay in the fact that candidate countries were effectively placed *inside the European Parliament's structures* whilst negotiations on accession were still at a very delicate stage. The EP was thus taking a stance and laying down a marker to member states as to where it stood and what should happen. European Parliament political families expanded with the inclusion of delegates representing candidate countries who had decided which groups they would align with.[44] Within the Parliament it was thought that the debate would also serve as an important functional test of the enlarged Parliament's operational capacity. For the first time simultaneous translation into 23 languages was utilized without any major difficulties being experienced.[45]

Another important component of the Parliament's enlargement entrepreneurship was the discursive support and public advocacy offered by EP presidents. Certainly there were striking differences between the various holders of the office. In the 1994–9 Parliament, Klaus Hänsch was more active than his successor Gil-Delgado Gil-Robles, and, in the 1999–2004 Parliament, Pat Cox was much more prominent than his predecessor, Nicole Fontaine. Cox's energy, enthusiasm and commitment were a remarkable asset, which the Parliament deployed to some effect.[46] Even as head of the Liberal group in Parliament Cox had invested considerable time and energy in cross-crossing the candidate states explaining the EP's attitude to enlargement and encouraging movement on the Copenhagen criteria. Cox's view was that politicians had to get out and make the political case for enlargement to the widest possible audience.[47] He succeeded in forging a dynamic working partnership with the Commission that worked particularly well during the final critical part of the negotiating process. Indeed Cox is on record describing his relationship with Commissioner Verheugen and his Enlargement Task Force as unprecedented in its closeness and intensity. Clearly, the Commission saw an ally in a Parliament which was consistently supportive of its enlargement aims and strategy; all the more so where certain member states were somewhat obstructionist in their attachment to national interests. Cox also enjoyed an excellent working relationship with the Danish Presidency. Cox's public discourse mirrored that of the enlargement 'drivers' within the Commission and Council, stressing the importance of extending the EU Community of values to the east and presenting enlargement both as a viable economic opportunity and a moral imperative for the EU.[48] At earlier periods he actively cautioned against postponement where that was being considered in some quarters.[49] Parliament was thus one arm of a formidable cross-institutional advocacy network within the internal EU debate on enlargement.

Equality of treatment

The second identifiable norm that the EP sought to embed in the enlargement process developed gradually. That was an insistence on the equal treatment of candidates in a rational and non-discriminatory process centred exclusively on the ability to meet the Copenhagen criteria and transpose the *acquis communautaire*. In a 1996 resolution the Parliament stressed the importance of beginning negotiations *simultaneously* with all countries of Central and Eastern Europe which had applied for membership and which were aiming to fulfil both the economic and the political criteria as set out by the Copenhagen European Council in 1993, so as to prevent the emergence of first- and second-class groups of applicant countries. This was at a time when the Council and Commission had effectively embraced a strategy of differentiation or 'enlargement in waves'.[50]

Therefore, while the Parliament welcomed, in principle, the opening of the enlargement process in March 1998 with all of the candidate countries, as well as the opening of negotiations with a first group of five plus one (Poland, Hungary, Czech Republic, Slovenia, Estonia and Cyprus), it reminded the Council that the enlargement process must 'remain open at all times' to all applicants. This was pointed out on 3 December 1998, when the Parliament adopted a series of reports on the five applicant countries that had not yet begun accession negotiations with the EU (Romania, Bulgaria, Latvia, Lithuania and Slovakia). The Parliament similarly endorsed the views of its rapporteurs who – with regard to the two Baltic states and Slovakia – distanced themselves from the recommendations the European Commission made in its Progress Reports.[51] Thus the EP stance was one of keeping the door to membership open whilst insisting that candidate states maintain real progress toward reform.

The Parliament's position was made even clearer in the run-up to the Helsinki Council in December 1999, when it called on the Council 'to put an end to the invidious divide between two classes of applicant countries'.[52] Again in the wake of the Gothenburg European Council and the Irish rejection of Nice in the summer of 2001, which placed the timetable for accession in some doubt, the Parliament staked out its position in its own annual progress reports by insisting firmly that the CEE countries should be welcomed by 2004. This should happen irrespective of whether Ireland ratified the Nice treaty or not. This forthright and consistent stance demonstrated clearly an institution that was independent-minded and more embracing of the European interest than the Council.[53]

The Parliament's greater willingness to accommodate CEE interests was also in evidence on the issue of institutional representation. Perhaps the most facile of the institutional negotiations at Nice had been that on the future voting rights in the EP. Against the ceiling of 700 members set at Amsterdam, the Danish Presidency came up against the desire of some member states to compensate themselves for other institutional concessions by accruing additional representation in the enlarged Parliament. To the irritation of the Council the European Parliament demonstrated its support for Hungary and the Czech Republic when both demanded the same number of seats in the EP as Belgium and Portugal.[54] For the Parliament there could be no justification for any institutional re-calibration that did not, as a solid principle, recognize the new member states as full partners in the integration process.

The Parliament's inclusive approach to enlargement was also manifest in its decision to invite 162 observers from the ten candidate countries to take part in its work after the signing of the Accession Treaty in April 2003. This continued the process of involving what Cecilia Malmström of the ELDR termed the 'virtual MEPs' in the work of the Parliament, which had been ongoing for a number of years.[55] These representatives from the accession countries would, until 1 May 2004, have a national mandate without formal status within the European Parliament. This meant they had only limited rights to participate in its work.[56] In late 2004 the Parliament again staked out a collectivist and courageous position on Turkish membership of the Union. In the run-up to a Brussels summit dedicated to the issue of whether or not to open negotiations with Turkey, MEPs in a vote in plenary session in Strasbourg on 15 December voted 407 to 262 on a resolution calling for membership talks with Turkey to begin as soon as possible. Amendments that offered Turkey associate membership or such as a 'privileged partnership' (favoured by conservative MEPs) were rejected.[57] In the middle of a contentious EU-wide debate on the merits of opening negotiations the EP again sought, as it had done during the eastern enlargement process, to press the member states into agreeing a collective EU position that was inclusive and open rather than partial and selective. Again the European Commission lined up as an ally of the EP in supporting the non-member in question. Commission President José Manuel Barroso told MEPs that, after 40 years, 'it is now time for the European Council to honour its commitment to Turkey and announce the opening of accession negotia-tions'.[58] Enlargement watchers recognized in this a familiar alliance between Commission and Parliament. Where there existed division among the member states the Parliament was consistently willing to take a lead and urge a more inclu-sive and forward-looking engagement with the prospective member state.

Protecting the integrity of the EU enlargement process

The third discernible element of parliamentary enlargement activity was that of the promotion of specific ideas about the protection of EU institutional capacity, the need for enlargement to be facilitated by internal institutional reform and adjustments to the Union's financial framework, and the preservation of inter-insti-tutional balance within the enlarged Union's structures.[59] From the outset the Parliament stressed that expansion and internal institutional reform both revolved around the key concept of legitimacy. The European Parliament, the national parliaments of the member states, as well as the national parliaments of the candi-date countries, were considered the vehicles for the harnessing of such legitimacy. Thus the need to strengthen the role of parliaments was stressed when the Parlia-ment gave its Opinion on the general outline for the Association Agreements in 1991.[60] Starting with the Hänsch report of 1993, the position of the Parliament can be found in several resolutions, which all focus on one or more aspects of demo-cratic legitimacy and created the basis for the Parliament's resolutions on *Agenda 2000* in 1997.[61] The main message of the report was that the Parliament consid-ered enlargement as inevitable but that it would also be necessary to ensure that the Union remained intact as a viable institutional and political system. Indeed enlargement could not proceed without transparent institutional reform. As the enlargement process developed the Parliament remained insistent that the EU had to reform itself in advance of the accessions.

The belief in ensuring a sound financial structure for an enlarged EU repre-sented the second foundation stone of the Parliament's position on the internal EU preparation for enlargement and was spelt out in a resolution that was adopted in 1996.[62] Parliament concluded that the accession of the CEE states would give rise to additional needs, and that the system of own resources would be inadequate to fund enlargement. In particular the agricultural and structural policies needed reform. In this sense the Parliament took the middle ground, manoeuvring between those member states who felt that the financial strain to be endured as a result of (even limited) CEE accession was simply too great and the Commission view, laid down in *Agenda 2000* that enlargement was affordable.[63] The various strands of the Parliament's position finally came together in the reaction to the new reinforced pre-accession strategy as proposed by the Commission in *Agenda 2000* and adopted by the Council at the Luxembourg summit in December 1997. In three different resolutions it expressed its most significant views.[64] The Parliament stated that the institutional framework that had emerged from the Amsterdam Treaty did not meet the necessary conditions for achieving enlargement without endangering the operation of the Union and the effectiveness of its institutions.

A good example of the Parliament's doggedness on the matter of financial soundness and respect for inter-institutional agreements can be evinced in the stand-off with the Council on the Parliament's right to approve the budget component of the 2002 Copenhagen deal. This dragged on through the early part of 2003 and threatened at various junctures to result in the withholding of the EP's consent. This was the so-called 'Annex XV' struggle. The Parliament argued that the Copenhagen deal did not respect the Inter-Institutional agreement (IIA) of May 1999 on budgetary discipline because the EP was not consulted before it was agreed at Copenhagen.[65] Under the IIA, the EP has a right to negotiate with the Council actual spending amounts within agreed spending limits. The EP argued that this right was not respected in the Copenhagen deal. The annex effectively meant a restriction of the EP's powers to establish payment appropriations, a power conferred on it by the Treaty for non-compulsory spending, i.e. other than agriculture. MEPs were of the view that the issue could be compared to the ground-breaking *Isoglucose* case in 1981.[66] Through February and March 2003 the EP threatened to withhold consent. On 11 March the EP's legal service informed President Pat Cox that the Copenhagen deal not only encroached upon Parliament's prerogatives under co-decision, but also could cause legal problems with the budgetary procedure in the future.[67] Cox was appalled by the failure of the Presidency under Greek Prime Minister Costas Simitis to take Parliament's concern seriously.[68]

The prospect of re-opening what had been a difficult budgetary negotiation deal needless to say frightened many, not least many MEPs who understood what might ensue. The Parliament's Committee on Budgets subsequently engaged in a 'trialogue' with the Commission and Council in an effort to resolve the stand-off, but in the end obtained no substantive change regarding the principle of parliamentary input on the Copenhagen budgetary deal. Although more money was again found for the new member states, the Council did not concede the substantive issue. Given the tight schedule for gaining Parliament's assent and the signing in Athens within one week it seems likely that the Council dared the Parliament to withhold or at least delay granting its consent (the so-called 'nuclear option') and risk being castigated by the new member states as the villain of the piece. On this issue at least the Parliament's sabre-rattling simply did not work.[69] Budget Committee Chairman Terry Wynn (PES, UK) captured the mood by describing the agreement as a 'second best solution' and a direct attack on the European Parliament's rights.[70] Daniel Cohn-Bendit of the Greens went further in referring to the episode as one of 'institutional rape'.[71] If nothing else the episode demonstrated the European Parliament's determination to safeguard the integrity of the EU's internal institutional boundaries and responsibilities.

The EP vote on accession of candidate states

The principal reports guiding MEPs on the enlargement vote was that drawn up by Elmar Brok on behalf of the powerful Foreign Affairs Committee and that drawn up by Reimer Böge and Joan Colom i Naval on behalf of the Budgets Committee.[72] The EP insisted on consultation on any modifications to the accession treaty. The reports were mostly uncontroversial, except for that on the Czech Republic, which again expressed concerns about the surviving laws and decrees associated with Beneš issues.[73] A clear statement of the Parliament's self-understanding of the EU as a 'community of values' underpinned the report on the Czech Republic. 'Putting the principles of respect for human rights and the rule of law into practice is a continuing challenge which is one of the fundamental obligations of the member states of the European Union', the report declared. And the report laid down a marker as to post-accession monitoring of minority rights: 'Parliament *will make sure* that the stated fundamental values of the Czech Republic *will not be undermined* in the future', i.e. after its accession.[74] The definitive tone of the language should leave no doubt as to Parliament's determination to remain the European Union's guardian of fundamental freedoms and human rights. In some ways it is remarkable that diplomatic protocol can be so casually cast aside, especially in a context where the earlier asymmetry of the enlargement process had been much reduced by the time of the Copenhagen deal.

As Table 7.1 demonstrates, the European Parliament voted overwhelmingly in support of enlargement in a plenary session in Strasbourg on 9 April.[75] This followed an agreement with the Council on the financing of enlargement the previous day. Article 49 of the EU treaty required the Assent of the EP voting by an absolute majority (i.e. 314 out of 626 votes). The Parliament considered the accession of each country separately and voted on ten different legislative resolutions. These were accompanied by a non-legislative resolution where Parliament expressed its political opinion. A vote on a separate resolution drawn up by Reimer Böge and Joan Colom i Naval confirmed the Parliament's endorsement of the solution reached the previous day on the budgetary disagreement with the Council that had been casting a shadow over the enlargement vote for several weeks.[76] To those present the event, which might have been expected to produce a lightning-charged atmosphere, came off as rather a dull occasion. Some speakers undoubtedly did capture the sense of realization and historic significance. The leader of the EPP-ED group, Hans Gert Pöttering, for example, invoked the spirit of Willy Brandt's *Ostpolitik* when declaring that 'those who should always have been together are now converging'. President Pat Cox asserted that 'the political message is now clear and very straightforward: the hour of enlargement has now

Table 7.1 European Parliament vote on accession, 9 April 2003

Country	In favour	Against	Abstention
Czech Republic	489	39	37
Cyprus	507	29	26
Estonia	520	22	24
Hungary	522	23	23
Latvia	522	22	24
Lithuania	521	22	24
Malta	521	23	23
Poland	509	25	31
Slovakia	521	21	25
Slovenia	522	22	22

Source: European Parliament

struck'.[77] The votes on individual candidate states were unremarkable, save perhaps for the 39 votes cast against Czech accession (with another 37 abstentions). Overall the support for accession was overwhelming.

Conclusions

Since its foundation, Parliament has had a long history of supporting integrationist EU perspectives on enlargement. This was no less true of eastern enlargement than any previous round. In some ways the role of the European Parliament in the eastern enlargement process was still a minor one. Testimony for such is provided by Parliamentary pleas for greater responsibility and involvement in various aspects of the negotiations and, on occasion, a sense of powerlessness at negotiation outcomes. The Parliament's formal role came at the very end of the enlargement process, where it voted to give assent to the accession of the candidate states. That formal power, however, represented just one aspect of the European Parliament's role. It also exercised all kinds of informal power throughout the enlargement process which meant that the Commission and the Council had to pay attention to Parliament's concerns on enlargement issues. Thus concessions to Parliament's position were granted at various stages of the process. But it may well be in the long-term impact of creating a pan-European parliamentary network and supporting ideas about democracy, oversight and control over executive politics that the real value of the Parliament's contribution to the eastern enlargement process may lie. Certainly the Parliament's insistence on full and unequivocal transposition and implementation of EU human rights norms influenced the content of legislation in the candidate states and identified the EP as the most vocal and stalwart champion of democratic norms within the enlargement process. The

Parliament was also keen to involve itself as substantially as possible in different components of the EU strategy for enlargement as it developed. It was not simply content to pronounce on the fitness of the candidates after the issuing of regular reports much less the final vote on accession.[78] The Parliament's willingness to push the Council toward greater accommodation of candidate state preferences was not unimportant in the 'push' for a conclusion to negotiations in 2002. The activism and public role of EP President Pat Cox raised the profile of the EP within enlargement deliberations and also helped remind both insiders and outsiders of the normative importance of enlargement. None of this is meant to overstate the importance of the Parliament's role within the eastern enlargement process. For much of the long negotiation period it remained a junior partner within the internal EU process. What the chapter demonstrates, however, is that contrary to the passive role implied by Article 49 of the treaties, the European Parliament proved itself capable of contributing in important ways to the enlargement process. As it has increased its legislative and oversight powers within the broad integration process, so has it also ensured that it can, in different ways, influence an enlargement negotiation. In the final analysis this ensured that the parliamentary dimension of the EU's most ambitious expansion was anything but marginal.

Part III

Conceptualizing eastern enlargement

8 Geopolitical explanations of eastern enlargement

Introduction

If the eastern enlargement of the European Union generated a significant flow of academic analysis it was only belatedly that scholars began to produce conceptual research. The neglect of enlargement by scholars of integration theory led, amongst others, Phillippe Schmitter and Helen Wallace to observe that the discussion of the enlargement issue was taking place in a 'theoretical vacuum'.[1] This was surprising in that eastern enlargement was clearly going to change the EU in important ways and represented a major new foreign policy and geopolitical challenge for the Union, consisting of nothing less than the potential reconstitution of the map of Europe.[2] Furthermore, if eastern enlargement constitutes but a first step, with further enlargement to the Balkans, and, as importantly, Turkey, to follow, the process will eventually entirely reshape the territorial, political, institutional, economic, and perhaps even, cultural contours of the European and Eurasian landmass. EU borders might potentially reach Iran, Iraq, Syria, large swathes of Russia and the Caucasus. Thus no serious analysis of the eastern enlargement can ignore the geopolitical dimension to the process.[3]

Notwithstanding the functional and technocratic basis of the European integration process, and the fact that the accession criteria hardly mention security issues, eastern enlargement brought to the forefront of EU politics important geopolitical and security issues at every stage. In short, geopolitics mattered. It mattered to the decision taken by the EU to embark on expansion in the early 1990s, and thereafter security issues remained prominent in enlargement debates. This chapter seeks to analyse the most important geopolitical issues which eastern enlargement brought to the fore. In the process it utilizes realist and neorealist theories of International Relations (IR). Realist scholars frame their approach to the study of international relations in ideas focusing on power, the role of the state, and the structural distribution of power and resources in the international system. In seeking realist and neorealist explanations of eastern enlargement the chapter foregrounds some key issues, including the potential power realignments in Europe triggered by enlargement, the EU relationship with Russia and its importance to the unfolding of the enlargement process, and how, if at all, eastern enlargement augmented and increased EU power in the international arena. The chapter begins, however, by introducing a range of realist precepts and their arguments about the nature of international politics.[4]

The realist worldview

As a way of thinking about the world, realism is distinguished by its pessimism regarding moral progress and the perfectibility of the human condition.[5] Realists are sceptical that human beings and collectivities can overcome recurrent conflict and establish cooperative or peaceable relations on a durable basis. This pessimism is rooted in both the nature and history of the international system itself and, at a deeper level, in human nature.[6] Hans Morgenthau began his classic text *Politics Among the Nations* by observing that the conflict-ridden international arena was the consequence of 'forces inherent in human nature', and that the best humanity could hope for was the 'realization of the lesser evil rather than of the absolute good'.[7] For contemporary realists the absence of a leviathan in the international system inevitably and tragically leads to insecurity, conflict, and the routine resort to organized violence.[8] States can mitigate the consequences of anarchy by relying on time-honoured instruments such as diplomacy and the balance of power. But they cannot escape it altogether. Statecraft is more a matter of damage limitation than of fundamental problem-solving. Both classical and contemporary realists would accept the following set of assumptions as central to their intellectual and scholarly endeavour.

In the first place, the most important actors in international politics are 'territori-ally-organized entities' – city states in antiquity, empires in the late modern period, and nation states in the contemporary arena.[9] Nation states are not the only actors that count in international politics, but realists assume that more can be under-stood about world politics by focusing on the behaviour of and interaction among nation states than by analysing the behaviour of individuals, social classes, transna-tional firms, or indeed international organizations. Second, realists believe that relations among nation states are inherently conflictual. States compete most intensely in the realm of military security, but coexist uneasily in other realms as well, in particular in economic areas and competition for trade and international investment. When analysing the nature of interstate competition realists draw a sharp distinction between domestic and international politics. For realists, it is self-evident that the level of violence is greater at the international than the domestic level. The international system is a self-help system in which states hold security as their primary concern in order to protect their autonomy. According to Hans Morgenthau, the fundamental national interest of any state is always the protection of its physical, political and cultural identity against encroachments by other nations. In fact Morgenthau's view of politics in the international arena was one of a Manichean contest for power and resources.[10]

From this perspective states are capable of cooperation but this is extremely diffi-cult. Cooperation is undertaken only to specific ends and always with the need to protect or enhance the state's power in the interstate system.[11] Competition is a consequence of anarchy, which forces states ultimately to rely on themselves to ensure their survival and autonomy. This does not imply that cooperation is impossible, only that states will approach cooperation with a concern for their impact on relative power positions.[12] Third, realists emphazise the close connection between state power and interests. States seek power in order to achieve their interests, and they calculate their interests in terms of their power and in the context of the international environment they confront. The key point for realists is that in defining the so-called national interest, state officials look outward and respond to the opportunities and constraints of the international environment. Finally, realists assume that state behaviour can be explained as the product of rational decision-making. As Robert Keohane puts it: for the realist 'world politics can be analyzed as if states were unitary rational actors, carefully calculating the costs of alternative course of action and seeking to maximise their expected utility, although doing so under conditions of uncertainty'.[13] States act strategically and instrumentally, in an arena in which the 'noise level' is high.[14]

Summing up, power is crucial to the realist lexicon and traditionally has been defined narrowly in military and geopolitical terms. It is the ability to get what you want either through the threat or use of force. Yet irrespective of how much power a state may possess, the core national interest of all states must be survival. These assumptions constitute the starting point for realist analysis. They do not lead to a single, unified theory of contemporary world politics or to a single conceptualization of state behaviour. Each realist image however embraces these core assumptions. The chapter now goes on to apply key realist and neorealist concepts to the eastern enlargement process. In doing so it poses important questions regarding the nature, exercise and ubiquity of power within the process. It also addresses key issues of geopolitics and foreign policy decision-making which eastern enlargement brought to the fore.

Post-1989 Europe: the return of anarchy?

In the period following the collapse of Communism and the bipolar system the academic community rushed to contribute to the debate on the future of international politics. Whilst Francis Fukuyama proclaimed the 'End of History', and Samuel Huntington the 'Clash of Civilizations', realist scholars, although themselves divided on any number of issues, were generally very pessimistic about the prospects for progress. Some indeed forecast a return to the pre-1914 or interwar period, characterized by multipolarity and a new balance of power model. Although realists (and especially neorealists) had little to say about the European integration process,[15] John Mearsheimer for one predicted that Europe (along with much of the rest of the world) would remain mired in history and indeed go 'back to the future'.[16] This was a world of historical *déjà vu*, as Jim George put it, characterized by elementary and structurally induced threat.[17] And that future would inevitably bring a fracturing of the European compact, power balancing against perceived threats to state security, and the return of irredentist conflict.

These pessimistic predictions seemed apposite as Yugoslavia imploded and Europeans caught a glimpse of the disturbing new reality of fratricidal interstate ethno-nationalist conflagrations. As the violence spiralled out of control in the Balkans, European political élites worried about similar conflicts breaking out in other parts of the continent. The disturbing legacy of European history meant the potential re-emergence of irredentism, and the presence of sizeable minorities in many of the new states left many fearful that the Yugoslav imbroglio rather than the relative harmony of the EU model was the template for the future. The realist argument was based on a view that, with the removal of the artificial straitjacket provided by the Cold War, the new European geopolitics would, for Europe's nation states, be one of competitive coexistence, a return to a more pure form of Hobbesian anarchy. Where in 1989 there existed 27 states in Europe, by 1992 this had risen to 42 with the break up of the Soviet Union and Yugoslavia.[18] One estimate suggested that 8,000 miles of new borders were created out of the old demarcations.[19] And where there were new borders there existed the manifest potential for conflict. New international frontiers were created such as those of the Baltic States, the Yugoslav successor states, and out of the break-up of Czechoslovakia. Some were reconfigured as a result of war, others by democratic agreement.[20] The Cold War, some argued, had provided Western Europe with a secure and stable eastern frontier.[21] But where the Cold War had provided the critical leviathans for each geopolitical bloc in the US and USSR, this new world seemed to herald the return of self-help attitudes straight from the canon of classical realist thinking. Neorealists identified these new states as new units in a reconfigured and still reconfiguring international system, all of them responding to the new climate on the basis of the distribution of power in the system and seeking to balance against existential threats to state security.

Although these new states proclaimed their attachment to the European integration model and pursued membership of the European Community, realists argued that this was simply a strategic effort to guard against instability and potential threats and ensure economic gains from the process of integration. Interstate cooperation along the lines of the West European integration system would prove extremely difficult to achieve. This was not least because this system had been developed under the protective military shield of the United States, which would now turn its attention away from Europe, as it redefined its own security interests in the new world order.[22] Thus hopes of an extension of that successful post-war cooperative model on a pan-European basis were simply illusory given the absence of the Cold War stabilizer and the return of multipolarity. The sceptics pointed, for example to the failure of the Visegrad group of states (Hungary, Poland and Czechoslovakia) to maintain a collective approach to the question of EU membership in the early 1990s. Each state preferred to deal directly with the EU rather than establish unified positions, which might better have aided their membership ambitions. Indeed each Visegrad state consistently demonstrated suspicion of its fellow Central Europeans and sought to enhance its own standing with Brussels. For its part the EU, even when it had decided on membership for CEE as the best option, persisted with a policy of differentiation between candidate states, at least up to the Helsinki European Council meeting in December 1999.

Realist perspectives also offered the view that enlargement presented an enormous challenge to the task of preserving the balance of power in Europe. In short, the new geopolitical environment brought into sharp focus a new set of security externalities that threatened the achievements of the successful post-1945 European compact. For one thing the 1989 revolutions had brought the German Question back to the centre of European politics. The question of how German power might reassert itself occupied the minds of many policy-makers, not least the Germans themselves. The mantra that what German élites sought was 'not a German Europe but a European Germany' was consistently deployed to assuage the concerns of those who feared a resurgence of German power. Similarly, German commitment to the deeper integration embedded in the Maastricht Treaty was presented as evidence of German bona fides. Despite such assurances, however, there were many who argued that, in the long run, the worst German tendencies would re-assert themselves and Central and Eastern Europe would become again, either directly through the projection of military and political power, or indirectly through the projection of Germany's vast economic power, a zone of vassal states, which over time would help destabilize the peaceable interstate system built up through the integration process. The prospect of the Bonn–Paris axis being replaced by a Berlin–Warsaw axis was one which triggered fears in particular about the continued viability of the Franco-German alliance. But for all of these concerns, paradoxically, enlargement represented at the same time the only viable solution to the new balance of power problem. Eastern enlargement, notwithstanding parallel developments in respect of NATO enlargement, could become the primary mechanism for buttressing the European integration process against renewed German power ambitions. Locking in both the CEE states and the new Germany to the institutional and political commitments of the enlargement process and wider integration framework would represent the best means of guarding against this important security externality weakening the commitment to the new Europe.

States as central actors in the enlargement process

Realists are agreed on a core proposition regarding international politics – that its central actors are and continue to be nation states. Despite the claims made by advocates of globalization, and despite the existence of layers of important networks and institutions of international governance, states remain at the core of the realist worldview. Thus, for realists, the new European system of international relations to emerge in the wake of 1989's geopolitical revolutions was fashioned by states pursuing their own interests in the new geopolitical climate. State actors and their concerns dominated this system. It was state actors who took the lead in reconstituting EU relations with Central and Eastern Europe, both on a bilateral and multilateral basis, and, crucially, it was state actors who proved pivotal at all times to the key decisions which emerged from the eastern enlargement process.

Supranational institutions, to the extent that they mattered at all, were significant only in so far as they were delegated specific tasks by the member state governments whose control over the enlargement process was enshrined in Article 49 of the treaties and remained intact right up to the conclusion of negotiations. The European Commission and European Parliament in this view remained marginal to the process throughout because state actors dominated on both the EU and CEE sides. All of the important enlargement decisions, whether with respect to issues such as trade, agriculture, migration, or institutional recalibration, emerged out of key intergovernmental summit meetings such as Copenhagen in 1993, Luxembourg in 1997, Helsinki in 1999 and Copenhagen again in 2002. Very often enlargement-related outcomes relating to, for example, CAP or budgetary matters were resolved by meetings of heads of state and government at the last minute.[23] Realists would also argue that the structure of the enlargement negotiations favoured national actors. The role of the Presidency proved crucial as time went on, and very often this involved bilateral internal as well as external talks between the Presidency and national administrations. In fact the *tour des capitals* by the Presidency was consistently important in moving the internal EU deliberation on enlargement forward and establishing (or making clearer) negotiating positions. In Brussels the Permanent Representations and their contact with candidate state representatives also proved highly significant. All of this suggests that the most convincing explanations of enlargement are those that privilege the role of governments and classical interstate bargaining models.

Power and geopolitics in the enlargement process

A second principal preoccupation of realist perspectives on international politics is that of the exercise of power. Enlargement, from this perspective, can be viewed as part of an ongoing project – to turn the EU into a superstate and a genuine great power that could compete with the United States and emerging powers such as China and India. The EU, in this view, instrumentally used eastern enlargement as the primary vehicle for this geopolitical advance, which brought into the Union eight new states in Central and Eastern Europe, moved the EU border hundreds of miles east from Berlin to Tallinn (within miles of St Petersburg), and added 80 million new citizens. Territorial expansion will only continue as the addition of Romania and Bulgaria in 2007 will bring the Union's borders right up to the shore of the Black Sea. Christopher Hill suggests that the EU already shows signs of behaving like a great power. In evidence he points to the EU's increasingly prioritizing its own 'near abroad' through the Euro Mediterranean Partnership and a common strategy on Russia.[24] Further evidence for this conclusion, Hill suggests, is provided by the reaction to Europe's relative impotence in the face of the Balkan Wars of the 1990s. The EU, many argue, can only hope to manage these problems successfully by attaining the attributes (military and political) of a great power. Thus the Rapid Reaction Force (RRF) is, in this view, a first step towards the formation of a European army with significant capability and geopolitical reach. The ESDP has developed because of the EU desire to compete as a great power on the world stage.

Such a power perspective presents the EU's Stabilization and Association

Process (SAP) for the Western Balkans as a mirror image of the early eastern enlargement process. It is designed to ensure that EU influence over the Balkans proves decisive in the medium to long term. At the Thessaloniki Summit in June 2003 the EU effectively committed itself (at least rhetorically) to membership for the Western Balkans.[25] The EU SAP has been highly interventionist and indicative of a much more robust and proactive geopolitical approach to the region than had been evident earlier during the Bosnia War.[26] As it becomes clear that the United States is slowly disengaging from the region the EU will increasingly seek responsibility for conflict resolution and crisis management and assert regional leadership. Indeed, this was already apparent in the EU decision to take over responsibility for security in Bosnia.[27] The French view, that the enlarging EU should become a real geopolitical power in the world, although not widely shared, was still a recurring theme in the enlargement debate. French political élites worried that an over-ambitious enlargement would compromise European power; they thus fretted about any expansion that would take the Union beyond 25 members. They especially opposed the principle of Turkish membership for this reason.[28] For realists, however, the important point is that the continual expansion of the EU is reflective of a general desire for security and power maximization.

Further evidence for EU power ambitions can be gleaned from the rhetoric and public discourse of key actors. Former Commission President Romano Prodi, for example, in a speech to the European Parliament in 2001, pointed out that a key advantage of eastern enlargement was the fact that it would boost the EU's power in the world. Already, he suggested, 'we are an emerging power, dare I say, a potential power'. He then suggested that enlargement had the potential to 'transform the Union into a continental power'.[29] Similarly, Karen Smith argues that EU policy toward Central and Eastern Europe could be viewed as a desire to preserve and enhance its position in a rapidly changing geopolitical environment. She cites the EU stance on negotiating the Europe Agreements with the CEE states and policy toward Russia that suggests a power-based approach by the Union.[30] Irrespective of whether or not the intention exists to use enlargement as a springboard to greater geopolitical power on a global level, the enlarged EU will figure prominently in the cognitive maps of decision-makers worldwide from 2004 onwards.[31] It is also true to say that outsiders such as Russia, China and the United States simply will not remain indifferent to the way in which enlargement changes the fundamentals of EU power.[32] Thus, even if security and power did not feature prominently initially in the calculus of EU decision-makers, the enlargement process could not but trigger important geopolitical questions for the Union.

Whether in response to internal or external considerations, the EU, throughout the enlargement process, presented important security and geopolitical arguments as part of the underlying rationale for justifying expansion. Atsuko Higashino, for example, cites the declaration at the Helsinki European Council in 1999, which portrayed enlargement as a means to 'lend a positive contribution to security and stability on the European continent'. The rhetoric of EU leaders was as focused on security issues, she argues, as on economic or normative ones.[33] Her analysis of the speeches and statements of EU leaders throws up a rhetorical structure that consistently highlights the 'existential threats' to European security as a specific opportunity cost of failure to enlarge. Enlargement represented the only viable alternative to the various threat scenarios. CEE state representatives, of course, also deployed this form of discourse strategically as a supplementary weapon used in conjunction with their more usual norm-based appeals for membership.[34] EU leaders routinely invoked a combination of the dreadful European past, the spectre of instability and conflicts such as the Yugoslav conflagration or the instability of Russia, as central to the enlargement logic. In addition, a 'soft security' discourse, which focused on the social disorder deriving from trans-European organized crime, the trafficking of drugs and people, and endemic corruption in Central and Eastern Europe, regularly featured in the public commentary of EU leaders, both supranational and national. In particular the Kosovo war in 1999 focused attention on the potential for recurrent interstate and intrastate conflicts in the absence of concrete EU institutional relationships (with the prospect of membership attached) and EU leadership for states in the region. Later, after what Georgian President Mikheil Saakashvili termed 'Europe's third wave of liberation', the EU's attention would turn to Georgia and Ukraine.[35] Security and geopolitics would constitute as central a part of EU policy toward these states as it had earlier in respect of Central and Eastern Europe.

Eastern enlargement and CFSP/ESDP

Another important way of conceptualizing eastern enlargement in geopolitical terms arises out of the potential if not actual political muscle it adds to the EU's fledgling security and defence policy.[36] Conceivably the addition of ten new states, most of them already members of NATO, could boost the security dimension of the integration process, not least in the increase in potential military resources available for CFSP/ESDP operations. Just as the events of 1989 played an important part in the initial development of a CFSP, enlargement adds new momentum to the process by providing critical mass, where it has, for most of its history, been lacking. One important study of voting trends at the United Nations General Assembly demonstrates a dramatic increase in the 1990s in convergence among EU15 member states.[37] The same study challenges the rationalist view that enlargement inevitably compromises the search for common positions by demonstrating that the trend of convergence also applies to the new member states. Voting convergence has been most apparent in the case of the Czech Republic, Hungary, Poland, Slovakia and Slovenia, with the Baltic States catching up in recent years.[38] Thus enlargement at the least does not appear to hinder the search for collective solutions in the area of foreign and security policy.

The empirical evidence, however, also suggests that the growing pains experienced in the foreign policy-making domain in the 1990s have not receded and that enlargement may in fact compound them. The difficulties in establishing a common EU position on important international issues was underlined most dramatically by the split on Iraq in the latter part of 2002 and early 2003. With enlargement negotiations completed, a majority of CEE states sided with the United States and

Britain, and against Germany and France on the question of an attack on Baghdad. Some commentators argued that the former communist states had been far too easily drawn into the US orbit as a consequence of the weakness of existing CFSP/ESDP structures.[39] An unseemly row was then triggered by President Chirac's description of CEE behaviour as 'infantile' and 'reckless'.[40] Thus enlargement can hardly be said to have helped overcome the problem of political will in CFSP.[41] The aspiration to speak with one voice was no closer to being realized in 2004 than ten years earlier during the height of the Yugoslav crises. Realist perspectives which highlight the impossibility of meaningful interstate military and security cooperation suggest that the capacity of CFSP and ESDP to deal with the security agenda will be further reduced as a result of enlargement. Christopher Hill, indeed, expresses the fear that the enlarged EU may lose any distinction it now possesses with, for example, the OSCE or the Council of Europe.[42] Those making the pessimistic argument doubt that the decision-making machinery of CFSP/ESDP has the capacity to cope and suggest that the efficacy of systemic decision-making in the enlarged Union of 25 will be so sub-optimal as to further compromise the overall scope of foreign policy activity by the EU.

The selection of candidate states

Another important focus of attention for realist scholars of eastern enlargement was the distinct geopolitical dimension to the decisions on *which countries* were to be favoured with candidate status and the *timeframe* in which they could expect to successfully conclude negotiations. Although the Commission and Council for long adhered to a policy of differentiation on the grounds of merit and progress in transposition of the *acquis communautaire*, it is clear that at least some of the candidate states were included for purely geopolitical reasons. Some decisions proved contentious within the internal EU deliberations. Others caused tension in the negotiations with the candidate states and with important regional powers such as Russia. Across every dimension of the process of selecting candidates geopolitics mattered.

The recommendations made by the Commission in *Agenda 2000*, and subsequently acted upon by the Council, to include both Estonia and Slovenia in the first wave of accession, represent a textbook example of the significance of geopolitics. In this case, as Baun points out, the Commission favoured a geographically balanced enlargement that would not be limited to just Central Europe but would also include a country from the north (Estonia) and one from the south (Slovenia).[43] It is clear now that the decision subsequently to open up the eastern enlargement process to those countries placed on the slow lane at Luxembourg in 1997 was also one largely influenced by geopolitical considerations. After the decisions at Luxembourg the Romanian and Bulgarian governments argued that the double rejection shock of exclusion from the first wave of both NATO and EU expansion would consign them to a 'geopolitical grey zone' between Western Europe and Russia.[44] The consequences for them (and by implication for the EU also) might be extreme if it resulted in a retardation of the democratic process and further economic decline. It is clear that these factors, in addition to the new situation arising out of the Kosovo crisis, were instrumental in the decision to open negotiations with them at the Helsinki summit in December 1999. This was, in large part, a geopolitical response on the part of the EU to fears of Bulgarian and Romanian drift.[45] Bulgaria and Romania went on to conclude their membership negotiations with the EU in late 2004. Although both countries had made demonstrable progress toward fulfilling the obligations of membership, there remained the lingering conviction that they had been subject to a much less exacting critique than the states that had acceded in 2004. Indeed the accession treaties included so-called safeguard clauses that allowed the EU to postpone or delay entry into the EU in the absence of further improvement in implementation capacity. But for all of that the opportunity cost of their continued exclusion was simply too great for the EU to justify refusal or continued prevarication.

Balancing against existential threats

If the internal EU debate on questions of inclusion, exclusion, and the possible geographical limit of eastern enlargement proved important, no less so were the arguments which stressed the expansion process as an instrument for guarding against both conventional and more contemporary threats to European security and stability. A core enlargement proposition for neorealists in particular, as Frank Schimmelfennig has pointed out, was that expansion was a desirable option if it represented a necessary and efficient means of balancing superior power or perceived threats. And where neorealists would emphasize the threat represented by Russian military power, other realists favoured expansion as a means of guarding against other forms of instability on the EU's eastern borders. Both justifications for eastern enlargement are intimately connected with the end of Communism as a competing political system and the emergence of a 'zone of instability' in Central and Eastern Europe and the former Soviet Union. Ensuring that the 'zone of instability' had at least the *prospect* of becoming a 'zone of stability' thus represented a key reason for expansion.[46] And the eastern enlargement process represented, if not the best or indeed the only mechanism in fighting existential threats or security externalities, at least an important component of EU policy.

Russia as existential threat

The principal existential threat to be considered here is that of Russian power, both actual and potential. The power-based approach suggests that although the implosion of the Soviet Union and the loss of its satellite states left the successor state – the Russian Federation – weaker, it still represented a considerable security threat to EU interests. In 1994 Richard Ned Lebow had argued that 'post-Soviet Russia is a smaller less populous state, consumed with the problems of political instability, ethnic fragmentation and precipitous economic decline'. With respect to Russian military capacity, he pointed out that most armoured divisions lacked spare parts and effective maintenance, with much of the former Soviet navy 'rotting in port and unable to put to sea'.[47] With the economic disruption that followed the break-up of the Soviet Union, Russia has fallen further and further behind the West in the development and deployment of state-of-the-art weaponry and has lost for the foreseeable future the ability to exploit and utilize military technology on a large scale. According to UN projections, Russia's population will plummet from about 146 million in 2000 to about 104 million in 2050. Russia will go from being the sixth-most-populous country in the world to being the 17th.[48] The ongoing Russian failure to tame the Chechen insurgency also brought Russian military weakness into sharp focus. The botched response to Chechen terrorist operations such as the *Nord-Ost* (Dubrovka) theatre siege in October 2002 and the Beslan school massacre in September 2004 reinforced the view of Russian military incompetence deriving from post-Soviet decline.[49] Lebow's observations were thus no less relevant in 2004 than they had been ten years previously.

For all of the evidence of Russian decline, however, Russia still arguably represents the greatest potential 'existential threat' to the power of the EU and to the peace and stability of the continent. In the first place Russia retains a formidable military capacity and significant natural resources.[50] It provides over a fifth of EU energy needs and almost one-third of Germany's.[51] It boasts the largest standing army on the European continent, a significant air, land and naval capability and, most crucially, a nuclear arsenal far in excess of those of the UK and France, the EU's only nuclear powers. Enlargement thus could be viewed as a straightforward power-balancing and power-maximization act by the EU in response to both the dangers that accompany Russian military retrenchment and fear of a resurgence in Russian power. This is despite the fact that it is NATO and not the EU which is the primary repository of EU members' security interests. The addition of ten new member states, most of which are already NATO members, immeasurably boosts the EU's geopolitical position vis-à-vis Russia.

In simple terms enlargement encompassed a straight geopolitical switch of allegiance by Russia's former vassal states, from the Russian or Soviet sphere of influence to the EU sphere. The EU might have chosen to placate and assuage Russian concerns by offering the former Soviet satellites something short of membership such as a 'privileged partnership' or associate membership, which would effectively have rendered them once again a buffer zone between Western Europe and Russia. The EU, however, sought to absorb them fully and wholly in EU structures, including defence and security structures. The swing in the power pendulum has been such that, more often than not, it is now the EU that dictates to Russia rather than the other way around, on matters of regional security. At the least, Russia had to accommodate itself to the changes happening on its western borders without having any influence over developments. Or to put it in explicitly realist terms: the EU acted as it did because it could and did not compromise when asked to by Russia. Russia acted as it could but what it could do was much more limited than in Soviet or Romanov times.

Changing the focus somewhat from pure power politics and geopolitical competition, the eastern enlargement of the EU might also be viewed as an effort to balance against the instability created by the fragmentation of Russian power and the lack of stability in Russia's domestic politics. Russia, for Georg Sørensen, is akin to a drifting supertanker, uncertain of what kind of statehood it will end up with. Political institutions outside of the Presidency are impotent and citizenship has little substantive meaning.[52] The success of Vladimir Zhirinovsky in the Russian parliamentary elections of December 1992, and the popularity of the 'red/brown' alliance (communist and nationalist) raised early concerns within the EU about the prospects for democracy in Russia, and increased fears in Central and Eastern Europe that a more nationalist and aggressive Russia would upset the geostrategic balance in the new Europe by seeking to reclaim its Empire.[53] This triggered new demands from CEE and a EU response that privileged CEE accession as the only credible strategy whilst developing a new EU–Russia strategic partnership.[54] It is not too difficult to envisage a sclerotic Russia turning toward a revived nationalism in whatever new form, increasingly causing difficulties with the Baltic States or Ukraine, for example.[55] As Christopher Hill argues, it would not be too dramatic a leap then for the EU and Russia to seem to each other like real security threats.[56] President Putin's rhetoric in the run-up to the 60th anniversary of victory in the Great Patriotic War unnerved many with its nostalgia for Russia's imperial past and its message that Russia continued to define its interests at the expense of its neighbours.[57]

Of equal concern throughout the eastern enlargement process was the fact that Russian central government was extremely weak, under both Yeltsin and Putin. And where Vladamir Putin acted to restore Moscow's prerogatives within the Russian Federation this had the effect of convincing western policy-makers that he was taking Russia back to a more authoritarian and hostile form of state.[58] The Putin government's actions against Mikhael Khodorkovsky and Yukos in 2004 only reinforced this perception. Putin's determination to reassert Russian power manifested itself most obviously in the 'near abroad' and on the Chechen question. Russian military adventurism in the Caucasus both undermined Russian power and contributed to growing instability on the EU's eastern frontiers. Continued interference in Georgia and manifest interference in Ukrainian domestic politics (especially during the Presidential election in 2004), left EU policy-makers convinced that the Russian threat was now defined by its propensity for creating instability as much as by any military threat it could wield. Thus EU policy-makers acknowledged this type of security externality and presented eastern enlargement as in part an effort to 'lock in' the CEE states into the EU orbit and guard against the westward migration of the problems generated by Russian instability.

Instability in Central and Eastern Europe as existential threat

If Russian power and instability created one set of geopolitical motivations for eastern enlargement, then of equal weight was the EU's concern about instability within Central and Eastern Europe itself. In the wake of 1989 the Yugoslav conflict provided convincing evidence of the potentially fratricidal nature of future interstate relations in the region. The volatility of Central and Eastern Europe was a function of longstanding historical grievances regarding territory, irredentist border claims, the presence of significant ethnic minorities in neighbouring states and their treatment by those states, and the weakness of the emerging governance structures in the new democracies. Together these issues constituted both a reason for EU caution regarding enlargement and also one of the primary geopolitical motivations for expansion. At the macro-level only the real prospect of membership could be used to good effect. But at the micro-level the EU sought to put in place a substantive instrument for guarding against the possible corrosion of interstate relations. This represented a crucial part of the EU's pre-accession strategy and was introduced, as we saw in chapter 2, at the Essen summit in 1994 and further developed through the 'Pact on Stability in Europe'.[59] In this the EU sought to minimize the security risk attached to enlargement and thus it constituted a substantive process of preventative diplomacy.[60] All these developments were of course heavily influenced by the ongoing carnage in Bosnia.

The Pact on Stability can be viewed as rational from the EU perspective in two crucial ways. First, it represented an act of balancing against potential Russian power in the Balkans. The EU, after an initial period of inaction during the 1992–1995 Bosnian war, was much more forceful and proactive on Kosovo in 1998 and 1999, and, later, Macedonia. Especially during Kosovo the Russian government sought to establish itself as an important presence on the ground in the Balkans. From an early policy, which sought recognition and equal status, later Russian interventions looked to Europeans to be obstructionist and belligerent, backed up by a more bellicose rhetoric than had been in evidence since Soviet times.[61] An impasse over a Russian move to 'take' Pristina airport was indicative to Europeans not just of Russian perfidy but also its continued aggressive posture. EU actions were to a large degree designed to ensure that Russia could not establish itself as a presence and exert influence. The Pact on Stability was thus one crucial mechanism for ensuring that all states in the troubled Balkan region would gravitate toward Brussels and not Moscow in the emerging geopolitical landscape.

The EU approach was again evident in the proactive diplomacy that brought about a direct solution to the Macedonian crisis in 2001, and in the EU taking over direct responsibility for policing from NATO in Bosnia in 2004.[62] But the more obvious and well publicized reason behind the Pact on Stability was to ensure that the EU model of peaceful coexistence and stable interstate relations could be expanded east and south so as to ensure the elimination of all significant security issues.[63] It would put an end to irredentist claims, encourage trans-border economic development and cooperation and help inculcate the European spirit in a region more traditionally defined by ethnic tensions and lingering post-war hostilities. In the early 1990s many commentators argued that the worst potential flashpoint in Europe was that between Hungary and Romania. This dated back to the Treaty of Trianon in 1920 under which Hungary lost two-thirds of its territory and 60 per cent of its population. In the aftermath of 1989 ethnic Hungarian populations of significance remained not only in Romania but also in Slovakia and Vojvodina in Yugoslavia. Bulgaria contained within its territory a significant Turkish population that had been subject to a programme of discrimination and deportation under the Todor Zhikov regime in the 1980s. Although there were real differences manifest in the attitudes of different states to the welfare of their co-nationals in non-national settings, EU attitudes clearly weighed heavily with each. Hungary had the most important concerns with an estimated 2.7 million ethnic Hungarians in Romania and about 500,000 in Slovakia. The sizeable Russian minorities in the Baltic States also presented a challenge to EU strategists.[64] And EU policy, whilst it encompassed different instruments in different contexts and jurisdictions, was undertaken in the spirit of the original 1994 formulation of the Pact. The combination of capacity-building and coercion through conditionality was used throughout. And although as time went on the EU focused its efforts more on the transformation of domestic conditions as the optimum strategy, the Pact's significance in terms of norm generation and diffusion was of the utmost significance.[65] It certainly contributed to the building of trust and the dissipation of geopolitical tensions.

Eastern enlargement and terrorism

No geopolitical approach to enlargement can be considered without examining the change in conceptions of security after the atrocities of 11 September 2001. For one thing the attacks led some commentators to argue that enlargement would be delayed on the grounds that the EU would place yet more stringent conditions before the candidate states to counter the threat of importing new internal security problems into the Union. New demands concerning the tightening of border controls especially loomed large.[66] Others worried that enlargement would be superseded by terrorism as the EU's most important priority in the years ahead. But this did not happen and the enlargement timetable was realized as scheduled on 1 May 2004. Clearly the normative desire to complete the accession process prevailed over any lingering fears regarding new terrorism-based security externalities.

In the immediate aftermath of 11 September the support offered the United States by the EU and the candidate states was substantial and not unimportant to the US-led campaign against the Taliban and Al Qaeda.[67] On the one hand, enlargement offered the opportunity of institutionalizing in a much deeper way existing modes of transnational cooperation on such issues as border controls, organized crime, and asylum and migration flows. The EU took many steps towards tracking down and freezing terrorist funds. All the member states and candidate states undertook to ratify the UN Convention on the suppression of the financing of terrorism.[68] In a more defined way the enlargement process offered the opportunity for tackling the pervasive problem of trans-European terrorist and criminal mafia money-laundering.[69] Thus one important effect of September 11 was to recognize that if markets had become globalized then so had terrorism and the threat it represented. Therefore the concepts of internal and external security, which had hitherto been quite separate, now became bound up with each other to a much more significant degree. If September 11 was the main catalyst for that then eastern enlargement provided both the opportunity and the instruments to reconceptualize European security in a more holistic manner.

The advantages of cooperation might, however, be cancelled out by the greater vulnerability to terrorism of an enlarged transterritorial space and the greater access to Europe offered potential terrorist cells. Europe, because of its porous borders, it could be argued, is much more difficult to defend than North America.[70] In particular the Balkans and Southeast Europe represent in this sphere, as in others, the 'soft underbelly' of Europe. Already the most common routes into Europe for illicit drugs, illegal immigrants and trafficked people were through the Balkans. So would not terrorist groups use exactly those same well-established routes in planning their operations?[71] Enlargement to Southeastern Europe potentially exacerbated the existing difficulties by many degrees. Yet it has to be acknowledged that Al Qaeda's assaults on North America and Europe have to date been accomplished mainly with the aid of operatives (sleepers) based in Britain, Germany and Spain and not the Balkans, much less Central and Eastern Europe.[72]

In another sense the support that many of the new member states offered the United States regarding the War on Terror and the invasion of Iraq meant that the new Europe became more vulnerable to attacks by militant Islamic groups in particular. The professed Euro-Atlanticism and NATO membership of these states also made them more conspicuous. Indeed Romania and Bulgaria both sought to site American military bases on their territory as the US contemplated full-scale withdrawal from Germany. The March 2004 bomb attacks on the Madrid commuter rail lines simultaneously highlighted the danger and contributed to a strengthening of EU defences.[73] Thus late in the day the enlargement debate became fused with that on the terror threat to Europe. And whilst terrorism did not feature largely in the calculus of policy-makers on eastern enlargement, it loomed larger in their thoughts as further enlargement became a realistic prospect.

The distribution of power in the enlargement process

The realist conception of the enlargement process as grounded in fundamental questions of material power and interests has also been demonstrated in the power gap between the EU and the candidate countries. Specifically the clear power asymmetry in the EU–CEE relationship was such that enlargement appeared as a 'take it or leave it' proposition from the larger, more powerful entity to the (mostly) small and vulnerable states which sought membership. Haggard *et al.* are correct to point out that the transitioning countries were 'impelled to seek close association with the West' in the search for aid and resources to help overcome the daunting problems they faced. Economic difficulties left them as 'regime-takers' in their negotiations with the EU.[74] This study suggested there would be no fundamental modification of policies by the EU to accommodate the CEE states. Rather the expectation was that the regime-takers would adapt to existing norms. This is consistent with the view expressed elsewhere by Moravcsik that 'Western Europe is likely to be stable no matter what happens in the East' and that 'the West is likely to gain little by opening up to these countries'.[75] The asymmetric relationship was very evident in two other respects also. First, the applicant states had no choice but to accept in full the entire corpus of EU legislation – the 80,000 pages of the *acquis communautaire*. This was considered non-negotiable. Second, the introduction of conditionality as a key instrument of EU negotiating strategy again is suggestive of the EU states as 'regime-makers' and the applicants as classic 'regime-takers', even if, as within the EU itself, the precise domestic impact of different forms of conditionality is difficult to specify. To the candidate states it must have seemed that there was little room for manoeuvre and little inclination on the part of the EU to compromise. Yet the evidence also demonstrates that EU negotiating positions were often watered down in response to the canvassing of CEE representatives or their internal EU allies. CEE preferences were accommodated to a much more significant degree than realists suggest.

Conclusions

Eastern enlargement of the EU arose out of the dramatic changes wrought by the 1989 revolutions. Enlargement quickly became a priority for the Union, if indeed others such as Economic and Monetary Union (EMU) were more quickly realized. From the outset geopolitical issues featured strongly in the calculus of EU leaders. Enlargement increased both the size of the EU population and the territory it covers by a significant degree (about one-third in each case). In terms of area that meant the European Union now stretched from the Atlantic in the west to within miles of St Petersburg in the east, and after 2007, to the Black Sea coast in the southeast. Enlargement thus brought with it new dangers and new geopolitical opportunities for the Union. Some saw it as a vehicle for turning the EU into a global geopolitical power that would match the EU's power in the economic realm. Enlargement would thus transform the Union as a presence not just in Europe and Eurasia but also in the world. The chapter analysed EU motivations for eastern enlargement utilizing realist concepts of power and interests. While undoubtedly geopolitical motivations can be found in many aspects of EU activity, there are also unsatisfactory outcomes to many of the questions posed. While eastern enlargement may have been a vehicle for containing both Russian power and the consequences of Russian state weakness, EU policy toward Russia was both assertive *and* conciliatory. Enlargement is better understood as a specific geopolitical response to instability in Central and Eastern Europe and a determination to avoid the fragmentation and horrors of Yugoslavia. It was an indication of the success of the eastern enlargement that Serbia and Montenegro, for long outside the loop of European integration, began to gravitate toward the very geopolitical model which they had for long disdained. Eastern enlargement helped stabilize and then normalize interstate relations in Eastern Europe and ensure a peaceful transition from Communism to European integration. Security considerations were especially important in both moving the enlargement process forward at critical junctures and also changing the contours of enlargement in specific ways. The Kosovo war of 1999 especially stood out in this regard. Kosovo was a warning shot to the EU about the dangers of excluding the Balkans from the integration process. This not only accelerated the eastern enlargement process, it also produced a much more sure-footed and concrete EU model for the integration of the Balkans. The same political-institutional mix employed for eastern enlargement began to be deployed in Southeast Europe also, albeit allowing for very different economic and political circumstances in some states. Thus geopolitical factors certainly counted in the timing and nature of enlargement policy-making, even if they were frequently superseded by economic and normative considerations on the part of the EU. Realist concepts thus help to explain an important dimension of the process but in their exclusive and narrow focus on security and power explanations also limit our understanding of what was an extraordinarily multifaceted process. Eastern enlargement was built upon and unfolded from a much wider set of motivations on the EU's part.

9 Economic explanations of eastern enlargement

Introduction

There seems little doubt that the gradual deepening of the European integration process, leading to a cumulatively more unified political and institutional environment, has been underpinned to a very significant degree by the willingness of the member states to pool sovereignty in the economic sphere. Just as specific steps such as the Single European Act and the 1992 programme advanced the process of economic integration, so each successive enlargement of the EU has had its own important economic logic and in different ways also changed the contours of EU economic activity and contributed to the process of institutionalizing supranational decision-making. This was no less true of the eastern enlargement than the three previous expansions of the EU. This chapter examines the economic dimension to eastern enlargement, and more specifically, the different economic motivations that influenced the EU's approach to enlargement. It investigates the nature of economic power and how it manifested itself in EU decisions. It analyses the importance of key economic issues in the enlargement process, ranging from agriculture and the EU financial framework to the challenges posed by cross-border environmental externalities and EU perspectives on future immigration from Central and Eastern Europe. All of these issues featured strongly in EU enlargement debates, even if they were interpreted differently depending on the jurisdiction and the context. The chapter relies heavily on the theoretical framework developed by Andrew Moravcsik in his contributions to European integration theory.[1] It begins by outlining the importance of economic power within the eastern enlargement process.

Economics and power

Consideration of the geopolitical dimension to eastern enlargement reminds us of the ongoing importance of power and security in international politics, but no less important is the domain of economic power. For some indeed the international political economy follows the same logic of power competition and rivalrous coexistence as does the international political system. This approach asserts that material resources such as oil, natural gas, nuclear power, and financial strength represent an indispensable component of the national resource base and that the state pursues foreign economic policies in order to maintain and strengthen its autonomy, security and position in the international power structure.[2] Economic organization then serves much the same purpose as military alignment. The greater the economic power and influence of the state the safer and more prominent it is in a competitive world system. Or, as Christopher Hill puts it when analysing the EU, 'even without the development of a single military policy economic power cannot avoid being political in its use and implications'.[3] Whatever the arguments about the EU as an emerging global political power, it is inarguable that the Union constitutes the world's foremost economic bloc.

Viewed in this way, the EU's motivations for eastern enlargement centre on the protection and enhancement of the Union's position in the world market and augmenting and enhancing its economic power relative to peer competitors. Extending the economic community eastward would, first, guard against cheap competition from Central and Eastern Europe, in what are perceived to be vital economic sectors in the EU.[4] These include agriculture, steel, and textiles – the so-called 'sensitive sectors' – the sectors most protected within the EU and, also, during the early negotiation process with the candidate countries, the most contentious. The enlargement process would ensure that CEE producers would gradually become subsumed into EU regulatory structures, thus ensuring that CEE advantages in respect of the costs of inputs would dissolve over time. As chapter 2 demonstrated, much of the evidence from the early 1990s and, in particular, during the negotiation of the Europe Agreements with the CEE states, suggests that this was indeed the EU position. Markets had to be protected even if it meant retarding EU–CEE relations and weakening the overall commitment to eastern enlargement.

Another important economic power explanation for eastern enlargement may be found in the EU's positive expectations of increased market share in emerging CEE markets. The opportunity for EU firms and industries to take advantage of the great possibilities presented as Central and Eastern Europe began to realize its growth potential and generate new business for EU companies seems obvious. In this respect it should hardly surprise that large and medium-sized European and global corporations were among the most enthusiastic supporters of Eastern enlargement.[5] Similarly, Helene Sjursen points out that access to primary resources and low cost labour in the CEE states further strengthens the competitiveness of the EU, even if there is uneven distribution of benefits in the short to medium term.[6] By transferring some labour-intensive production to CEE, EU companies made sure they stayed competitive on a global scale and continued to expand in home markets. Foreign Direct Investment (FDI) in CEE therefore helped to some extent to preserve jobs in Germany, France and the UK.[7] Potentially, the trade creation effects of eastern enlargement outweigh those of trade diversion within the EU and act to boost EU economic power in the world economy, vis-à-vis both existing rivals and emerging trade competitors such as China and India. In addition, enlargement boosts the EU's negotiating muscle within institutions of international trade such as the World Trade Organization (WTO). Already the EU can claim to be the most significant economic bloc in the world; in the medium to long term, eastern enlargement would solidify and enhance that position.[8]

If we analyse the extent of economic integration between the EU15 and the new member states it is striking to note the extent of economic liberalization which had taken place in CEE even prior to accession in 2004. EU–CEE trade grew exponentially throughout the 1990s. Czech exports, for example, grew by 230 per cent after 1993 and Hungarian exports by more than 400 per cent. By 2000 the accession countries were trading with the EU just as much as the EU members were trading with each other.[9] Further, in the decade preceding accession growth in the CEE states, at an average of almost 4 per cent per year, was double that of the EU15 area. While the EU increasingly threw open its markets to CEE goods, it also exploited growing export opportunities in the candidate states. In fact by the time of accession the EU sold much more to the newcomers than it bought in return. The result has been consistently large EU trade surpluses with CEE. According to the Osteuropainstitut, a German research institute, this trade surplus created as many as 114,000 jobs in the EU during the 1990s.[10]

EU companies not only sold their goods in the new markets but they also bought existing businesses there and launched new ones. Since 1990 the new members have received about €130 billion in FDI. Most of this came from the large eurozone countries.[11] The Osteuropainstitut calculated that German FDI alone created almost 450,000 jobs in CEE. But crucially this did not come at the expense of existing German jobs. FDI was largely directed at the new emerging businesses in CEE and not displaced across EU borders. Where Coca Cola set up new bottling plants to service the Hungarian market it retained such plants in Germany and Austria. Financial institutions bought banks and insurance companies exclusively to service emerging domestic markets in CEE rather than as cost-cutting or downsizing measures. So most FDI came in addition to, not instead of, investments in the existing EU. By investing abroad, EU companies mostly sought to access new and fast-growing markets rather than to cut costs at home.[12]

Eastern enlargement also offered the possibility to revisit (and reform) existing EU policies. If enacted, the reforms would render the EU more efficient and competitive in the global economic market. This was especially the case with the CAP, where enlargement-inspired reforms, although threatening to reduce the power of important producer interests within the EU, equally promised to enhance the efficiency of the notoriously wasteful agricultural regime. Enlargement would thus provide another significant transformative dynamic which potentially boosted the EU's global economic power and influence. And although WTO-related pressure was at least as important in triggering ideas about CAP reform, it was only the prospect of eastern enlargement which prompted the substantive moves to streamline the CAP in 2002.

At official level the EU consistently presented arguments justifying eastern enlargement as boosting EU power vis-à-vis competitors in an increasingly competitive global market. EU documents on enlargement or specific sectoral aspects of the process consistently stressed the beneficial effects of expansion over time. Frequently it was described as a 'win–win' process, as economically positive for both incumbents and incoming states, and as a potential boon to the EU's macroeconomic performance.

These assertions seemed hollow to many who pointed to the yawning gap in economic performance between insiders and outsiders, which, it was frequently asserted, could not be easily overcome, even through accession of the outsiders. Enlargement after all added about one-third to EU territory, slightly less in population terms, but crucially, less than 10 per cent to EU GDP. Even the most optimistic assessments suggested that the average CEE 'catch-up' with Greece, Portugal and Spain would take at least 20 years to achieve. The internal EU debate on the economic merits of eastern enlargement, however, was much more diverse and wide-ranging than such simplified measurements suggest. It needs to be understood in more nuanced terms encompassing consideration of winners and losers in important economic sectors within the EU, regional variations in levels of interdependence with the countries of CEE, the degree of embeddedness of specific EU policies such as CAP and regional policy and different national attachments to each, and also, the distribution of bargaining power among EU member states and transnational interest groups. All these issues are best understood viewed through a key body of integration theory – Andrew Moravcsik's liberal intergovernmental model.

The liberal intergovernmental model of European integration

In the neoliberal perspective the international system is characterized by complex patterns of economic interdependence. States are concerned about the implications of such interdependence and international institutions are therefore instituted as functional regimes, for the purpose of transnational management of common problems.[13] Andrew Moravcsik's application of neoliberal theory to the European integration process – liberal intergovernmentalism (LI) – represents a sophisticated model of EU preference formation and bargaining, predicated on the assumption of the crucial importance to state behaviour of domestic interests (principally domestic producer interests). Bargaining power is determined by the relative intensity of member state preferences and not by military or other material power considerations. Economic issues and interstate economic competition dominate all others in the international political arena.

Moravcsik's theory is a tripartite one. It assumes rational behaviour on the part of the state; it asserts a liberal theory of national preference formation; and it utilizes an intergovernmental analysis of interstate negotiation where the distribution of power among the member states is a key determinant of outcomes.[14] Combining the three constituent elements, Moravcsik explains how the costs and benefits of economic interdependence primarily determine national preferences on EU issues. Governments act as domestic gatekeepers and aggregate those domestically generated preferences and then deliberate on and negotiate those preferences at EU level. The most important negotiations are those which fall under the flagship of what Lee Miles terms 'super-systemic' Intergovernmental Conferences (IGCs), which pave the way for the so-called 'grand bargains' of the integration project.[15] And where neofunctionalist approaches to integration argued for a so-called 'spillover motor' which drove the integration process forward, Moravcsik asserts the centrality of interstate bargains and the convergence of domestic preferences at international level as crucial to the unfolding of the integration process.

In *The Choice for Europe* Moravcsik posits the notion that 'economic (and) in particular, commercial interests have been the "drivers" of European integration' and that 'the foreign policy goals of national governments are viewed as varying in response to shifting pressure from domestic social groups'.[16] The social groups that receive most attention are business organizations such as the Confederation of British Industry (CBI), the Bundesverband der Deutschen Industrie (BDI), the trade union organizations, and agricultural producer lobbies. All are concentrated in the economic sphere in national settings. Moravcsik then presents European integration historically as:

> a series of rational adaptations by national leaders to constraints and opportunities stemming from the evolution of an interdependent world economy, the relative power of states in the international system, and the potential for international institutions to bolster the credibility of interstate commitments.[17]

The question then is whether we might view EU enlargement policy in such a light. If one were to trace the evolution of the process would we observe a 'series of rational policy adaptations' arising out of rising interdependence between the EU and CEE, and mediated at EU level by bargains which resulted from disparities in relative power? Was the politics of eastern enlargement a battle between competing producer groups? If enlargement was dominated by such interstate clashes what then of the role played by the European Commission in the process?

It is worth noting that analysis of previous enlargement rounds hardly features in *The Choice for Europe*, save for extended commentary on British efforts to join the Community and French policy of obstructing Britain. In a 2003 paper on eastern enlargement, however, Moravcsik and Milada Ana Vachudova present three reasons to support an LI perspective on enlargement. In the first place they argue that the overall effect of eastern enlargement is rather benign from the EU's perspective. Second, distinct material benefits, even if modest, and only likely to kick in over the medium to long term, do indeed accrue to the EU15. The addition of 100 million new consumers to the EU market, and, in addition, the macro stability garnered through the management of EU–CEE interdependence, guarantee at least a benign and potentially a positive outcome for the EU. Third, the EU managed during the negotiations with the CEE applicant states to limit the costs to itself even if some member states and groups would bear a disproportionate share of the costs of enlargement.[18] In addition, they argue that the role of ideas and norms was only important in a subordinate context. Only when the normative ran parallel to and supported EU material self-interest did normative arguments influence key decisions. Thus in contrast to some interpretations of enlargement, the LI view is that eastern enlargement was only of marginal importance to the EU. A deeper application of liberal intergovernmentalism seems apposite, however, and in particular, an investigation of the dynamics of national preference formation and both EU internal bargaining and the inside–outside bargaining that followed during the actual negotiations.

Domestic enlargement preference generation and aggregation

The LI model suggests that governments in each member state of the European Union aggregate domestic preferences and establish positions on individual issues of interstate economic governance as a result of a competitive intra-state bargaining process. Important economic interest groups compete to shape national preferences on everything from fishing quotas to telecoms regulation. Moravcsik's theory offers the benefit of a parsimonious model of domestic preference formation. We should expect that national preference formation on enlargement follows the pattern and that national preferences will primarily derive from each state's dominant economic interest groups and from relative expectations of 'exogenous increase in opportunity for cross-border trade and capital movements'.[19]

Although a full analysis of all 15 member state enlargement debates and modes of preference generation lies beyond the scope of this book, there is potential in a more limited application of LI that examines preference formation and aggregation in key member states. Among the key issues to be considered are the differential impact of enlargement arising from perceptions of positive and negative interdependence with Central and Eastern Europe; geographical proximity and its relation to levels of economic interdependence; and variations in socioeconomic structure among the EU15, in the context of the uneven distribution of costs associated with enlargement. The distributional consequences of eastern enlargement fall on member states rather differently and crucially influence national preferences.[20] Enlargement threatened to create particularly high costs, resulting from trade and budgetary competition, for the poorer, less developed and more dependent member states such as Greece, Portugal and Spain.[21] This is because these states largely specialize in the same traditional and resource-intensive industries as many of the CEE states and were thus more likely to be adversely affected by trade diversion effects than more developed member states. A second key distributional issue was the expected recalibration of structural and cohesion funding, where the prospect of competing for subvention in a much enlarged Union meant that those same states stood to suffer disproportionately from any redirection of funds to the accession states, especially in a context where the net contributing states were now consistently stating their opposition to the idea of any increase in the size of the EU budget. But eastern enlargement, equally, presented challenges and opportunities to the larger and wealthier EU states, challenges which crucially influenced attitudes to enlargement in those member states.

British and German enlargement preferences

Analysis of the macroeconomic implications of eastern enlargement demonstrates that it is the net contributors to the EU budget that stand to gain the most. It seems hardly surprising then that Germany, the UK and the Nordic states all consistently supported enlargement, if indeed they simultaneously held some doubts about certain implications of the process.[22] From a German perspective, analysis suggests that the argument of economic gains is especially apparent. This is also the case with Finland, which has close economic ties with the Baltic States, and also for Austria whose geographic proximity to CEE makes it an important economic player in the region.[23] Germany is the main trading partner for all of the CEE states and the largest contributor of humanitarian aid as well as the largest foreign investor in the region.[24] One survey conducted in 2004 found that 40 per cent of all German manufacturing firms had already diversified into CEE, and 90 per cent were planning to institute production over the next five years.[25] German FDI alone was responsible for the creation of 450,000 jobs in CEE by 2004. Crucially, this was not a case of job displacement as most investment was aimed at the construction and development of domestic markets in the accession states rather than shifts in production from Germany. A study by Baldwin, Francois and Portes demonstrated that, among EU member states, Germany had much more to gain in terms of increased trade than any other EU state.[26] This was confirmed subsequently in numerous studies, including those conducted by the European Commission. Thus interdependence with CEE was and is much more of a fact for Germany (and Austria) than for any other EU15 state. For German governments that meant that eastern enlargement did not present any fundamental conflict, at least in terms of the trade effects anticipated.

Given the underlying factors encouraging the expected increase in trade it is hardly surprising that a powerful network of German multinational corporations headed by Volkswagen and Siemens, and financial institutions such as Deutsche Bank, which had invested substantially in the candidate countries in advance of accession, made for a significant corporate influence on German policy. Indeed Bohle points out that in the run-up to accession the Audi plant in Győr, Hungary, contributed around 12 per cent of the group's entire turnover, and with a generous Hungarian government tax break, 74 per cent of Audi profits.[27] Management of important negative externalities such as environmental problems and migration flows associated with increased interdependence also helps explain German advocacy of enlargement. As Zaborowski points out: 'EU and NATO enlargements to the east represent a stabilization of (Germany's) external environment, therefore an improvement on its own security.'[28]

Notwithstanding these factors, however, German governments consistently adopted a schizophrenic attitude to enlargement. This anomaly is understandable perhaps in the context of a balancing act between the 'high politics' and 'low politics' of enlargement, with Germany particularly fearful of having to bear a disproportionate part of the cost of the extension of EU distributive policies. German governments also worried about negative public opinion toward eastern enlargement. As accession approached the German public increasingly linked high and persistent domestic unemployment and the generally depressed economic climate in their country with such issues as low labour costs and unfair tax competition in CEE. All of this made for a difficult balancing act in German attitudes to enlargement. Neoliberal approaches, while very useful in highlighting the issues mentioned here, also have difficulties in explaining German enlargement policy, and in particular the consistent normative framing of eastern enlargement by German policy-makers.[29] For Germany enlargement was not simply, or even primarily, about the extension of markets but a matter of historical justice and moral retribution.[30] So while acknowledging the influence of important German producer interests it is important to emphasize how this complemented rather than singularly framed German policy.

In the UK case the economic gains from eastern enlargement are expected to be lower. It does not have the substantial local trade interests in Central and Eastern Europe that Germany does. Having said that, there is no suggestion that the UK would be a significant loser from enlargement, at least not in economic terms. If the argument were to turn to institutional issues and the question of whether widening, as a matter of course, produces further deepening, then one might expect a different attitude from the UK. It may also be that the UK's neoliberal economic outlook is important here. The extension of the internal market and the market creed may have proved decisive for the UK in encouraging deregulation, privatization, and the vigorous pursuit of microeconomic reform in the candidate countries. Certainly the CBI and the Institute of Directors consistently promoted early and wide enlargement. The change in government from Conservative to Labour in 1997 produced no appreciable change in direction. In some ways, in fact, the Labour government was even more attached to the neoliberal model of economic development. While some commentators continually sought to paint British support for enlargement in negative terms as support for a diluted form of European integration (that further widening would effectively cripple the Federalist project), the evidence suggests more that UK governments evaluated national preferences in terms of economic benefits to the UK and the normative benefit of ensuring peace and prosperity in Central and Eastern Europe. Prime Minister Tony Blair in particular was conspicuous in publicly supporting the candidate states and calling for the acceleration of the enlargement process at important junctures.[31]

In one important respect the prospect of eastern enlargement did bring about a convergence of German and British preferences. Both countries sought to change the shape and financial burden of the CAP and saw eastern enlargement as a golden opportunity to pursue their national preferences by arguing that the CAP in its present design simply could not be transferred to the new member states without bankrupting the EU. In fact British and German attachment to CAP reform was so strong that in the final negotiations with the candidate states both countries set out their stall against paying direct income subsidies to the new member states because this would slow down the reform of the CAP.[32] This presented an extraordinary paradox in that, at a vital period in the negotiations, both countries appeared to be the main obstruction to achieving a deal, when both had in fact been unwavering supporters of enlargement throughout the process. Both the UK and Germany also consistently pushed the goal of reining in spending on the EU budget. In both jurisdictions the dominant interest groups that influenced governmental enlargement positions were industrial conglomerates which saw enlargement as a significant opportunity for market expansion and investment. Their positions were based on arguments that stressed the size of the new markets, the availability of relatively cheap pools of skilled labour, and economies of scale to be realized from transnational production processes. But against those arguments, in both Britain and Germany, different normative logics also influenced policy-makers to quite a degree. The enlargement discourse of state representatives stressed the importance of securing peace and stability in Central and Eastern Europe as much as market share and financial gain.

French enlargement preferences

If expectations of economic gain and the influence of important domestic producer groups significantly influenced British and German enlargement preferences, then one can plausibly argue that the reluctance of successive French governments to embrace eastern enlargement resulted from the ability of French agricultural interests in particular to shape national preferences. Smaller states such as Ireland were quite content to have the French fight the major battles on agriculture in the knowledge that no major change in the status quo could be effected without French consent. The prospect of a radical overhaul in the CAP drove the French government to protect French interests at the expense of the normative desire to expand the EU's democratic club. Later on, opposition to the European Commission's proposed services directive, which would have liberalized the provision of services across the enlarged EU, was again based on a French fear of domestic service providers being undercut by *arriviste* Easterners, who would accept far lower rates than local architects or plumbers, for example, for the same work. The attachment of the CEE states to the Anglo-Saxon rather than European social model meant that the fabric of French socioeconomic structures would inevitably fray as CEE influence began to assert itself within the Council of Ministers. In early 2005 President Chirac (in an offhand comment) suggested that 'ultra-liberalism is the communism of our times'. For many in Central and Eastern Europe this jibe seemed targeted at them rather than the allegedly neoliberal-obsessed Barroso Commission. They made a direct connection with Chirac's earlier insult about them behaving 'in an infantile manner' in their earlier support for the American-led invasion of Iraq. If nothing else the episode represented the culmination of a pattern of French behaviour demonstrating 'how out of sympathy is France with the newly enlarged EU'.[33] The rejection of the Constitutional Treaty on 29 May 2005 was in some measure a rejection of eastern enlargement, or at least a demonstration of serious concern at its impact on France.

French obstructionism manifested itself in different ways but French fears about the impact of enlargement on the nature of the integration project were regularly aired, not least after the Helsinki decision to open up the process to Bulgaria, Romania and Turkey in 1999.[34] Earlier, in September 1998, the French government had sought to delay the beginning of negotiations by requesting that the Commission draw up a full political assessment of the accession process, including an analysis of the Cyprus situation. According to the then French Minister for

European Affairs, Pierre Moscovici, the accession process should be 'under polit-ical control', not on 'automatic pilot'.[35] This was a less than subtle reference to the role and influence of the Commission within the accession process. The French requests were viewed as an attempt to postpone the beginning of substantive nego-tiations and to delay enlargement. The French government, however, angrily denied any suggestions that it wanted to delay enlargement. Instead, it claimed that it was merely trying to get its fellow member states to focus on the real problems created by enlargement.

There is little doubt that the French Presidency of 2000 did much less than other EU Presidencies to advance the enlargement timetable and agenda. In the dispute between Germany and Spain over the future financing of the structural funds, for example, France hardened its position on agriculture rather than seek a compro-mise solution.[36] Notwithstanding the difficulties presented by the unique character-istics of the French foreign policy machinery (*Cohabitation*), and the normal large state EU presidency juggling of national and collective interests, outside observers could not but conclude that defending French interests overrode the collective desire to progress the enlargement process.[37] Such a perspective also had a distinc-tive geopolitical dimension in the shape of French fears that eastern enlargement would produce a more German Europe by moving the centre of gravity of the new EU eastward with Berlin at its core. In short, enlargement changed the funda-mental dynamic that had powered the integration process, namely the Franco-German relationship. Liberal intergovernmental theory therefore, although it does capture the essential basis for French preferences on eastern enlargement, also falls short in its relative neglect of geopolitics. Rather, a complex interplay of economic and geopolitical issues crucially influenced French policy on eastern enlargement.

Spanish and Irish enlargement preferences

With regard to the states that were consistently identified as the most reluctant to embrace eastern enlargement, liberal intergovernmentalism might most usefully be applied to Spain. Spain for long held major concerns about the impact of enlargement on the existing arrangements for regional spending and agriculture and at various important junctures argued against producing a timetable for acces-sions, and against the provision of financial appropriations that would disadvan-tage Spain or reduce the levels of subvention it enjoyed from the EU budget.[38] Before taking over the presidency in 2001 the Swedish foreign minister attacked Spain as especially 'irresponsible' in blocking negotiations by demanding guaran-tees for its national interests.[39] And Spain 'did not refrain from manipulative and forcing strategies' even during the course of its own EU Presidency in 2002.[40]

In the first place Spain stood to gain much less from the expansion of trade which accompanied enlargement. As late as 2000, Spanish exports to CEE amounted to only 2 per cent of the EU total exports. And this amounted to less than 8 per cent of Spanish exports outside the EU. This pattern was as evident in CEE exports to the EU, which showed that Spain only accounted for about 2.5 per cent of the total, making it one of the least important trading partners for the accession states within the EU bloc. The relative paucity of economic contact was also evident in the figures for FDI, which showed that Spanish investment in CEE was very low, and had barely increased as CEE had opened up to new investment.[41] Spanish preferences also turned on the consequences of enlargement for EU structural funding. By 1999 Spain had become the highest net recipient of structural funds, and the fourth largest recipient of CAP monies leaving it with a net EU financial balance of €6 billion.[42] The 2000–6 financial framework guaranteed Spain €55 billion from the EU budget. This represented more than double the amount distributed to all of the CEE states combined. Thus the redistributive consequences of any reorganization of the existing structural fund regime particularly threatened Spanish subvention.

A determination to protect Spanish prerogatives was in evidence as early as 1989 when Spain vetoed the EC budget in order to force agreement on doubling the structural funds as a compensatory side payment for accepting the Single European Act. A similar strategy was employed in the Maastricht negotiations, which eventually yielded the Cohesion fund agreed at Edinburgh in December 1992.[43] This massively boosted Spanish receipts from the EU budget. In November 1991 the Spanish government had threatened to veto the conclusion of Europe Agreements with Poland, Hungary, and Czechoslovakia because the agreements included provision for aid to CEE iron and steel production which could negatively affect the Spanish sector, which was undergoing a troublesome restructuring process at home.[44] Former Prime Minister Felipe Gonzalez put it forcefully in an interview with the *Financial Times* in 1992: 'we should not pull the wool over our own eyes. I don't think Lech Walesa realizes that Western Europe is not going to foot the bill for forty years of Communism. Just like it didn't pay for forty years of Franquismo. No one feels obliged to pay this bill.'[45] Again, during the Amsterdam negotiations, Spain sought to prevent any decision that would harm Spanish subsidies. It fiercely opposed the extension of Qualified Majority Voting (QMV) to Structural and Cohesion funding, for example, and in 1999 it again blocked the reform of the cohesion funds and claimed further financial compensation for its less developed regions to counteract the negative impact of prospective eastern enlargement on its financial position.[46]

The Spanish argument, formally expressed in a 2001 memorandum to Romano Prodi, President of the European Commission, stated that the admission of 12 or 13 countries would lower average per capita incomes across the EU, and 'enlargement will therefore produce an artificial acceleration of economic convergence of those states and regions which do not match average incomes in the European Union of today'.[47] Spanish policy was to 'minimize' or 'neutralize' this effect and Spanish negotiators did not refrain from forcing and manipulative bargaining strategies.[48] The Barcelona Process was one important concession wrung from the EU for accepting eastern enlargement. Thus Spanish enlargement preferences seem to fall much more favourably into Moravcsik's framework than do those of Britain or France.

The Spanish case, however, also demonstrates how political élites also conceived of enlargement in normative terms and struggled to balance their commitment to the process with the need to defend important national economic interests. Piedrifita Tremosa shows that Spanish policy-makers were extremely concerned throughout the eastern enlargement process with their reputation within the EU. They considered enlargement as much an issue of justice and legitimacy as economic utility. In particular Spanish élites felt they could not legitimately oppose eastern enlargement 'given the similarity of its own accession to the moral foundation – peace, stability, and support for democracy – of this round of enlargement'.[49] Whereas EFTA enlargement was deemed different in that the candidates were rich countries which did not need accession as a means of consolidating democracy, to block or threaten to veto the eastern enlargement was morally unacceptable to successive Spanish governments.[50]

Similarly, Portugal and Greece were faced not just with a potential reduction in subvention but also the prospect of serious competition from CEE producers in certain industries and redirection of FDI. Along with France and Italy they were also inclined toward the protection of existing privileges over the collective pursuit of enlargement objectives.[51] Ireland was also identified as one of the states most reluctant to accommodate the preferences of the candidate states. Indeed Schimmelfennig and others categorize Ireland as one of the 'brakemen' along with Spain, Portugal and Greece.[52] Ireland had benefited quite disproportionately from the EU budget over the years and largely succeeded in protecting its subvention even as it shot up the EU wealth table from about 1995 on. For some the rejection in 2001 by Irish voters of the Treaty of Nice was viewed as deriving from unwillingness on the part of the Irish electorate to offer substantial economic support to the applicant countries and general fears regarding the economic implications of enlargement. Will Hutton, for example, made an explicit link between the No vote and enlargement: 'Italy's Berlusconi is openly sceptical about the costs of enlargement; the Irish voted against it in their referendum for the same reason.'[53] George Soros, in an address in Budapest, suggested that one of the reasons Ireland rejected the Nice Treaty was 'over fears aid to EU states would dwindle after eastern candidates joined'.[54] Conservative MEP Daniel Hannan argued that 'asked to endorse a Treaty that would turn them into net contributors, Irish voters were unimpressed'.[55] Another editorial asserted that 'there is no reciprocal sense that Irish GDP having ballooned, a similar effort should now be made on behalf of Eastern Europe. Geo-politics and geo-gratitude do not go together, it seems'.[56]

Irish preferences on eastern enlargement, however, did not only flow from determinations of economic interest. While Irish governments sought to protect EU subvention flows they also offered consistent support for enlargement. And while one might argue that the radical change in its economic position after 1995 may have led to a more benign outlook on enlargement, it is clear that normative considerations also crucially influenced Irish governments. Indeed the Irish government effectively turned the second referendum on Nice in October 2002 into a referendum on enlargement. The question mutated from 'Are you in favour of the ratification of the Treaty of Nice?' to 'Are you in favour of eastern enlargement?'. To argue against enlargement would be to deny to the countries of Central and Eastern Europe all the benefits of membership that had flowed to Ireland since it acceded in 1973. It would be hypocritical and morally unacceptable to deny the CEE states the same opportunities to prosper. This suggests that ideational or normative issues were at least as important as material issues in the construction of Irish enlargement preferences.

More convincing support for Moravcsik's view is provided by analysis of the role of the European Roundtable of Industrialists (ERT), which was forceful in arguing for a full and substantive EU commitment to enlargement from the beginning and actively lobbied for acceleration in the pace of negotiations in the late 1990s. For the ERT (and other such nationally located groups also), enlargement meant access to new production facilities, comparatively cheap labour and well educated workforces and opportunities to reorganize production chains on a more effective and rational trans-European basis, thus increasing global competitiveness.[57] Enlargement meant that foreign investors could gradually and more fully exert control over strategic sectors of CEE economies and provide a reliable and consistent regulatory framework which made investment attractive.[58] The EU also employed different forms of conditionality in its relations with CEE to ensure the direct transposition of its deregulatory economic framework while withholding commitment to the great subventions granted its own poorer member states. In contrast to the Mediterranean round, where the acceding member states were expected to open their markets on entry to the EU or thereafter with exemptions granted, EU treatment of CEE was very different and consistent with views which sought to support EU industry at the expense of a level playing field. In sum, therefore, liberal intergovernmental analysis is well equipped to account for the preferences of transnational capital in the eastern enlargement process.

The interstate level: internal EU bargaining and EU–CEE bargaining

In its third part Moravcsik's framework focuses on the strategic state interaction and bargaining which takes place in Brussels. *The Choice for Europe* revolves around the key interstate 'grand bargains', which, Moravcsik asserts, decisively shaped the trajectory and form of the European integration process; these were, respectively, the Common Market, the CAP, the European Monetary System (EMS), the Single European Act, and the Maastricht Treaty including European Monetary Union (EMU). If Moravcsik's central thesis regarding interstate bargaining is to hold then there is no reason one cannot identify similar 'grand bargains' which characterized the development of enlargement policy, encompassing as it did every conceivable aspect of the wider integration process. The 'grand bargains' which stand out in the eastern enlargement process include crucial summit meetings such as Copenhagen (June 1993), Essen (December 1994), Cannes (June 1995), Luxembourg (December 1997), Helsinki (December 1998), Gothenburg (June 2001), Brussels (October 2002) and Copenhagen (December 2002). If Moravcsik is correct those European Council summit meetings should have proved crucial to enlargement outcomes. Intergovernmental bargaining should have proved consistently more important than supranational entrepreneurship. Interstate negotiation should have been relatively straightforward with governments having aggregated preferences at domestic level and pursued them in intergovernmental settings. Enlargement outcomes should reflect the distribution of power at EU level and result in so-called 'side payments' to those member states who held a veto on enlargement but for domestic reasons were not supportive of expansion and needed to be 'bought off' to ensure their cooperation. The EU enjoyed a significant bargaining advantage over the candidate states and outcomes should reflect that also.

Moravcsik and Vachudova argue that, consistent with past enlargement rounds, EU leaders promoted eastern enlargement because they considered it to be in their long-term economic and geopolitical interests. They see the same bargaining patterns, which have for long characterized the bargaining process within the EU, similarly evident in the enlargement negotiations. In particular, specific interstate concessions and compromises have 'tended to reflect the priorities of the EU's core countries, and disproportionately the most powerful among them'.[59] In previous enlargement rounds, bargaining demands by applicant states were effectively 'stripped away one by one until a deal was struck that disproportionately reflected the priorities of existing member states'.[60] Further, they see in the asymmetry in power relations between the insider (EU) and outsiders (CEE applicant states), evidence that the distribution of power impacts on the enlargement negotiations in much the same fashion as LI suggests with respect to the integration process. The Copenhagen criteria for membership were non-negotiable and reflected the deep chasm of power between the EU and the outsiders who simply had to accept the demands made upon them. Financial aid to the candidate states compared very poorly with that awarded the EU's Cohesion four.[61]

The EU was unrelenting in defending its interests in the negotiations with the candidate states and the final outcome was clearly reflective of the yawning power gap. In addition they cite the imposition, in the course of the eastern enlargement process, of additional requirements to be met by the candidate states. This is in keeping with the core of LI thinking about the integration process. EU conditions were narrowly self-interested in their design and intrusive in their implementation. Applicants were forced to forgo, at least in the short to medium term, some of the significant benefits of membership available to member states. Moravcsik and Vachudova cite the outcome of negotiations in late 2002 in support of their contention. They argue that the acceding CEE member states will receive 'lower (albeit still substantial) subsidies from the CAP and from the structural and cohesion funds than did the previous poorer applicants'. In this instance they cite the fact that transfers to the CEE states will be capped at 4 per cent of GDP, far lower than their predecessors, some of which received up to 8 per cent per year of GDP through EU funds. The authors argue that not only does this limit potential CEE receipts from the EU. It also protects the prerogatives of both richer and poorer EU15 members.[62] The richer states succeeded in the negotiations in limiting the amount of aid to be transferred to the new member states whilst Cohesion states such as Spain managed to protect their subventions going forward. Thus the interstate context in which the enlargement negotiations reached a conclusion chimes perfectly with LI predictions.

While it is not difficult to assert that the sheer asymmetrical power of the EU vis-á-vis the applicant states proved important throughout the process, and certainly in the final negotiations, one could also argue that the outcome of the Brussels and Copenhagen negotiations in the autumn of 2002 did not entirely coincide with LI expectations. After all, the CAP was extended to the applicant states, albeit in a reduced form and after delays. The budgetary deal struck also suggests that the applicant states did not simply have to take what was being offered to them. They bargained and in some cases (such as Poland) managed to pull off a better than expected outcome. Against LI one might also ask why it was that, with the extraordinary asymmetrical advantage enjoyed by the EU (regarding material bargaining capacity) vis-à-vis the applicant states, the option was for full integration of CEE into EU structures? Neoliberal theory would suggest that something short of outright enlargement, such as a preferential free trade arrangement, a customs union or even association status would be the EU's preferred option. Yet the EU–CEE relationship moved quickly from trade and cooperation agreements (early 1990s), through Association agreements (mid 1990s), and advanced political dialogue and impending accession (late 1990s), to eventual accession. This evolution cannot be accounted for satisfactorily by liberal intergovernmentalism.

Liberal intergovernmental theory proves better able to account for the internal EU bargaining and decision-making, which accompanied and facilitated eastern enlargement. Even if eastern enlargement prompted new thinking about important EU policies such as CAP, the outcome of negotiations suggests, first, that the usual EU vested interests succeeded in protecting their transfers and, second, that the decisions on CAP reflected as much external and ongoing pressure for reform, which Moravcsik argues, has been a longstanding one. This has been in evidence through WTO reform proposals and from pressure from EU member states such as the UK and Germany. Thus enlargement-influenced or related CAP outcomes coincide exactly with what LI would predict – the protection of resources and privileges by dominant producer interests within the EU, postponement of any radical decisions on the recalibration of the CAP and an EU outcome that was reflective of the distribution of power in bargaining and negotiations.

Migration

Because economic interpretations of eastern enlargement revolved largely around perceptions of positive and negative interdependence with the candidate countries, two particular types of economic externalities played an important part in the calculations of EU actors. These were expectations about how enlargement would impact on migration flows into EU member states and, second, the considerable challenge posed by the candidate states' environmental degradation. EU fears about the possibility of large flows of migrants from east to west in the wake of accession were not consistent across the member states but were crucial in the determination of some member state preferences such as Austria and Germany. West European publics increasingly viewed crime, asylum and immigration, although quite separate issues, as inseparable. Migration thus became a dominant theme in a large number of European countries just in the period when eastern enlargement was reaching a critical negotiating point. In many EU member states alarmist projections relating to an influx of 'eastern hordes' were propagated. At the extreme margin of this discourse the United Kingdom's viciously xenophobic tabloid press hysterically claimed that after 1 May 2004, millions of East European 'scroungers' or welfare tourists would come to Britain.[63]

These existential fears derived to some degree from the fact that people in Europe seem to harbour an unfocused, general anxiety about frontiers no longer providing the protection they once did. Some might even look back to the Cold War days with nostalgia. Organized cross-border crime, drug and people trafficking, smuggling and prostitution seemed to indicate that frontier controls are no longer as effective as they once were.[64] In some states such as Germany and France, eastern enlargement was increasingly viewed through the prism of the immigration threat as accession loomed. Further migration threatened domestic wage levels, welfare expenditure and the domestic socioeconomic compact, it was frequently stated. In addition, in the aftermath of the 11 September attacks, the new salience of international terrorism means that in many jurisdictions 'foreigners' were now viewed with unrelenting suspicion. Thus the debate on eastern enlargement became entangled with the various strands of debate on transnational migration.

In their analysis of the enlargement negotiations Moravcsik and Vachudova argue that the inclusion in the accession treaties of special provisions including transition measures on inward migration to the EU15 'reflect the demands of special interests or the concerns of voting publics in the existing members'. Their argument is that the outcome of the accession negotiations closely follows that which LI would have predicted. Candidate states found it difficult to have their preferences accommodated by the EU and in most instances found themselves having to accept less than favourable terms. The costs of non-membership were simply too great not to compromise on the EU's terms. Thus applicants made concessions even where no coercion was threatened.[65] Back in 2001 in the run-up to the Gothenburg summit, a number of EU member states, led by Sweden, Denmark, and the Netherlands, had announced that they would unilaterally deviate from EU policy by granting unrestricted access to their labour markets for job seekers from the new member states after accession. The three countries announced they would not apply the seven-year transition period which had been proposed by Austria and Germany in the negotiations.[66] By late 2002, however, all member states except for the UK, Ireland, and Sweden had insisted on some restrictions being placed on free movement.[67] This was entirely consistent with LI expectations in that even those member states which had earlier displayed a benign attitude to CEE labour migration changed their stance as accession loomed. The German and Austrian governments were the most active in insisting upon a protectionist stance as they considered themselves to come under the most serious threat.[68]

Where migration featured strongly in the calculation of EU actors in the direct sense of legislative iniatives and constitutional safeguards, it also mattered in other informal ways. The EU, for example, sought to connect the Pact on Stability to its

Justice and Home Affairs *acquis*. Unlike previous enlargements, eastern enlargement was the first to include a specific JHA *acquis*, which covered asylum, migration and border controls, organized crime, terrorism, drug and people trafficking, as well as police, customs and judicial cooperation. The *acquis* also included the Schengen Agreement on the internal EU removal of border controls.[69] All of this suggests an EU which viewed enlargement, at best, nervously, and sought the most substantive legal protections against mass inward migration. This was despite all the economic evidence from the Mediterranean enlargement (the only comparable expansion on this issue), which showed that even after the lifting of restrictions on free movement, out-migration from Greece, Portugal and Spain to the rest of the EU simply did not materialize.

EU attitudes hardened as the enlargement process unfolded; officials from the member states routinely presented cross-border organized crime in particular as an important existential threat to the integrity and legitimacy of the integration process. The interesting observation here is that the EU offered little or no flexibility to the candidate states during enlargement negotiations. The Union was the 'regime-maker' and the candidate states the 'regime-takers'. This, of course, created serious difficulties for many CEE states, especially those such as Hungary, which had large ethnic diaspora communities in neighbouring states that were not part of the enlargement process.[70] CEE states resented the Schengen-related demands in particular, as they had no part in designing the rules of the Schengen regime.[71] Implementation of tough new border rules often came with a real economic cost. This was certainly the case with the Polish re-bordering of its frontier with Ukraine.[72] Although one might view this as purely a security-related issue, the nature of globalization meant that the EU also looked at these issues from a pronounced economic and welfare perspective and as a problem of domestic governance rather than external relations. The huge flows of money generated by human trafficking, prostitution rackets, narco-transportation and other forms of organized crime were seen as a destabilizing phenomenon. Ensuring these did not become an even bigger problem for the EU after enlargement was thus a key concern of policy-makers. Thus the liberal intergovernmental framework also helps account for attitudes to migration externalities within the enlargement process.

Environmental externalities

While control over migration flows represented one key negative externality, the issue of transnational and cross-border environmental problems also occupied EU policy-makers throughout the eastern enlargement process. Environmental problems, because of their transnational nature, are by definition classic collective action problems. As Hill points out, eastern enlargement promised the opportunity of institutional regulation of the environmental problems associated with the old smokestack industries in Eastern Europe, and created new possibilities for protecting the peoples of both candidate states and existing member states from any future environmental disasters on their borders.[73] The candidate states inherited daunting environmental challenges, however. Before 1989 air pollution was a major problem, particularly in the northern region (Poland, the Czech Republic and former East Germany), due to heavy industries and reliance on brown coal for energy. Water pollution in the form of hazardous substances and nutrients affected all CEE countries, and soil degradation was also part of the negative inheritance from the past. As the transition process took hold economic and social restructuring presented new environmental problems, arising from particularly mass consumerism, the increase in all forms of transportation and sharp rises in waste disposal. In addition, the candidate states, faced with multiple economic challenges, did not prioritize environmental issues to the same degree as other western states and the NGO sector that emerged in this area was generally weak.[74] So, in a myriad of ways, eastern enlargement threatened to impose a significant economic cost on the EU, and especially on those states which shared borders with the candidate countries.

EU policy, in insisting on candidate state adoption of the entire environmental *acquis* prior to accession, was forceful and intrusive. The EU is frequently described as the most progressive environmental zone in the world. Given the problems manifest in CEE there were many who feared that enlargement would lead to a slowdown or even reversal of EU environmental policy. Where the 1995 EFTA enlargement seemed to strengthen the environmental lobby within the EU, eastern enlargement could only compromise it. Or so the argument went. Therefore EU policy, at least those parts driven by the environmental leaders, was to insist on transposition and implementation in advance of membership. On this same point one could also cite the strong pro-enlargement positions adopted by the Nordic states of the EU – Sweden, Denmark and Finland. These states had taken the lead on such issues as reducing emissions of carbon dioxide and other pollutants. Their consistent advocacy of eastern enlargement was not unconnected to their strong attachment to multilateralizing environmental issues. Without enlargement the ability of the EU to institutionalize the management of common environmental problems would be significantly impaired. The experience of previous enlargements suggested that those states that were not as environmentally conscious were slowly socialized into more robust norms of performance through institutionalized regulation. One of the best examples was Ireland, which had progressively improved its levels of environmental protection through its membership of the EU. One must ask, however, whether management of perceived common problems of this nature would have evolved *anyway* even without a structured accession process? The answer to this is probably yes. The asymmetrical nature of the negotiations meant, however, that the CEE states were vulnerable to more pressure from the EU in a negotiation and accession context.[75]

Among other things *Agenda 2000* outlined a strategy that required the candidate countries to upgrade nuclear installations to best international safety standards, and stipulated that those installations that could not be upgraded at a reasonable cost would be shut down. The Kosovo War and the problems it presented to the Danubian CEE states, especially Bulgaria and Romania, reinforced the fears about environmental degradation impacting as seriously on Austria, Germany and other countries. The Danube is the second largest river in Europe and in one way or another binds together 80 million people. Thirteen separate countries share its catchment area. It became a major focus of attention in the enlargement process.[76] Moreover, on the front of energy and the security of its supply, the eastern enlargement was likely to worsen the ratio of consumers to producers within the EU. The CEE states may have coal and steel, but they lack oil and gas. Many of the CEE states remained dependent on Russia for energy supplies.[77] This may not matter too much in a period of stability and free trade, but things might look very different in the event of foreign policy crises with Russia or the Middle East. Even a rise in the price of energy for economic and ecological reasons might cause an enlarged and more variegated EU significant problems.[78] Again liberal intergovernmentalism presents a plausible set of arguments from which to analyse EU preferences on environmental issues.

Conclusions

For all of the explanatory power which derives from these applications of liberal intergovernmentalist theory, there are also some important problems which it has difficulties explaining. Firstly, if economic rationalism lay at the core of the EU's approach there is reason to doubt the benign outcome predicted. While the anticipated surge in trade certainly took place (even in advance of 2004) the potential budgetary cost of eastern enlargement may be difficult to contain, for all the determination displayed by the net contributors to limit EU spending. Although the Commission insisted throughout the process that the cost of enlargement could be met within the terms of the current financial arrangements (1.27 per cent of Union GDP) there are reasons to believe that this may not be the case. One could cite the impact on the budget of the accession of the Mediterranean countries in the 1980s, or, more dramatically, the absorption of the GDR by West Germany in 1990. In each case much more money ended up being transferred than had been envisaged. Thus the negative dynamic arising out of domestic dissatisfaction produced in member states such as Portugal and Spain on the one hand (the prospect of reduced subvention), and Germany and Britain (increased budgetary burden) on the other, should have been enough to derail the entire enlargement project or at least severely limit its potential cost. And where Moravcsik and others have argued that the member states succeeded in doing just that in the 2002 negotiations, the increase in bargaining power of the new member states may well produce significant friction over future financial frameworks, beginning with the negotiation of the 2007–13 budget. This suggests a less than rational approach to enlargement on the part of member states and weakens the case for LI at a number of levels.

The asymmetric nature of inside–outside bargaining that accompanied eastern enlargement, and which LI privileges, also prompts the question of why the EU was backed into a corner on agriculture reform. As one of the world's foremost agricultural powers, it might have been expected that the EU would not be willing to renegotiate (internally) its own longstanding agriculture regime. LI projects a recalcitrant position from the big domestic agriculture concerns which in turn would decisively shape member state behaviour on the CAP. And although Moravcsik argues that the Copenhagen deal effectively locked in the prerogatives of those producer interests until 2013, the concession on direct subsidies, which will be gradually extended to the new member states, is more difficult for LI to explain, except perhaps as a short-term measure designed to postpone dealing with a very divisive issue.

A further problem with liberal intergovernmentalism lies in its attachment to the so-called 'grand bargain' model of European integration. The focus on the grand bargains (the Treaty of Rome, the consolidation of the Common Market, the founding of the European Monetary System, the Single European Act and the Treaty on European Union) is simply too narrow, tending to vitiate the role of everyday activity at EU level, and means that liberal intergovernmentalism is consequently ill equipped to account for the sheer density of issues and level of institutionalized cooperation evident in the EU.[79] In short, Moravcsik tends to marginalize *process*. The liberal intergovernmental model cannot adequately depict the enlargement process, characterized as it has been by an ever-expanding range of institutional arrangements and commitments. Applying the Moravcsikian 'logic' to the 'enlargement grand bargains' over the past decade – the European Council Summits from Copenhagen (1993), through to Copenhagen (2002) – the outcomes demonstrate not just or even primarily the decisive import of domestic producer interests and unchanging national preferences, but rather an ongoing process characterized by member state uncertainty, complex patterns of intra-EU bargaining, and an important entrepreneurial role played by the European Commission. In this connection Moravcsik's 'bias against supranationalism' prevents a rounded analysis of eastern enlargement and its institutional context.[80] It may be especially the case that LI is simply blind to the proactive role played by the EU's institutions and denies them the status of purposive actors. Chapters 6 and 7 demonstrated how the Commission and, to a lesser extent, the European Parliament, contributed effectively, sometimes decisively, to enlargement decision-making. Wincott asks whether 'the application of state theories to European integration begs the question of why the political institutions of states can have an impact, but those of the EC cannot'.[81] The argument is not one that replaces Moravcsik's with a straightforward swap to a supranational model. Rather, it is that there is a complex process of interaction between member states, EU institutions and candidate states with preferences sometimes quite identifiable but at other times undecided and susceptible to pressure in the process of interaction. Reductionism, of the state-centric or any other variety, does not help to explain our enlargement questions.

Acknowledging these deficiencies of LI does not lead one to disregard explanations of eastern enlargement which centre on economics and rational cost–benefit calculation. Important parts of the process can only be properly understood by reference to the desire of important EU companies for market penetration and neoliberal reform measures in CEE, and the classical predictions of regional economic integration theory. Economic studies consistently demonstrated that the effect of enlargement would be benign, if not entirely negligible. If the economies of the new member states were too small to trigger real disruption or change within the old EU, there would be an uneven distribution of costs which member states would have to bear. LI also helps us depict the complex pattern of transnational enlargement advocacy, especially the influence in key member states of powerful multinational corporations. It is less successful in explicating how eastern enlargement was negotiated in a complex terrain which was *simultaneously* intergovernmental and supranational. While the early stages of the enlargement process certainly lend empirical confirmation to liberal intergovernmentalism and neoliberal institutionalism, being characterized on the EU side by blockage of trade liberalization measures, an obsession with side payments issues and continued prevarication on the question of a clear membership perspective for the CEE states, it is clear that it cannot account for what appears after the Helsinki (1999) and especially the Copenhagen (2002) summits to be a normatively determined outcome. This is what Schimmelfennig referred to as the major puzzle of EU enlargement. The collective outcome is as explicable by the constitutive values of the EU as the relative power or pursuit of interests by the member states.[82] Indeed, as the next chapter will demonstrate, normative factors proved consistently more important than any others in determining the shape and trajectory of eastern enlargement.

10 Normative explanations of eastern enlargement

Introduction

In recent years the study of European integration has broadened considerably beyond the previously rather narrow debate between neofunctionalism and classical (and later liberal) intergovernmentalism. In fact a rich and diverse set of competing claims about the fundamental nature of the European integration process has encouraged the sense that Europe's great diversity is now reflected in European scholarship also. One of the most important approaches to EU politics has developed out of a normative literature which itself breaks down into two identifiable camps. The first explores EU decision-making through rational choice institutionalism and focuses particularly on the interactions of member states and institutional actors under specific constitutional and institutional rule structures. The second normative approach revolves around sociological institutionalism and highlights the nature of state interaction within international forums, and in particular the relationship between state identity and interests under conditions of international interaction and intersubjectivity. Scholarship from both camps has become increasingly sophisticated and responded to calls to test claims empirically.[1] The eastern enlargement of the EU provides an important test case for the rival claims. On the one hand, *rules* – devised by the Commission, shaped by the Council, and imposed on the candidate states – played an important part in the enlargement process. On the other hand, *norms* – sometimes framed as rules, but more usually considered cognitive guides to appropriate behaviour, reflecting EU values and collective identity – also helped shape the EU approach to eastern enlargement to a considerable degree. And whilst there is little doubt that both geopolitical and economic motivations were instrumental in guiding EU policy, it is equally clear that eastern enlargement was driven by a normative logic which proved more decisive to outcomes than arguments about power, territory or new markets. In short, enlargement was conceived in a normative environment, governed by specific norms and rules, and carried forward to a successful conclusion by attachment to those norms. This chapter examines eastern enlargement with the aid of constructivist ideas about ideational factors in international politics, the EU self-conception as a 'community of values', the norm-rich environment which has underpinned the integration process and helped produce a distinct EU identity in world politics.

The constructivist worldview

Constructivist approaches to international politics are distinguished by the effort to seek some sort of understanding between the natural world and the human or social world. Nicholas Onuf points to a 'world of our making' and suggests that social relations make or construct people into the kind of beings that we are.[2] Alexander Wendt, in his seminal *Social Theory of International Politics,* tries to understand 'social kinds' and 'natural kinds'.[3] The constructivist approach, although increasingly diverse, is made up of three important hypotheses. First, it is contended that the structures of international life are not exclusively material but also consist of a substantial ideational dimension; this means that the security dilemma traditionally associated with anarchy is, in fact, what Wendt suggests it is – *what we make of it* – in other words, an ideational construct rather than a material reality. Second, the contribution made by intersubjective shared meanings between purposive state actors decisively determines identities and interests in the international system. In other words, as Risse-Kappen suggests, actors' interests and preferences cannot simply be treated as unproblematic and exogenous to structure. To a great extent those interests are made clearer as a result of interaction with other states and membership of international organizations.[4] Wendt refers to this approach as 'structural idealism' (in opposition to existing structural realist theories such as those of Waltz).[5] Finally, it is contended that ideas and norms have to be taken more seriously in IR than traditional approaches have allowed.

Combining these elements of the constructivist approach, a key feature of international politics is the co-constitution of the material and ideational in human life. Constructivism does not deny the importance of material structures or a phenomenal world external to thought but rather seeks to understand that world in relation to human behaviour or social structure. The differences between and among the different streams of constructivist thought are significant.[6] Nevertheless all constructivist approaches share the basic claim that the 'neo-neo' synthesis (and by implication most IR theory) is 'undersocialized' in the sense that it pays insufficient attention to the ways in which international life is socially constructed.[7] And for constructivists one of the most important features of contemporary international politics is the way in which community-building and security-enhancing possibilities arise out of state engagement with multilateral international institutions. International institutions open up new opportunities for interstate cooperation, change the patterns of state behaviour, and can create the conditions under which the structural quicksand that is international anarchy may be overcome.

Security and peace communities and the democratic peace

Constructivists interested in exploring the links between state identities and interests have re-discovered the concept of security community in seeking to develop ideas about the norm-generating potential of international organizations. In the original formulation by Karl Deutsch, a security community was defined as a collection of states that had become integrated to such a point that there is a 'real assurance that the members of that community will not fight each other physically, but will settle their disputes in a peaceful way'.[8] The concept thus revolves around 'dependable expectations of peaceful change'. That is that states within the community possess a compatibility of core values derived from common institutions and mutual responsiveness – a matter of mutual identity and loyalty, a sense of 'we-ness' – and are integrated so closely that the aforementioned 'dependable expectations of peaceful change' has become the norm.[9]

Deutsch distinguished between an 'amalgamated security community' (formal unity) and so-called 'pluralistic security communities' (where sovereignty is retained). Building on Deutsch, Adler and Barnett identify three important characteristics of modern transnational political communities. First, members of the community have as a starting point a set of shared values and meaning to underpin their collective identity. State interaction is thus informed to a crucial degree by such common values. Second, interaction among members takes place in a multitude of forums, concerning transactions of every kind (material and non-material). As the pace of globalization has quickened since the 1980s a great acceleration in both the quantity and quality of contact has encouraged the deepening of regional groupings, especially of the European Union. This in turn has produced new forms of legal regulation which are designed to institutionalize and manage such interdependence. Third, members of the community exhibit a reciprocity that expresses, if not pure altruism, then acknowledgement of long-term collective interests. These in turn derive from the process of interaction and prompt a sense of obligation and collective responsibility.[10] One key element of the neo-Deutschian security community argument is that centred on the 'democratic peace', the idea that democracies do not fight each other. Thus for democratic peace theorists Immanuel Kant's postulate, developed in his *Perpetual Peace* (1795), has been empirically substantiated. Wendt's *Social Theory* (chapter 6) argues that at its core the international system is being slowly transformed into a Kantian culture. In this sense we have moved from Hobbesian state rivalries (defined by enmity), to a Lockean culture (defined by rivalrous competition), to one where we see the emergence of a growing number of states that are predisposed toward external self-restraint and interdependence.[11] The implication of such emerging communities might be profound:

> quasi-Kantian peaceful change without its teleological and universal elements might be presently evolving. If so, peaceful change need not rely on the transcendence of the nation state or the elimination of existing cultural and ethnic loyalties and identities; what matters is the creation of social cognitive and normative bonds that can encourage peoples to identify, and to expect their security and welfare to be intimately intertwined with those that exist on the same side of spatial and cognitive borders.[12]

For most analysts the European Union is the best example of a pluralistic security community in today's international system. Indeed, member states tend to take 'dependable expectations of peaceful change' and EU core values for granted.[13]

These core values have become a central referent for member state conceptions of their own identities and interests. Since the foundation of the European Communities in the 1950s, European integration was meant to create and stabilize a security community that would replace the traditional rivalries and contestation for power and resources between and among the European states. In its course, the Community members not only established a stable democratic peace amongst themselves but also a unique set of institutions and legal order. This is indeed a type of regional organization representing a community of values. Often, arguments about low politics, as Gardner Feldman points out, succeed in diverting attention from the real achievement of the EU, which has been lasting reconciliation between former enemies.[14] Since 1989 European security has revolved almost exclusively (if not always directly) around the institutional settings of the EU.[15] And the eastern enlargement of the European Union became the most direct and important instrument for extending the existing security community eastward.

Enlarging the European security community

Eastern enlargement as such duplicated the earlier processes of interstate cooperation and community-building which shaped the early integration process in Western Europe. Its aim was that of transforming former adversaries into allies and transporting the CEE states directly into the heart of the European security community, which, although comprising a range of different institutions,[16] nevertheless has a distinct centre of gravity in the EU. Enlargement would facilitate the transmission of new norms from the EU to the candidate states, thus helping to transform the 'Eastern' European states into 'European' states'.[17] This is surely what Commission President Romano Prodi meant when he said that 'our enlargement strategy ensures that these values are enshrined in the candidate countries before they can join the EU. Democracy, the rule of law and respect for human rights will become the norm throughout the expanding Union.'[18] The cognitive model was one which highlighted the transformation in Franco-German relations after the Second World War, as one which could be emulated in the re-constitution of German–Polish relations, Hungarian–Romanian relations, indeed any interstate relationship previously characterized by tensions over territory, ethnic minorities, or disputed versions of history. Thus the earlier patterns of peace building have been replicated in Central and Eastern Europe and indeed extended far beyond what was initially envisaged in the early 1990s. The EU has employed a virtually identical political-institutional mix in Southeastern Europe (Stabilization and Association Process), the Euro-Mediterranean area (the Barcelona Process) and beyond (the Wider Neighbourhood policy), even if different (non-accession) outcomes are likely. The very success of EU community-building in Central and Eastern Europe thus promoted the extension of community-enhancing instruments to the wider Europe.

Analysis of the enlargement discourse employed by EU representatives indicates a clear attachment to the concept of an expanding political community. Former enlargement Commissioner Hans van den Bröek, in a 1997 speech, for example, referred to the EU as a 'genuine security community in which the very idea of war between any members can be dismissed out of hand'.[19] This is a direct articulation of the academic concept of the security community as a Deutschian 'non-war community'.[20] It was of a pattern where the European Commission actively sought to create a we-feeling both amongst the applicant states from CEE and also, obviously, between the EU member states and the individual applicant states. The building of trust through institutional engagement and capacity-building became a central preoccupation of EU strategists.[21] This assertion is supported by a stream of Commission documentation that emphasizes that the EU wanted to create in the East a 'psychological environment of mutual trust', and a 'feeling of belonging'.[22] Council and Commission officials regularly reiterated the importance of extending the post-1945 model of reconciliation and legitimacy. Sometimes it was stated explicitly by officials such as Commissioner van den Bröek when he again stated that 'enlargement can thus be seen as an extension of the EU's zone of stability to the East'.[23] Commissioner Verheugen similarly suggested that 'all the experience shows that the projection of political stability and economic prosperity implicit in enlargement enhances the security of Europe as a whole'. He went on to stress that 'the EU is by definition pacific'. It is, among other things, 'a highly successful example of conflict prevention and dispute settlement'.[24] Thus from the beginning eastern enlargement was conceptualized as a contemporary security enhancing project, one which would embed EU norms in the former Communist states and ensure a successful extension of the existing pluralistic security community. To a large extent, however, this process was dependent for success on a genuine coalescence between insiders and outsiders around a particular set of values and shared collective identity.

European collective identity

Constructivism emphasizes the ways in which membership of international organizations offers the possibility of transforming member states' identities as well as interests. Governance clearly involves shaping identities in different ways. Preferences, expectations, and beliefs relating to a state's identity and interests are not immune from or exogenous to political history associated with different levels of international embeddedness.[25] Identities and interests indeed, according to constructivists, are created and changed with that history and through different forms of international interaction. Notwithstanding the difficulties in making claims for a unified European identity, constructivists argue that the European integration process has facilitated the construction of a different type of collective identity around EU processes and normative practice.[26] This identity is neither national nor supranational. Rather it is constructed around transnational institutional and civic politics and encourages ever-deeper identification between state actors and EU structures. It is fundamentally an identity built around real and substantive commitments on the part of member states to the principles of collective decision-making and contractual obligation, and embedded in perceptions of shared values, and a commitment to diffuse those values internationally. This evolving EU identity is also one that challenges cultural essentialists such as Pope Benedict XVI and Samuel Huntington, who argue that Europe remains one indivisible (Christian) civilizational entity.[27] The debate on God and whether or not the preamble to the Constitutional Treaty should contain a reference to Europe's Christian heritage saw the triumph of the constructivist over the essentialist definition of EU identity. The enlarged EU was not to be defined in a cultural or religious sense but rather as a shared civic and secular European consciousness.[28]

Beginning with François Duchêne's description of the EU as a 'civilian power', scholars have sought to articulate and analyse the meaning of the EU's international identity as it has developed.[29] This posited the EU as a different sort of international entity, less concerned with material power and hard security than with seeking to domesticate foreign policy along the successful domestic post-1945 template of progressive politics. This is a representation of an international actor which seeks to encourage civic virtue, transparent representative institutions, and the highest standards of democratic governance, on the basis of shared commitment to a specific value set. Most recently, Ian Manners borrowing from Duchêne in depicting a 'normative power' Europe, has analysed how EU policies and activities shape our understandings of the EU, and the different ways in which the EU can be viewed as a political and social agent embedded in and employing economic, political, and social institutions.[30] As Manners puts it:

> The concept of normative power is an attempt to suggest that not only is the EU constructed on a normative basis, but importantly this predisposes it to act in a normative way in world politics. It is built on the crucial, but usually overlooked observation, that the most important factor shaping the international role of the EU is not what it does or what it says, but what it is.[31]

The EU's constitutional norms represent the crucial foundations determining its international identity. The principles of democracy, rule of law, and respect for human rights and fundamental freedoms were first made explicit in the 1970s although only given constitutional expression in the 1990s.[32] Within the European Union these core norms have been elaborated through a series of declarations, treaties, policies, and the development of an explicit set of membership conditions. These norms helped define the *acquis communautaire* and *acquis politique* and by definition the EU's international identity. It is no coincidence that these norms were placed at the heart of EU enlargement policy during the 1990s. Eastern enlargement unfolded from and thus was a product of what Helen Wallace termed the 'affiliational' or normative dimension of the European integration process.[33] In other words expansion could not have been undertaken without such a solid affiliational connection between insider and outsider.

This is a Europe that even American neoconservatives such as Robert Kagan admit has moved away from power toward a 'self-contained world of laws and rules and transnational negotiation and cooperation'. The territory with the European Union at its core has entered a 'post-historical paradise of peace and relative prosperity, the realization of Immanuel Kant's "perpetual peace"'.[34] In the aftermath of the attacks on the United States on 11 September 2001, and in particular the American-led invasion of Iraq in 2003, it became clear that the European Union's collective international identity had evolved to such a point that it now diverged radically from the United States. Notwithstanding EU support offered the US in the campaign against the Taliban in Afghanistan and European divisions on Iraq, subsequent events gave support to the view that European norms and values (as manifested in the EU) were now significantly different from those of the United States. Where the EU had embraced a Kantian international identity the United States remained mired in history and attached to a Hobbesian *Weltanschauung*.

If the development of a norm-based collective European identity laid the basis for a successful enlargement of the Union to Central and Eastern Europe then a number of important themes stand out as worthy of further attention. In particular three important phenomena can be identified as crucial to the normative underpinning of the eastern enlargement process. Each contributed to the progression of the process by providing cognitive road maps for policy-makers, which, although competing with other non-normative templates, proved decisive to enlargement decision-making. First, enlargement emerged fundamentally from the EU self-understanding and collective identity based on the values which had come to define 'Europeanness'. Second, the eastern enlargement process was driven by an explicit moral dimension, which manifested itself in the 'return to Europe' argument deployed by the Central and East European states, and on the EU side, by acceptance of those claims for membership on the basis that accession was a natural right for and could not be denied to the CEE states. Finally, another 'logic of appropriateness' can be identified in the institutional path dependency of EU enlargement history and in particular, the precedents set by previous enlargement rounds. All three phenomena can only be understood as emanating from understandings of the EU as a contemporary pluralistic security community.

Enlargement and the EU – self-understanding

The EU's self-understanding and the importance to this of a core set of values is reflected in the principles of governance that have grown up around the integration process. This self-understanding and self-representation cannot simply be dismissed as cognitive or rhetorical as rationalist scholars frequently suggest. Rather, as Sedelmeier argues, eastern enlargement reflected a sense of what EU institutional actors and member state representatives considered appropriate behaviour for the role that they collectively ascribed to themselves – as representatives of the EU – in their relationships with Central and Eastern Europe (and indeed other non-member states on the eastern and southeastern fringes of the EU) and the behavioural obligations implied for this particular relationship.[35] The normative basis for this self-understanding can be analysed through a number of different phenomena most of which can be sourced to earlier processes of norm construction within the European integration process. The Laeken Declaration of 2001 provided an important representation of EU self-understanding and its role in international politics:

Does Europe not, now that it is finally unified, have a leading role to play in a new world order, that of a power able to play a stabilizing role worldwide and to point the way ahead for many countries and peoples? Europe as a continent of humane values, the Magna Carta, the Bill of Rights, the French Revolution and the fall of the Berlin Wall; the continent of liberty, solidarity and above all diversity, meaning respect for others' languages, cultures and traditions.[36]

This representation includes the key ideational and philosophical influences that helped mould today's European Union and frame its international identity. At regular intervals during the eastern enlargement process key actors on both the EU and candidate state side made reference to the values and principles that arose out of those ideational influences and the behavioural obligations they implied.

If the core of this EU self-understanding lies in such commitment to its constitutive values and norms then this creates an obligation to diffuse them internationally and to grant membership to the states that share them.[37] Crucially, that process of diffusion can only be implemented with the voluntary acceptance of these norms by outside states. These norms are constitutive for the political culture and collective identity of democratic societies; democratic states tend to externalize them. They want their international relations to be governed by the same norms of non-violence and rule-based conflict management as their domestic politics. For the constructivist the constitutive character of liberal norms is reflected in the basic treaties of the European Union.[38] This point is underscored by Lykke Friis, who suggests that the EU can sit down to negotiate with applicant states not simply in response to pressures of economic interdependence and worries about stability, (though of course these are important factors), but also because of its own self-understanding. The system of international cooperation breaks down – or loses prestige – if the member states have difficulty solving their national questions through supranational means. This logic is reflective of a system where over time national interests also develop a 'system interest'.[39] Or, as Roy Ginsberg puts it, 'a synthesis between regional and national interests develops'.[40]

Thus the effort to export the core EU norms of peace, economic cooperation and legal interdiction was a natural outgrowth of systemic change within the European integration process. Had the EU failed to respond positively to the requests for membership from Central and Eastern Europe, it would have constituted a negation of the integration process itself and the values upon which the member states structured their cooperative interstate relations. This central truth of the enlargement process was captured by Joschka Fischer's observation that 'following the collapse of the Soviet Empire, the EU had to open to the East, otherwise the very idea of European integration would have undermined itself and eventually self-destructed'.[41]

In the immediate aftermath of the 1989 revolutions the search for recognition by the new democracies of Central and Eastern Europe was met by a European Union that found it difficult to depart from the ideals it supposedly stood for throughout the entire period of the Cold War. In their examination of 'norm construction' within both the EU and NATO enlargement processes, Fierke and

Wiener identified a complex relationship between identity, norms and practices.[42] Their analysis suggested the central importance of the Helsinki Final Act of 1975, the significance of which lay 'less in the force of the law than in constructing a moral obligation' toward the CEE states.[43] The goal was to translate the promise of Helsinki into reality. Patricia Chilton also underscores the importance of the Helsinki accords for both Western and Eastern European states. At their core they reflected and progressively reified a certain image of Western Europe. That image captured the imagination of dissidents in Central and Eastern Europe. Even if a primarily rhetorical device, the consistent declarations of attachment to those ideals by western policy-makers meant that after 1989 the rhetorical commitments came in for substantive scrutiny and the promises made could not be reneged upon.[44]

It is also worth remembering that while the Cold War may have artificially cut off east from west Europe, it may also in fact may have led to a greater awareness across Europe of what a collective European identity actually consisted of. Throughout the Cold War period, two things were stressed in official statements from EU and national representatives. First, there were consistent expressions of solidarity with what Milan Kundera called the 'kidnapped west', and, second, the there was the involuntary nature of the eastern exclusion from western structures, and specifically from the evolving integration process.[45] Reinforcement of this normative discourse was usually supported by assertions that if and when geopolitical circumstances were to change, this would be met on the Community side by a clear commitment to bringing the states of Central and Eastern Europe into the Community structures. The implication of a natural right to accession was always there, if indeed it seemed very unlikely that such a scenario could ever be realized in the dark days of domination by the Soviet Union.

A perusal of communiqués and official statements from European Council meetings throughout the late 1970s and 1980s reveals a strong attachment to a perception of special responsibility for Central and Eastern Europe. It was taken for granted that this implied an obligation to support economic and political development in CEE, and potentially, integration into the EU. These notions of affiliation and an EU 'special responsibility' can clearly be evinced from the discourse of EU political élites and from Commission officials. This affiliational discourse, which would help lock the EU into a commitment to eastern enlargement, was already to the fore in the pledge of full support for the transformation process in Central and Eastern Europe, offered at the Strasbourg European Council in December 1989:

> The Community and its member states are fully conscious of the common responsibility which devolves on them in this decisive phase in the history of Europe ... They are prepared to develop ... closer and more substantive relations in all areas ... The Community is at the present time the European identity which serves as the point of reference for the countries of Central and Eastern Europe.[46]

The importance to the EU of its own self-image is also reflected in the sensitivity to criticism, especially when it originated with political representatives and public intellectuals in Central and Eastern Europe. This criticism, although often quite guarded and moderate in tone, was very obvious with respect to the perceived protectionist tendencies of the EU on the negotiation of the Europe Agreements. Despite the prominence of EU material interests (and the activities and influence of important interest groups), the criticism did have an impact on policy and led to a speedier resolution of issues in favour of CEE interests. Continued reference to EU special responsibility to CEE made this possible. Schimmelfennig's emphasis on 'rhetorical argument' and CEE officials 'exposing inconsistencies' in EU policy provides striking evidence for such a supposition with these representatives using emotive language in phrases such as 'economic Yalta' and 'a new economic Iron Curtain'.[47] Later, in deploring the various delays imposed on the enlargement process, and in seeking to bring the negotiations to a successful conclusion, CEE state representatives would consistently deploy the language of shared values, community, and normative resonance in an effort to move the process forward. Their success in exposing inconsistent EU behaviour could not have been achieved without reference to the shared values which underpinned the European integration process and the EU desire to uphold its own self-image and self-understanding.

Membership conditions

The EU self-understanding and value system was made manifest within the enlargement process in the membership conditions laid down before the candidate states. These conditions represented not just the 'rational' or functional basis for the incorporation of non-member states into the EU, but also a cogent representation of the EU's own self-identification. The core values of the EU are all cited in the membership criteria first enunciated at the Copenhagen summit in June 1993 and are worth recalling. They include the need for a functioning market economy governed by rules of credible legal enforcement, open and transparent representative democratic institutions and respect for minorities and fundamental human rights.[48]

These membership conditions had only evolved slowly since the inception of the European Communities in the 1950s. The basic condition for membership stipulated in Article 237 of the Rome Treaty – European identity ('any European state may apply') – was always very ambiguous. How was 'European' to be defined? Was this a geographic-territorial definition? Or a political definition? During the Cold War, eligibility was not a troubling issue, as membership for the Warsaw Pact states, which happened also to be European, was not on the cards. But Sjursen and Smith point out that even in the 1970s the adherence to democratic norms as a basis for Community membership represented an important signal that the EEC was not just an economic integration bloc or free trade zone: deeper values pervaded the Community and bound member states together. This interpretation is reinforced if one bears in mind that Portugal and Spain asked to open negotiations in the early 1960s but their candidatures were not at that time taken seriously.

It would only be a return to the democratic fold that would render these states eligible for membership.[49] So despite the fact that no substantive membership criteria existed outside of the vague Article 237, it was clear that a commitment to democratic institutions and fundamental freedoms constituted an implicit basis for consideration of a membership request.

If such an informal values-based criterion governed Community attitudes to membership requests then it is clear that the development of more explicit and formal conditions followed from and in response to both the internal deepening of the Community and changes in external conditions. Helen Wallace, for example, demonstrates that the EU value-set (and thus the template by which membership requests would be judged) was developed only very slowly over the years. The Treaty of Rome (Article 237), as we have seen, had simply noted that 'any European state' could apply for EU membership. The 1987 Joint Declaration by the Council, the Commission, and the European Parliament on fundamental rights was, in Wallace's view, a 'rather feeble attempt' at a rhetorical statement of shared democratic values. Not until the Treaty on European Union in 1993 (Article F) did the member states note that their Union was founded on the principles of democracy and their 'respect for fundamental rights'.[50]

In the aftermath of the June 1993 Copenhagen summit more general statements concerning membership conditions were forthcoming. The Amsterdam Treaty formalized the political conditions of membership and in effect, codified the Copenhagen criteria. Article 6 of the Amsterdam Treaty set out the basic membership conditions. It stated: 'The Union is founded on the principles of liberty, democracy, respect for human rights and fundamental freedoms, and the rule of law.' Further, 'any European state that respects these principles may apply to become a member of the Union' (Article 49). It is these two treaty articles that provided the legal basis for the conduct of the negotiations on eastern enlargement. And if, as some scholars argued, Article 6 still remained somewhat vague and ambiguous, it at least provided the basis and justification for the Commission's close monitoring of reform of political institutions, public administration, judicial systems and rights legislation in Central and Eastern Europe.

Technically the treaty articles would seem to rule out even the acceptance of an *application* from states deemed in violation of such principles. Article 7, in setting out a sanctions regime to be deployed against member states which fail to uphold the value-set outlined in Article 6, seems just as salient, however, in setting out a constitutional instrument for the protection of those values, not just with respect to the applicant states but also to the existing members of the Union. The haphazard way in which the Union sought to impose sanctions on Austria after the formation of a coalition including the far-right Freedom Party in early 2000 perhaps represented a poor initial effort (poorly executed at least) in the defence of those principles. Its failure, however, should not detract from the fact that the reaction of the member states of the EU to the Haider phenomenon demonstrated clearly the universal attachment to those principles set down in Article 6 within the Union.

In insisting on various forms of conditionality, but especially binding conditionality with respect to the political criteria laid down at Copenhagen, the EU acted robustly to uphold its own value system. For example, when framing the Europe Agreements, the Commission included an explicit suspension clause that effectively hardened political conditionality.[51] As the enlargement process deepened the framework of political conditionality made more and more demands on the candidate states. Even though the use of political conditionality has been much criticized,[52] one cannot but argue that the strict application of the principle was reflective of a deep attachment within the EU to the democratic process.

The substance of EU enlargement policy also stipulated, and, over time, increased, the salience of the EU's role in the protection of human rights and democracy. This should be understood in the context of the wider attachment to democracy promotion within the EU, as Tanja Börzel and Thomas Risse point out. Democracy promotion has become a centrepiece of EU foreign policy activity and is backed up by considerable financial resources. Eastern enlargement, however, stands out as by far the most ambitious effort by the EU to promote democracy, human rights and the rule of law in third countries.[53] The remarkable success of democratization in much (but far from all) of Europe in the post-1989 period is undoubtedly linked to the demands of the enlargement process and the values of the integration project.[54]

Sedelmeier identifies two specific aspects of EU enlargement policy, which, in highlighting the importance of human rights norms, underpin the importance of such to the EU value-set and self-understanding.[55] The first was the consistent assertion of the promotion and protection of democratic norms as a core rationale for enlargement and the explicit establishment of respect for democracy and human rights as a precondition for membership. The European Parliament, in particular, consistently sought to expose inconsistencies in applicant state behaviour and inadequate adaptation to democratic norms and practices. The Commission's annual reports on applicant state progress also placed compliance with democracy norms at the top of its agenda. As Marc Maresceau put it, the publication of progress reports created 'an atmosphere of permanent follow-up and contributed considerably to the enhancement in the candidate countries of an awareness that the necessary measures must be taken'.[56] Measuring the extent of EU success in this regard is undoubtedly difficult. But there exists some evidence that local political élites in Central and Eastern Europe assessed seriously the opportunity-cost of non-compliance with EU norms and in many cases shifted their positions substantially on such issues as ethnic minority rights and constitutional protections to make their parties and political programmes accord with the new 'pro-EU space' in their domestic political systems.[57]

EU enlargement policy practice also spelled out more explicitly as time went on the principles that underpin membership.[58] Certain aspects of EU policy were aimed at directly promoting democracy and human rights, such as the PHARE Democracy Programme. And even if the EU privileged capacity-building within CEE public sectors more than democracy promotion, over time the latter strengthened local civil society groups, helped change the preferences of domestic political élites, and undermined the claims to legitimacy of populist nationalist regimes. As importantly, through articulating the promotion of human rights and democracy as a distinct and central rationale for its eastern enlargement policy, EU policy-makers affirmed a self-image of the EU as progressive, internationalist and normative.[59]

The seriousness attached to the democracy norm was underlined by the EU's refusal to open membership negotiations with Slovakia in 1997 on the basis of concerns over the Mečiar government's emasculation of political institutions and independent media in that country. And although, as Vachudova points out, the EU démarches did not succeed in compelling the Mečiar government to end its chauvinist practices and concentration of political power, they did help tone down the anti-democratic excesses.[60] Even if the EU did not take the 'nuclear option' of suspending Slovakia's Europe Agreement the Commission's criticisms made it clear that membership of the EU was certainly at risk. Negotiations had to wait until Mečiar's administration was replaced with a new administration committed to transparent democratic norms. In this situation therefore the weapon of political conditionality was 'entirely credible'.[61] One prominent Slovak, Pavol Demes, of the German Marshall Fund in Bratislava, attested: 'we would not have got rid of Mečiar, were it not for the vision of the EU'.[62]

Later the EU was much more explicit in spelling out its expectations and demands regarding reform of democratic institutions in Bulgaria and Romania and in the Balkans.[63] Concerns about human rights infringements arose regularly in EU–Turkish relations and constituted a significant barrier to progress even if in its 2004 Report, the Commission judged that Turkey did fulfil the political criteria for membership.[64] Even after the EU agreed to open negotiations with Turkey it very publicly criticized the country on a range of issues, including the heavy-handed police response to an International Women's Day march in early 2005. Perhaps the most dramatic demonstration of EU attachment to democratic norms, however, was the decision not to proceed to the opening of membership talks with Croatia. Widely expected to open negotiations for membership in March 2005, Croatia's failure to arrest General Ante Gotovina, indicted by the International Criminal Court for former Yugoslavia (ICTY) for alleged war crimes, was taken by the EU to represent so serious an instance of non-compliance as to warrant at least the temporary postponement of negotiations.[65] This decision spelled out clearly for Croat élites the potential cost of non-compliance and at the same time represented the clearest statement of EU principles.

As Wallace suggests the recent articulation within the Union of core principles of democracy and the sketching of key elements of a European Citizenship programme assert the importance of the 'affiliational' dimension of European integration. This is the context around which the normative dimension of eastern enlargement developed. This does not mean that prior to the 1990s there was not a deep attachment to these values. Rather they had a 'taken for granted quality' about them. The prospect of CEE enlargement meant rethinking and refashioning the EU's own self-understanding. The enlargement process in this sense has thus helped clarify what the EU represents – a peaceable international community dedicated to preserving peace within its borders and projecting its value system on to the world outside.[66]

Enlargement as moral imperative

The argument about EU values and self-understanding is reinforced if one considers that there was also a powerful moral argument for enlargement deployed in both the candidate countries in Central and Eastern Europe and by their supporters within the European Union. The evidence suggests that the 'moral imperative' argument had a very significant impact and this partly explains why eastern enlargement was eventually realized in 2004. From a constructivist perspective, there is an interesting link between the construction and presentation of the moral obligation on the EU side, the strategic use of moral arguments by the candidate countries and the way in which both of these phenomena fed into other normative elements of the integration process such as the EU self-understanding.

In the first instance the moral argument surfaced in the ideas and discourse of important EU actors, as previous chapters demonstrated. It is clear that many within the EU (individual citizens, individual policy-makers, governments) felt a strong sense of moral obligation toward the former Communist states, believing that the West's freedom and prosperity was somehow paid for by Eastern Europe's subjugation during the Cold War.[67] The 1989 revolutions had been successfully realized because of the brave self-sacrifice of many thousands of individuals, who had, in many instances, cited West European norms as their yardsticks for reform. After the fall of the Berlin Wall commitments entered into had to be honoured with a firm perspective on membership for those countries which desired it. Thus from an early stage in the new EU–CEE relations a moral discourse was developed and deployed by advocates of enlargement. Sometimes this discourse was free-standing and designed to appeal solely to the moral conscience of the target audience. More usually it was deployed in combination with economic and utilitarian arguments for enlargement.

Whatever the context in which the moral argument was presented the content can be unpacked quite easily. As chapter 5 demonstrated, foremost among those making the moral argument were senior German politicians and policy-makers. Helmut Kohl, Gerhard Schröder and Joschka Fischer appealed, within their own borders, to the German sense of shame at the misdeeds of Nazism and the need to offer EU membership as the principle form of political reparation for such. Outside Germany, they stressed the shared values which underpinned the European integration process and acceptance of CEE accession as a collective affirmation of those values. And although German policy-makers, no less than other EU actors, sought to protect German prerogatives to the fullest extent possible, they were also much more willing to accommodate the preferences of the CEE states, as a demonstration of their moral commitment to enlargement.

The guiding force that was the sense of moral obligation was not confined to German élites however. In fact it permeated the discourse and policies of government representatives throughout the European Union. For some, eastern enlargement was necessary to demonstrate solidarity with the states that, in historical terms, were demonstrably part of the shared European historical experience and had involuntarily been shut out of the integration process in the 1950s. That process had yielded enormous benefits to the participating states and should not now be denied the CEE states. Another variant of this argument harked back to the freedom fighters who opposed both Nazism and Communism during the Second World War and now steadfastly proclaimed attachment to Western models of government and institutional practice. Others highlighted the potential hypocrisy of the EU position, in having consistently supported the reform efforts of the Warsaw Pact states, and then seemingly failing to reach out adequately to anchor their transition to EU norms and practices.

The vast disparity in economic wealth between insiders and outsiders also contributed to the moral framing of enlargement. From the outset the integration process had privileged the narrowing of regional gaps in income and general prosperity. Whilst relatively unimportant in the relatively homogeneous EEC of six states, previous enlargements had added a much poorer set of countries to the Union. In time this produced a new consensus on social and economic cohesion and the imperative of reducing economic disparities between the richest and the poorest regions. Indeed the EU budget became as focused on providing subvention to its poorest regions as on its traditional concentration of CAP support. The obvious need for infrastructural support and human capacity-building in CEE also stood out. Thus the dual combination of existing practice within the EU and the manifest wealth gap with the candidate countries provided a dual moral argument to candidate states and it is also one that found significant support within the EU.

Acknowledgement of this discourse and the impact it had on the process of enlargement should not blind one to the fact that progress was, from the perspective of the applicant states, painfully slow. That would suggest that the moral dimension should not be over-emphasized. After all if it were the only logic which mattered the CEE accessions would have taken place much earlier than they did. The moral argument to some extent competed in policy-makers' cognitive frames with others such as utility arguments and security arguments. The difficult thing is gauging exactly when and how the force of the moral arguments really mattered. The constructivist answer is that viewed as one important component of the normative understanding of eastern enlargement, and one which also fed off and into the EU's own self-understanding, the moral argument was a convincing one. At the very least it made it difficult to refuse an application for membership, or justify continued obstruction of accession, even if other logics permeated the actual negotiations for accession.

Historical precedent and path dependency

If the process of eastern enlargement was driven to some extent by the logic of appropriateness inherent in moral arguments then such a logic also found expression in the EU's own experience of enlargement. On the one hand a form of institutional path dependency could be traced through the evolution of EU handling of applications for membership and subsequent negotiations for accession. On the other hand individual member states also conceptualized enlargement and their own preferences through the lenses of their own specific experiences of past enlargements. Constructivist approaches, borrowing from sociologically-driven historical-institutionalist theories, alert us to the importance of both phenomena within the eastern enlargement process.

In the first place eastern enlargement can be viewed as governed by specific forms of institutional path dependency. Paul Pierson has emphasized the ways in which initial institutional or policy decisions – even sub-optimal ones – can become self-reinforcing over time.[68] Elsewhere, Emanuel Adler and Michael Barnett write that 'Path dependent patterns are characterized by self-reinforcing positive feedback'.[69] These can arise from different combinations of deliberate advocacy and unintended consequences and lead to 'gaps' in member state control.[70] These initial choices encourage the emergence of elaborate social and economic networks, greatly increasing the transaction costs of change and therefore inhibiting exit from the current policy path. Collective commitments can be subsequently adduced from even modest statements of intent. Thus the path dependent analysis of enlargement politics suggests that outcomes depend not only on the current environment and the important policy and institutional choices at issue in a given negotiation. The 'shadow of the past', in historical-institutional-speak, also looms large in collective decision-making.

Enlargement negotiations take place in the shadow of institutional deals from past enlargement rounds which give shape and form to the negotiation agenda. Everything from the structure of association agreements to programmes of capacity-building and the formal institutional structuring of negotiations draws to some extent from past experience. And while institutional innovation is not uncommon, the history of enlargement does indeed demonstrate important evidence for path dependent outcomes. Perhaps the most important path dependent phenomenon is that once negotiations have been opened with a candidate state they have always been brought to a successful conclusion and accession usually followed.[71] This feature of the EU's enlargement history encouraged many to oppose the opening of negotiations with Turkey in 2004, aware that to proceed to the opening of negotiations would almost certainly invite substantive negotiations in the medium term. When the EU eventually agreed to the opening of negotiations with Turkey it included a crucial caveat that allowed for a suspension of negotiations should Turkey not make substantial progress in its reform process.[72]

Other variants of normative path dependency can be sourced to the eastern enlargement process itself. Each makes the case for a gradual 'lock-in' of the EU to the process and each is based on different suppositions. For one thing there was the issue of just how many applications for membership would be submitted. In the early 1990s the 'official queue' consisted of only about 8 or 10 states in total.[73] By 2005 in the aftermath of the accession of 10 new states to the Union, there were still at least another 10 states which had either negotiated successfully (Bulgaria, Romania), or opened negotiations (Turkey), or were actively pursuing membership (Croatia, Bosnia-Herzegovina, FYR Macedonia, Serbia and Montenegro, Albania, Georgia, Ukraine). Clearly one of the unintended consequences of the original decision to open up membership to Central and Eastern Europe was the triggering of a much larger number of applications from a much wider geographical area. The development of a meritocratic and rational process for judging applications within the EU, which was to a large extent culturally neutral, made it difficult to determine where the process might end. The pluralistic security community centred on the EU was and remains a regional magnet for states aspiring to modernize, democratize and Europeanize their countries.

Another variant of path dependency evident within the enlargement process related to the credibility of EU commitments and efforts to enforce those by outsiders. Sjursen, for example, makes the case for the importance of publicity and the ability to 'shame' any one party during the enlargement process, for not living up to expectations and commitments. She invokes Elster's 'civilising force of hypocrisy' to demonstrate the importance of this. Elster had argued that 'the effect of an audience is to replace the language of interest by the language of reason ... the presence of a public makes it especially difficult to appear motivated merely by self-interest ... publicity does not eliminate base motives, but forces or induces speakers to hide them'.[74] Schimmelfennig's 'rhetorical entrapment' should be similarly understood.[75] When does rhetorical support turn into rhetorical entrapment? At what point do considerations of credibility and legitimacy come into play on the EU side? How did the applicants seek to gain leverage by manipulating the supportive rhetoric of EU policy representatives? In this respect the importance of the rhetorical commitments made in the course of the EU enlargement process stand out. The very acknowledgement that there existed a right to accession, allied to promises of membership from the EU (even if insincerely meant), created a framework where over time the EU became 'locked in' to an accession process that for short-term economic and political reasons might prove difficult. The argument is premised on the supposition that one cannot go on making promises and statements of support without compromising one's credibility if there is a failure to deliver on those commitments.

On the CEE side, the case can also be made for another type of path dependency specific to this enlargement process. The candidate states were progressively locked into a set of commitments from the Copenhagen summit onwards. Some of these had been passed down from previous enlargement rounds, some derived from developments in the integration process. Others still were introduced in response to specific problems 'on the ground' in the applicant states. As Sedelmeier and Wallace suggest, the scope for accommodating the preferences of the CEE states was predetermined by existing arrangements among and for the incumbent members of the EU.[76] But it also evolved in the specific context of the enlargement process itself and the challenges it generated. Individual candidate states struggled to achieve 'wiggle room' in the accession negotiations in particular, as more and more parts of the policy process demonstrated path dependent features.

Eastern enlargement also highlighted another form of path dependent structural feature. That was the experience of the EU's non-original members who themselves had experienced being outside the club, negotiated with the EU, and succeeded in attaining membership. Being an alumnus of this particular club made it exceptionally difficult to act toward the CEE applicant states in anything other than a supportive fashion. In this respect the accessions in the 1980s of the

Mediterranean states set an especially important historic precedent. The Southern accessions were thus to some extent negotiating cards in the arsenal of the applicant states. After all Greece, Spain and Portugal had all been in a similar position in the 1970s. Just emerging from years of authoritarian rule they sought membership in the West European club as a means of buttressing their emerging democracies. Then they themselves invoked arguments related to rights and the return to the European fold. The precedent meant that they could hardly deny the same to other returning states. CEE representatives were not slow to remind the EU of this. Already in 1990, Hungarian Foreign Minister Kodolonyi argued that the Iberian enlargement 'had been the result of a political settlement' (the European Council's decision to over-ride the Commission's ruling on Greece) and that 'the Community would do the right thing now to take a similar decision'.[77]

The arguments related to historical precedent were even more cogent when highlighting how membership of the EU had 'worked' for those states that had acceded in previous enlargement rounds. Perhaps the outstanding example here was the Republic of Ireland which had benefited enormously from EU membership and had catapulted itself up the EU wealth table as a consequence. Central and East European political representatives consistently held up Ireland as a shining example of the transformative potential offered by membership. For Ireland that made it all the more difficult to invoke its material interests at crucial stages of the eastern enlargement negotiations. And although lagging behind Ireland in terms of socioeconomic advance, Greece, Portugal and Spain had also manifestly transformed their countries through membership of the EU, which made it all the more difficult for them to block or obstruct CEE accession. Spain in particular had experienced significant economic growth in the decade prior to 2004, to some extent underpinned by the inflow of structural and cohesion funding from the EU, making it extremely difficult for Spanish officials to make a simple 'rational' or interest-based objection to CEE accession. When combined with the other outlined forms of path dependency this structural feature of the enlargement process exerted an important degree of influence on outcomes.

Conclusions

Well before eastern enlargement even came onto the EU's agenda there existed what might be called a customary enlargement practice within the EU, which had developed through previous enlargement rounds with only a minimum legal guide on how to conduct an enlargement process provided by the treaties. Thus the eastern enlargement developed out of an existing set of norms and practices but itself developed in a way which both helped better define existing practice and created a new more concrete normative template for future enlargement rounds. In developing a normative conceptualization of the eastern enlargement process this chapter introduced constructivist explanations of international politics and particularly those which focus on the normative reach and influence of international organizations. The constructivist worldview, although itself increasingly variegated, highlights the importance of both material and human/social dimensions of the European integration process and is especially useful in identifying the complex relationship between state identities and interests at EU level. Eastern enlargement, no less than the wider integration process, saw member states continually seeking to clarify their preferences, and achieve an acceptable fit between the claims made for the normative importance of enlargement against the need to protect vital national interests. The chapter argued that although interests mattered in the determination of outcomes, the enlargement process was governed by a more fundamental norm-set which prevailed over interest-based cost–benefit calculation and other conceptualizations of expansion. The norms that ultimately proved most important to the realization of eastern enlargement were those of representative democracy, fundamental freedoms and minority rights – precisely those norms which emanated from the EU self-understanding as a pluralistic security community and a community of values in the international political system. The primacy of these democracy norms was such that the EU was not prepared to compromise with the candidate states on their implementation in the way that it was prepared to overlook the deficiencies in economic preparedness or in other areas. The legitimacy of the EU itself increasingly turned on its identification (and self-identification) as a transnational organization committed to the community-building and security-enhancing norms which both flowed from and guided its efforts to democratize the wider Europe. And although the eastern enlargement process, and EU motivations for enlargement, can only be understood as a complex combination of geopolitical, economic and normative reasoning, it is clear that the normative desire to ensure a peaceful, law-governed, democratic wider Europe consistently triumphed over narrower and more instrumentalist logics within the enlargement process and ultimately facilitated the 2004 accessions.

11 Conclusions

The accessions to the EU of the Central and East European states on 1 May 2004 brought to a close a series of processes that had been instituted by the democratic revolutions of 1989. While some of these developments (such as NATO enlargement) took place outside the EU, most of them converged around structures put in place by Brussels: these structures would in time become the main vehicles for 'Europeanizing' the new democracies. And while transitologists studied the different forms that transition took on in CEE, it became increasingly difficult to disentangle each and every mode of transition from the institutional structures developed under the eastern enlargement process. From the outset the new democracies represented their endeavours as designed to deliver their 'return to Europe', a rhetorical construction loaded with historical and normative symbolism. The 'return' was finally secured on 1 May 2004 but only after an extended period of protracted negotiations, characterized by long periods of uncertainty and no little tension on both sides.

Eastern enlargement, although closely modelled on the EU's previous enlargements, especially the southern (Mediterranean) enlargement round of the 1980s, was also manifestly different in its fundamental constituent elements. This became increasingly clear as time went on. Never before had the EU engaged so closely and negotiated with so many countries simultaneously. Never before had the negotiations extended for so long. Never before had the EU introduced such a large range of extra measures to be implemented by the candidate states in advance of accession. Undoubtedly also eastern enlargement was disruptive for the EU, forcing it to recalibrate both major policies and decision-making rules in a way which had not occurred in any previous enlargement round. The sheer scale of the process dwarfed anything previously attempted by the EU – enlargement added 100 million new EU citizens from ten extremely diverse countries but added only just over 5 per cent to EU GDP. The scale of the challenge of economic integration was particularly visible in the stark differences in wealth between old and new member states. Average GDP per head in the ten new members (including Cyprus and Malta) was only 46 per cent of the EU average. Only one newcomer – Slovenia – was as wealthy as the poorest EU15 state – Greece. The poorest new country – Latvia – had a GDP per head of only 36 per cent of the EU average.[1]

Accession took place against a backdrop of distinct unease about the direction of the EU in many member states and part of that unease was rooted in a fear of the consequences of eastern enlargement (and potential future enlargements). Sclerotic economic growth in many of the old member states and a failure to tackle structural domestic economic problems meant that eastern enlargement was more often than not presented as another economic problem inflicted on the old EU. The much higher rates of growth and evident embrace of the market left the new member states vulnerable to the charge that they represented an Anglo-Saxon fifth column within the enlarged Union, ready to tear apart German wage-bargaining mechanisms or undermine the role of the state in social protection in France. EU politicians for the most part had not bothered to explain the enlargement process and the important benefits it offered to their citizens, either before 1 May 2004 or after.[2] Thus eastern enlargement became something of a convenient foil for politicians in France and Germany who refused to embrace a more laissez faire approach to economic organization. The communication gap was not significant in the ratification process as that was exclusively the privilege of executives and parliaments within the old EU, but one year after enlargement its impact had become a serious issue in the domestic politics of many member states, not least in France and the Netherlands where it was prominent in the Constitutional treaty referendum campaigns.[3] Indeed, for some enlargement had resulted in a sort of theft – 'they are taking our jobs' (or they will in the future), 'they are living off our welfare systems', 'stealing from our limited resource pool'. It did not help that unemployment levels had increased across the board in Europe in the intervening year. On 1 May 2004 German unemployment stood at 9.3 per cent, in France 9.4 per cent. One year later it was 11.1 per cent in Germany and 10.2 per cent in France. It was little wonder then that the defeat of the Constitutional Treaty referendum in France was attributed in some part to French unease with the enlarged EU. Accusations of 'social dumping' abounded and the French political classes choose to minimize enlargement as an issue rather than highlighting its benefits for the European Union.

The public misunderstanding of eastern enlargement and its impact on the EU was at odds with the early evidence of its effects – all indications point in fact to a smooth transition by both old and new member states. Despite the fact that trade integration was almost complete by the time of accession, exports and imports between the EU and CEE grew at double digit rates in 2004, spurred by the removal of remaining trade barriers.[4] Though investments in manufacturing made headlines it was clear that agriculture in the new member states did at least as well. The first tranches of EU farm aid were distributed with fewer bureaucratic tangles than expected, especially in Poland, where 1.4 million farmers successfully applied for direct payments. The European Commission estimated that farmers' incomes in CEE had risen 50 per cent across the board.[5] Exports of food from Poland and the Czech Republic roughly doubled from 2003 to 2004, while Slovakia's food exports trebled.[6] The new member states saw economic growth increase 5 per cent in 2004 after an increase of 3.7 per cent in 2003. And although FDI into Central and Eastern Europe increased exponentially this was not at the expense of the old member states. The greater profitability of enterprises operating in the new member states helped EU companies toward better results and probably saved jobs in their home countries. De-localization of jobs remained more a myth than reality in the old member states. Neither was there anything like the expected wave of migration, even to the UK, Ireland, and Sweden, whose labour markets were open to citizens of the new member states. But if enlargement had indeed proved a positive economic project for the EU (with more discernible benefits down the line) citizens in the old member states were either not aware of it or did not believe the evidence.

One of the great paradoxes of the European integration process which eastern enlargement magnified was that of the different value attached to membership by citizens of 'insider' states and those of 'outsider' states. While those outside desperately want to get in, those inside increasingly express frustration with 'Europe' and indeed in many states a desire to exit the process. Whilst those outside readily proclaim their allegiance to the EU and demonstrate a willingness to accept the demanding measures of implementation implicit in the process, insider citizens feel increasingly remote from Brussels and in many jurisdictions blame the EU for everything from the imposition of allegedly neoliberal economic policies which threaten the social fabric, to the standard charge of 'Brussels Bureaucrats' seeking to create a vast nanny-state by imposing regulation on every conceivable variant of social market activity. Swedish prime minister Göran Persson summed up this paradox in 2001 during the Swedish Presidency of the EU when he attested that while so many countries wanted nothing else but to get in, all the Swedes wanted was to get out. Perhaps the luxury of being able to gripe is one reserved for members of the club – the cynicism of the secure – but nevertheless it seems strange that such disaffection did not spill over into public opinion in the candidate states. The CEE states saw membership as the only viable means of securing their 'return to Europe', of embedding themselves in the successful structures of the European integration process.

In some ways enlargement further added to the democratic deficit which the EU is alleged to suffer from, and perhaps even created new such deficits. After all the process was undertaken by both CEE and Western élites without any significant input from their societies. Enlargement was driven forward largely by the bureaucratic expertise of the Commission and most issues remained removed from any form of public deliberation. The negotiations of 1998–2002 were classic Euroelite talks. CEE publics only got a say after the completion of negotiations with no chance to influence the content of the accession treaties. EU publics did not even get a vote, despite opinion polls showing great concern about the impact of enlargement. And while this may not have mattered too much to the course of negotiations the evidence cited above about perceptions in the old member states suggests a large gap between the public and their representatives. At the very least it will make further enlargement more difficult to negotiate than previously.

Some saw enlargement as a natural consequence of the geopolitical changes wrought by the 1989 revolutions and the collapse of the Soviet Union. As such it represented the reunification of the continent. This argument is often accompanied by claims that enlargement was facilitated primarily by cultural connectedness, that 'Europe' was and remains an indivisible civilizational and religio-cultural entity simply waiting for circumstances to allow it to be made whole through political unification. Such a view entirely misreads the eastern enlargement process and indeed the fundamental nature of the European integration process. Cultural affiliation undoubtedly helped the process of reconstituting political relations among the European states. But this view underestimates the degree to which the contemporary integration process is neutral as to culture, religion and history. Enlargement proceeded on the basis of agreed norms and shared values regarding state behaviour, interstate reciprocity and legal interdiction. The process was entirely secular and rule-governed. Just as private morality has largely ceased to count as a factor in the determination of attitudes to individual politicians across Europe, so cultural essentialism (or reductionism) played no part in the framework of enlargement decision-making.

In the aftermath of the election of Cardinal Joseph Ratzinger to the Papacy in April 2005 (coinciding, incidentally, almost exactly with the first anniversary of the eastern enlargement of the EU), there were some commentators who sought to expressly link the two events. The German cardinal succeeded the Polish Pope. Europe's twentieth-century history was thus manifest in the succession – the Polish tragedy, the horrors of Nazi empire, Europe's cataclysmic wars. Just as eastern enlargement helped heal the continent's wounds Ratzinger's election symbolized Germany's rehabilitation in international politics and the wider process of interstate reconciliation.[7]

At an abstract level this was a consoling thought. But it concealed an important truth, which underlined the extraordinary difference between the two events. Ratzinger's worldview was that of the cultural essentialist. This was most apparent in his view that Turkey should not be admitted to the European Union because 'Europe is a cultural continent, not a geographic one'.[8] For good measure he stressed that Europe's roots were Christian and it was these roots that gave legitimacy to current political structures. Eastern enlargement was undertaken on a premise which was exactly opposite to that put forward by Ratzinger – that the EU was not an exclusive club, much less a defined civilizational or religious entity. In fact eastern enlargement highlighted the degree to which the EU marginalized culture and religion as criteria for membership. The Copenhagen criteria were and remain genuinely secular in their scope, privileging technocratic capacity, representative government and market capitalism. EU membership is no different for Orthodox Greece than for Catholic Poland, nor a secular France which includes a growing Muslim population.

Why norms mattered

While this book has sought to describe the eastern enlargement process, its important structural features, and the way in which negotiations unfolded, its more important contribution lies in its institutional and conceptual analysis. The arguments presented centre on three important and interrelated phenomena, which, it is claimed, can only be properly understood by embracing constructivist and ideational interpretations of the European integration process. The first argues that the EU should be understood as a genuine pluralistic security community and that eastern enlargement represented an extension of that community, and especially its value system, to the new democracies of Central and Eastern Europe. The second argument concerns norms and their centrality to the enlargement process. A core set of norms developed in and around the European integration process and influenced the EU's enlargement policy in a decisive way. Finally, the institutional politics of the eastern enlargement, although intricate and multifaceted, reveal a complex division of responsibilities between the EU's three leading institutions – the Council, Commission, and Parliament. In particular the European Commission played the decisive role in shaping and guiding the enlargement process to a conclusion.

We can summarize each of the component parts of each of these three interlinked arguments. First, eastern enlargement constituted an extension of the EU-centred security community in Europe. The book argued for an emerging Kantian environment in the interstate and supranational politics of pan-Europe, characterized by deep and still developing economic interdependence and a high level of cooperation between states. The security community centred on the EU acted as a magnet for outside states and, in the aftermath of the Cold War, represented a formidable guarantor of 'dependable expectations of peaceful change'. In effect the eastern enlargement process became the main instrument by which the EU sought to export its constitutive order to Central and Eastern Europe and beyond. Thus the EU expanded the framework under which lasting peace and reconciliation was achieved in Western Europe after 1945 to the eastern part of the continent which had been cut off from those developments involuntarily for the duration of the Cold War. The enlargement policies adopted by the member states were characterized not just by the egoistic pursuit of national interests but a real endogenization of the European interest also, and this greatly facilitated agreement on enlargement. Member states did not refrain from pushing their own preferences but they also demonstrated remarkable attachment to the community-building and security-enhancing potential of the eastern enlargement process. Although the early stages of the process seemed suggestive of ambiguity (if not recalcitrance) on the part of the EU (protectionism, delaying tactics, unwillingness to consider real and substantive institutional and policy reforms), it is also clear that the EU might have opted for some other form of institutional and political relations with Central and Eastern Europe such as associate membership, privileged partnerships or purely economic links. That it did not demonstrates the profound attachment to the Deutschian model of community. The wider Europe was not just a space to exploit market potential but a genuine community centred on a set of core values and norms.

The second argument made in this book is that, consistent with constructivist thinking about the European integration project, the eastern enlargement process was dominated by a set of normative logics. Chapters 8, 9 and 10 examined EU motivations for enlargement from the perspectives of geopolitics, economics, and norms. The process demonstrated a complex mix of all three motivations on the EU's part, and the mix varied from member state to member state, as did the degree of enthusiasm for enlargement, and the degree of acceptance of CEE claims for membership. What is extraordinary is that the less enthusiastic or indeed outrightly obstructionist states among the EU15 were persuaded to consent to an expansion which threatened their economic interests either directly or indirectly by changing the nature of the underlying bargains which characterized the integration process. Whether one argues that such consent was garnered through a process of social learning, rhetorical entrapment, unintended consequences or path-dependent institutional factors, one can manifestly single out member states such as France, Spain and Greece and ask why, in the face of specific integration preferences, they agreed to something which, on the surface, appeared inimical to their interests.

Andrew Moravcsik argues that member state consent was secured along the familiar lines of liberal intergovernmental bargaining. The prerogatives of Britain, France and Germany took precedence; smaller, less powerful member states were effectively bought off with the ring fencing of existing side payments and a modest recalibration of institutional arrangements. Preferences and power dominated the enlargement process as they had for long dominated most important parts of the integration process in Europe. This seems at best a partial explanation. It may account for French or Spanish acquiescence if their state representatives simply conceptualized eastern enlargement within a short timescale. It may well explain some recurrent features of the process. But it is much less convincing as a macro-explanation of outcomes.

The book argues that throughout the eastern enlargement process norms mattered as much as interests, and indeed that normative explanations of the eastern enlargement prove much more compelling than either geopolitical or economic-centred arguments. To argue that the actors within the enlargement process conformed mostly to logics of appropriateness is not to suggest that these very logics did not themselves change over time. Certainly the content and meaning of 'appropriate behaviour' was contested and challenged. These logics also adapted to, *inter alia*, the external environment, domestic political dynamics and the ongoing institutional politics of the EU. However, the most significant logics of appropriateness – in this case justice, legitimacy, reciprocity, shared values – remained more or less constant throughout and proved decisive to enlargement outcomes.

Within the enlargement process some norms mattered more than others. Clearly those of democracy, representative and transparent political institutions, fundamental freedoms, and minority rights were of much greater significance than others. This became more and more evident as the enlargement process progressed and the political criteria took on an importance outweighing economic or security criteria. These norms were of the highest importance to the EU's own constitutional order and to its own self-understanding. They represented its very *raison d'être* as a transnational community of values. In fact such norms were so deeply rooted that they could be considered part of the EU's DNA, and they were increasingly codified in its constitutional order. To fail to live up to the behavioural characteristics implied by these norms represented a negation not just of the membership aspirations of fellow European states but also of the very norms from which the EU itself drew its legitimacy. The EU simply could not exist if it refused membership to the CEE states, which shared the same value-set as the EU, and had made extraordinary efforts, carrying a high domestic social cost, to complete the necessary transition to accommodate the EU's *acquis communautaire*.

Although the process of transposition and implementation of EU norms was cumbersome, contested, and sometimes placed enormous strain on the emerging systems of public administration in Central and Eastern Europe, there was no fundamental norm conflict that may have caused serious difficulties. The process may have been asymmetrical but CEE élites, even if they complained of logistical difficulties and arbitrary imposition of new rules, rarely contested the norms being transferred in a serious way. Thus norm entrepreneurship and diffusion succeeded not just because of the asymmetry of positions between insider and outsider but also because of the resonance of the norms being transferred domestically in CEE. Even where they imposed significant economic and social costs in the short term there was usually acknowledgement that in the medium term they could only benefit the economy and society. Sedelmeier and Schimmelfennig suggest that the key factor in candidate state compliance was not norm resonance but the strict conditionality applied by the EU and the lack of room for manoeuvre of the candidates. Logics of rational action and consequentiality thus dominated the process of norms transfer and diffusion.[9] The evidence, however, suggests a much more complex picture. The sort of changes which accompanied these measures simply could not have been entertained without a consensus in the receiving countries that these measures simply had to be adopted, or that they could not be adopted if there was any fundamental conflict with local norms and societal practices.

Eastern enlargement was also governed on the EU side by a certain moral dimension, especially the notion of having a 'special responsibility' for Central and Eastern Europe and incorporating the region into EU structures. There is strong evidence that German enlargement policy in particular was driven by a sense of shame at Nazi tyranny in CEE and the need to atone for such. A similar view cast enlargement as potentially 'rescuing' CEE in the same way that Germany had been rescued by the European integration process and restored its reputation in the world. The normative explanation also provides a powerful explanation of the policies of those member states which themselves had acceded to the Union in the course of previous enlargements. In particular Greece, Ireland, Portugal and Spain, although they sought to protect their prerogatives within the integration process, were also deeply influenced by their own experiences of acceptance into the club, and general experience of membership, which because it was overwhelmingly positive, made it difficult to obstruct CEE aspirations. Although this might represent a negative cognitive assessment of enlargement on the part of these élites, it was nevertheless an analysis governed by normative logics of appropriateness.

The normative dimension to the process also manifested itself in some more subtle ways. Eastern enlargement helped define the criteria for membership and especially the norms and rules which govern enlargement processes. Previously the process was quite ad hoc and lacking in structure. The development of a specific set of practices and rules under the rubric of eastern enlargement led to much more concrete (and realistic) expectations of what was expected of aspiring members. And even if enlargement law remained, in the wake of eastern enlargement, more customary than treaty-defined, the practices, institutional rules and behavioural expectations surrounding the process had all evolved to such a point that substantive enlargement practice existed and was itself being utilized as further enlargement began to occupy the EU's attention.[10] Indeed, the same identifiable mix of political and institutional practices began to define the EU's efforts to integrate the Western Balkan states and, in a slightly different sense, relations with the Wider Europe.

Why institutions mattered

The third argument the book makes relates to the institutional management of eastern enlargement. This concerns the roles played by the three primary EU institutions – the Council, Commission and Parliament. The European Union constitutes one of the most densely institutionalized interstate negotiating arenas in international politics. In many ways the intra-EU institutional politics of enlargement were the most important feature of the process. It is therefore puzzling that this subject has been so neglected within studies of eastern enlargement. In fact only one article to date has sought to measure the influence of an institutional actor within the eastern enlargement process.[11] Analysis of the internal EU bargaining on enlargement reveals an enormous amount about such issues as how power is exercised within the EU, how the complex institutional design works in a charged negotiation setting, and the relative importance of specific elements of the enlargement process. It is also true that we know much more about how the eastern enlargement process was conceptualized, deliberated and negotiated than any previous enlargement of the EU.

Chapters 5, 6 and 7 sought to analyse the roles played within the eastern enlargement process by the Council, Commission and Parliament. The first striking observation to be made is the great disjunction between the sparse and highly ambiguous legal-formal hierarchy of responsibilities laid down in the EU treaties and what has evolved as customary enlargement practice. The sheer scale of the eastern enlargement round encouraged the development of a clear, if not entirely transparent, set of guidelines or enlargement rules, which although developed in a rather ad hoc manner nevertheless came to constitute *la règle du jeu* for all participants. In developing those rules each of the institutions sought to maximize its own input and influence and shape the process to the best degree possible. For different reasons, however, it was the Commission who emerged from the eastern enlargement process as the most important, or at least, the most effective, institutional actor.

Although the Council is identified in the treaties as the primary institutional actor in the process, its role is complex and hampered by a number of different structural problems, not least of which is the fragmentation of its power along territorial and sectoral lines. The differentiated sharing of responsibilities across the Council meant that enlargement decisions were discussed, deliberated, problematized and negotiated in a context where such territorial and sectoral divisions weakened the coherence of Council positions. In addition to confusing the candidate states as to desired modes of action this fragmentation of power ensured that the Commission enjoyed a much greater role in policy and in the negotiations than the treaty provisions suggested. The European Council, consisting of heads of state and government, plays an increasingly important role in EU politics and certainly provided much of the loosely framed political direction which guided eastern enlargement. Its role, however, was frequently undermined by one of the structural weaknesses of customary EU deliberation, the tendency to leave important policy-making decisions to the high-octane summit meetings which take place about four times per year. If on some occasions there was enough political will to provide real momentum, there were many other summit meetings that produced nothing but stasis and left the candidate states exasperated and the process itself in limbo. The European Council only really contributed effectively within the enlargement process when the Presidency galvanized opinion and effectively mediated between parties, enabling the problem of fragmentation within the Council to be overcome.

Chapter 5 suggested that the EU Presidency played a crucial institutional role in the eastern enlargement process. Presidencies were able to shape the enlargement agenda by using a range of instruments and deploying them effectively within the largely informal and arbitrary decision-making structures. While there were important differences in the way the member states approached enlargement during their Presidencies, it is clear that those of Sweden and Denmark in particular used innovative institutional measures and a not inconsiderable amount of political entrepreneurship in moderating between insiders and outsiders, and between member states, as the negotiations drew to a conclusion. The ability of the Presidency to exploit the very ambiguity of its own institutional functions was hugely important in creating political space where positions could be assessed, deliberated and moderated if necessary. The analysis suggests that it also more difficult for large states to put their interests aside in an enlargement negotiation. Small states were manifestly more successful in promoting bargains which accommodated candidate state preferences and collective outcomes over partisan attachments. That may be because of the realities of power asymmetry within the internal EU negotiation setting, or because small states often do not have the same range of issues or intensity of preferences in the negotiations. It is clear, however, that the Presidency plays an increasingly important role within enlargement decision-making.

The proactive and very effective role played by the European Commission within the eastern enlargement process also stands out in the institutional context. Whilst member states (through the European Council and the various parts of the Council machinery such as Coreper) may have seemed to be in command of the enlargement process, the conclusions presented in chapter 6 suggest that the Commission was consistently able to shape the policy agenda and structure negotiations in a way which proved decisive. Facing the challenge of managing relations with the new democracies the Commission was confronted with an environment it had never previously encountered. That led to many mistakes in the early part of the enlargement process where the Commission found itself as much student as teacher. But gradually a more sure-footed approach developed. The Commission's influence stemmed principally from two sources. The first was its formal power to initiate policy proposals, which helped it set and shape the enlargement policy agenda. And although as in the general integration framework it sought to incorporate and adjust for the specific concerns of member states, as frequently it found itself the sole policy innovator and thus the best placed EU actor within the process. As importantly it deployed a formidable range of informal agenda-shaping instruments as it sought to progress the enlargement process. Most importantly it consistently sought to frame eastern enlargement as a 'win–win' process for both candidates and the EU, and as community-enhancing and morally just. From the outset of the process member states were dependent on the Commission for leadership and policy advice. It was the Commission which took responsibility for managing the initial aid programmes for CEE, produced the Opinions on the ability of the candidate states to meet the criteria for membership, and oversaw the screening process, that is, the analysis of the transposition and implementation efforts by candidate states. Even in the latter stage of negotiations where the member states were in the ascendancy and the Presidency played a crucial role, the Commission continued to promote its enlargement strategy to both insiders and outsiders, with a mixture of cajolery, debate and persuasion. Crucially the Commission's socialization of the candidate states into EU norms and practices was achieved through its dual responsibility for capacity-building in the candidate states and ensuring compliance with EU norms and legal regulations. This dual role allowed it to exert an extraordinary degree of influence on both the candidate states and on the enlargement process itself as it developed. Indeed it is not going too far to suggest that the Commission emerges as the unsung hero of the process, guiding enlargement from behind the scenes and demonstrating a sureness of diplomatic touch which helped mediate between parties and bring the process to a successful conclusion.

Another part of the eastern enlargement's institutional story emerges in the activity of the European Parliament, for long, as Pat Cox attests, the Cinderella of the European integration process. It is clear that the Parliament is now a major institutional force within the EU, empowered as it has been by successive processes of constitutional revision. And although within the enlargement process the Parliament's role remains somewhat marginal, chapter 7 suggested that it managed to carve out for itself an influential role both with the candidate states and with the Council and Commission. While the Parliament's role remained confined to issuing its assent on completion of negotiations there is plenty of evidence that it managed also to exert informal power throughout the process, not least in shaping parliamentary practice as it developed in Central and Eastern Europe. The Parliament was insistent from the beginning of the process that the EU's core norms of democracy, legitimacy, justice, and fundamental freedoms be placed at the forefront of both EU policy and CEE transition. There were many occasions throughout the process when the Parliament asserted the importance of EU values. And while it did not refrain from challenging the candidate states to up their performance in given areas, it also remained throughout the most consistent advocate of enlargement and of the accommodation of candidate state preferences within the negotiation process. At the very least the Parliament's formal power to withhold assent guaranteed that other actors within the process desisted from taking actions which provoked it and potentially resulted in its refusal to sanction the accession of any one country or indeed all candidates.

Eastern enlargement emerged out of the dramatic changes in the European landscape after 1989. It consisted of a geopolitical dimension that revolved around the construction of a new security architecture in Europe. This developed in the shadow of NATO structures, which assumed much more importance for the management of Europe's new security relations. But the eastern enlargement of the EU also threw up important security issues and was partly governed by security logics, even if these were more 'soft' than 'hard'. Enlargement also grew out of a set of economic pressures or logics. The EU saw enlargement both as an instrument for enhancing market opportunities and entrenching the market economic system in Central and Eastern Europe and as a means of managing a range of economic externalities such as environmental problems, immigration and social dumping. In the final analysis, however, eastern enlargement of the EU is best understood as a norm-driven phenomenon, representing, as Vaclav Havel has suggested, an attempt to extend the European community of values to the eastward part of the continent. That such enlargement was only realized 15 years after the new dawn of 1989 says something about the shifting sands of European politics and the continued tension between national interests and collective values. It is difficult to speculate how eastern enlargement will change the EU. It is clear, however, that the process by which enlargement was realized will continue to fascinate scholars and political commentators long into the future. Such a profound change in the status quo, effected by such a diverse range of actors in a dense and complex institutional environment perhaps constitutes one of the most remarkable achievements of the European integration process to date.

Notes

Chapter 1

1   The EU was established by the 1992 Maastricht Treaty (Treaty on European Union), which came into force in November 1993. Preceding the EU was the European Economic Community (EEC), which was created by the 1957 Treaty of Rome. The European Coal and Steel Community (ECSC), established by the 1951 Paris Treaty, preceded the EEC itself. The term European Union (EU) will be used throughout this book. Where a distinction with the old EEC or ECSC is deemed necessary that will be made clear in the text.

2   I do not include the accession of the old East Germany (GDR), which formally acceded to the EU after its absorption into the Federal Republic of Germany (FRG) in 1991. This is considered a purely domestic matter.

3   William Wallace, 'Where Does Europe End? Dilemmas of Inclusion and Exclusion', in Jan Zielonka (ed.), *Europe Unbound: Enlarging and Reshaping the Boundaries of the European Union* (London: Routledge, 2002), p. 88.

4   See Hussein Kassim and Anand Menon, 'European Integration Since the 1990s: Member States and the European Commission', ARENA Working Papers, WP 6/04, Oslo: ARENA.

5   Fraser Cameron, 'Widening and Deepening', in Fraser Cameron (ed.), *The Future of Europe: Integration and Enlargement* (London; Routledge, 2004), p. 1.

6   'EU delays Croatian entry talks', *Guardian*, 17 March 2005; 'EU makes Croatia suffer for allowing war criminal to flee EU', *European Voice*, 10–16 March 2005; 'Postponed, but Croatia talks still on if Gotovina is found', *European Voice*, 17–23 March 2005.

7   Graham Avery, 'The Enlargement Negotiations', in Fraser Cameron (ed.), *The Future of Europe: Integration and Enlargement*, pp. 35–62; Graham Avery and Fraser Cameron, *Enlarging the European Union* (Sheffield: Sheffield Academic Press, 1998); Michael J. Baun, *A Wider Europe: The Process and Politics of European Union Enlargement* (Lanham, MD: Rowman & Littlefield, 2000); Peter Ludlow, *The Making of the New Europe: the European Councils on Brussels and Copenhagen 2002*, European Council Commentary, vol. 2/1 (Brussels: EuroComment, 2004).

8   Karen Hendersen (ed.), *Back to Europe: Central and Eastern Europe and the European Union* (London: University of London Press, 1999); Hillary Ingham and Mike Ingham (eds), *EU Expansion to the East: Prospects and Problems* (Cheltenham: Edward Elgar, 2002); Mike Mannin (ed.), *Pushing Back the Boundaries: The European Union and Central and Eastern Europe* (Manchester: Manchester University Press, 1999); Marc Maresceau, *Enlarging the European Union* (Harlow: Longman, 1997); Neil Nugent (ed.), *European Union Enlargement* (Basingstoke: Palgrave, 2004); Jan Zielonka (ed.), *Europe Unbound: Enlarging and Reshaping the Boundaries of the European Union* (London: Routledge, 2002).

9   Atila Ágh, 'Europeanization of Policy-Making in East Central Europe: the Hungarian Approach to EU Accession', *Journal of European Public Policy* 6/5, 1999: 839–54; Irene Brinar and Marjan Svetlicic, 'Enlargement of the European Union: the Case of Slovenia', *Journal of European Public Policy* 6/5, 1999: 802–21; Petr Bugge, 'Czech Perceptions of the Perspective of EU Membership: Havel versus Klaus', *EUI Working Papers*, RSC No. 2000/10; Jerzy Buzek, 'Poland's Future in a

United Europe', *ZEI Discussion Paper*, Centre for European Integration Studies, Bonn, 1998; Rachel Cichowski, 'Choosing Democracy: Citizen Attitudes and the Eastern Enlargement of the European Union', *EUI Working Papers*, RSC No. 2000/12; Martin Ferry, 'The EU and Recent Regional Reform in Poland', *Europe–Asia Studies* 55/7, 2003: 1097–116; Vello Pettai and Jan Zielonka (eds), *The Road to the European Union. vol. 2: Estonia, Latvia and Lithuania* (Manchester: Manchester University Press, 2003); Frederik Pflueger, 'Poland and the European Union', *Aussen Politik* 46/3, 1995: 228–38; Jacques Rupnik and Jan Zielonka (eds), *The Road to the European Union, vol. 1: The Czech and Slovak Republics* (Manchester: Manchester University Press, 2003); Renata Stawarska, 'EU Enlargement from the Polish Perspective', *Journal of European Public Policy* 6/5, 1999: 822–38; Aleks Szcerbiak and Paul Taggart (eds), *EU Enlargement and Referendums* (London: Routledge, 2005).

10   Stephen D. Collins, *German Policy-Making and Eastern Enlargement of the EU During the Kohl Era* (Manchester: Manchester University Press, 2002); John O'Brennan, 'Enlargement as a Factor in the Irish Referendum on the Nice Treaty', *Perceptions: Journal of International Affairs* VII/III, 2002: 78–94; Henning Tewes, 'Between Deepening and Widening: Role Conflict in Germany's Enlargement Policy', *West European Politics* 21/2, 1998: 117–33; Sonia Piedrafita Tremosa, 'The EU Eastern Enlargement: Policy Choices of the Spanish Government', *European Integration online Papers* 9/3, 2005, http://eiop.or.at/eiop/texte/2005-003a.htm; Jean Marc Trouille, 'France, Germany and the Eastwards Expansion of the EU: Towards a Common Ostpolitik', in Hillary Ingham and Mike Ingham (eds), *EU Expansion to the East: Prospects and Problems*, pp. 50–64.

11   Richard E. Baldwin, *Toward an Integrated Europe* (London: Centre for Economic Policy Reform, 1994); Richard E. Baldwin, Jean E. Francois and Ricardo Portes, 'The Costs and Benefits of Eastern Enlargement: the Impact on the EU and Central Europe', *Economic Policy* 24, 1997: 125–76; Niklas Baltas, 'The Economy of the European Union', in Neil Nugent (ed.), *European Union Enlargement*, pp. 146–57; Dorothee Bohle, 'The Ties That Bind: Neoliberal Restructuring and Transnational Actors in the Deepening and Widening of the European Union', Paper presented at the ECPR Joint Session Workshops 'Enlargement and European Governance', Turin, 22–27 March 2002; Fritz Breuss, 'Macroeconomic Effects of EU Enlargement for Old and New Members', *WIFO Working Papers* 143/2001 (Vienna: Austrian Institute of Economic Research (WIFO), 2001); Terry Caslin and Laszlo Czaban, 'Economic Transformation in CEE', in Mike Mannin (ed.), *Pushing Back the Boundaries: The European Union and Central and Eastern Europe*, pp. 70–98; ERT (European Roundtable of Industrialists), *Opening Up: The Business Opportunities of EU Enlargement*, ERT Position Paper and Analysis of the Economic Costs and Benefits of EU Enlargement (Brussels: ERT, 2001); Alan Mayhew, *Recreating Europe* (Cambridge: Cambridge University Press, 1998); Alan Mayhew, 'The Financial and Budgetary Impact of Enlargement and Accession', *SEI Working Paper* no. 65 (Brighton: Sussex European Institute, 2003).

12   David Bailey and Lisa de Propris, 'A Bridge too PHARE? EU Pre-Accession Aid and Capacity Building in the Candidate Countries', *Journal of Common Market Studies* 42/1, 2004: 77–98; Marise Cremona (ed.), *The Enlargement of the European Union* (Oxford: Oxford University Press, 2003); Antoaneta Dimitrova, 'Enlargement, Institution Building and the EU's Administrative Capacity', *West European Politics* 25/4: 171–90; Michael Emerson and Gergana Noutcheva, 'Europeanization as a Gravity Model of Democratization', *CEPS Working Document* no. 214, (Brussels: Centre for European Policy Studies, 2004); Heather Grabbe, 'Europeanization Goes East: Power and Uncertainty in the EU Accession Process', Paper presented at the ECPR Joint Sessions Workshop 'Enlargement and European Governance', Turin, 22–27 March 2002; James Hughes, Gwendolyn Sasse and Clare Gordon, 'Conditionality and Compliance in the EU's Regional Policy and the Reform of Sub-National Government, *Journal of Common Market Studies* 42/3, 2004: 523–51; Dimitry Kochenov, 'Behind the Copenhagen Façade: The Meaning and Structure of the Copenhagen Political Criteria of Democracy and the Rule of Law, *European Integration online Papers* 8/10, 2004, http://eiop.or.at/texte/2004-010.htm; Marc Maresceau, 'The EU Pre-Accession Strategies: a Political and Legal Analysis', in Marc Maresceau and Erwan Lannon (eds), *The EU's Enlargement and Mediterranean Strategies: A Comparative Analysis* (Basingstoke: Palgrave, 2001); Phedon Nicolaides, 'Preparing for Accession to the European Union: How to Establish Capacity for Effective and Credible Application of EU Rules', in

Marise Cremona (ed.), *The Enlargement of the European Union*, pp. 43–78; Dimitri Papadimitriou and David Phinnemore, 'Europeanization, Conditionality and Domestic Change: The Twinning Exercise and Administrative Reform in Romania', *Journal of Common Market Studies* 42/3, 2004: 619–39; Frank Schimmelfennig and Ulrich Sedelmeier, *The Europeanization of Central and Eastern Europe* (Ithaca, NY: Cornell University Press, 2005); Frank Schimmelfennig and Ulrich Sedelmeier, 'Governance by Conditionality: EU Rule Transfer to the Candidate Countries of Central and Eastern Europe', *Journal of European Public Policy* 11/4, 2004: 661–79; Frank Schimmelfennig, Stefan Engbert, and Heiko Knobel, 'The Conditions of Conditionality: The Impact of the EU on Democracy and Human Rights in European Non-Member States', Paper presented at the ECPR Joint Sessions Workshop 'Enlargement and European Governance', Turin, 22–27 March 2002; Karen E. Smith, 'The Evolution and Application of EU Membership Conditionality' in Marise Cremona (ed.), *The Enlargement of the European Union*, pp. 105–40; Milada Ana Vachudova, 'The Leverage of International Institutions on Democratizing States: Eastern Europe and the European Union', RSC No. 2001/33, Robert Schuman Centre for Advanced Studies, Florence: European University Institute.

13 Stefanie Bailer and Gerald Schneider, 'The Power of Legislative Hot Air: Informal Rules and the Enlargement Debate in the European Parliament', *Journal of Legislative Studies* 6/2, 2000: 19–44; Thomas Bräuninger and Thomas König, 'Enlargement and the Union's Institutional Reform', Paper presented at the Conference on Enlargement and Constitutional Change in the European Union, Leiden University, Netherlands, 26–28 November 1999; Herbert Hubel, 'The EU's Three-Level Game in Dealing with Neighbours', *European Foreign Affairs Review* 9, 2004: 347–62;

14 Andrew Moravcsik, *The Choice for Europe: Social Purpose and State Power from Messina to Maastricht* (Ithaca, NY: Cornell University Press, 1998); Andrew Moravcsik and Milada Ana Vachudova, 'National Interests, State Power, and EU Enlargement', *East European Politics and Society* 17/1, 2003: 42–57.

15 Karen Fierke and Antje Wiener, 'Constructing Institutional Interests: EU and NATO Enlargement', *Journal of European Public Policy* 6/5, 1999: 721–42; Ulrich Sedelmeier, 'East of Amsterdam: The Implications of the Amsterdam Treaty for Eastern Enlargement', in Karlheinz Neunreither and Antje Wiener (eds), *European Integration After Amsterdam: Institutional Dynamics and Prospects for Democracy* (Oxford: Oxford University Press, 2000).

16 Iver T. Berend, 'The Further Enlargement of the European Union in a Historical Perspective', *European Review* 7/2, 1999: 175–81; Iver B. Neumann, 'European Identity, EU Expansion, and the Integration/Exclusion Nexus', *Alternatives* 23, 1998: 397–416; Ulrich Sedelmeier, 'EU Enlargement, Identity and the Analysis of European Foreign Policy: Identity Formation through Policy Practice', *EUI Working Papers*, RSC No. 2003/13.

17 Ronald H. Linden (ed.), *Norms and Nannies: The Impact of International Organizations on the Central and East European States* (Lanham, MD: Rowman & Littlefield, 2002); Frank Schimmelfennig, *The EU, NATO, and the Integration of Europe* (Cambridge: Cambridge University Press, 2003); Frank Schimmelfennig, 'The Community Trap: Liberal Norms, Rhetorical Action and the Eastern Enlargement of the European Union', *International Organization* 55/1, 2001: 47–80; Frank Schimmelfennig and Ulrich Sedelmeier, 'Governance by Conditionality: EU Rule Transfer to the Candidate Countries of Central and Eastern Europe', *Journal of European Public Policy* 11/4, 2004: 661–79; Antje Wiener, 'Contested Compliance: Interventions on the Normative Structure of World Politics', *European Journal of International Relations* 10/2, 2004: 189–234.

18 See Tanja A. Börzel and Thomas Risse, 'One Size Fits All: EU Policies for the Promotion of Human Rights, Democracy and the Rule of Law', Paper presented to the Workshop on Democracy Promotion, Centre for Development, Democracy, and the Rule of Law, Stanford University, 4–5 October 2004. See also Antje Wiener, op. cit.

19 See Dimitri Kochenov, 'EU Enlargement Law: History and Recent Developments', *European Integration online Papers* 9/6, 2005, http://eiop.or.at/eiop/texte/2005-006a.htm.

20 Desmond Dinan, 'The Commission and Enlargement', in John Redmond and Glenda Rosenthal (eds), *The Expanding European Union: Past, Present and Future* (Boulder, CO: Lynne Rienner, 1998), p. 20.

21 Ibid., p. 36.

22   Ulrich Sedelmeier and Helen Wallace, 'Eastern Enlargement: Strategy or Second Thoughts?' in Helen Wallace and William Wallace (eds), *Policy-Making in the European Union*, 4th edn (Oxford: Oxford University Press, 2000), p. 446.

23   See, for example, Markus Jachtenfuchs, 'Deepening and Widening Integration Theory', *Journal of European Public Policy* 9/4, 2002: 650–57.

24   Jan Zielonka, 'Ambiguity as a Remedy for the EU's Eastward Enlargement', *Cambridge Review of International Affairs* XII/1, 1998: 15.

Chapter 2

1   John Pinder, *The European Community and Eastern Europe* (London: Pinter/RIIA, 1991), pp. 8–23; Ulrich Sedelmeier and Helen Wallace, 'Eastern Enlargement: Strategy or Second Thoughts?' in Helen Wallace and William Wallace (eds.), *Policy-Making in the European Union*, 4th edn (Oxford: Oxford University Press, 2000), pp. 427–60.

2   The CMEA, or Comecon as it was more popularly referred to, was the economic arm of the Warsaw Pact Alliance. For analysis of its demise see 'East Europeans meet to bury Warsaw Pact', *Independent*, 25 February 1991; 'Comecon: life after death', *Economist*, 20 April 1991; 'Comecon put out of its misery after 42 years', *Financial Times*, 29 June 1991.

3   The 'Return to Europe' quickly emerged as the central pillar upon which membership bids by the CEE states were founded. The 'Return' has been the subject of an exhaustive range of academic analysis. For our purposes it is sufficient to note the extent to which CEE political leaders deployed the phrase and the reigning idea very regularly in the early 1990s. For some examples, see Iver B. Neumann, 'European Identity, EU Expansion, and the Integration/Exclusion Nexus', *Alternatives* 23, 1998: 397–416; Frank Schimmelfennig, 'The Community Trap: Liberal Norms, Rhetorical Action and the Eastern Enlargement of the European Union', *International Organization* 55/1, 2001: 68–9.

4   Ulrich Sedelmeier and Helen Wallace, op. cit., p. 433.

5   See, for example, 'Poll finds yearning to join Community', *The European*, 30 November 1990.

6   'EC dilemma over Eastern Europe', *Guardian*, 10 April 1990.

7   See 'Thatcher urges closer EC ties with East bloc nations', *Financial Times*, 15 November 1989; 'Thatcher seeks commitment on EC entry for Eastern Europe', *Financial Times*, 6 August 1990; 'Thatcher defies EC over East bloc members', *Independent on Sunday*, 12 August 1990.

8   See, for example, 'Hurd foresees East Europe joining EC', *Independent*, 28 February 1990; 'Hurd pushes for EU expansion', *Guardian*, 1 May 1995; 'Major promises to help Poland join the twelve', *Independent*, 27 May 1992. Major visited Czechoslovakia, Hungary and Poland between 26 and 28 May 1992 and pledged support for early entry to the Community.

9   'Eastern Europe "threatens to destabilise EC"', *Financial Times*, 7 November 1990. Mitterand was not alone. During the Irish Presidency of the Community in 1990, Taoiseach Charles Haughey ruled out membership of the EC for Eastern Europe and instead advocated special individual links, *Financial Times*, 6 February 1990. On Mitterand's position see Jean-Marc Trouille, 'France, Germany and the Eastwards Expansion of the EU: Towards a Common Ostpolitik', pp. 50–64. On differences between Thatcher and Mitterand see 'Umpteen ways to spell Europe', *Independent*, 22 September 1990.

10   'Delors frames EC "Ostpolitik"', *Independent*, 16 November 1989; 'Brussels urges wider links with East bloc', *Financial Times*, 2 February 1990.

11   Iver T. Berend, *Central and Eastern Europe 1944-1993: Detour from the Centre to the Periphery* (Cambridge: Cambridge University Press, 1996), p. 335.

12   Desmond Dinan, *Ever Closer Union? An Introduction to the European Community*, (Basingstoke: Macmillan, 1994), p. 475.

13   European Council, Presidency Conclusions, Strasbourg European Council, *Bulletin of the European Communities*, EC 12– 1989.

14   Ulrich Sedelmeier and Helen Wallace, op. cit., p. 432.

15 See, for example, Wim Duisenberg's contribution: 'Lessons from the Marshall Plan', *European Affairs* 5/3, 1991: 21–5.

16 Werner Ungerer, 'The Development of the EC and its Relationship with Central and Eastern Europe', *Aussen Politik* 41/3, 1990: 278.

17 See, for example, 'EC pushes for fresh trade pacts with East Europe', *Financial Times*, 4 January 1990; 'Brussels to widen trade favours in East Europe', *Financial Times*, 18 October 1990; 'EC takes stock of eastern promise', *Financial Times*, 6 March 1991.

18 'EC to offer Eastern Europe new links', *Financial Times*, 2 August 1990.

19 One of the interesting side effects of the eventually successful conclusion to the enlargement negotiations was the virtual collapse of CEFTA. It lost most of its members on 1 May 2004 leaving only three members – Bulgaria, Croatia and Romania. This has its parallel in the reduction in size of the EFTA through successive enlargements of the European Community/Union. It is left with three members also – Norway, Iceland and Liechtenstein. See 'CEFTA trading bloc to collapse?' *European Report*, No. 2826, 6 December 2003, V.11.

20 'Linking arms on the march to Europe', *Independent*, 15 February 1991.

21 Iver T. Berend, op. cit., p.336.

22 'G 24 may offer more aid to Eastern Europe', *Financial Times*, 17 February 1990; 'EC proposes to offer £1.7 billion aid package to Eastern Europe', *Financial Times*, 22 February 1990; 'Twelve plan more aid to Eastern Europe', *Independent*, 29 October 1990.

23 Alan Mayhew, *Recreating Europe* (Cambridge: Cambridge University Press, 1998), pp. 134–7.

24 Iver T. Berend, op. cit., pp. 334–5.

25 See Neal Ascherson, 'A new Iron Curtain in Europe is dividing rich from poor', *Independent on Sunday*, 11 November 1990. See also 'Eastern promise betrayed by latter-day Marshall Plan', *Guardian*, 8 May 1994.

26 The amount applies not for three whole financial years but two and a half approximately, taking into account the date of accession of 1 May 2004.

27 Heather Grabbe, 'The Copenhagen Deal for Enlargement', Briefing Note, Centre for European Reform, London, December 2002.

28 The UN target figure for aid to developing countries is 0.7 per cent of GDP. Among the EU states only Denmark, Luxembourg, the Netherlands, and Sweden contribute at or above the UN figure. The United Kingdom contributes less than 0.4 per cent of its GDP to developing countries, Germany 0.3 per cent, whilst Italy is the worst performer, donating only 0.15 per cent of GDP. See *The Economist*, 7 May 2005.

29 Hubert Leipold, 'The Eastwards Enlargement of the European Union: Opportunities and Obstacles', *Aussen Politik* 46/2, 1995, p. 131.

30 The figures are cited by Heather Grabbe, op. cit.

31 The Irish government was very successful in arguing for and then maintaining a disproportionate share of the Cohesion funds. Helpfully for Ireland the negotiation of the 2000–6 financial framework took place at a time when Irish GDP, although growing rapidly, had not yet reached a point where the country could be excluded from the poorer cohort of member states. The Irish government also argued successfully that Ireland was the only country in the industrialized world to demonstrate a marked difference between GDP and GNP, a phenomenon attributable to the transfer-pricing activities of multinational companies operating in the Republic. The Irish government argued that the country's entitlement should be based on the lower figure of GNP rather than the normal GDP. Thus Ireland managed to hold on to a much more significant share of Structural and Cohesion funding over the period 2000–6 than might have been expected.

32 See *The Economist*, 17 June 1995.

33 ERT (European Roundtable of Industrialists), *Opening Up: the Business Opportunities of EU Enlargement*, ERT Position Paper and Analysis of the Economic Costs and Benefits of EU Enlargement (Brussels: ERT, 2001), p. 32.

34 Arnuf Baring, *Germany's New Position in Eastern Europe: Problems and Perspectives* (Oxford: Berg, 1996), p. 68.

35 The French acronym for: 'Poland and Hungary: Assistance for Restructuring Economies'. See

'PHARE: a beacon of hope', *The Courier*, 121, 1990; 'Coordinated aid to Poland and Hungary', *Bulletin of the European Communities* 10, 1989.

36   'EC to extend its financial aid', *Financial Times*, 3 May 1990; 'Directing aid at an explosive situation', *Guardian*, 27 November 1991.

37   European Commission, *Second Annual Report from the Commission to the Council and the European Parliament: On the Implementation of Community Assistance to the Countries of Central and Eastern Europe*, COM (93) 172 final, Brussels, 1993.

38   By early 2004 the EIB had lent over €23 billion to Central and Eastern Europe.

39   European Commission DG Enlargement, *From Pre-Accession to Accession: Interim Evaluation of PHARE Support Allocated in 1999–2002 and Implemented until November 2003*, Consolidated Summary Report, March 2004, p. 3.

40   See Alan Mayhew, op. cit., pp. 138–50.

41   Frederick Pflueger, 'Poland and the European Union', *Aussen Politik*, 46/3, 1995, p. 229.

42   The Vice-President of the EIB, Wolfgang Roth, for example, urged the EU to cut funds to the myriad range of advisers and contractors. See *Financial Times*, 15 November 1996.

43   Court of Auditors, Annual Report, *Official Journal of the European Communities*, No. 309, 16 November 1993, pp. 179–80.

44   See 'Watchdog urged to halt aid swindlers', *The European*, 1 June 1990; 'Aid hit by fraud', *The European*, 30 November 1990.

45   Cited in Desmond Dinan, op. cit., p. 475.

46   'EC aid to the East – Good intentions, poor performance', *The Economist*, 10 April 1993.

47   For a retrospective evaluation of PHARE see European Commission DG Enlargement, 2004, op. cit.

48   Alan Mayhew, op. cit., pp. 154–6.

49   Ibid., p. 14.

50   Council Decision of 19 November 1990 on the conclusion of agreement establishing the European Bank for Reconstruction and Development, 90/674/EEC, OJ L372, 31 December 1990 (includes the text of the agreement). For commentary see 'Big ambitions are born with pan-European bank', *Financial Times*, 18 September 1990; 'EBRD has 200 projects in hand', *Financial Times*, 3 January 1991; 'European bank aims to start lending by June', *Financial Times*, 15 April 1991.

51   'European bank site sparks deep row', *Financial Times*, 21 May 1990; for a profile of Attali see the *Independent*, 22 June 1991.

52   See 'Attali and his bank fail to match up to expectations', *Guardian*, 27 August 1991.

53   'EBRD spends more on itself than on loans to Eastern Europe', *Financial Times*, 13 April 1993; *European Report*, No. 1850, 8 April 1993, V.8; 'EBRD lending falls far short of targets', *Financial Times*, 24 May 1993.

54   'Attali quits as EBRD chief "in bank's interest"', *Financial Times*, 26 June 1993. See also *Guardian*, 26 June 1993; *European Report*, No. 1870, 26 June 1993.

55   'De Larosière's new Banque de France', *Euromoney*, April 1996.

56   'EBRD casts off its profligate image', *Financial Times*, 7 March 1996; 'EBRD lends a helping hand', *European Dialogue*, 4, July–August 1997.

57   On association and association agreements see David Phinnemore, *Association: Stepping-stone or Alternative to EU Membership?* (Sheffield: Sheffield Academic Press, 1999); Alan Mayhew, op. cit., Part II, Association, pp. 41–59.

58   See European Commission, *Communication on the Association Agreements with the Countries of Central and Eastern Europe: a General Outline*, COM (90) 398 final, Brussels, 18 November 1990; European Commission, *Proposals Concerning the Conclusion of the Interim Agreements between the EC and Poland, Czechoslovakia and Hungary*, COM (91) 524 final, Brussels, 13 December 1991. See also 'Central Europeans sign EC trade deal', *Financial Times*, 17 December 1991; 'EC paves way for free trade with Eastern Europe', *Financial Times*, 23 November 1991. See also *Independent*, 23 November 1991; *European Report*, No. 1721, 16 November 1991, V.5; 'The shape of agreements to come', *Financial Times*, 5 December 1991.

59 European Commission, *Third and Fourth Annual Reports From the Commission to the Council and the European Parliament*, COM (95) 13 final, Brussels, 1995.

60 Ibid.

61 An early and cogent criticism of the EC's protectionist stance came in the form of a *Financial Times* editorial, 'With friends like these', on 9 September 1991. See 'Open Up', *The Economist*, 3 August 1991; 'A new Iron Curtain descends', *Independent*, 30 September 1992; 'Fortress Europe keeps Eastern neighbours out', *Financial Times*, 19 October 1992.

62 Ernst Wistrich, *The United States of Europe* (London: Routledge, 1994), p. 129.

63 'East Europe hopes of EC integration being dashed', *Financial Times*, 26 March 1991; 'East Europeans hit at EC barriers', *Guardian*, 8 June 1991. See also *Financial Times*, 10 June 1991; 'Steel dumping duties upset Eastern Europe', *Financial Times*, 20 November 1992.

64 'Delay angers East Europe', *Guardian*, 10 April 1991.

65 'Brussels opens its doors to trade with Eastern Europe', *Financial Times*, 19 April 1991; 'Food surplus war looms', *The European*, 19 July 1991; 'EEC industry wants limits to Association Agreements', *European Report*, No. 1704, 18 September 1991, V.5–7; 'French retreat stiffens east's EC links', *Guardian*, 1 October 1991; 'Polish dispute threatens EC hopes for East Europeans', *The European*, 1 November 1991.

66 ERT, op. cit.

67 Anders Inotai, 'The "Eastern Enlargements" of the European Union', in Marise Cremona (ed.), *The Enlargement of the European Union* (Oxford: Oxford University Press, 2003), pp. 90–1.

68 Desmond Dinan, op. cit., p. 428.

69 Alan Mayhew, op. cit., p. 99.

70 Quoted in Desmond Dinan, op. cit., p. 478.

71 See also 'East Europe calls EC's bluff over free trade', *Financial Times*, 16 April 1993; *European Report*, No. 1851, 17 April 1993, V.4; 'Iron curtain in the way of trade', *Financial Times*, 29 April 1993.

72 David Phinnemore, op. cit., pp. 67–70; Sedelmeier and Wallace, op. cit., p. 438.

73 European Commission, op. cit., COM (90) 398 final, Brussels, 27 August 1990.

74 See 'Association Agreements under strain', *European Report*, No. 1794, 12 September 1992, V.4-5.

75 Perry Anderson identifies a triangular relationship between the removal of the Iron Curtain, which triggered the unification of Germany, which in turn necessitated locking Germany into a more integrated European Community. See *Independent*, 29 January 1996. For a detailed rejection of such a view see Andrew Moravcsik, *The Choice for Europe: Social Purpose and State Power from Messina to Maastricht* (Ithaca, NY: Cornell University Press, 1998), pp. 407–17.

76 'Absent friends frozen out of unity talks', *Guardian*, 7 December 1991; 'Eastern Europe keeps half an eye on the EC', *Financial Times*, 12 December 1991.

77 Ulrich Sedelmeier and Helen Wallace, op. cit., p. 435. See also Ulrich Sedelmeier, 'Sectoral Dynamics of EU Enlargement: Advocacy, Access, and Alliances in a Composite Polity', *Journal of European Public Policy*, 9/4, 2002: 627–34.

78 Ulrich Sedelmeier and Helen Wallace, op. cit., p. 439.

79 See, for example, Richard E. Baldwin, Joseph E. Francois and Ricardo Portes, 'The Costs and Benefits of Eastern Enlargement: the Impact on the EU and Central Europe', *Economic Policy* 24, 1997; Alan Mayhew, op. cit.; Karen Hendersen (ed.), *Back to Europe: Central and Eastern Europe and the European Union* (London: University of London Press, 1999).

80 Quoted by Lionel Barber, *Financial Times*, 16 November 1995. Headlines such as '2001 Is Too Late' (*The Economist*, 13 March 1993) and 'The EU Goes Cold On Enlargement' (*The Economist*, 25 October 1995) were representative of the concerns about the lack of priority accorded to eastward enlargement in EU circles.

81 See, for example, 'Unwilling to take no for an answer', *The European*, 23 July 1992; 'East European states put case for EC entry', *Financial Times*, 6 October 1992; 'Eastern Europe steps up pressure', *Financial Times*, 21 September 1992; 'Applicants knock loudly on EC door', *Guardian*, 30 September 1992.

82 Peter Ludlow, *The Making of the New Europe: The European Councils on Brussels and Copenhagen 2002*, European Council Commentary 2/1 (Brussels: EuroComment, 2004), p. 21.

83   European Commission, *Towards a Closer Association with the Countries of Central and Eastern Europe*, COM (93) 648 final, Brussels, 18 May 1993.
84   Michael J. Baun, *A Wider Europe: The Process and Politics of European Union Enlargement* (Lanham, MD: Rowman & Littlefield, 2000), p. 44.
85   Graham Avery, 'The Enlargement Negotiations', in Fraser Cameron (ed.), *The Future of Europe: Integration and Enlargement* (London: Routledge, 2004), p. 36.
86   European Council, Presidency Conclusions, Copenhagen European Council, *Bulletin of the European Communities*, EC 6–1993.
87   Ibid.
88   Ibid.
89   On help with market access see European Commission, *Follow-up to the European Council in Copenhagen: Market Access Measures to help the Central and Eastern European Countries*, COM (93) 321 final, Brussels, 7 July 1993.
90   In advance of Copenhagen Commissioner Leon Brittan was particularly forthright in calling for PHARE to be 'streamlined and decentralised' in order to improve its effectiveness. 'Brittan admits flaws in aid', *Financial Times*, 10 June 1993. See also *European Report*, No. 1863, 2 June 1993, Memo, page 1.
91   Michael J. Baun, op. cit., p. 45.
92   Cited in Anna Michalski and Helen Wallace, *The European Community: The Challenge of Enlargement* (London: RIIA, 1992), p. 114.
93   Michael J. Baun, op. cit., p. 46.
94   Quoted in the *Financial Times*, 5 February 1992.
95   *Financial Times*, 23 March 1993.

Chapter 3

1   Michael J. Baun, *A Wider Europe: The Process and Politics of European Union Enlargement* (Lanham, MD: Rowman & Littlefield, 2000): p. 53.
2   Switzerland, another EFTA state, had also applied for membership in May 1992, but its application was effectively withdrawn after Swiss voters rejected the European Economic Area (EEA) in a December 1992 referendum.
3   Ulrich Sedelmeier and Helen Wallace, 'Eastern Enlargement: Strategy or Second Thoughts?' in Helen Wallace and William Wallace (eds), *Policy-Making in the European Union*, 4th edn (Oxford: Oxford University Press, 2000), p. 442.
4   European Commission, *Communication on Relations with the Associated Countries of Central and Eastern Europe. Task force on Approximation of Laws*, COM (94) 391 final, Brussels, 16 September 1994.
5   Peter Ludlow, *The Making of the New Europe: The European Councils on Brussels and Copenhagen 2002*, European Council Commentary 2/1 (Brussels: EuroComment, 2004), p. 23.
6   See, for example, 'Big boost in EU trade with Central and Eastern Europe', Eurostat News Release, No. 53, 14 November 1994.
7   Hungary was the first state to apply for membership on 31 March 1994, followed by Poland on 5 April 1994. Romania was next on 22 June 1995, Slovakia on 27 June 1995, Latvia on 13 October 1995, Estonia on 24 November 1995, Lithuania on 8 December 1995, and Bulgaria on 14 December 1995. The following year, applications were formally lodged by the Czech Republic on 17 January and Slovenia on 10 June 1996.
8   European Commission, *The Europe Agreements and Beyond: A Strategy to Prepare the Countries of Central and Eastern Europe for Accession*, COM (94) 320 final, Brussels, 13 July 1994.
9   Michael J. Baun, op. cit., p. 56.
10   European Commission, *The Europe Agreements and Beyond*.
11   European Commission, *Follow Up to Commission Communication on The Europe Agreements and Beyond: A Strategy to Prepare the Countries of Central and Eastern Europe for Accession*, COM (94) 361 final, Brussels, 27 July 1994.

12 See Stephen D. Collins, *German Policy-making and Eastern Enlargement of the EU during the Kohl Era* (Manchester: Manchester University Press, 2002), pp. 100–5.

13 'Kohl wants East Europeans invited to EU summits', *Financial Times*, 19 July 994.

14 Michael J. Baun, op. cit., pp. 56–7.

15 Quoted by Lionel Barber, 'Kohl Invites Eastern States to EU Summit', *Financial Times*, 1 December 1994. See also 'Six ex-communist states take big step towards EU', *Guardian*, 1 November 1994.

16 See the *Financial Times* editorial, 'Europe's Big Challenge', 9 November 1994; 'When the East's dream evaporates', *Guardian*, 19 November 1994; 'EU's outstretched hand to the east begins to waver', *Financial Times*, 23 November 1994; 'East Europe impatient for seat at the table', *Financial Times*, 9 December 1994.

17 European Council, Presidency Conclusions, Essen Summit, *Bulletin of the European Union*, EU-12 1994.

18 Michael J. Baun, op. cit., p. 58.

19 The leaders of the six states that had signed Europe Agreements by that stage were present – Poland, Hungary, the Czech Republic, Slovakia, Bulgaria and Romania.

20 The Balladur Plan, named after its instigator, French Prime Minister Édouard Balladur.

21 *European Dialogue*, March–April 1995.

22 There is a solid case for arguing that the Pact on Stability ensured that potentially corrosive long-standing disputes relating to borders and extraterritorial national minority groups could find peaceful resolution. Many commentators point out that the Hungarian–Romanian relationship might easily have degenerated into a fratricidal conflict every bit as bloody as the break-up of Yugoslavia without the conditionality imposed by the EU in its enlargement design. Other disputes successfully settled before the International Court of Justice under the influence of the Pact included those between Hungary and Slovakia over a dam on the river Danube and the question of the maritime frontier between Lithuania and Latvia. See Jacek Saryusz-Wolski, 'Looking to the Future', in Antonio Missiroli (ed.), *Enlargement and European Defence after 11 September*, Chaillot Papers No. 53 (Paris: EU Institute for Security Studies), pp. 55–69.

23 Michael J. Baun, op. cit., p. 64.

24 European Commission, *White Paper: Preparation of the Associated Countries of Central and Eastern Europe for Integration Into the Internal Market of the Union*, COM (95) 163 final, Brussels, 3 May 1995.

25 Michael J. Baun, op. cit., pp. 64–5.

26 Quoted by Lionel Barber, 'East Europe's Reform Route to EU', *Financial Times*, 4 May 1995. See also 'A White Paper approved for nine CEECs', *European Report*, 14 June 1995, V.6–7.

27 Ulrich Sedelmeier and Helen Wallace, op. cit., p. 443.

28 Michael J. Baun, op. cit., p. 67. See also *Economist*, 15 July 1995.

29 For the internal German politics of eastern enlargement see Stephen D. Collins, op. cit., ch. 2.

30 European Council Presidency Conclusions, Madrid, *Bulletin of the European Union*, EU-12 1995.

31 Graham Avery and Fraser Cameron, *Enlarging the European Union* (Sheffield: Sheffield Academic Press, 1998), p. 39.

32 'Brussels keeps the gates to the east shut', *Financial Times*, 16 November 1995.

33 'Improvements proposed to EU–East Europe structured dialogue', *European Report*, No. 2111, 28 February 1996, V.7.

34 On preparation of the Commission's Opinions, see Graham Avery and Fraser Cameron, op. cit., pp. 35–43; Michael Baun, op. cit., pp. 78–95; Heather Grabbe and Kirsty Hughes, *Enlarging the EU Eastwards* (London: Royal Institute of International Affairs, 1998), pp. 41–54; and Alan Mayhew, *Recreating Europe: The European Union's Policy towards Central and Eastern Europe* (Cambridge: Cambridge University Press, 1998), pp. 174–6.

35 The Commission had supplied the CEE states with a very extensive questionnaire related to their legislative capacity. See 'CEEC's face extensive list of questions', *European Report*, No. 2128, 1 May 1996, V.4–6; 'Commission prepares to analyse mountain of enlargement replies', *European Voice*, 11 July 1996.

36 Michael J. Baun, op. cit., p. 78.

37 The assessment process was a difficult one for the Commission with an amount of technical detail and a degree of uncertainty about the accuracy of the information provided. See 'Officials find

the devil is in the detail', *European Voice*, 21 November 1996. See also Graham Avery and Fraser Cameron, op. cit., pp. 35–7.

38 European Commission, *Agenda 2000: For A Stronger and Wider Union, Bulletin of the European Union*, Supp. 5/97. The full texts of the ten Opinions can be found in Supps 6/97 to 15/97, in separate volumes.

39 Michael J. Baun, op. cit., p. 83.

40 Ibid., p. 84.

41 Cited in Lionel Barber, 'Brussels Unveils Plans for Reforms in an Enlarged EU', *Financial Times*, 17 July 1997.

42 'EU braced for enlargement war', *Financial Times*, 14 July 1997. See also Graham Avery and Fraser Cameron, 'Reactions to Agenda 2000', op. cit., pp. 121–39.

43 Ulrich Sedelmeier and Helen Wallace, op. cit., p. 448.

44 Marie Soveroski, 'Agenda 2000: A Blueprint for Successful EU Enlargement?', *Eipascope* 1998/1.

45 See the Commission Press Release on the new orientation of PHARE, IP/97/234, 19 March 1997. For background see also, 'New mandate sought for guarantees on CEEC loans', *European Voice*, 23 January 1997; 'EU takes firmer grip on PHARE funding', *European Voice*, 27 February 1997.

46 Marc Maresceau, 'The EU Pre-Accession Strategies: a Political and Legal Analysis', in Marc Maresceau and Erwan Lannon (eds), *The EU's Enlargement and Mediterranean Strategies: A Comparative Analysis* (Basingstoke: Palgrave, 2001), p. 7.

47 Council Regulation (EC) No. 622/98, 'Assistance to the applicant states in the framework of the pre-accession strategy, and in particular on the establishment of Accession Partnerships', OJ L85, 20 March 1998; the text of the Accession Partnerships can be accessed in OJC202, 29 June 1998. See also Commission Press Releases IP/98/117, 4 February 1998 and IP/98/274, 25 March 1998; *European Report*, No. 2301, 21 March 1998, V.1.

48 European Commission, 'Enlarging the European Union: Accession Partnerships with the Central European Applicant Countries', MEMO 98/21, Brussels, 27 March 1998.

49 'Accession partnership accord on fast track for approval', *European Voice*, 15 January 1998; 'Screening formula under scrutiny', *European Voice*, 19 February 1998; 'EU enlargement – Commission Task Force negotiations start work', *European Report*, No. 2305, 4 April 1998, I.1–2; 'Including the excluded: Screening the other applicants', *European Report*, No. 2309, 22 April 1998, V.3–4.

50 Michael J. Baun, op. cit., p. 102.

51 Ulrich Sedelmeier and Helen Wallace, op. cit., p. 452.

52 'Candidates gear up for structural funds', *European Report*, No. 2759, 15 March 2003, V.5.

53 Commission Press Release IP/00/1228, 27 October 2000.

54 Proposal for a Council Regulation (EC) establishing an Instrument for Structural Policies for Pre-Accession, OJC164, 29 May 1998. On ISPA's impact see, for example, 'EU spending on infra-structure tops one billion euro in 2001', *European Report*, No. 2660, 16 February 2002, V.6. For concerns about the efficacy of ISPA spending see *European Report*, No. 2692, 15 June 2002, V.11.

55 See the comments of Agriculture commissioner Franz Fischler in 'SAPARD can be showcase for restructuring', Commission Press Release IP/00/580, 6 June 2000.

56 See the feature on SAPARD in *European Report*, No. 2398, 10 April 1999, V.1–2; 'Commission gives green light to 2002 rural development programmes', *European Report*, No. 2721, 23 October 2002, V.7.

57 For an authoritative analysis of the Twinning exercise and its impact in Romania see Dimitris Papadimitriou and David Phinnemore, 'Europeanization, Conditionality and Domestic Change: The Twinning Exercise and Administrative Reform in Romania', *Journal of Common Market Studies* 42/3, 2004: 619–39.

58 'Need for stronger administration highlighted by Auditors' reports', *European Report*, No. 2779, 24 May 2000, V.2; 'Poland sent letter on food safety', *European Report*, No. 2775, 10 May 2003, V.8. Among the claims, supported by Poland's own audit office, were that Poland had only used 0.15 per cent of the ISPA environment funds at its disposal for 2000–2. It was also claimed that of the €575 million available for over 20 projects, only €28 million had actually been transferred to

Poland and under €1 million actually spent by mid-2002. The Commission subsequently argued that the take-up rate in Poland and elsewhere had been higher but that the substance of the report was correct.

59   Poland had the most number of such Twinning projects with 32, followed by Romania with 30, and the Czech Republic with 19. The concentration of these projects was in judicial and police cooperation, public finance, and agriculture and fisheries.

60   European Commission DG Enlargement, *From Pre-Accession to Accession: Interim Evaluation of PHARE Support Allocated in 1999-2002 and Implemented until November 2003*, Consolidated Summary Report, Brussels, March 2004, p. 1.

61   'Information trickles from PHARE', *European Report*, No. 286, 27 September 2003, V.7. See also 'PHARE, twinning and partnerships need refinement', *European Report*, No. 2259, 15 October 1997, V.8–9; 'Auditors launch renewed attack on aid schemes', *European Voice*, 6 November 1997; 'EU conditions for aid under attack', *Financial Times*, 22 December 1997.

62   A 2003 report by the OECD showed that in Poland pollutant emissions had been cut substantially with sulphur dioxide and nitrous oxide emissions falling by 53 and 35 per cent respectively. There was significant improvement in the provision of water supply and sewage systems and a decline in nitrogen and phosphorus presence in coastal waters. See 'Poland making progress on environment', *European Report*, No. 2786, 21 June 2003, V.6; 'Enlargement: PHARE helps clear the fog in the Czech Republic', *European Report*, No. 2794, 19 July 2003, V.4. See also 'New member states ahead on key environment law', EUobserver.com, 2 May 2005.

63   'New members wait in line for EU entry', *Financial Times*, 19 June 1997; 'EU talks boost for Slovenia and Estonia', *Financial Times*, 8 July 1997.

64   Michael J. Baun, op. cit., p. 86. See Mark Turner's analysis of the divisions: 'Split over accession candidates', *European Voice*, 2 October 1997; *European Report*, No. 2257, 8 October 1997, V.4; *European Report*, No. 2258, 11 October 1997, V.5.

65   'Key decisions imminent on EU applicants', *European Voice*, 16 October 1997; 'New battle over EU expansion', *European Voice*, 27 November 1997.

66   European Council, Presidency Conclusions, Luxembourg Summit, *Bulletin of the European Union*, EU-12 1997.

67   Ibid.

68   On screening see 'First wave screening will run to July 1999', *European Report*, No. 2319, 30 May 1998, I.1.

69   'Foreign ministers recommend no promotions to first wave', *European Report*, No. 2366, 9 December 1998; 'Encouraging signals are the most applicants can hope for', *European Voice*, 10 December 1998; 'EU hopefuls fear membership delay', *Independent*, 14 December 1998; 'Enlargement train slow to leave station', *European Voice*, 17 December 1998; interview with Bulgarian Foreign Ministry official, Sofia, 2 March 2001.

70   European Commission, 'Reports on Progress Towards Accession by Each of the Candidate Countries: Composite Paper', 4 November 1998, http://europa.eu.int/comm/enlargement/report_11_98/

71   On the impact of Kosovo see 'Kosovo raises enlargement hopes', *European Voice*, 22 July 1999; Timothy Garton Ash, 'An appeal to Europe: now is the moment to take the leap', *Independent*, 30 July 1999.

72   'Enlarging the European Union: a new pace', *Economist*, 2 October 1999; 'Commission opens door to all six applicants', *European Voice*, 14 October 1999.

73   Atsuko Higashino, 'For the Sake of Peace and Security? The Role of Security in the European Union Enlargement Eastwards', *Cooperation and Conflict* 39/4, p. 358.

74   'Signs that enlargement is increasingly on the political agenda', *European Report*, No. 2382, 13 February 1999, V.2–3; 'Enlargement talks on target despite crisis', *European Voice*, 25 March 1999.

75   Michael J. Baun, op. cit., p. 123; See also Joschka Fischer's linkage between enlargement and a potential Yugoslav-style imbroglio: 'Fischer in the Eurosceptics' den', *Guardian*, 25 January 2001.

76   'Romania Still Looks West in the Long Term', *Financial Times*, 14 May 1999; 'Bulgarians Start to Ponder Hidden Costs of the Conflict', *Financial Times*, 18 May 1999.

77 European Commission, *Composite Paper: Reports on Progress Towards Accession by each of the Candidate Countries*, COM (1999) 500 final, Brussels, 13 October 1999.

78 Verheugen quoted in Agence Europe, *Europe Daily Bulletin*, no. 7572, 14 October 1999.

79 Agence Europe, *Europe Daily Bulletin*, no. 7575, 18–19 October 1999.

80 European Council Presidency Conclusions, Helsinki Summit, *Bulletin of the European Union*, EU-12 1999.

81 'EU Paves the Way for Another Six', *Financial Times*, 11–12 December 1999.

82 Cited in Agence Europe, *Europe Daily Bulletin*, no. 7612, 11 December 1999.

83 Michael J. Baun, op. cit., pp.129–33.

84 'EU paves the way for another six members', *Financial Times*, 11 December 1999; 'Major headaches in prospect as talks with the applicant countries enter crucial phase', *European Voice*, 16 December 1999.

Chapter 4

1 See, for example, 'Britain to push for a firm deadline on next phase of EU expansion', *Independent*, 25 July 2000. See also the text of UK Foreign Secretary Robin Cook's speech in Budapest in the *Independent*, 27 July 2000.

2 European Commission, *Regular Reports from the Commission on Progress Towards Accession by Each of the Candidate Countries*, Brussels, 8 November 2000. The Regular Reports can be found on the Commission's Website at: http://www.europa.eu.int/comm/enlargement/report_11_00/index.htm

3 See, for example, 'Clean up your act, EU tells aspiring members', *Independent*, 9 November 2000; 'Bigger when?', *The Economist*, 11 November 2000; 'Onward to the Holy Land', *Transitions*, 13 November 2000.

4 European Commission, Enlargement Strategy Paper, Report on Progress Towards Accession by Each of the Candidate Countries, *Bulletin of the European Union*, Supp. No. 3, 2000. See also Commission Press Release IP/00/1264, 8 November 2000; 'Commission timetable for enlargement under attack', *European Voice*, 16 November 2000.

5 Graham Avery, 'The Enlargement Negotiations', in Fraser Cameron (ed.), *The Future of Europe: Integration and Enlargement* (London: Routledge, 2004), p. 48.

6 Peter Ludlow, *The Making of the New Europe: The European Councils on Brussels and Copenhagen 2002*, European Council Commentary 2/1 (Brussels: EuroComment, 2004), pp. 45–6.

7 Ibid., p. 47.

8 On Biarritz, see 'All in accord – on procrastination', *The Economist*, 21 October 2000.

9 See the *Financial Times*, 29 December 2000.

10 Peter Ludlow, op. cit., p. 54.

11 Ibid., p. 52.

12 'Védrine: Romania and Bulgaria in the "big bang"', EUobserver.com, 20 November 2001; 'Védrine's vision dismissed as speculation', EUobserver.com, 11 December 2001; see also Graham Avery, op. cit., p. 52.

13 See, for example, 'War of words erupts over enlargement', *European Voice*, 23–29 March 2000; 'Sound and fury in debate on Union's future', *European Voice*, 22–28 June 2000; 'Members in 2005?', *The Economist*, 10 June 2000. On the deliberations at Nice see 'Prodi reminds Europe of the importance of expansion', *Guardian*, 9 November 2000; 'EU leaders agree to reform package, opening way to negotiations', *Independent*, 11 December 2000; 'Commission timetable for enlargement under attack', *European Voice*, 16–22 November 2000.

14 See 'Enthusiasm for a larger Europe starts to wane', *Financial Times*, 5 June 2001.

15 'Sweden pushes for early breakthrough on EU expansion', *European Voice*, 4 January 2001; 'Sweden wants clear enlargement dates', *Financial Times*, 6 June 2001.

16 Quoted in the *Financial Times*, 11 January 2001.

17 European Council, Presidency Conclusions, Gothenburg, *Bulletin of the European Union*, EU-6 2001.

18 Peter Ludlow, op. cit., p. 52.

19 Quoted in 'Crowded field in race to join EU', *Financial Times*, 27 June 2001.
20 Graham Avery, op. cit., p. 51.
21 See also 'Enlargement agreed after Swedish push', *Financial Times*, 17 June 2001; 'Enlargement agreed for 2004 after Persson push', *Financial Times*, 18 June 2001; 'Progress amid the mayhem', *Guardian*, 18 June 2001. For a negative reading of Gothenburg see Will Hutton, 'The summit of Europe's ambitions?', *Observer*, 17 June 2001.
22 See 'Brussels Backs "Big Bang" Plan For 10 Nations', *Independent*, 29 June 2001; 'EU Expansion' (editorial comment), *Financial Times*, 13 November 2001; 'EU prepares for "big bang" entry of 10 countries', *Daily Telegraph*, 14 November 2001.
23 Peter Ludlow, op. cit., p. 56.
24 Persson engaged in an energetic campaign to discredit and draw out the opponents of enlargement. Led by the *Financial Times*, many newspapers that appeared on the Saturday of the summit gave the impression that German Chancellor Gerhard Schröder in particular 'was turning sour on enlargement'. See Peter Ludlow, ibid., 57–8.
25 'EU Agrees to Speed up Enlargement Momentum', *Financial Times*, 16 June 2001.
26 See European Commission, *Regular Reports from the Commission on Progress Towards Accession by Each of the Candidate Countries 2001*, http://europa.eu.int/comm/enlargement/report2001/
      See also 'Ten nations on track to join the EU', *Financial Times*, 13 November 2001; 'EU on course for big enlargement', *Guardian*, 14 November 2001; 'European Union facing "big bang" expansion in 2004', *Independent*, 14 November 2001; 'The European Union heads for "Big Bang" enlargement', *Financial Times*, 14 November 2001; 'Brussels' high hopes for EU candidates', *Financial Times*, 14 November 2001; 'Top German politicians call for radical EU shake-up', *Financial Times*, 19 November 2001.
27 Graham Avery, op. cit., p. 52.
28 Peter Ludlow, op. cit., pp. 84–5.
29 See *The Economist*, 28 August 2002, for a bleak analysis of the prospects of success of the Irish referendum. On the 2002 elections in France, Germany and some of the candidate states see *European Report*, No. 2652, 19 January 2002.
30 For a flavour of the issues and their interpretation in early 2002 see 'First year of EU expansion to cost €5.6bn', *Financial Times*, 27 January 2002; 'EU newcomers will receive less regional aid', *Financial Times*, 28 January 2002; 'Wider and dearer' (editorial comment), *Financial Times*, 30 January 2002; 'Prodi defends 2004 deal as Poles hit out', *European Voice*, 31 January 2002; 'Playing for real now the talk is of money', *European Report*, No. 2656, 2 February 2002, V.1; 'Paying for a bigger Europe', *Financial Times*, 10 February 2002; 'EU warns accession countries on agriculture', *Financial Times*, 19 March 2002; 'EU starts to stake out positions over aid', *Financial Times*, 4 April 2002.
31 European Commission, *Common Financial Framework 2004–06 for the Accession Negotiations*, SEC (2002) 102 final, Brussels, 30 January 2002.
32 Alan Mayhew, 'The Financial and Budgetary Impact of Enlargement and Accession', *SEI Working Paper* No. 65 (Brighton: Sussex European Institute, 2003), p. 13.
33 Commission figures showed the Czech Republic would suffer most: after receiving €158 million in 2003, it would be €342 million worse off in 2004 and €109 million in 2005. Slovenia would be a net contributor for three consecutive years. For the full range of calculations, see 'European Commission calculates net EU budgets for the candidates', *European Report*, No. 2712, 21 September 2002, V.3–4. See also 'Budget contributions worry applicants for EU', *Financial Times*, 12 September 2002.
34 Peter Ludlow, op. cit., p. 68.
35 Alan Mayhew, op. cit., p. 13.
36 In the case of Poland, for example, 350,000 farmers alone. Or, to put it another way, 60 per cent of Polish farmers hold plots as small as one hectare.
37 'Commission offers limited aid to accession-country farmers', *European Report*, No. 2654, 26 January 2002, V.11.
38 For candidate state reaction see 'Hungarian PM attacks EU subsidies offer', *Financial Times*, 31 January 2002; 'Trouble brews over regional policy on eve of negotiations', *European Report*, No.

2655, 30 January, V.6; 'Opposition leader very critical of Commission proposals on farm aid', *European Report*, No. 2657, 6 February 2002, V.6; 'Poles demand better deal for commercial farmers', *European Report*, No. 2659, 13 February 2002, V.8; 'Commission tells candidates their farmers will gain by joining', *European Report*, No. 2669, 20 March 2002, V.7; 'Czech farmers warn against EU package', *European Report*, No. 2709, 11 September 2002, V.3.

39   Peter Ludlow, op. cit., p. 72. See also 'Enlarging the European Union – to get them in cut the costs', *The Economist*, 2 February 2002; 'Member states sift the financing plan for the candidates', *European Report*, No. 2557, 6 February 2002, V.12; 'Cost of enlargement €7.5 billion too much, says Germany', *European Voice*, 7 February 2002; 'Paying for enlargement', *Financial Times*, 11 February 2002; 'Tremonti attacks EU expansion', *Financial Times*, 13 March 2002.

40   Schröder, quoted by Peter Ludlow, op. cit., p. 74. Germany's EU commissioner Michaele Schreyer disagreed, pointing out in an interview with the *Süddeutsche Zeitung* that the German contribution to the EU had fallen from 33 per cent of the EU household in the mid-1990s to about 23.5 per cent in 2002. She also claimed that Berlin had paid three billion euro less into the EU budget in the year 2000 than five years before – see EUobserver.com, 3 April 2002.

41   'Finance ministers split over funding plan', *European Report*, No. 2660, 16 February, V.6.

42   'EU debating how to handle agriculture negotiations', *European Report*, No. 2682, 8 May 2002, V.3; 'General Affairs Council fails to agree on farm payments for new members', *European Report*, No. 2691, 12 June 2002, V.1–2; 'Agreement on agriculture but not direct payments to farmers', *European Report*, No. 2693, 19 June, V.10–11; 'Large gap persists between EU and candidates on agriculture', *European Report*, 27 July 2002, V.3.

43   See 'Enlargement talks still on track despite hurdles', EUobserver.com, 11 June 2002; 'Divisions widen over costs of enlargement', *Financial Times*, 11 June 2002; Verheugen quoted in *European Report*, No. 2692, 15 June 2002, V.1.

44   European Commission, *Mid-Term Review of the Common Agricultural Policy*, COM (2002) 394 final, Brussels, 10 July 2002.

45   Peter Ludlow, op. cit., pp.129–30

46   Ibid.

47   European Commission, *Towards the Enlarged Union*, COM (2002) 700 final. Available online at http://europa.eu.int/comm/enlargement/report2002/Brussels, 9 October 2002.

48   Peter Ludlow, op.cit., p.136.

49   The difficulties associated with 'administrative capacity' of course varied from country to country. Perhaps the most manifest example of deficiency among the candidate states was Romania. 'Administrative capacity' takes on a whole new meaning, as one leader writer put it, in a country where the President earns only around €800 per month, and senior civil servants take home only €200. See 'Fitting Romania into the EU jigsaw', *European Report*, No. 2762, 26 March 2003, V.6–7.

50   For a cogent example of the 'transposition-implementation' gap see 'Telecoms battle in Slovenia exposes implementation gap', *European Report*, No. 2775, 10 May 2003, V.9. The article focuses on the problems faced by companies in the Slovenian telecommunications market in competing with the dominant market player, the state-owned Telekom Slovenije which held 75 per cent of the market.

51   On the Action Plans and their importance to the candidate's efforts see 'Verheugen sets high administrative hurdle for candidates', *European Report*, No. 2690, 8 June 2002, V.1–2.

52   'Commission confirms risk of delay on structural funding', *European Report*, No. 2794, 19 July 2003, V.3.

53   'Corruption is still a problem in most candidate countries', *European Report*, No. 2726, 9 November 2002.

54   On the emphasis placed by the Irish government on enlargement in the second referendum see John O'Brennan, 'Ireland's Return to "Normal" EU Voting Patterns: the 2002 Nice Treaty Referendum', *European Political Science* 2/2, 2003: 5–14.

55   Peter Ludlow, op. cit., p. 166. The three-party coalition was composed of six ministers from the Christian Democrats (CDA), four from the People's Party for Freedom and Justice (VVD) and four from the List Pim Fortuyn (LPF).

56 'Dutch government in crisis over enlargement', EUobserver.com, 15 October 2002; 'Dutch raise doubts over candidates' fitness to join EU', *Financial Times*, 15 October 2002.

57 See, for example, 'EU defers hot issues to late October', *European Report*, No. 2715, 2 October 2002, V.5; 'The high price of admission: why the eastern states' entry to the EU is not yet a done deal', *Financial Times*, 9 October 2002; 'Chirac and Schröder: no agreement on CAP reform', EUobserver.com, 15 October 2002.

58 Alan Mayhew, op. cit., p. 15.

59 Ibid.

60 The GAERC meeting of 21–22 October effectively narrowed the agenda for the European Council by achieving agreement on such important issues as the number of MEPs, the formula for structural fund spending and agreement on safeguard clauses. See 'Challenges for Brussels summit ... and beyond', *European Report*, No. 2721, 23 October 2002, V.6.

61 Alan Mayhew, op.cit., p.15.

62 Peter Ludlow, op. cit., p. 187.

63 Quoted in 'Enlargement to be delayed if Brussels summit fails', EUobserver.com, 23 October 2002.

64 'Round one to France in fight over cost of enlargement', *European Report*, No. 2722, 26 October 2002.

65 See the *Financial Times*, 29 October 2002; 'Enlargement: negotiations "end game" begins', *European Report*, No. 2723, 30 October 2002, V.6.

66 Peter Ludlow, op. cit., p. 219.

67 'Danish presidency shows its negotiating hand', *European Report*, No. 2732, 30 November 2002, V.1–2.

68 Unpublished paper, 8 November 2002. 'Elements for a negotiating package'. The paper was drafted by the Commission but was nevertheless a joint Presidency–Commission paper following on from their meeting of 7 November 2002.

69 Alan Mayhew, op. cit., p. 17.

70 Peter Ludlow, op. cit., p. 235.

71 Ibid., p. 238.

72 'Danish presidency shows its negotiating hand', *European Report*, No. 2732, 30 November 2002, V.1–2.

73 Of the ten countries that would join the EU on 1 May 2004, Lithuania was due to receive the largest amount of financial assistance per capita: €390 per head during the first years after accession. Estonia and Latvia would receive €360 and €350 per capita. By contrast, Poland would receive only €166 per capita, and the Czech Republic a meagre €87 per capita. The headline figures can be misleading however. In the case of Lithuania almost 10 per cent of the total would go toward the cost of decommissioning the Ignalina nuclear power plant. That reduced the per capita subvention to less than €350. The figures also do not indicate the massive differentials in funding within receiving countries. In Lithuania's case, for example, farmers benefit excessively, to the tune of €800 per capita. See 'Lithuania: Is EU largesse a victory or defeat?', Radio Free Europe, 16 December 2002, http://www.rferl.org/nca/features/2002/12/16122002171611.asp.

74 See, for example, 'EU entry talks test Polish PM's skills', *Financial Times*, 23 November 2002. See also 'EU candidates demand fair treatment from Brussels', *Financial Times*, 17 November 2002; 'Candidate countries unhappy with financial package', EUobserver.com, 18 November 2002.

75 'EU candidates accepting EU "realism" in Copenhagen countdown', *European Report*, No. 2729, 20 November 2002, V.10; 'Denmark pushes on towards deal at Copenhagen', *European Report*, No. 2734, 7 December 2002, V.12.

76 'EU presidency hands its final offer to candidates', *European Report*, No. 2731, 27 November 2002, V.5; 'Candidates maintain demands ahead of Copenhagen Summit', *European Report*, No. 2735, 11 December 2002, V.5–7.

77 Peter Ludlow, op. cit., p. 283.

78 Former Polish Premier Tadeusz Mazowiecki, quoted in the *Observer*, 15 December 2002.

79 Peter Ludlow, op. cit., pp. 286–8.

80   Alan Mayhew, op. cit., p. 18.
81   Peter Ludlow, op. cit., p. 299.
82   Ibid., p. 301.
83   See Heather Grabbe, 'The Copenhagen Deal for Enlargement', *Briefing note*, Centre for European Reform, London.
84   Peter Ludlow, op. cit., p. 303.
85   European Council, Presidency Conclusions, Copehagen Summit, *Bulletin of the European Union*, EU 12–2002.
86   See, for example, 'EU embraces 10 new members – and opens the door to Turkey', *Guardian*, 14 December 2002; 'Outstanding performance by Danish Presidency', EUobserver.com, 14 December 2002; 'The shake-up that Europe needs', *Observer*, 15 December 2002; 'Enlargement – cheap at the price', EUobserver.com, 17 December 2002; 'Big Bang achieved with little money', *European Report*, No. 2737, 18 December 2002, I.2–4.
87   'Duncan Smith slams EU on enlargement', *Guardian*, 17 December 2002.
88   'Furious Chirac hits out at "infantile" easterners', *Guardian*, 18 February 2003; 'Eastern Europe dismayed at Chirac snub', *Guardian*, 19 February 2003.
89   'Some Polish farmers still fear annihilation', *European Report*, No. 2747, 1 February 2003, V.10.
90   Council of the European Union, Treaty of Accession, AA 2003 final, Brussels, 3 April 2003. For commentary on the text of the Accession Treaty see Graham Avery, op. cit., p. 58.
91   'Bated breath for accession treaty', *European Report*, No. 2748, 5 February 2003, V.11.
92   See 'Ten countries sign on the dotted line in Athens', *Guardian*, 17 April 2003; 'Treaty seals Europe's historic expansion to the east', *Independent*, 17 April 2003; 'Emotions run high amid warm welcome', *Guardian*, 18 April 2003; Will Hutton, 'Why I back this Warsaw pact', *Observer*, 1 June 2003; Heather Grabbe, 'A Union of shifting coalitions', *Warsaw Business Journal*, 2 June 2003; Heather Grabbe, 'Shaken to the Core', *Prospect*, May 2003.
93   Quoted in the *Guardian*, 18 April 2003. For a detailed analysis of the content of the accession treaty, see also 'The terms of the accession treaty', *European Report*, No. 2752, 19 February 2003, V.1–3.
94   'Athens Declaration issued as leaders sign Accession Treaty', *European Report*, No. 2769, 18 April 2003, V.4–5.
95   In most of the CEE states the threshold level was set at 50 per cent of the turnout. In Lithuania, however, the initial figure had been set at 75 per cent for amendments to Article 1 of the Constitution which outlined the nature of Lithuania's independence. Concern over likely turnout and its implications for ratification of the Accession Treaty resulted in a reduction in the constitutional requirement to 50 per cent. See Anneli Albi, 'Referendums in Eastern Europe: the Effects on Reforming the EU Treaties and on the Candidate Countries' Positions in the Convention', *EUI Working Papers*, RSC No. 2002/65.
96   See 'Malta flags assent to EU membership', *Guardian*, 10 March 2003; 'Slovene double "yes" to Nato and EU leaves pollsters red-faced', *Guardian*, 24 March 2002.
97   'Poland votes yes to joining EU's big powers', *Guardian*, 9 June 2003.
98   'Estonia says Yes to EU', *European Report*, No. 2803, 17 September 2003, V.1; 'Latvian yes completes EU sweep', *Guardian*, 22 September 2003.
99   For an overview of the accession referendums see Alexs Szcerbiak and Paul Taggart (eds), *EU Enlargement and Referendums* (London: Routledge, 2005).
100 Quoted in the *Guardian*, 23 June 2003.
101 European Commission, *Regular Reports and Strategy Paper 2003*, http://europa.eu.int/comm/enlargement/report_2003/ See also 'An almost clear road for the ten', *European Report*, No. 2818, 8 November 2003, V.1.

Chapter 5

1   See, for example, Kenneth A. Armstrong and Simon Bulmer, *The Governance of the Single European Market* (Manchester: Manchester University Press, 1998); Wayne Sandholtz and Alec Stone Sweet (eds), *European Integration and Supranational Governance* (Oxford: Oxford University Press,

1998); Alec Stone Sweet, Wayne Sandholtz, and Neil Fligstein (eds), *The Institutionalization of Europe* (Oxford: Oxford University Press, 2001).

2 Article 49 of the Treaty on European Union (TEU). Article 6 (1) (Ex Article F) effectively codified the Copenhagen criteria for membership of the Union. It reads: 'The Union is founded on the principles of liberty, democracy, respect for human rights, and fundamental freedoms, and the rule of law, principles which are common to the Member States'. In the Constitutional Treaty, agreed by heads of State and Government of the Union in June 2004, Article 49 is replaced by Article I-58 of Title IX. The only significant change is the inclusion of notification of national parliaments on receipt of a membership application. Article 1-2 of Title I replaces Article 6. At the time of writing the Constitutional Treaty had not been ratified and so is only referred to in passing here. More importantly, the 2004 accessions were negotiated and agreed on the basis of the existing constitutional provisions, thus it is those to which the text here refers.

3 On the development of 'enlargement law' and in particular the differences between the way the EU enlargement process is inscribed in the treaties and customary enlargement practice as it has evolved, see Dimitry Kochenov, 'EU Enlargement Law: History and Recent Developments', *European Integration online Papers* 9/6, 2005, http://eiop.or.at/eiop/texte/2005-006a.htm

4 Article 213 of the Treaty on European Union (TEU).

5 Dimitry Kochenov, 'Behind the Copenhagen Façade: The Meaning and Structure of the Copenhagen Political Criteria of Democracy and the Rule of Law', *European Integration online Papers* 8/10, 2004, http://www.eiop.or.at/texte/2004-010.htm

6 Coreper itself is divided into two parts. Coreper I consists of deputy ambassadors and Coreper II consists of the ambassadors, or permanent representatives as they are known. Broadly speaking Coreper II meetings cover issues of external relations and 'high' politics while Coreper I, also known as the 'technical councils', broadly cover the sectoral councils or 'low' politics.

7 The European Council is considered here as part of the Council machinery even though it was designed as a purely intergovernmental forum and not as a Community institution. In respect of enlargement decision-making the structural dynamics of the European Council proved very similar to those of the Council of Ministers.

8 Jonas Tallberg, 'The Power of the Presidency: Brokerage, Efficiency and Distribution in EU Negotiations', *Journal of Common Market Studies* 42/5, 2004, p. 999.

9 John Peterson and Elisabeth Bomberg, *Decision-Making in the European Union* (Basingstoke: Macmillan, 1999), p. 34.

10 Maximilian Conrad, 'Persuasion, Communicative Action and Socialization after EU Enlargement', Paper presented to the Second ECPR Pan-European Conference, Bologna, 24-26 June 2004, p. 20.

11 John Pinder, *The European Community and Eastern Europe* (London: Pinter/RIIA, 1991), p. 25.

12 Ulrich Sedelmeier, 'Sectoral Dynamics of EU Enlargement: Advocacy, Access, and Alliances in a Composite Polity', *Journal of European Public Policy* 9/4, 2002, p. 631.

13 Ibid.

14 Ibid., p. 634.

15 See Fiona Hayes Renshaw, 'The Council of Ministers', in John Peterson and Michael Shackleton (eds), *The Institutions of the European Union* (Oxford: Oxford University Press, 2002), p. 55.

16 Peter Ludlow, *The Making of the New Europe: The European Councils on Brussels and Copenhagen 2002*, European Council Commentary 2/1 (Brussels: EuroComment, 2004), p. 115.

17 Lee Miles, 'Enlargement: From the Fusion Perspective', *Cooperation and Conflict* 37/2, 2002, p. 197.

18 Peter Ludlow, op. cit., pp. 224–5.

19 Ibid.

20 See, for example, Fiona Hayes Renshaw and Helen Wallace, *The Council of Ministers* (New York: St Martin's Press, 1997); Pippa Sherrington, *The Council of Ministers: Political Authority in the European Union* (London: Pinter, 2000); Jonas Tallberg, 'The Agenda-Shaping Powers of the Council Presidency', in Ole Elgström (ed.), *European Union Council Presidencies: A Comparative Perspective* (London: Routledge, 2003), pp. 18–37.

21 Jonas Tallberg, 'The Agenda-Shaping Powers of the Council Presidency', p. 19.

22   Dimitry Kochenov, 'EU Enlargement Law: History and Recent Developments', p. 17.

23   Jonas Tallberg, 'The Agenda-Shaping Powers of the Council Presidency', p. 21.

24   Jonas Tallberg, 'The Power of the Presidency: Brokerage, Efficiency and Distribution in EU Negotiations', p. 999.

25   Jonas Tallberg, 'The Agenda-Shaping Powers of the Council Presidency', p. 24.

26   Lee Miles points out that some 64 chapters were opened during the Swedish Presidency and a further 66 chapters provisionally closed by 27 June 2001. In particular the Presidency established EU positions on the nine chapters identified by the Nice 'road map'. See Lee Miles, op. cit., p. 194.

27   See Bo Bjurulf, 'The Swedish Presidency of 2001: A Reflection of Swedish Identity', in Ole Elgström (ed.), *European Union Council Presidencies*, p. 138.

28   Ibid., p. 140.

29   Graham Avery, 'The Enlargement Negotiations', in Fraser Cameron (ed.), *The Future of Europe: Integration and Enlargement* (London: Routledge, 2004), p. 57.

30   Jonas Tallberg, 'The Agenda-Shaping Powers of the Council Presidency', p. 24. On Kaliningrad and its importance in the later stages of the enlargement process, see 'Russia's hell-hole enclave', *Guardian*, 7 April 2001; 'Kaliningrad cuts deeper into EU-Russia relations', *European Report*, 2712, 21 September 2002; 'Still at loggerheads over Kaliningrad', *European Report*, 2684, 18 May 2002.

31   Jonas Tallberg, 'The Power of the Presidency: Brokerage, Efficiency and Distribution in EU Negotiations', p. 1004.

32   Jonas Tallberg, 'The Agenda-Shaping Powers of the Council Presidency', p. 25.

33   Jonas Tallberg, 'The Power of the Presidency: Brokerage, Efficiency and Distribution in EU Negotiations', p. 1004.

34   Ibid.

35   Ibid., p. 1017.

36   Peter Ludlow, op. cit., pp. 57–8.

37   Lee Miles, op. cit., p. 194.

38   Peter Ludlow, op. cit., p. 56.

39   Ole Elgström, 'The Honest Broker? The Council Presidency as a Mediator', in Ole Elgström (ed.), *European Union Council Presidencies*, p. 38.

40   Ibid., p. 45.

41   Ibid., p. 49.

42   Teija Tilikainen, 'The Finnish Presidency of 1999: Pragmatism and Promotion of Finland's Position in Europe', in Ole Elgström (ed.), *European Union Council Presidencies*, p. 111.

43   Ulrich Sedelmeier and Helen Wallace, 'Eastern Enlargement: Strategy or Second Thoughts?', in Helen Wallace and William Wallace (eds), *Policy-Making in the European Union*, 4th edn (Oxford: Oxford University Press, 2000), p. 457.

44   See the feature on Genscher: 'Turning a warhorse into a peacemaker', *The European*, 27 May 1994.

45   See, for example, former Polish Prime Minister Hanna Suchocka, 'Don't be greedy – let the prodigal sons of the East come home', *The European*, 3 June 1994.

46   For typical examples see 'EU Must reach out to Eastern Europe', *Financial Times*, 15 April 1994; 'For a bigger, better EU', *The Economist*, 3 August 1996.

47   European Council, Presidency Conclusions, Strasbourg European Council, *Bulletin of the European Communities*, EC 12-1989.

48   Michael J. Baun, *A Wider Europe: The Process and Politics of European Union Enlargement* (Lanham, MD: Rowman & Littlefield, 2000), p. 10.

49   Leon Brittan, *The Europe We Need* (London: Hamilton, 1994), p. 4.

50   Helmut Kohl, Address by Chancellor Kohl to the Bundestag, *Bulletin*, No. 103, 16 December 1996.

51   Joschka Fischer, 'From Confederacy to Federation – Thoughts on the Finality of European Integration', Humboldt University, Berlin, 12 May 2000.

52   Guy Verhofsdadt, 'The Enlargement of the European Union: A Unique Opportunity to Restore the Unity of Europe', Speech to the Hungarian Academy of Sciences, Budapest, 13 March 2001.

53 Aznar and Piqué, cited in Sonia Piedrafita Tremosa, 'The EU Eastern Enlargement: Policy Choices of the Spanish Government', *European Integration online Papers* 9/3, http://eiop.or.at/eiop/texte/2005-003a.htm

54 Guy Verhofstadt, op. cit.

55 Fischer, quoted in Agence Europe, *Europe Daily Bulletin*, 6 April 1999.

Chapter 6

1 The former privilege *statist* conceptions of inter-state relations within the European integration process while the latter argue for a significant *supranationalist* dimension to European integration and patterns of governance in Europe.

2 Dimitry Kochenov, 'Behind the Copenhagen Façade: The Meaning and Structure of the Copenhagen Political Criteria of Democracy and the Rule of Law', *European Integration online Papers* 8/10, 2004, http://eiop.or.at/eiop/texte/2004-010.htm

3 Mark Pollack, *The Engines of European Integration: Delegation, Agency and Agenda-Setting in the EU* (New York: Oxford University Press, 2002), pp. 48–9. In this respect, as Pollack points out, the use of Qualified Majority Voting (QMV) within the EU is of crucial importance in that it is much easier for the Commission to forge alliances with certain member states in an effort to get a measure through whilst it is much more difficult to amend proposals. In contrast, unanimity effectively means that the Commission is marginalized as a player in certain policy areas.

4 Andrew Moravcsik, 'Preferences and Power in the European Community: A Liberal Inter-governmentalist Approach', *Journal of Common Market Studies* 31/4, 1993, p. 480.

5 Paul Pierson, 'The Path to European Integration: A Historic-Institutionalist Analysis', in Wayne Sandholtz and Alec Stone Sweet (eds), *European Integration and Supranational Governance* (Oxford: Oxford University Press, 1998), p. 36.

6 Mark Pollack, op. cit., pp. 48–9 and pp. 84–5.

7 This view is challenged by a number of scholars who argue that the Commission has continually lost ground to the member states as the European integration process has been increasingly inter-governmentalized through constitutional revision from the early 1990s on. See, for example, Hussein Kassim and Anand Menon, 'European Integration Since the 1990s: Member States and the European Commission', ARENA Working Papers, WP 6/04 (Oslo: ARENA, 2004),p. 10.

8 Mark Pollack 'Delegation, Agency and Agenda-Setting in the Treaty of Amsterdam', *European Integration online Papers* 3/6, 1999, http://eiop.or.at/eiop/texte/1999-006.htm

9 Marlene Wind, 'Europe Toward A Post-Hobbesian Political Order: Constructivism and European Integration', *EUI Working Paper*, European University Institute, Florence, 1996, p. 2.

10 Lykke Friis, '"The End of the Beginning" of Eastern Enlargement – The Luxembourg Summit and Agenda-Setting', *European Integration online Papers* 2/7, 1998, http://eiop.or.at/eiop/texte/1998-007a.htm

11 Ibid.

12 Article 49 of the Treaty on European Union (TEU). The Constitutional Treaty, agreed by heads of state and government in June 2004, but not yet ratified at the time of going to print, does not change the European Commission's role in the enlargement process.

13 Desmond Dinan, 'The Commission and Enlargement', in John Redmond and Glenda Rosenthal (eds), *The Expanding European Union: Past, Present and Future* (Boulder, CO: Lynne Rienner, 1998), p. 21.

14 Marc Maresceau, 'The EU Pre-Accession Strategies: a Political and Legal Analysis', in Marc Maresceau and Ewart Lannon (eds), *The EU's Enlargement and Mediterranean Strategies: A Comparative Analysis* (Basingstoke: Palgrave, 2001), p. 3.

15 Ulrich Sedelmeier and Helen Wallace, 'Eastern Enlargement: Strategy or Second Thoughts?', in Helen Wallace and William Wallace (eds), *Policy-Making in the European Union*, 4th edn (Oxford: Oxford University Press, 2000), p. 438.

16 Ulrich Sedelmeier, 'Sectoral Dynamics of EU Enlargement: Advocacy, Access, and Alliances in a Composite Polity', *Journal of European Public Policy* 9/4, 2002, p. 638.

17 Ulrich Sedelmeier and Helen Wallace, op. cit., p. 443.

18   Frank Schimmelfennig, 'The Double Puzzle of EU Enlargement: Liberal Norms, Rhetorical Action, and the Decision to Expand to the East', *ARENA Working Papers*, No. 15, June 1999.

19   Jeffrey Checkel, 'International Norms and Domestic Politics: Bridging the Rationalist–Constructivist Divide', *European Journal of International Relations* 3/4, 1997, pp. 473–5.

20   Ulrich Sedelmeier, 'East of Amsterdam: The Implications of the Amsterdam Treaty for Eastern Enlargement', in Karl-Heinz Neunreither and Antje Wiener (eds), *European Integration After Amsterdam: Institutional Dynamics and Prospects for Democracy* (Oxford: Oxford University Press, 2000), p. 229.

21   See, for example, 'Brittan bangs drum for East European trade', *Financial Times*, 14 April 1993.

22   'Delors calls for closer ties to Eastern Europe', *Financial Times*, 29 January 1994; see also *European Report*, No. 1932, 9 March 1994, V.3.

23   Jacques Delors, 'An Ambitious Vision for the Enlarged Union', Speech delivered to the *Notre Europe* Conference, Brussels, 21 January 2002.

24   Peter Ludlow, *The Making of the New Europe: The European Councils on Brussels and Copenhagen 2002*, European Council Commentary 2/1, (Brussels: EuroComment, 2004), pp. 23–5. On van den Bröek's role see also 'Europe's expander' (profile), *The Economist*, 6 June 1998.

25   'Commission reorganizes on eve of regular reports', *European Report*, No. 2436, 22 September 1999, V.4-5.

26   Peter Ludlow, op. cit., p. 43.

27   See the interview with Landaburu in *European Voice*, 19 September 2002, in which he argues that enlargement is cheap at the price and to place it in its proper context would bring nothing like the problems with the war on terror.

28   Peter Ludlow, op. cit., pp. 43–4.

29   Ibid., pp. 34–5.

30   Quoted in *European Voice*, 10 February 2000.

31   Quoted in the *Financial Times*, 30 June 2000.

32   'Eastern land issue clouds EU negotiations', *Financial Times*, 3 April 2001; 'Verheugen supports applicants' right to delay sale of land to wealthy West', *European Voice*, 5 April 2001.

33   See, for example, 'Verheugen meets new Hungarian government', *European Report*, No. 2701, 17 July 2002, V.8.

34   'Verheugen warns Poles against "lies"', *European Report*, No. 2700, 13 July 2002, V.3.

35   Whilst addressing the European Parliament, for example, in early 2003, commissioner Verheugen was the subject of a withering attack by Spanish socialist María Izquierdo Rojo who accused him of being the commissioner for the candidate countries instead of representing the interests of the EU. See *European Report*, No. 2745, 25 January 2003, V.3. Former Czech Prime Minister Vaclav Klaus accused Verheugen of a 'tragic misuse of his position' after the Commissioner had warned that the Czech Republic's prospects of EU membership would be set back if the Klaus-led Civic Democrats won the 2002 general election. See 'Verheugen accused of meddling by former Czech PM', *European Voice*, 29 September 2001.

36   The one notable blip in Verheugen's smooth steering of enlargement policy came in an interview with the *Süddeutsche Zeitung* on 2 September 2000 when he suggested that a referendum on eastern enlargement should be held in Germany to ensure that the public there were not simply presented with a 'fait accompli'. The Commissioner claimed that the euro had been introduced 'behind the backs of the German people' and said that there should have been a referendum on the single currency to 'force the élites to come down from their ivory towers and campaign for the euro in a dialogue with the people'. Speculation that this constituted a German effort to delay enlargement was prompted by the close relationship Verheugen enjoyed with German Chancellor Gerhard Schröder, a former colleague in the Social Democratic Party. See 'EU enlargement row deepens', *Guardian*, 4 September 2000: 'Commissioner's comments spark furore', *Financial Times*, 4 September 2000; 'EU commissioner casts new doubts on enlargement', *Independent*, 4 September 2000; 'A row about a bigger EU', *The Economist*, 9 September 2000.

37   Peter Ludlow, op. cit., p. 225.

38   Ibid., p. 137.

39   Typical of the Commission's approach is the language to be found in the Regular Reports of

2002. See European Commission, *Towards the Enlarged Union: Strategy Paper*, COM (2002) 700 final. Available online at: http://europa.eu.int/comm/enlargement/report2002/, Brussels, 9 October 2002. These were the final monitoring reports to be released before the crucial end stage of the negotiations in November–December 2002.

40 Robert Kagan, *Paradise and Power: America and Europe in the New World Order* (New York: Alfred A. Knopf, 2003), p. 55.

41 David Phinnemore, *Association: Stepping-stone or Alternative to EU Membership?* (Sheffield: Sheffield Academic Press, 1999), p. 105; Jan Zielonka, 'Ambiguity as a Remedy for the EU's Eastward Enlargement', *Cambridge Review of International Affairs* XII/1, 1998, p. 17.

42 Romano Prodi, 'Catching the Tide of History: Enlargement and the Future of the Union', Paul Henri Spaak Foundation, Speech/00/374, Brussels, 11 October 2000.

43 Olli Rehn, 'Values define Europe, not Borders', *Financial Times*, 4 January 2005.

44 Ibid.

45 Ulrich Sedelmeier, 'East of Amsterdam', p. 219.

46 Günter Verheugen, 'Enlargement is Irreversible', Speech to the European Parliament, Speech 00/351, Brussels, 3 October 2000.

47 Frank Schimmelfennig, op. cit.

48 See, for example, European Commission, *Regular Reports from the Commission on Progress Towards Accession by Each of the Candidate Countries*, Brussels, 8 November 2000. Available online at: http://www.europa.eu.int/comm/enlargement/report_11_00/index.htm

49 See, for example, Prodi's 2001 speech to the Hungarian Academy of Sciences. Its title is indicative of the 'drivers' inclusive approach. Romano Prodi, 'Bringing the Family Together', Speech to the Hungarian Academy of Sciences, Speech/01/158, Budapest, 4 April 2001.

50 Jacques Delors, op. cit.

51 Günter Verheugen, op. cit.

52 Iver B. Neumann, 'European Identity, EU Expansion, and the Integration/Exclusion Nexus', *Alternatives* 23, 1998, p. 405.

53 Graham Avery, *The Commission's Perspective on the Negotiations*, SEI Working Paper No. 12, June 1995.

54 Tanja A. Börzel, 'Guarding the Treaty: The Compliance Strategies of the European Commission', in Tanja A. Börzel and Rachel A. Cichowski (eds), *The State of the European Union, vol. 6: Law, Politics and Society* (Oxford: Oxford University Press, 2003), pp. 198–202.

55 Brigid Laffan, 'The European Union and its Institutions as "Identity Builders" in R. K Hermann, Thomas Risse and Mark Brewer (eds), *Transnational Identities: Becoming European in the EU* (Lanham, MD: Rowman & Littlefield, 2004), p. 85.

56 Maximilian Conrad, 'Persuasion, Communicative Action and Socialization after EU Enlargement', Paper presented at the Second ECPR Pan-European Conference, Bologna, 24–6 June 2004, p. 2.

57 Dimitris Papadimitriou and David Phinnemore, 'Europeanization, Conditionality, and Domestic Change: The Twinning Exercise and Administrative Reform in Romania', *Journal of Common Market Studies* 42/3, 2004, p. 620.

58 See Commissioner Verheugen's retrospective overview of the PHARE Programme: Günter Verheugen, Speech at the 100th Meeting of the PHARE Management Committee, Brussels, 12 June 2003.

59 Tanja Börzel and Thomas Risse, 'One Size Fits All! EU Policies for the Promotion of Human Rights, Democracy and the Rule of Law', Paper Presented at the Workshop on Democracy Promotion, Stanford University, 2–4 October 2004.

60 Dimitris Papadimitriou and David Phinnemore, op. cit., p. 623.

61 Ibid., p. 625.

62 Günter Verheugen, Speech at the 100th Meeting of the PHARE Management Committee, Brussels, 12 June 2003.

63 Milada Ana Vachudova, 'The Leverage of International Institutions on Democratizing States: Eastern Europe and the European Union', RSC No. 2001/33, Robert Schuman Centre for Advanced Studies (Florence: European University Institute, 2001), p. 2.

64 Phedon Nicolaides, 'Preparing for Accession to the European Union: How to Establish Capacity for Effective and Credible Application of EU Rules', in Marise Cremona (ed.), *The Enlargement of the European Union* (Oxford: Oxford University Press, 2003), p. 46.
65 See, for example, European Commission, *Towards the Enlarged Union: Strategy Paper 2002*, http://europa.eu.int/comm/enlargement/report2002/, Brussels, 2002.
66 Phedon Nicolaides, op. cit., p. 48.
67 Ibid., p. 49.
68 Dimitry Kochenov, op. cit.
69 Marc Maresceau, op. cit..
70 Martin Ferry 'The EU and Recent Regional Reform in Poland', *Europe–Asia Studies* 55/7, 2003, p. 1107.
71 Phedon Nicolaides, op. cit., p. 43.
72 Milada Ana Vachudova, op. cit., p. 27.
73 Marc Maresceau, op. cit., pp. 32–4.
74 'Poland sent letter on food safety', *European Report*, No. 2775, 10 May 2003, V.8.
75 'Preparing for accession safeguards', *European Report*, No. 2816, 1 November 2003, V.5.
76 European Commission, *Comprehensive Monitoring Report 2003*, http://europa.eu.int/comm./enlargement/report_2003/
77 'Monitoring reports warn of "serious concern"', *European Report*, No. 2817, 5 November 2003, V.1. On food safety and Polish efforts to comply with the Commission's demands see 'Poland aims to ease its passage', *European Report*, No. 2834, 14 January 2004, V.8
78 'Candidate countries receive warning letters', *European Report*, No. 2761 22 March 2003, V.3; 'Latvia needs to do more work in the social field', *European Report*, No. 2789, 2 July 2003, V.9.
79 'Preparing for accession safeguards', *European Report*, No. 2816, 1 November 2003, V.5.
80 Phedon Nicolaides, op. cit., p. 47.

Chapter 7

1 David Phinnemore, *Association: Stepping-stone or Alternative to EU Membership?* (Sheffield: Sheffield Academic Press, 1999), pp. 31–2.
2 Ibid.
3 Ibid., p. 70.
4 Karlheinz Neunreither, 'The European Parliament and Enlargement, 1973–2000' in John Redmond and Glenda Rosenthal (eds), *The Expanding European Union: Past, Present and Future* (Boulder, CO: Lynne Rienner, 1998), pp. 70–1.
5 On the advances made by the European Parliament, see Uwe Diedrichs and Wolfgang Wessels, 'A New Kind of Legitimacy for A New Kind Of Parliament', *European Integration online Papers* 1/6, 1997, http://eiop.or.at/eiop/texte/1997_006a.htm; Anders Rasmussen, 'Institutional Games Rational Actors Play – The Empowering of the European Parliament', *European Integration online Papers* 4/1, 2000, http://eiop.or.at/eiop/texte/2000-001a.htm; on the Convention Process and Constitutional Treaty see Giacomo Benedetto, 'How Influential was Europe's Parliament during the Convention and IGC, 2002–2004?', Paper presented to the Second ECPR Pan European Conference, Bologna, 24–26 June 2004; http://www.jhubc.it/ecpr-bologna
6 Mark Pollack, *The Engines of European Integration: Delegation, Agency and Agenda-setting in the EU* (New York: Oxford University Press, 2002), p. 229. The majority threshold for EP assent in the case of an Article 7 breach is stronger (at two-thirds of the members) than the majority required for the Parliament's assent on accession decisions. In the Constitutional Treaty Article 7 is replaced by Article I-59, which does not alter the European Parliament's role within the sanctioning process.
7 Article 49 of the Treaty on European Union (TEU). In the Constitutional Treaty, agreed by heads of state and government in June 2004 (but at the time of going to press not yet ratified), the European Parliament's role does not change.
8 One crucial difference between the role of the European Parliament and that of national parliaments of the member states in the ratification process is that the latter ratify the Accession

Treaty after it has been signed and approve all the accession states en bloc, whereas the EP has to give its assent to each country's application individually before the Accession Treaty can be signed. Thus the EP has the opportunity in theory to block the accession of any individual state while national parliaments can only register disapproval by voting down the entire enlargement.

9 In the case of eastern enlargement ratification by EU member states took place exclusively by parliamentary approval. This has been the norm in all previous enlargements, except in the case of British entry into the Community, when the French government decided that the issue was too important for simple parliamentary approval. A referendum was held in France, which approved British entry, by a large majority. More recently, in the aftermath of the EU decision to begin accession negotiations with Turkey, attention has turned to the desirability of approval through popular referendums and these have been proposed for a number of EU member states such as Austria and France.

10 Stefanie Bailer and Gerald Schneider, 'The Power of Legislative Hot Air', *Journal of Legislative Studies* 6/2, 2000, p. 21.

11 Richard Corbett, Frances Jacobs and Michael Shackleton, *The European Parliament*, 4th edn (London: John Harper, 2000), p. 204; David Judge and David Earnshaw, *The European Parliament* (Basingstoke: Palgrave, 2003), p. 210.

12 Ulrich Sedelmeier and Helen Wallace, 'Eastern Enlargement: Strategy or Second Thoughts?' in Helen Wallace and William Wallace (eds), *Policy-Making in the European Union*, 4th edn (Oxford: Oxford University Press, 2000), p. 433.

13 See, for example, 'Romania Warned of EU Entry Block Over Anti-Gay Laws', *European Voice* 7/23, 7–13 June 2001; 'Anti-Gay Laws Could Return, Warn MEPs', *European Voice*, 28 June–4 July 2001.

14 See European Parliament Committee on Foreign Affairs, Human Rights, Common Security and Defence Policy, *The Committee's Enlargement Activities During the Fifth Legislature (1999–2004)*, Notice to Members No. 08/2004, PE 329.317, Brussels, 5 May 2004, p. 2.

15 Interviews, PSE and ELDR MEPs, Brussels, October 2002.

16 On Viktor Orban's grilling before the Committee see *European Report*, No. 2662, 23 February 2002, V.1. See also 'Hungarian minorities a big problem, Verheugen admits', *European Report*, No. 2662, 23 February 2002, V.4.

17 European Parliament, *The Committee's Enlargement Activities During the Fifth Legislature (1999–2004)*, p. 10.

18 Interview, ELDR MEP, Brussels, October 2002.

19 Maximilian Conrad, 'Persuasion, Communicative Action and Socialization after EU Enlargement', Paper presented at the Second ECPR Pan-European Conference, Bologna, 24–6 June 2004, p. 15.

20 For a more precise examination of socialization within the European Parliament see Roger Scully, *Becoming Europeans? Attitudes, Behaviour, and Socialization in the European Parliament* (Oxford: Oxford University Press, 2005).

21 Trine Flockhart, 'Masters and Novices: Socialization and Social Learning through the NATO Parliamentary Assembly', *International Relations* 18/3, 2004: 361–80.

22 Trine Flockhart, op. cit., p. 372.

23 Interviews PPE-DE and ELDR members, Brussels, October 2002.

24 On the EP's relations with national parliaments see European Parliament, *National Parliaments and Enlargement/Accession*, Briefing No. 45, PE 186.571, Brussels, 10 November 1999.

25 Peter Ludlow, *The Making of the New Europe: The European Councils on Brussels and Copenhagen 2002*, European Council Commentary 2/1 (Brussels: EuroComment, 2004), p. 65.

26 Interviews PPE-DE and ELDR members, Brussels, October 2002.

27 Simon Hix, Abdul Noury, and Gerard Roland, 'Power to the Parties: Competition and Cohesion in the European Parliament, 1979–2001', *British Journal of Political Science* 34/4: 767–93; Tapio Raunio, *Party Group Behaviour in the European Parliament: An Analysis of Transnational Political Groups in the 1989–1994 Parliament* (Tampere: University of Tampere Press, 1996), pp. 202–5.

28 Stephen Day and Jo Shaw, 'The Evolution of Europe's Transnational Political Parties in the Era

of European Citizenship', in Tanja A. Börzel and Rachel A. Cichowski (eds), *The State of the European Union, vol. 6: Law, Politics and Society* (Oxford: Oxford University Press, 2003), pp. 161–2.

29 See Stefanie Bailer and Gerald Schneider, op. cit., for an in-depth analysis of these divisions.

30 Interview PES MEP, Brussels, October 2002.

31 I thank Tapio Raunio for this point.

32 Geoffrey Harris, 'The Democratic Dimension of EU Enlargement: the Role of Parliament and Public Opinion', in Ronald. H. Linden (ed.), *Norms and Nannies: The Impact of International Organizations on the Central and East European States* (Lanham, MD: Rowman & Littlefield, 2002), p. 46.

33 For a comprehensive exposition of the Parliament's position on the Beneš Decrees see European Parliament, *The Committee's Enlargement Activities During the Fifth Legislature (1999–2004)*, pp. 11–12.

34 Geoffrey Harris, op. cit., p. 46.

35 Interview UEN MEP, Dublin, March 2004.

36 There is demonstrable proof for this hypothesis in the final reports of each country Rapporteur, which were delivered in advance of the key enlargement debate on 9 April 2003. The great majority of Rapporteurs waxed lyrical on the achievements of the candidate states and the historic sense of occasion that permeated the EP vote. The only exception was the Report of the Rapporteur for the Czech Republic, Jürgen Schröder (PPE), whose criticism mainly revolved around the Czech failure to respond positively (or positively enough) on the Beneš Decrees.

37 See 'MEPs back candidate's stance on farm talks', *European Report*, No. 2688, 1 June 2002, V.1.

38 'MEPs back Sofia on nuclear power plant closure', *European Report*, No. 2690, 8 June 2002, V.4. On a similarly supportive JPC position on Slovakia see 'Parliamentarians call for democratic continuity', *European Report*, No. 2690, 8 June 2002, V.7.

39 At the EP debate on enlargement on 9 April 2003, Minister Yiannitsis, representing the Greek Presidency of the European Union, specifically cited the work carried out by the JPCs as 'invaluable' to the process.

40 European Parliament, *Draft Report on the Financial Impact of EU Enlargement* (Rapporteur Reimer Böge), A5-0178/2002, Brussels, 13 June 2002; European Parliament, *Draft Report on the State of the Enlargement Negotiations* (Rapporteur Elmar Brok), A5-0190/2002, Brussels, 13 June 2002. For detailed analysis see 'MEPs give their backing against sombre background', *European Report*, No. 2686, 25 May 2002, V.6–7.

41 'MEPs pleased with progress in accession negotiations', *European Report*, No. 2692, 15 June 2002, V.11.

42 Turkey was not represented in the debate because the Turkish Grand Assembly was not able to select the 12 members of parliament it was allocated for the debate, as the Turkish Parliament had not been constituted after parliamentary elections.

43 Quoted by EUobserver.com, 19 November 2002. See also 'European Parliament debate with candidates', *European Report*, No. 2729, 20 November 2002, V.14–15; 'MEPs back plans for accession negotiations', *European Report*, No. 2730, 23 November 2002, V.3–4.

44 The biggest gain within the Parliament was recorded by the socialist grouping (PES). It gained 79 new deputies, one third of the total number of new deputies. Of this figure 26 deputies were from Poland. See 'Socialists to get most candidate deputies', EUobserver.com, 19 November 2002.

45 The logistical impact of eastern enlargement on the Parliament should not be underestimated. The Parliament's estimate for spending on such as extra administrative and infrastructural support would amount to €90 million in 2003, €156 million in 2004, €186 million in 2005 and almost €200 million in 2006. Extra office space would also be needed, thus the EP set about the construction of two new office blocks to be ready by the end of 2006. Extra personnel would amount to about 1,120 posts of which approximately 70 per cent would be accounted for by translation services. The increase in membership naturally would add many new languages, in fact ten new languages, from 11 to 21. The EP decided to guarantee multilingualism through a policy known as 'controlled multilingualism'. This would mean that MEPs would still be able to speak in their mother tongue to other MEPs through interpretation. On recruitment and the spread of post-enlargement positions see *European Report*, No. 2678, 24 April 2002.

46 Peter Ludlow, op. cit., p. 64–5.

47 Interview, Pat Cox, March 2005.

48   See, for example, Pat Cox, Speech at the Conference on EU Enlargement Day, Dublin Castle, 1 May 2004.

49   See Cox's speech at the Seville summit, *Bulletin of the European Union*, EU 6-1999, 19 June 2002.

50   See European Parliament, *Resolution on the Commission's White Paper: Preparation of Associated Countries of Central and Eastern Europe for Integration into the Internal Market of the Union* (Rapporteur Arie Oostlander), A4-0101/1996, Brussels, 17 April 1996. See also European Parliament, *Resolution on the Communication of the Commission on 'Agenda 2000' – the 2000-06 Financial Framework for the Union and the Future Financing System* (Rapporteur Colom i Naval), A4-0331/97, PE 223.701/def, Brussels, 1997.

51   See European Parliament, *Resolution on the Commission Proposals for Council Decisions on the Principles, Priorities, Intermediate Objectives and Conditions Contained in the Accession Partnerships*, A4-0081/1998, A4-0087/1998, Brussels, 11 March 1998.

52   Peter Ludlow, op. cit., p. 64. See also European Parliament, *Resolution on the Preparation of the Meeting of the European Council in Helsinki on 10 and 11 December 1999*, B5-0308/99, B5-0309/99, B5-0311/99, B5-0312/99, Brussels, 2 December 1999; European Parliament, *Resolution on the Helsinki European Council*, B5-0327/99, B5-0353/99, B5-0354/99, B5-0357/99, Brussels, 16 December 1999.

53   See 'MEPs call for enlargement with or without Nice', EUobserver.com, 4 September 2001. See also Stefanie Bailer and Gerald Schneider, op. cit., p. 28.

54   'Council to defer institutional chapter until end of negotiations?', *European Report*, No. 2713, 25 September 2002, V.4–5.

55   Cecilia Malmström, European Parliament Debate on Enlargement, 9 April 2003; available online at: http://europarl.eu.int/enlargement/default_en.htm

56   In practice this meant that observers from the accession states would be able to attend plenary sessions of the European Parliament but would not have the right to vote or speak. However, within the EP's committees they had the right to speak – although again not to vote. In addition observer status meant second-class status when it came to claiming expenses for the year before formal accession. They were only able to claim for actual travel expenses incurred – rather than the lucrative regime enjoyed by the EU15 MEPs who could claim a sum derived from the mileage travelled, sometimes well in excess of the actual cost incurred.

57   'EU leaders to offer Turkey deal on membership talks', *Independent*, 16 December 2004; 'EU chiefs set for late 2005 talks start date', *Irish Times*, 16 December 2004.

58   Quoted in the *Irish Times*, 16 December 2004.

59   For an overview of the Parliament's position on institutional recalibration see European Parliament, *The Institutional Aspects of Enlargement of the European Union*, Briefing No. 15, PE 167.299/rev.1, 21 June 1999.

60   European Parliament, *Resolution on the Association Agreements*, A3-0055/1991, Brussels, 18 April 1991.

61   European Parliament, *Resolution on the Structure and Strategy for the European Union with Regard to its Enlargement and the Creation of a Europe-Wide Order* (Hänsch Report), A3-0189/1992, Brussels, 20 January 1993.

62   European Parliament, *Resolution on the Financing of the Enlargement of the European Union* (Rapporteur Efthymios Christodoulou), A4-0353/1996, Brussels, 12 December 1996.

63   At the time German finance minister Theo Waigel and his Dutch counterpart, Gerrit Zalm, led the way in suggesting cuts in the structural and cohesion funds as the appropriate means to finance eastern enlargement. See 'MEPs count the cost of enlargement', *European Voice*, 28 November 1996.

64   European Parliament, *Resolution on the Communication of the Commission on 'Agenda 2000' – the 2000–2006 Financial Framework for the Union and the Future Financing System* (Rapporteur Colom i Naval), A4-0331/1997; European Parliament, *Resolution on the Communication from the Commission 'Agenda 2000 – For a Stronger and Wider Union'* (Rapporteurs Oostlander/Baron Crespo), A4-0368/1997, Brussels, 4 December 1997; European Parliament, *Enlargement: Pre Accession Strategy for Enlargement of the European Union*, Briefing no. 24 of the Parliament's Secretariat's Task Force, PE 167.631, Luxembourg, 17 June 1998.

65   European Union, *Interinstitutional Agreement between the European Parliament, the Council and the European Commission on Budgetary Discipline and Improvement of the Budgetary Procedure*, 1999/C 172/01, Brussels,

6 May 1999. On the significance of the IIA to the Parliament's budgetary powers see David Judge and Robert Earnshaw, op. cit., pp. 216–17.

66 In 1980 the Council of Ministers agreed on a Commission proposal for a Community Regulation before the EP had delivered its opinion, which was mandated under the treaty's consultation procedure. When the Council proceeded with the legislative proposal without Parliament's opinion, the EP took the issue to the ECJ claiming that the Council had exceeded its powers under the treaties. The ECJ agreed and in effect granted the Parliament the power to delay legislation to ensure the consultation procedure could be properly carried out.

67 'Parliament could delay approval of accession treaty', *European Report*, No. 2758, 12 March 2003, V.15; 'Parliament insists on renegotiating Copenhagen deal', *European Report*, No. 2759, 15 March 2003, V.10.

68 Cox wrote to Simitis urging the Presidency to re-open the issue of the budget, underlining how seriously Parliament was taking the issue. He got no reply to his letter.

69 See 'Parliament resigned to compromise on financing of enlargement', *European Report*, No. 2766, 9 April 2003, V.5.

70 Quoted in 'European Parliament gives its assent', *European Report*, No. 2767, 12 April 2003, V.13.

71 Daniel Cohn-Bendit, European Parliament Debate on Enlargement, 9 April 2003; available online at: http://europarl.eu.int/enlargement/default_en.htm.

72 European Parliament, *Report by the Committee on Foreign Affairs, Human Rights, Common Security and Defence Policy on the Conclusions of Negotiations with the Candidate States in Copenhagen* (Rapporteur Elmar Brok), A5-0081/2003; European Parliament, *Report by the Committee on Budgets on the Financial Perspective on Enlargement presented by the Commission in accordance with point 25 of the Inter-institutional Agreement of 6 May 1999 on Budgetary Discipline and Improvement of the Budgetary Procedure* (Rapporteurs Reimer Böge and Joan Colm I Naval), A5-0117/2003.

73 In particular the Foreign Affairs Committee singled out the so-called Law No.115 of 8 May 1946, which granted blanket legitimacy to the most serious criminal acts and even post-war crimes. The Committee held a special exchange of views with the Czech Foreign Minister, Cyril Svoboda, on 11 February 2003, which was dominated by the Beneš Decrees.

74 'Parliament makes its check on candidates before historic vote', *European Report*, No. 2764, 2 April 2003, V.8–10. The emphasis is my own.

75 The plenary debate and the historic vote were disturbed by an unofficial strike by session staff at the Parliament who were protesting over EU public service staff rules. Work in the interpreters' booth was stopped from time to time. One MEP, Maes of the Greens, commented that although he had every sympathy for the strikers he did think it 'a bit steep that the best paid officials in Europe should be expressing themselves in this way on a day on which we are welcoming the worst paid and the least prosperous people in Europe'. See European Parliament Debate on Enlargement, 9 April 2003.

76 'European Parliament gives its assent', *European Report*, No. 2767, 12 April 2003, V.12–13.

77 Ibid., V.13.

78 See, for example, 'MEPs seek role in enlargement conference', *European Voice*, 6 November 1997; 'European Parliament to demand input on Accession Partnerships', *European Report*, No. 2296, 4 March 1998, V.7–9

Chapter 8

1 Phillippe Schmitter, 'Examining the Present Euro-Polity with the Help of Past Theories', in Gary Marks, Fritz W. Scharpf, Phillippe Schmitter, and Wolfgang Streek, *Governance in the European Union* (London: Sage, 1996), p. 14; Helen Wallace, 'EU Enlargement: A Neglected Subject', in Maria Green Cowles and Mike Smith (eds), *The State of the European Union, vol. 5: Risks, Reforms, Resistance and Revival* (Oxford: Oxford University Press, 2000), pp. 149–63.

2 Christopher Hill, 'The Geopolitical Implications of Enlargement' in Jan Zielonka (ed.), *Europe Unbound: Enlarging and Reshaping the Boundaries of the European Union* (London: Routledge, 2002), p. 96.

3 Jan Zielonka, 'Introduction', in Jan Zielonka (ed.), *Europe Unbound*, p. 9.

4   The realist school of International Relations is of course extremely diverse. The chapter does not privilege any particular branch of the realist school but rather takes the central propositions advanced by both classical and contemporary realists as the basis for analysis.

5   Robert Gilpin, 'The Richness of the Tradition of Political Realism', in Robert Keohane (ed.), *Neorealism and its Critics* (New York: Columbia University Press, 1986), p. 304.

6   See Jack Donnelly, *Realism and International Relations* (Cambridge: Cambridge University Press, 2002). Chapter 2 deals with human nature and how it influences state motivations.

7   Hans J. Morgenthau, *Politics Among the Nations: The Struggle for Power and Peace*, 6th edn (New York: Alfred Knopf, 1985), pp. 3–4.

8   See, for example, John Mearsheimer, *The Tragedy of the Great Powers* (New York: Norton, 2001).

9   Robert Gilpin, op. cit., pp. 304–5.

10   Hans Morgenthau, op. cit., p. 12.

11   See, for example, David Baldwin (ed.), *Neorealism and Neoliberalism: The Contemporary Debate* (New York: Columbia University Press, 1993); Joseph M. Grieco, 'The Maastricht Treaty, Economic and Monetary Union and the Neorealist Research Programme', *Review of International Studies* 21, 1995: 21–40; Kenneth Waltz, *Theory of International Politics* (New York: Random House, 1979).

12   Joseph Grieco, *Cooperation Among Nations: Europe, America and Non-Tariff Barriers to Trade* (Ithaca, NY: Cornell University Press, 1990).

13   Robert O. Keohane, 'Theory of World Politics: Structural Realism and Beyond', in Robert O. Keohane (ed.), op. cit., p. 165.

14   John Mearsheimer, 'Back to the Future: Instability after the Cold War', *International Security* 15/1, 1990, pp. 5–9.

15   Within the discipline of IR European integration for a long time was treated as an insignificant and provincial terrain unworthy of the interest of (mostly American) scholars. See Knud Erik Jørgensen, 'Continental IR Theory: the Best Kept Secret', *European Journal of International Relations* 6/1, 2000, pp. 9–42.

16   John Mearsheimer, 'Back to the Future', p. 5.

17   Jim George, 'Back to the Future?', in Greg Fry and Jacinta O'Hagan (eds), *Contending Images of World Politics* (Basingstoke: Macmillan, 2000), p. 33.

18   My estimate includes all of the new states of Croatia, FYR Macedonia, Bosnia-Herzegovina, Serbia (later the State Union of Serbia and Montenegro) and Slovenia, which emerged after the break-up of Yugoslavia. It also includes Estonia, Latvia, Lithuania, Moldova, Ukraine, Belarus, Georgia, Armenia, Azerbaijan, and Russia as the states to emerge from the old Soviet Union. The Central Asian states to emerge from the Soviet Union are excluded. Finally, the Czech and Slovak republics are included as separate entities, as are Cyprus, Malta, and Turkey.

19   Alina Mungiu-Pippidi, 'Facing the "desert of Tartars": The Eastern Border of Europe', in Jan Zielonka (ed.), *Europe Unbound*, p. 52.

20   Eberhard Bort, 'Illegal Migration and Cross-Border Crime: Challenges at the Eastern Frontier of the European Union', in Jan Zielonka (ed.), *Europe Unbound*, p. 191.

21   William Wallace, 'Where Does Europe End? Dilemmas of Inclusion and Exclusion', in Jan Zielonka (ed.), *Europe Unbound*, p. 78.

22   The early foreign policy of the Clinton administration brought a new emphasis to the Asia-Pacific region. This was reflected in IR scholarship of the period, a significant body of which focused on the coming twenty-first century as the 'Pacific Century'.

23   A classic example is the agreement on CAP between President Chirac and Chancellor Schröder thrashed out at the Hotel Conrad in advance of the crucial Brussels summit in October 2002.

24   Christopher Hill, op. cit., p. 96.

25   European Council, Presidency Conclusions, Thessaloniki European Council Summit Meeting, *Bulletin of the European Union*, EU 6-2003.

26   See Christian Pippan, 'The Rocky Road to Europe: The EU's Stabilization and Association Process for the Western Balkans and the Principle of Conditionality', *European Foreign Affairs Review* 9, 2004, p. 243.

27   Operation ALTHEA, the EU military operation in Bosnia and Herzegovina, was launched on 2

December 2004, following adoption of United Nations Resolution 1575. Operation ALTHEA is an EU-led operation making use of NATO common assets and capabilities.

28   Pierre Hassner, 'Fixed Borders or Moving Borderlands: A New Type of Border for a New Type of Entity', in Jan Zielonka (ed.), *Europe Unbound*, p. 38.

29   Romano Prodi, 'After Stockholm': Speech to the European Parliament, Speech/01/156, Strasbourg, 4 April 2001.

30   Karen Smith, *The Making of European Foreign Policy: The Case of Eastern Europe* (Basingstoke: Macmillan, 1999).

31   Christopher Hill, op. cit., p. 96.

32   Ibid., p. 97.

33   Atsuko Higashino, 'For the Sake of "Peace and Security"? The Role of Security in the European Union Enlargement Eastwards', *Cooperation and Conflict* 39/4, p. 348.

34   Ibid., p. 351.

35   Mikheil Saakashvili, 'Europe's Third Wave of Liberation', *Financial Times*, 20 December 2004.

36   Since its coinage in 1999 European Security and Defence Policy (ESDP) has come to cover a specific policy and set of institutional arrangements. Primarily identified as a crisis management instrument it has translated into a series of operations, both civilian and military. ESDP is an integral part of the EU's Common Foreign and Security Policy (CFSP), which in turn is but one arm of EU external action. See Antonio Missiroli, 'EDSP – How it Works', in Nicole Gnesotto (ed.), *EU Security and Defence Policy: The First Five Years (1999–2004)* (Paris: EU Institute for Security Studies, 2004), pp. 55–72.

37   Elisabeth Johansson-Nogués, 'The Fifteen and the Accession States in the UN General Assembly: What Future for European Foreign Policy in the Coming Together of the "Old" and the "New" Europe?', *European Foreign Affairs Review* 9/1, 2004, p. 72.

38   Ibid., pp. 76–7.

39   See, for example, 'The New Vassals', *Guardian*, 7 February 2003.

40   'Furious Chirac hits out at "infantile" easterners', *Guardian*, 18 February 2003; 'Eastern Europe dismayed at Chirac snub', *Guardian*, 19 February 2003.

41   Elisabeth Johansson-Nogués, op. cit., p. 67.

42   Christopher Hill, op. cit., p. 107.

43   Michael Baun, *A Wider Europe: The Process and Politics of European Union Enlargement* (Lanham, MD: Rowman & Littlefield, 2000), p. 86.

44   Anatol Lieven, 'Romania presses its case', *Financial Times*, 30 September 1997.

45   Consider that in the mid-1990s Boris Yeltsin made an ostensibly serious suggestion that Bulgaria forget about EU membership and join the Commonwealth of Independent States (CIS). This suggestion was not taken seriously in Bulgaria (despite very close historic ties, which predated the Soviet period). Arguably, however, Yeltsin's 'offer' gave Bulgarian leaders extra leverage in discussions with the EU.

46   Frank Schimmelfennig, 'The Double Puzzle of EU Enlargement: Liberal Norms, Rhetorical Action, and the Decision to Expand to the East', *ARENA Working Papers* 15, Oslo, June 1999.

47   Richard Ned Lebow, 'The Long Peace, the End of the Cold War, and the Failure of Realism', *International Organization* 48/2, 1994, pp. 258–9.

48   David Brooks, 'Mourning Mother Russia', *International Herald Tribune*, 29 April 2005.

49   See Anna Politkovskaya, *Putin's Russia* (London: Harvill Press, 2004), chapter 1, 'My Country's Army, and its Mothers', and chapter 5, 'Nord-Ost: the Latest Tale of Destruction'. See also Dov Lynch (ed.), *What Russia Sees*, Chaillot Papers, No. 74, January 2005 (Paris: EU Institute for Security Studies); Dov Lynch, *Russia Faces Europe*, Chaillot Papers, No. 60, May 2003 (Paris: EU Institute for Security Studies); Richard Sakwa, *Putin: Russia's Choice* (London: Routledge, 2004).

50   See Neil Robinson, *Russia: A State of Uncertainty* (London: Routledge, 2002), chapter 5, 'The Politics of Failed Grandeur: Russia's new international relations'; Richard Sakwa, *Russian Politics and Society* (London: Routledge, 2002), part 5. See also Rick Fawn (ed.), *Realignments in Russian Foreign Policy* (London: Routledge, 2003).

51   'Russian Gas to Flow to Europe via Baltic Sea', *International Herald Tribune*, 11 April 2005.

52   Georg Sørensen, *Changes in Statehood: The Transformation of International Relations* (Basingstoke: Palgrave, 2001), p. 46.

53   See Thomas Parland, *The Extreme Nationalist Threat in Russia* (London: Routledge, 2004).

54   Michael Baun, op. cit., p. 54.

55   The Russian minorities in Latvia and Estonia represent respectively 29.6 per cent and 28.1 per cent of the population, while the proportion is much smaller in Lithuania at 8.7 per cent. See Dov Lynch, 'Russia Faces Europe', p. 84.

56   Christopher Hill, 'The Geopolitical Implications of Enlargement', p. 105.

57   Putin referred to the Nazi–Soviet Pact of 1939 as a measure to enhance Russia's national security and went on to describe the collapse of the Soviet Union as the 'greatest geopolitical catastrophe of the 20th century'. See Janusz Bugajski, 'History is politics in Putin's Russia', *Financial Times*, 27 April 2005.

58   This was most obviously demonstrated in the decision post-Beslan (the justification) to replace Russia's directly elected regional governors with governmental appointees.

59   See European Council, Presidency Conclusions, Essen Summit, 9–10 December 1994. The text of the 'Concluding Document' from the inaugural conference for a Pact on Stability in Europe is reprinted in *Bulletin of the European Union* 12-1994, pp. 100–1.

60   Michael Baun, *A Wider Europe*, p. 61.

61   Neil Robinson, *Russia: A State of Uncertainty*, p. 141.

62   The EU Police Mission to the former Yugoslav Republic of Macedonia (FYROM) was called PROXIMA and was given the mandate of supporting the development of an efficient and professional police service in FYROM based on European standards of policing. This was accompanied by CONCORDIA, a military crisis mission. The EUPM in Bosnia-Herzegovina was the first civilian crisis management operation under ESDP. See Gustav Lindstrom, 'On the Ground: ESDP Operations', in Nicole Gnesotto (ed.), op. cit., pp. 111–30.

63   One of the many double standards evident in the eastern enlargement process was that the principle of achieving lasting resolution of border disputes was not applied to the accession of the Republic of Cyprus (Greek Cyprus). Although prior to the 2004 accessions one final effort was made to resolve the question (through the UN), the Greek threat to veto the entire eastern enlargement process was sufficient to ensure that the Cyprus question was treated differently to similar (if not as protracted) problems in Central and Eastern Europe. Greek Cypriot accession did not require an a priori resolution of the Cyprus problem.

64   Andre Liebich, 'Ethnic Minorities and Implications of EU Enlargement', in Jan Zielonka (ed.), *Europe Unbound*, p. 131–4.

65   Bruno de Witte, 'Politics vs Law in the EU's Approach to Minorities', in Jan Zielonka (ed.), *Europe Unbound*, p. 142.

66   Timothy Garton Ash, cited in Jacek Saryusz-Wolski, 'Looking to the Future', in Antonio Missiroli (ed.), *Enlargement and European Defence after 11 September*, Chaillot Papers, No. 53, June (Paris: EU Institute for Security Studies, 2003), p. 56.

67   Charles Grant, 'The Eleventh of September and Beyond: the Impact on the European Union', in Lawrence Freedman (ed.), *Superterrorism: Policy Responses* (Oxford: Blackwell, 2002), p. 135.

68   Ibid., p. 137.

69   One headline-grabbing example of the loose alliances between terrorist groups and criminal organizations was that of the IRA and a Bulgarian mafia group, which made the headlines in early 2005. The IRA sought out the Bulgarian group in order to help launder the bulk of the money stolen from the Northern Bank in Belfast (up to €40 million) in December 2004. The two organizations were alleged to be behind a plan to buy a Bulgarian bank as an instrument for their joint operations.

70   Christopher Hill, op. cit., p. 106.

71   See, for example, 'Al Qaeda's Balkan Links', *Wall Street Journal Europe*, 1 November 2001; 'Warning on Balkan Bases for Al Qaeda', *Irish Times*, 12 January 2005.

72   On the Al Qaeda presence in Western Europe and the threat it poses see Therese Délpèch, *International Terrorism and Europe*, Chaillot Papers, No. 56, December (Paris: EU Institute for Security Studies, 2002), pp. 16-21.

73 Gijs de Vries, 'Europe must Unite to end Terror', *Financial Times*, 30 November 2004.
74 Stephen Haggard, M. A. Levy, Andrew Moravcsik and Kalypso Nicolaidis, 'Integrating the Two Halves of Europe: Theories of Interests, Bargaining and Institutions', in Stanley Hoffmann, Robert O. Keohane and Joseph S. Nye (eds), *After the Cold War: International Institutions and State Strategies in Europe, 1989–1991* (Harvard, MA: Harvard University Press, 1991), p. 187.
75 Andrew Moravcsik, 'Studying Europe After the Cold War: A Perspective from International Relations', *TKI Working Papers on European Integration and Regime Formation* (Esbjerg: South Jutland University Press, 1996).

Chapter 9

1 Andrew Moravcsik, 'Preferences and Power in the European Community: A Liberal Inter-governmentalist Approach', *Journal of Common Market Studies* 31/4, 1993: 473–524; Andrew Moravcsik, 'Studying Europe After the Cold War: A Perspective from International Relations', *TKI Working Papers on European Integration and Regime Formation* (Esbjerg: South Jutland University Press, 1996); Andrew Moravcsik, *The Choice for Europe: Social Purpose and State Power from Messina to Maastricht* (Ithaca, NY: Cornell University Press, 1998); Andrew Moravcsik, 'A New Statecraft? Supranational Entrepreneurs and International Cooperation', *International Organization* 53/2, 1999: 267–306; Andrew Moravcsik, 'Is Something Rotten in the State of Denmark? Constructivism and European Integration', *Journal of European Public Policy* 6/4, 1999: 669–81; Andrew Moravcsik, 'The European Constitutional Compromise and the Legacy of Neofunctionalism', *Journal of European Public Policy* 12/2, 2005: 1–37.
2 Frank Schimmelfennig, 'The Double Puzzle of EU Enlargement: Liberal Norms, Rhetorical Action, and the Decision to Expand to the East', *ARENA Working Papers* 15, June 1999.
3 Christopher Hill, 'The Geopolitical Implications of Enlargement', in Jan Zielonka (ed.), *Europe Unbound: Enlarging and Reshaping the Boundaries of the European Union* (London: Routledge, 2002), p. 99.
4 Frank Schimmelfennig, op. cit.
5 See, for example, ERT, *Opening Up: The Business Opportunities of EU Enlargement*, ERT Position Paper and Analysis of the Economic Costs and Benefits of EU Enlargement (Brussels, 2001).
6 Helene Sjursen, 'Why Expand? The Question of Justification in the EU's Enlargement Policy', *ARENA Working Paper* WP 01/6, Oslo.
7 Katinka Barysch, 'EU Enlargement: How to Reap the Benefits', *Economic Trends* 2, 2004.
8 Fritz Breuss, 'Macroeconomic Effects of EU Enlargement for Old and New Members', *WIFO Working Papers* 143/2001, Austrian Institute of Economic Research (WIFO), Vienna, 29 March 2001.
9 Katinka Barysch, op. cit.
10 Ibid.
11 Ibid.
12 Ibid.
13 Frank Schimmelfennig, op. cit.
14 Andrew Moravcsik, *The Choice for Europe*, p. 3.
15 Lee Miles, 'Theoretical Considerations', in Neil Nugent (ed.), *European Union Enlargement* (Basingstoke: Palgrave, 2004), p. 257.
16 Andrew Moravcsik, *The Choice for Europe*, p. 473.
17 Ibid., p. 472.
18 Andrew Moravcsik and Milada Ana Vachudova, 'National Interests, State Power, and EU Enlargement', *East European Politics and Society* 17/1, p. 50.
19 Andrew Moravcsik, *The Choice for Europe*, p. 26.
20 Lee Miles, op. cit., p. 257.
21 Frank Schimmelfennig, *The EU, NATO, and the Integration of Europe* (Cambridge: Cambridge University Press, 2003), p. 180.
22 Helene Sjursen, op. cit.
23 Fritz Breuss, op. cit.

24 See figures in Michael Baun, *A Wider Europe: The Process and Politics of European Union Enlargement* (Lanham, MD: Rowman & Littlefield, 2000), chapter 7, for example.

25 Cited in Katinka Barysch, op. cit.

26 Richard E. Baldwin, Joseph E. Francois, and Ricardo Portes, 'The Costs and Benefits of Eastern Enlargement: the Impact on the EU and Central Europe', *Economic Policy* 24, April 1997, pp. 125–76.

27 Dorothee Bohle, 'The Ties that Bind: Neoliberal Restructuring and Transnational Actors in the Deepening and Widening of the European Union', Paper presented at the ECPR Joint Session Workshops 'Enlargement and European Governance', Turin, 22–27 March 2002, p. 31.

28 Marcin Zaborowski, 'Poland, Germany and EU Enlargement: The Rising Prominence of Domestic Politics', *ZEI Discussion Paper* C 51, Centre for European Integration Studies, Bonn, 1999.

29 For analysis of the paradoxical positions of both Germany and Austria see Kirsty Hughes, 'A Most Exclusive Club', *Financial Times*, 11 August 1999. For juxtaposed views of the German policy stance on eastern enlargement see Thomas Banchoff, 'German Identity and European Integration', *European Journal of International Relations* 5/3, 1999: 259–89; and Marcin Zaborowski, op. cit. See also Stephen D. Collins, *German Policy-Making and Eastern Enlargement of the EU During the Kohl Era* (Manchester: Manchester University Press, 2002).

30 German EU Commissioner, Günter Verheugen, in a 2000 speech, stressed that enlargement was 'not a project whose aim is bigger markets, more economic opportunities and more competition'. Rather, the fundamental aim was, he said, 'lasting peace between the peoples of Europe'. See Günter Verheugen, 'Enlargement is irreversible', Speech to the European Parliament, Speech 00/351, Brussels, 3 October 2000. This point is also emphasized repeatedly in the discourse of German Foreign Minister Joschka Fischer and his officials.

31 See 'Britain to champion enlargement of EU', *The Times*, 29 June 2000.

32 Alan Mayhew, 'The Financial and Budgetary Impact of Enlargement and Accession', *SEI Working Paper* No. 65 (Brighton: Sussex European Institute, 2003), p. 15.

33 Paul Gillespie, 'French Disenchanted with the EU', *Irish Times*, 26 March 2005. See also 'Are They Winning?', *The Economist*, 23 March 2005; 'The New Infantilism', *The Times*, 24 March 2005.

34 Pierre Hassner, 'Fixed Borders or Moving Borderlands: A New Type of Border for a New Type of Entity', in Jan Zielonka (ed.), *Europe Unbound: Enlarging and Reshaping the Boundaries of the European Union* (London: Routledge, 2002), p. 38.

35 Quoted by Quentin Peel, 'EU States Try to Slow Enlargement', *Financial Times*, 30 September 1998.

36 'France has firmly rejected calls for a firm date for accessions', *European Voice*, 3 August 2000; 'France to launch charm offensive with applicants to silence critics', *European Voice*, 12 April 2001; 'France joins EU enlargement dispute', *Financial Times*, 21 May 2001.

37 See Olivier Costa, Anne Couvidat and Jean Pascal Daloz, 'The French Presidency of 2000', in Ole Elgström (ed.), *European Union Council Presidencies: a Comparative Perspective* (London: Routledge, 2003), pp. 129–31.

38 See, for example, 'Spain's cash plea threatens EU enlargement talks', *Financial Times*, 14 February 1994; 'Aznar digs in for a fight', *Financial Times*, 17 May 2001; 'Madrid casts doubt over target date for enlargement', *European Voice*, 15 November 2001.

39 See, for example, 'Rich EU citizens oppose enlargement', *Guardian*, 30 April 2001; 'Expansionist dream turns into nightmare for Europe's leaders', *Independent*, 7 May 2001; 'EU ministers at odds over funding for enlargement', *Financial Times*, 7 May 2001; 'Sweden scolds Spain for guarding its EU money', *Guardian*, 16 May 2001.

40 Francesc Morata and Ana-Mar Fernandez, 'The Spanish Presidencies: 1989, 1995 and 2002', in Ole Elgström (ed.), *European Union Council Presidencies: a Comparative Perspective* (London: Routledge, 2003), p. 174.

41 Sonia Piedrafita Tremosa, 'The EU Eastern Enlargement: Policy Choices of the Spanish Government', *European Integration online Papers* 9/3, http://eiop. or.at/eiop/texte/2005-003a.htm

42 Ibid.

43   Francesc Morata and Ana-Mar Fernández, op. cit., p. 177.

44   Sonia Piedrafita Tremosa, op. cit.

45   Cited in Dorothee Bohle, op. cit., pp. 25–6.

46   Francesc Morata and Ana-Mar Fernández, op. cit., p. 178.

47   'Spain spells out stance on aid in bigger EU', *Financial Times*, 23 April 2001. The Spanish Government insisted that the European Council Summit at Gothenburg (14–15 June 2001) adopt a political declaration that specified development aid received by Spain would not fall significantly after enlargement. In the event no such declaration was adopted.

48   Francesc Morata and Ana-Mar Fernández, op. cit., p. 184.

49   Sonia Piedrafita Tremosa, op. cit.

50   Ibid.

51   See 'Italy warns against speedy enlargement of the EU to the east', *Financial Times*, 18 May 2001; 'Tremonti attacks EU expansion', *Financial Times*, 13 March 2002.

52   Frank Schimmelfennig, 'The Community Trap: Liberal Norms, Rhetorical Action and the Eastern Enlargement of the European Union', *International Organization* 55/1, p. 52.

53   *The Observer*, 17 June 2001.

54   Quoted in the *Irish Times*, 19 June 2001.

55   *Daily Telegraph*, 10 June 2001.

56   *Guardian*, editorial, 11 June 2001.

57   Dorothee Bohle, op. cit., p. 23.

58   Ibid., p. 24.

59   Andrew Moravcsik and Milada Vachudova, op. cit., p. 45.

60   Ibid.

61   Ibid.

62   Ibid.

63   The *Sun*, *Mail*, and *Daily Express* led the ceaseless anti-immigrant campaign. But some of the broadsheets were just as prominent (if a little more subtle) in presenting eastern enlargement as primarily about the immigration threat. See, for example, 'Adverts to deter Euro dole seekers', *Sunday Times*, 8 February 2004. The *Sun* argued, *inter alia*, that hundreds of thousands of migrants would arrive on 1 May 2004 to take advantage of Britain's healthcare system. See 'See you on 1 May', *Sun*, 19 January 2004; 'Sick Britain', *Sun*, 24 February 2004. The *Daily Express* argued in the same week that the 'work-shy of Europe', 'tens of thousands of them', would be facilitated in their desire to decamp to the UK by new low cost airlines expanding their operations into Eastern Europe. See 'Migrants will fly for just £2', *Daily Express*, 25 February 2004. The 'flood' scenario was one the tabloid suggested would follow on from the decision of Easyjet to introduce just one new route to Ljubljana, Slovenia, ironically one of the wealthiest cities among the accession capitals. For a summary of the tabloid commentary on eastern enlargement see Peter Preston, 'Tabloids brimming with bile', *Observer*, 29 February 2004.

64   Eberhart Bort, 'Illegal Migration and Cross-Border Crime: Challenges at the Eastern Frontier of the European Union', in Jan Zielonka (ed.), *Europe Unbound: Enlarging and Reshaping the Boundaries of the European Union* (London: Routledge, 2002), p. 199.

65   Andrew Moravcsik and Milada Vachudova, op. cit., p. 48.

66   See *Financial Times*, 12 June 2001.

67   Both the UK and Ireland, although they granted full rights of residency and work, placed restrictions on CEE citizens' entitlements to benefits. The benign economic environment in both states may account for the greater generosity of access. In 2004 and 2005, for example, the unemployment rate in the UK hovered at under 5 per cent. In Ireland, the unemployment rate dropped to 4.2 per cent by the end of 2004, despite the entrance into the labour market of up to 80,000 workers from the new EU member states. In both countries important parts of industry had become hugely dependent on low cost migrant labour.

68   Alina Mungiu-Pippidi, 'Facing the "desert of Tartars": the Eastern Border of Europe', in Jan Zielonka (ed.), *Europe Unbound: Enlarging and Reshaping the Boundaries of the European Union* (London: Routledge, 2002), pp. 57–8.

69   Ibid., p. 66.

70 Ibid., p. 67.
71 Eberhart Bort, op. cit., p. 194.
72 Ibid., p. 195.
73 Christopher Hill, op. cit., p. 106.
74 Jon Birger Skjaerseth and Jorgen Wettestad, 'EU Enlargement: Challenges to the Effectiveness of EU Environmental Policy', Paper presented at the ECPR Second Pan-European Conference, Bologna, 24–26 June 2004, http://www.jhubc.it/ecpr-bologna, p. 9–12.
75 Consider the case of Bulgaria. In the Commission's Regular Reports on the progress of enlargement negotiations Bulgaria's nuclear power plant at Kozludy has been consistently cited as a thorn in the negotiations. The Commission insisted that Bulgaria close it down. This was difficult for Bulgaria as the plant contributed about 25 per cent of the country's electricity and the issue provoked strong reactions in Bulgaria.
76 The European Commission set up a River Danube Task Force in the aftermath of a major silage spillage in Romania in 2001. The Task Force brought together ministers from all the Danubian states to work together on cleaning up the river.
77 See, for example, Poland's decision to buy natural gas from Denmark: 'Poland, Denmark to Sign Deal for New Baltic Pipe Gas Link', *Central Europe Online*, 3 July 2001.
78 Christopher Hill, op. cit., p. 106. For the Commission view see former Environment Commissioner Margot Wallström, Speech to the Polish Parliament, Speech 00/77; Warsaw, 9 March 2000; Margot Wallström, Speech to the Environment Committee of the European Parliament, Speech 00/228, Brussels, 20 June 2000.
79 Daniel Wincott, 'Institutional Interaction and European Integration: Towards an Everyday Critique of Liberal Intergovernmentalism', *Journal of Common Market Studies* 33/4, 1995, p. 602.
80 Ibid., p. 600.
81 Ibid., p. 602.
82 Frank Schimmelfennig, op. cit.

Chapter 10

1 Antoeneta Dimitrova and Mark Rhinard, 'The Power of Norms in the Transposition of EU Directives', Paper Presented at the ECPR Joint Sessions, Grenada, Spain, 14–19 April 2005, p. 5.
2 Nicholas Onuf, *World of Our Making: Rules and Rule in Social Theory and International Relations* (Columbia: University of South Carolina Press, 1989), p. 59.
3 Alexander Wendt, *Social Theory of International Politics* (Cambridge: Cambridge University Press, 1999), pp. 69–71.
4 Thomas Risse-Kappen, 'Democratic Peace – War-like Democracies? A Social Constructivist Interpretation of the Liberal Argument', *European Journal of International Relations* 1/4, 1995, p. 502.
5 Alexander Wendt, op. cit., p. 24.
6 On differences within the Constructivist school see Jeffrey Checkel, 'Social Constructivisms in Global and European Politics', *ARENA Working Paper* 15/03, 2003; Stefano Guzzini, 'A Reconstruction of Constructivism in International Relations', *European Journal of International Relations* 6/2, 2000: 147–82; John Kurt Jacobsen, 'Duelling Constructivisms: A Post-Mortem on the Ideas Debate in Mainstream IR/IPE', *Review of International Studies* 29/1, 2003: 39–60; John Gerard Ruggie, 'What Makes the World Hang Together? Neo-Utilitarianism and the Social Constructivist Challenge', *International Organization* 52/4, 1998: 855–85; Steve Smith, 'Social Constructivisms and European Studies: A Reflectivist Critique', *Journal of European Public Policy* 6/4, 1999: 682–91.
7 Alexander Wendt, op. cit., p. 4.
8 Emmanuel Adler and Michael Barnett, 'Security Communities in Theoretical Perspective', in Emmanuel Adler and Michael Barnett (eds), *Security Communities* (Cambridge: Cambridge University Press, 1998), p. 6.
9 Bruce Russet, 'A Neo-Kantian Perspective: Democracy, Interdependence and International Organizations in Building Security Communities', in Emmanuel Adler and Michael Barnett (eds), *Security Communities*, p. 373.

10 Emmanuel Adler and Michael Barnett, 'A Framework for the Study of Security Communities' in Emmanuel Adler and Michael Barnett (eds), *Security Communities*, p. 31.

11 Alexander Wendt, op. cit., p. 174.

12 Emmanuel Adler and Michael Barnett (eds), op. cit., p. 59.

13 Ole Wæver, 'Insecurity, Security and Asecurity in the West European non-war Community', in Emanuel Adler and Michael Barnett (eds), *Security Communities*, pp. 69–70.

14 Lily Gardner Feldman, 'Reconciliation and Legitimacy: Foreign Relations and Enlargement of the European Union', in Thomas Banchoff and M. P. Smith (eds), *Legitimacy and the European Union: The Contested Polity* (London and New York: Routledge, 1999), p. 66.

15 Ole Wæver, op. cit., p. 99.

16 These include the non-EU organizations the Council of Europe (CoE), the Organization for Security and Cooperation in Europe (OSCE), and NATO. The legal obligations inherent under CoE membership include adherence to the European Convention on Human Rights and Fundamental Freedoms, supported by the European Court of Human Rights in Strasbourg. The European Union's Constitutional Treaty, if ratified, will see the EU itself accede to the European Convention on Human Rights and Fundamental Freedoms thus establishing a formal identity between the hitherto separate behavioural codes.

17 Emmanuel Adler and Michael Barnett, 'Studying Security Communities in Theory, Comparison, and History', in Emanuel Adler and Michael Barnett (eds), *Security Communities*, p. 420.

18 Romano Prodi, 'Catching the Tide of History: Enlargement and the Future of the Union', Paul Henri Spaak Foundation, Speech/00/374, Brussels, 11 October 2000.

19 Hans van den Bröek, Speech to the EU Enlargement Conference organized by the International Press Institute, Speech 97/264, Brussels, 27 November 1997.

20 For more see Ole Wæver, op. cit., p. 6–70.

21 Lily Gardner Feldman, op. cit., p. 81.

22 European Commission, 'The Europe Agreements and Beyond: A Strategy to Prepare the Countries of Central and Eastern Europe for Accession', COM (94) 320 final, Brussels, 1994.

23 Hans Van den Bröek, Speech to 'Forum 2000' Conference, Speech 98/198, Prague, 13 October 1998.

24 Günter Verheugen, Speech at the University of Tartu, 'Changing the History, Shaping the Future', Speech 01/215, Tartu, Estonia, 19 April 2001.

25 James G. March, and Johan P. Olsen, 'Institutional Perspectives on Governance', *ARENA Working Paper* 94/2, Oslo, 1994.

26 On efforts to construct a European identity see Lars Erik Cederman, 'Nationalism and Bounded Integration: What it Would Take to Construct a European Demos', *EUI Working Papers*, RSC No. 2000/34; Iver B. Neumann, 'Self and Other in International Relations', *European Journal of International Relations* 2/2, 1996: 139–74; Iver B. Neumann, 'European Identity, EU Expansion, and the Integration/Exclusion Nexus', *Alternatives* 23, 1998: 397–416; Iver B. Neumann and Jennifer Welsh, 'The "Other" in European Identity: An Addendum to the Literature on International Societies', *Review of International Studies* 17: 327–45; Thomas Risse *et al.*, 'To Euro or Not To Euro? The EMU and Identity Politics in the European Union', *European Journal of International Relations* 5/2: 147–87; Anthony D. Smith, 'National Identity and the Idea of European Unity', *International Affairs* 68: 55–76; Anthony D. Smith, 'A Europe of Nations – Or the Nations of Europe?', *Journal of Peace Research* 30: 129–35.

27 Samuel P. Huntington, 'The Clash of Civilizations?', *Foreign Affairs* 72, 1993: 22–49; Samuel P. Huntington, *The Clash of Civilizations and the Remaking of World Order* (New York: Simon & Schuster, 1996).

28 See Augustin José Menéndez, 'A Pious Europe? Why Europe Should Not Define Itself as Christian', *ARENA Working Paper* No. 10/04, Oslo, 2004. The article critiques Joseph Weiler's view that there should be an explicit reference to the Christian roots of European identity in the Preamble of the Constitutional Treaty.

29 François Duchêne, 'The European Community and the Uncertainties of Independence', in Max Kohnstamm and Walter Hager (eds), *A Nation Writ Large? Foreign Policy Problems before the European Community* (Basingstoke: Macmillan, 1973).

30   Ian Manners, 'Normative Power Europe: A Contradiction in Terms?', *Journal of Common Market Studies* 40/2, 2002: 235–58.

31   Ibid., p. 252.

32   Ibid., p. 241.

33   Helen Wallace, 'Which Europe Is It Anyway?' (The 1998 Stein Rokkan Lecture), *European Journal of Political Research* 35, 1998, p. 294.

34   Robert Kagan, *Paradise and Power: America and Europe in the New World Order* (New York: Knopf, 2003), p. 3.

35   Ulrich Sedelmeier, 'EU Enlargement, Identity and the Analysis of European Foreign Policy: Identity Formation through Policy Practice', *EUI Working Papers*, RSC No. 2003/13, p. 4.

36   European Council, Presidency Conclusions, Laeken European Council, *Bulletin of the European Union* 12-2001, Brussels, 14 and 15 December 2001.

37   Frank Schimmelfennig, *The EU, NATO, and the Integration of Europe* (Cambridge: Cambridge University Press, 2003), p. 267.

38   Frank Schimmelfennig, 'The Community Trap: Liberal Norms, Rhetorical Action and the Eastern Enlargement of the European Union', *International Organization* 55/1, 2001, p. 59.

39   Lykke Friis, 'When Europe Negotiates: From Europe Agreements to Eastern Enlargement', PhD Dissertation (Copenhagen: Department of Political Science, University of Copenhagen, 1996), pp. 84–90.

40   Roy Ginsberg, *Foreign Policy Actions of the European Community: The Politics of Scale* (Boulder, CO: Lynne Rienner, 1989), p. 36.

41   Joschka Fischer, 'From Confederacy to Federation - Thoughts on the Finality of European Integration', Humboldt University, Berlin, 12 May 2000.

42   Karen Fierke and Antje Wiener, 'Constructing Institutional Interests: EU and NATO Enlargement', *Journal of European Public Policy* 6/5, 1999: 721–42.

43   Ibid., p. 727.

44   Patricia Chilton, 'Mechanics of Change in Eastern Europe', in Thomas Risse-Kappen (ed.), *Bringing Transnational Relations Back In: Non-State Actors, Domestic Structures and International Institutions* (Cambridge: Cambridge University Press, 1999), p. 201.

45   Ulrich Sedelmeier, 'East of Amsterdam: The Implications of the Amsterdam Treaty for Eastern Enlargement', in Karlheinz Neunreither and Antje Wiener (eds), *European Integration After Amsterdam: Institutional Dynamics and Prospects for Democracy* (Oxford: Oxford University Press, 2000), p. 228.

46   European Council, Presidency Conclusions, Strasbourg European Council, *Bulletin of the European Communities*, EC 12-1989.

47   Frank Schimmelfennig, 'The Community Trap', op. cit., pp. 68–9.

48   European Council, Presidency Conclusions, Copenhagen European Council, *Bulletin of the European Communities*, EC 6-1993.

49   Helene Sjursen and Karen E. Smith, 'Justifying EU Foreign Policy: The Logics Underpinning EU Enlargement', *ARENA Working Paper* WP 01/1, Oslo, 2001.

50   Helen Wallace, op. cit., p. 294.

51   Ulrich Sedelmeier and Helen Wallace, 'Eastern Enlargement: Strategy or Second Thoughts? in Helen Wallace and William Wallace (eds), *Policy-Making in the European Union*, 4th edn (Oxford: Oxford University Press, 2000), p. 435.

52   See, for example, Antoeneta Dimitrova, 'Enlargement, Institution Building and the EU's Administrative Capacity', *West European Politics* 25/4, 2001: 171–90; James Hughes, Gwyndelon Sasse, and Claire Gordon, 'Conditionality and Compliance in the EU's Regional Policy and the Reform of Sub-National Government, *Journal of Common Market Studies* 42/3, 2004: 523–51; Jan Zielonka, 'Ambiguity as a Remedy for the EU's Eastward Enlargement', *Cambridge Review of International Affairs* XII/1, 1998: 14–29.

53   Tanja Börzel and Thomas Risse, 'One Size Fits All! EU Policies for the Promotion of Human Rights, Democracy and the Rule of Law', Paper Presented at the Workshop on Democracy Promotion, Stanford University, 2–4 October 2004.

54   Michael Emerson and Gergana Noutcheva, 'Europeanization as a Gravity Model of Democratization', *CEPS Working Document* No. 214 (Brussels: Centre for European Policy Studies, 2004), p. 21.

55   Ulrich Sedelmeier, 'EU Enlargement, Identity and the Analysis of European Foreign Policy: Identity Formation through Policy Practice', p. 7.

56   Marc Maresceau, 'Pre-accession', in Marise Cremona (ed.), *The Enlargement of the European Union* (Oxford: Oxford University Press, 2003), pp. 32–4.

57   Milada Ana Vachudova, 'The Leverage of International Institutions on Democratizing States: Eastern Europe and the European Union', RSC No. 2001/33, Robert Schuman Centre for Advanced Studies, Florence: European University Institute, p. 28; Michael Emerson and Gergana Noutcheva, op. cit., pp. 6–7.

58   Ulrich Sedelmeier, 'EU Enlargement, Identity and the Analysis of European Foreign Policy: Identity Formation through Policy Practice', p. 7.

59   Ibid.

60   Milada Ana Vachudova, op. cit., p. 27.

61   Michael Emerson and Gergana Noutcheva, op. cit., p. 6.

62   Quoted in *The Economist*, 30 April 2005.

63   On a visit to Sofia enlargement commissioner Ollie Rehn reminded the Bulgarian Parliament that the safeguard clauses included in the accession treaty would be invoked 'where the country is manifestly unprepared in an important number of areas'. These included fighting crime and corruption and protecting the rights of the Roma minority. See the *Irish Times*, 19 March 2005.

64   European Commission, *Recommendation of the European Commission on Turkey's Progress Toward Accession, Communication from the Commission to the Council*, COM (2004) 656 final, Brussels, 6 October 2004.

65   Tim Judah, 'Want to join the EU? Turn in your war criminals', *Observer*, 20 March 2005; 'EU shelves Croatia talks over war crimes dispute', *Financial Times*, 15 March 2005; 'Juncker presents Croatia with ultimatum', EUobserver.com, 15 March 2005; 'EU delays Croatian entry talks', *Guardian*, 17 March 2005; 'EU makes Croatia suffer for allowing war criminal to flee EU', *European Voice*, 10–16 March 2005; 'Postponed, but Croatia talks still on if Gotovina is found', *European Voice*, 17–23 March 2005; 'Croatia's chances dim as Hague says state is protecting war criminal', *International Herald Tribune*, 27 April 2005.

66   Helen Wallace, op. cit., p. 294.

67   Michael J. Baun, *A Wider Europe: The Process and Politics of European Union Enlargement* (Lanham, MD: Rowman & Littlefield, 2000), p. 10.

68   Paul Pierson, 'The Path to European Integration: A Historic-Institutionalist Analysis', in Wayne Sandholtz and Alec Stone Sweet (eds), *European Integration and Supranational Governance* (Oxford: Oxford University Press, 1998), p. 46.

69   Emanuel Adler and Michael Barnett, *Security Communities*, p. 49.

70   Ulrich Sedelmeier, 'EU Enlargement, Identity and the Analysis of European Foreign Policy: Identity Formation through Policy Practice', p. 15.

71   The only exception to this rule has been Norway, where after the successful conclusion of negotiations on two occasions the Norwegian people voted against membership.

72   European Council, Presidency Conclusions, Brussels European Council, *Bulletin of the European Union*, 12-2004, Brussels, 16–17 December 2004.

73   Milada Ana Vachudova, op. cit., p. 11.

74   Helene Sjursen, 'Why Expand? The Question of Justification in the EU's Enlargement Policy', *ARENA Working Paper* WP 01/6, Oslo, 2001.

75   Frank Schimmelfennig, 'The Community Trap', op. cit., pp. 72–6.

76   Ulrich Sedelmeier and Helen Wallace, op. cit., p. 457.

77   Cited by Frank Schimmelfennig, 'The Community Trap', op. cit., pp. 70–1.

Chapter 11

1   'A club in need of a new vision', *The Economist*, 29 April 2004.

2   Christine Ockrent, 'The price of arrogance', *International Herald Tribune*, 23–24 April 2005.

3   See, for example, Katinka Barysch, 'One year after enlargement', *CER Bulletin*, No. 41, April/May 2005; 'How can France's elite sell the EU constitution?', *International Herald Tribune*, 26 April

2005; 'As Poles take jobs, bitterness in Germany', *International Herald Tribune*, 27 April 2005; 'Mixed feelings one year after enlargement', EUobserver.com, 1 May 2005.

4   Katinka Barysch, op. cit.

5   Stefan Wagstyl, 'Accession states reap rewards of EU membership', *Financial Times*, 27 April 2005.

6   'In EU, boons and optimism after expansion', *International Herald Tribune*, 25 April 2005.

7   See, for example, Roger Cohen, 'Guilt, reconciliation and the German Pope', *International Herald Tribune*, 23–24 April 2005.

8   Ibid.

9   See Frank Schimmelfennig and Ulrich Sedelmeier, *The Europeanization of Central and Eastern Europe* (Ithaca, NY: Cornell University Press, 2005); Frank Schimmelfennig and Ulrich Sedelmeier, 'Governance by Conditionality: EU Rule Transfer to the Candidate Countries of Central and Eastern Europe', *Journal of European Public Policy* 11/4, 2004: 661–79.

10   Dimitry Kochenov, 'EU Enlargement Law: History and Recent Developments', *European Integration online Papers* 9/6, 2005, http://eiop.or.at/eiop/texte/2005-006a.htm

11   Stefanie Bailer and Gerald Schneider, 'The Power of Legislative Hot Air: Informal Rules and the Enlargement Debate in the European Parliament', *Journal of Legislative Studies* 6/2, 2000: 19–44.

Bibliography

Adler, Emanuel, 'Seizing the Middle Ground: Constructivism in World Politics, *European Journal of International Relations* 3/3, 1997: 319–63.

Adler, Emanuel, and Barnett, Michael (eds), *Security Communities* (Cambridge: Cambridge University Press, 1998).

Adler, Emanuel, and Barnett, Michael, 'Security Communities in Theoretical Perspective', in Emanuel Adler and Michael Barnett (eds), *Security Communities* (Cambridge: Cambridge University Press, 1998).

Adler, Emanuel, and Barnett, Michael, 'A Framework for the Study of Security Communities', in Emanuel Adler and Michael Barnett (eds), *Security Communities* (Cambridge: Cambridge University Press, 1998).

Adler, Emanuel, and Barnett, Michael, 'Studying Security Communities in Theory, Comparison, and History', in Emanuel Adler and Michael Barnett (eds), *Security Communities* (Cambridge: Cambridge University Press, 1998).

Ágh, Atila, 'Europeanization of Policy-Making in East Central Europe: The Hungarian Approach to EU Accession', *Journal of European Public Policy* 6/5, 1999: 839–54.

Albi, Anneli, 'Referendums in Eastern Europe: the Effects on Reforming the EU Treaties and on the Candidate Countries' Positions in the Convention', *EUI Working Papers*, RSC No. 2002/65, 2002.

Armstrong, Kenneth A., and Bulmer, Simon, *The Governance of the Single European Market* (Manchester: Manchester University Press, 1998).

Avery, Graham, 'The Enlargement Negotiations', in Fraser Cameron (ed.), *The Future of Europe: Integration and Enlargement* (London: Routledge, 2004), pp. 35–62.

Avery, Graham, *The Commission's Perspective on the Negotiations*, SEI Working Paper No. 12, June 1995.

Avery, Graham, and Cameron, Fraser, *Enlarging the European Union* (Sheffield: Sheffield Academic Press, 1998).

Bailer, Stefanie, and Schneider, Gerald, 'The Power of Legislative Hot Air: Informal Rules and the Enlargement Debate in the European Parliament', *Journal of Legislative Studies* 6/2, 2000: 19–44.

Bailey, David, and de Propris, Lisa, 'A Bridge too PHARE? EU Pre-Accession Aid and Capacity Building in the Candidate Countries', *Journal of Common Market Studies* 42/1, 2004: 77–98.

Baldwin, David (ed.), *Neorealism and Neoliberalism: The Contemporary Debate*, (New York: Columbia University Press, 1993).

Baldwin, Richard E., *Toward an Integrated Europe* (London: Centre for Economic Policy Reform, 1994).

Baldwin, Richard, Francois, Joseph E., and Portes, Ricardo, 'The Costs and Benefits of Eastern Enlargement: the Impact on the EU and Central Europe', *Economic Policy* 24, 1997: 125–76.

Baltas, Niklas, 'The Economy of the European Union', in Neil Nugent (ed.), *European Union Enlargement* (Basingstoke: Palgrave, 2004), pp. 146–57.

Banchoff, Thomas, 'German Identity and European Integration', *European Journal of International Relations* 5/3, 1999: 259–89.

Baring, Arnuf, *Germany's New Position in Eastern Europe: Problems and Perspectives* (Oxford: Berg, 1994).

Barysch, Katinka, 'EU Enlargement: How to Reap the Benefits', *Economic Trends* 2, 2004.

Baun, Michael J., *A Wider Europe: The Process and Politics of European Union Enlargement* (Lanham, MD: Rowman & Littlefield, 2000).

Benedetto, Giacomo, 'How Influential was Europe's Parliament during the Convention and IGC, 2002–2004?', Paper presented to the Second ECPR Pan European Conference, Bologna, 24–26 June 2004.

Berend, Iver T., 'The Further Enlargement of the European Union in a Historical Perspective', *European Review* 7/2, 1999: 175–81.

Berend, Iver T., *Central and Eastern Europe 1944–1993: Detour from the Centre to the Periphery* (Cambridge: Cambridge University Press, 1996).

Bjurulf, Bo, 'The Swedish Presidency of 2001: A Reflection of Swedish Identity', in Ole Elgström (ed.), *European Union Council Presidencies: A Comparative Perspective* (London: Routledge, 2003).

Bohle, Dorothee, 'The Ties That Bind: Neoliberal Restructuring and Transnational Actors in the Deepening and Widening of the European Union', Paper presented at the ECPR Joint Session Workshops 'Enlargement and European Governance', Turin, 22–27 March 2002.

Bort, Eberhardt, 'Illegal Migration and Cross-Border Crime: Challenges at the Eastern Frontier of the European Union', in Jan Zielonka (ed.), *Europe Unbound: Enlarging and Reshaping the Boundaries of the European Union* (London: Routledge, 2002), pp. 191–212.

Börzel, Tanja A., 'Guarding the Treaty: The Compliance Strategies of the European Commission', in Tanja A. Börzel and Rachel A. Cichowski (eds), *The State of the European Union, vol. 6: Law, Politics and Society* (Oxford: Oxford University Press, 2003), pp. 197–220.

Börzel, Tanja A., and Risse, Thomas, 'One Size Fits All! EU Policies for the Promotion of Human Rights, Democracy and the Rule of Law', Paper Presented at the Workshop on Democracy Promotion, Stanford University, 2–4 October 2004.

Bräuninger, Thomas, and König, Thomas, 'Enlargement and the Union's Institutional Reform', Paper Presented at a Conference on Enlargement and Constitutional Change in the European Union, Leiden University, Netherlands, 26–28 November 1999.

Breuss, Fritz, 'Macroeconomic Effects of EU Enlargement for Old and New Members', *WIFO Working Papers* 143/2001 (Vienna: Austrian Institute of Economic Research (WIFO)), 29 March 2001.

Brinar, Irene, and Svetlicic, Marjan, 'Enlargement of the European Union: the Case of Slovenia', *Journal of European Public Policy* 6/5, 1999: 802–21.

Brittan, Leon, *The Europe We Need* (London: Hamilton, 1994).

Bugge, Petr, 'Czech Perceptions of the Perspective of EU Membership: Havel versus Klaus', *EUI Working Papers*, RSC No. 2000/10, 2000.

Buzek, Jerzy, 'Poland's Future in a United Europe', *ZEI Discussion Paper*, Centre for European Integration Studies, Bonn, 1998.

Cameron, Fraser, (ed.), *The Future of Europe: Integration and Enlargement* (London: Routledge, 2004).

Cameron, Fraser, 'Widening and Deepening' in Fraser Cameron (ed.), *The Future of Europe: Integration and Enlargement* (London: Routledge, 2004).

Caslin, Terry, and Czaban, Laszlo, 'Economic Transformation in CEE', in Mike Mannin (ed.), *Pushing Back the Boundaries: The European Union and Central and Eastern Europe* (Manchester: Manchester University Press, 1999), pp. 70–98.

Cederman, Lars Erik, 'Nationalism and Bounded Integration: What it Would Take to Construct a European Demos', *EUI Working Papers*, RSC No. 2000/34, 2000.

Checkel, Jeffrey T., 'Social Constructivisms in Global and European Politics', *ARENA Working Paper* WP 15/03, Oslo, 2003.

Checkel, Jeffrey T., 'Social Construction and Integration', *ARENA Working Paper*, 98/14, Oslo, 1998.

Checkel, Jeffrey T., 'International Norms and Domestic Politics: Bridging the Rationalist-Constructivist Divide', *European Journal of International Relations* 3, 1997: 473–95.

Chilton, Patricia, 'Mechanics of Change in Eastern Europe', in Thomas Risse-Kappen (ed.), *Bringing Transnational Relations Back In: Non-State Actors, Domestic Structures and International Institutions* (Cambridge: Cambridge University Press, 1999).

Christiansen, Thomas, Jørgensen, Knud Erik, and Wiener, Antje (eds), 'The Social Construction of Europe', Special Issue, *Journal of European Public Policy* 6/4, 1999.

Cichowski, Rachel, 'Choosing Democracy: Citizen Attitudes and the Eastern Enlargement of the European Union', *EUI Working Papers*, RSC No. 2000/12, 2000.

Collins, Stephen D., *German Policy-Making and Eastern Enlargement of the EU during the Kohl Era* (Manchester: Manchester University Press, 2002).

Conrad, Maximilian, 'Persuasion, Communicative Action and Socialization after EU Enlargement', Paper presented at the Second ECPR Pan-European Conference, Bologna, 24–26 June 2004.

Corbett, Richard, Jacobs, Frances, and Shackleton, Michael, *The European Parliament*, 4th edn (London: John Harper, 2000).

Costa, Olivier, Couvidat, Anne, and Daloz, Jean Pascal, 'The French Presidency of 2000: An Arrogant Leader?', In Ole Elgström (ed.), *European Union Council Presidencies: A Comparative Perspective* (London: Routledge, 2003), pp. 120–37.

Council of the European Union, Treaty of Accession, AA 2003 final, Brussels, 3 April 2003.

Court of Auditors of the European Communities, Annual Report, *Official Journal of the European Communities*, No. 309, Brussels, 16 November 1993.

Cowles, Maria Green, and Smith, Mike (eds), *The State of the European Union, vol. 5: Risks, Reforms, Resistance and Revival* (Oxford: Oxford University Press, 2001).

Cremona, Marise (ed.), *The Enlargement of the European Union* (Oxford: Oxford University Press, 2003).

Cremona, Marise, 'The Impact of Enlargement: External Policy and External Relations', in Marise Cremona (ed.), *The Enlargement of the European Union* (Oxford: Oxford University Press, 2003), pp. 161–208.

Day, Stephen, and Shaw, Jo, 'The Evolution of Europe's Transnational Political Parties in the Era of European Citizenship', in Tanja A. Börzel and Rachel A. Cichowski (eds), *The State of the European Union, vol. 6: Law, Politics and Society* (Oxford: Oxford University Press, 2003), pp. 149–69.

Delors, Jacques, 'An Ambitious Vision for the Enlarged Union', Speech delivered to the *Notre Europe* Conference, Brussels, 21 January 2002.

Délpèch, Therese, *International Terrorism and Europe*, Chaillot Papers No. 56 (Paris: EU Institute for Security Studies, 2002).

Diedrichs, Uwe, and Wessels, Wolfgang, 'A New Kind of Legitimacy for A New Kind Of Parliament', *European Integration online Papers* 1/6, http://eiop.or.at/eiop/texte/1997-006a.htm

Dimitrova, Antoeneta, 'Enlargement, Institution Building and the EU's Administrative Capacity', *West European Politics* 25/4, 2001: 171–90

Dimitrova, Antoeneta, and Rhinard, Mark, 'The Power of Norms in the Transposition of EU Directives', Paper Presented at the ECPR Joint Sessions, Grenada, Spain, 14–19 April 2005.

Dinan, Desmond, 'The Commission and Enlargement' in John Redmond and Glenda Rosenthal (eds), *The Expanding European Union: Past, Present and Future* (Boulder, CO: Lynne Rienner, 1998).

Dinan, Desmond, *Ever Closer Union? An Introduction to the European Community* (Basingstoke: Macmillan, 1994).

Donnelly, Jack, *Realism and International Relations* (Cambridge: Cambridge University Press, 2002).

Duchêne, Francois, 'The European Community and the Uncertainties of Independence', in Max Kohnstamm and Walter Hager (eds), *A Nation Writ Large? Foreign Policy Problems before the European Community* (Basingstoke: Macmillan, 1973).

Duisenberg, Wim, 'Lessons from the Marshall Plan', *European Affairs* 5/3, 1991: 21–5.

Elgström, Ole (ed.), *European Union Council Presidencies: A Comparative Perspective* (London: Routledge, 2003).

Elgström, Ole, 'The Honest Broker'? The Council Presidency as a Mediator', in Ole Elgström (ed.), *European Union Council Presidencies: a Comparative Perspective* (London: Routledge, 2003).

Emerson, Michael, and Noutcheva, Gergana, 'Europeanization as a Gravity Model of Democratization', *CEPS Working Document* No. 214 (Brussels: Centre for European Policy Studies, 2004).

European Commission, *Recommendation of the European Commission on Turkey's Progress Toward Accession, Communication from the Commission to the Council*, COM (2004) 656 final, Brussels, 6 October 2004.

European Commission DG Enlargement, *From Pre-Accession to Accession: Interim Evaluation of PHARE Support Allocated in 1999–2002 and Implemented until November 2003*, Consolidated Summary Report, Brussels, March 2004.

European Commission, *Comprehensive Monitoring Report 2003*, http://europa.eu.int/comm/enlargement/report_2003/

European Commission, *Towards the Enlarged Union: Strategy Paper*, COM (2002) 700 final. Available online at: http://europa.eu.int/comm/enlargement/report2002/Brussels, 9 October 2002.

European Commission, *Mid-Term Review of the Common Agricultural Policy*, COM (2002) 394 final, Brussels, 10 July 2002.

European Commission, *Common Financial Framework 2004–06 for the Accession Negotiations*, SEC (2002) 102 final, Brussels, 30 January 2002.

European Commission, *Regular Reports from the Commission on Progress Towards Accession by Each of the Candidate Countries* 2001, http://europa.eu.int/comm/enlargement/report2001/

European Commission, *Regular Reports from the Commission on Progress Towards Accession by Each of the Candidate Countries*, Brussels, 8 November 2000. Available online at: http://www.europa.eu.int/comm/enlargement/report_11_00/index.htm

European Commission, *Composite Paper: Reports on Progress Towards Accession by each of the Candidate Countries*, COM (1999) 500 final, Brussels, 13 October 1999.

European Commission, *Agenda 2000: For A Stronger and Wider Union, Bulletin of the European Union*, supplement 5/97.

European Commission, *Third and Fourth Annual Reports From the Commission to the Council and the European Parliament*, COM (95) 13 final, Brussels, 1995.

European Commission, *White Paper: Preparation of the Associated Countries of Central and Eastern Europe for Integration Into the Internal Market of the Union*, COM (95) 163 final, Brussels, 3 May 1995.

European Commission, *Communication on Relations with the Associated Countries of Central and Eastern Europe. Task force on Approximation of Laws*, COM (94) 391 final, Brussels, 16 September 1994.

European Commission, *The Europe Agreements and Beyond: A Strategy to Prepare the Countries of Central and Eastern Europe for Accession*, COM (94) 320 final, Brussels, 13 July 1994.

European Commission, *Follow Up to Commission Communication on The Europe Agreements and Beyond: A Strategy to Prepare the Countries of Central and Eastern Europe for Accession*, COM (94) 361 final, Brussels, 1994.

European Commission, *Follow-up to the European Council in Copenhagen: Market Access Measures to help the Central and Eastern European Countries*, COM (93) 321 final, Brussels, 7 July 1993.

European Commission, *Towards a Closer Association with the Countries of Central and Eastern Europe*, COM (93) 648 final, Brussels, 18 May 1993

European Commission, *Second Annual Report from the Commission to the Council and the European Parliament: On the Implementation of Community Assistance to the Countries of Central and Eastern Europe*, COM (93) 172 final, Brussels, 1993.

European Commission, *Communication on the Association Agreements with the Countries of Central and Eastern Europe: a General Outline*, Brussels, COM (90) 398 final, Brussels, 18 November 1990.

European Council, Presidency Conclusions, *Bulletin of the European Communities/Bulletin of the European Union*, various years.

European Parliament Committee on Foreign Affairs, Human Rights, Common Security and Defence Policy, *The Committee's Enlargement Activities During the Fifth Legislature (1999–2004)*, Notice to Members No. 08/2004, PE 329.317, Brussels, 5 May 2004.

European Parliament, *Report by the Committee on Budgets on the Financial Perspective on Enlargement presented by the Commission in accordance with point 25 of the Inter-institutional Agreement of 6 May 1999 on Budgetary Discipline and Improvement of the Budgetary Procedure*, Report A5–0081/2003, Brussels, 2003.

European Parliament, *Draft Report by Reimer Böge and Joan Colom i Naval on behalf of the Committee on Budgets, on the Proposal for a Decision on the Financial Perspective for Enlargement*, Report A5–0117/2003, Brussels, 2003.

European Parliament, *Draft Report on the State of the Enlargement Negotiations* (Rapporteur Elmar Brok), A5–0190/2002, Brussels, 13 June 2002.

European Parliament, *Draft Report on the Financial Impact of EU Enlargement* (Rapporteur Reimer Böge), A5–0178/2002, Brussels, 13 June 2002.

European Parliament, *Resolution on the Helsinki European Council*, B5–0327/99, B5–0353/99, B5–0354/99, B5–0357/99, Brussels, 16 December 1999.

European Parliament, *Resolution on the Preparation of the Meeting of the European Council in Helsinki on 10 and 11 December 1999*, B5–0308/99, B5–0309/99, B5–0311/99, B5–0312/99, Brussels, 2 December 1999.

European Parliament, *National Parliament's and Enlargement/Accession*, Briefing Paper No. 45, Luxembourg, 10 November 1999, PE 168.571, Brussels, 10 November 1999.

European Parliament, *The Institutional Aspects of Enlargement of the European Union*, Briefing No. 15, PE 167.299/rev.1, 21 June 1999.

European Parliament, *Enlargement: Pre Accession Strategy for Enlargement of the European Union*, Briefing No. 24 of the Parliament's Secretariat's Task Force, PE 167.631, Luxembourg, Brussels, 17 June 1998.

European Parliament, *Resolution on the Commission Proposals for Council Decisions on the Principles, Priorities, Intermediate Objectives and Conditions Contained in the Accession Partnerships*, A4–0081/1998, A4–0087/1998, Brussels, 11 March 1998.

European Parliament, *Resolution on the Communication of the Commission on 'Agenda 2000'- the 2000–2006 Financial Framework for the Union and the Future Financing System* (Rapporteur Colom i Naval), A4 – 0331/97, PE 223.701/def, Brussels, 1997.

European Parliament, *Resolution on the Communication from the Commission "Agenda 2000- For a Stronger and Wider Union" of 4 December 1997* (Rapporteur Oostlander/ Baron Crespo), A4 – 0368/97, PE 224.336/def, Brussels, 1997.

European Parliament, *Resolution on the Financing of the Enlargement of the European Union* (Rapporteur Efthymios Christodoulou), A4 – 0353/96, PE 218.268/def, Brussels, 12 December 1996.

European Parliament, *Resolution on the Commission's White Paper: Preparation of Associated Countries of Central and Eastern Europe for Integration into the Internal Market of the Union* (Rapporteur Arie Oostlander), A4–0101/96, PE 215.521/def, Brussels, 17 April 1996.

European Parliament, *Resolution on the Structure and Strategy for the European Union with Regard to its Enlargement and the Creation of a Europe-Wide Order* (Hänsch Report), A3–0189/1992, Brussels, 20 January 1993.

European Parliament, *Resolution on the Association Agreements with Hungary, Poland, Czechoslovakia*, A3–0055/1991, Brussels, 18 April 1991.

ERT (European Roundtable of Industrialists), *Opening Up: the Business Opportunities of EU Enlargement*, ERT Position Paper and Analysis of the Economic Costs and Benefits of EU Enlargement (Brussels: ERT, 2001).

European Union, Interinstitutional Agreement between the European Parliament, the Council and the European Commission on Budgetary Discipline and Improvement of the Budgetary Procedure, 1999/C 172/01, Brussels, 6 May 1999.

Fawn, Rick (ed.), *Realignments in Russian Foreign Policy* (London: Routledge, 2003).

Ferry, Martin, 'The EU and Recent Regional Reform in Poland', *Europe-Asia Studies* 55/7, 2003: 1097–116.

Fierke, Karen, and Wiener, Antje 'Constructing Institutional Interests: EU and NATO Enlargement', *Journal of European Public Policy* 6/5, 1999: 721–42.

Fischer, Joschka, 'From Confederacy to Federation – Thoughts on the Finality of European Integration', Humboldt University, Berlin, 12 May 2000.

Flockhart, Trine, 'Masters and Novices: Socialization and Social Learning through the NATO Parliamentary Assembly', *International Relations* 18/3, 2004: 361–80.

Friis, Lykke, 'Approaching the Third Half of European Grand Bargaining: The Post-Negotiation Phase of the Europe Agreement Game', *Journal of European Public Policy* 5/2, 1998: 322–38.

Friis, Lykke, '"The End of the Beginning" of Eastern Enlargement – The Luxembourg Summit and Agenda-Setting', *European Integration online Papers* 2/7, 1998, http://eiop.or.at/eiop/texte/1998–007a.htm

Friis, Lykke, *When Europe Negotiates: From Europe Agreements to Eastern Enlargement*, Ph.D. Dissertation, Department of Political Science, University of Copenhagen, 1996.

Friis, Lykke, and Murphy, Anna, 'Turbo-charged Negotiations: the EU and the Stability Pact for South Eastern Europe', *Journal of European Public Policy* 7/5, 2000: 767–86.

Friis, Lykke, and Murphy, Anna, 'The European Union and Central and Eastern Europe: Governance and Boundaries', *Journal of Common Market Studies* 37/2, 1999: 211–32.

Gardner Feldman, Lily, 'Reconciliation and Legitimacy: Foreign Relations and Enlargement of the European Union' in Thomas Banchoff and Michael P. Smith (eds), *Legitimacy and the European Union: The Contested Polity* (London: Routledge, 1999), pp. 66–90.

Garton Ash, Timothy, *History of the Present: Essays, Sketches and Dispatches from Europe in the 1990s* (London: Penguin, 2000).

George, Jim, 'Back to the Future?', in Greg Fry and Jacinta O'Hagan (eds), *Contending Images of World Politics* (Basingstoke: Macmillan, 2000), pp. 33–47.

Gilpin, Robert, 'The Richness of the Tradition of Political Realism', in Robert Keohane (ed.), *Realism and its Critics* (New York: Columbia University Press, 1986).

Ginsberg, Roy, *Foreign Policy Actions of the European Community: The Politics of Scale* (Boulder, CO: Lynne Rienner, 1989).

Gnesotto, Nicole (ed.), *EU Security and Defence Policy: The First Five Years (1999–2004)* (Paris: EU Institute for Security Studies, 2004).

Grabbe, Heather, 'The Copenhagen Deal for Enlargement, *Briefing Note* (London: Centre for European Reform, December 2002).

Grabbe, Heather, 'Europeanization Goes East: Power and Uncertainty in the EU Accession Process', Paper presented at the ECPR Joint Sessions Workshop 'Enlargement and European Governance', Turin, 22–27 March 2002.

Grabbe, Heather, and Hughes, Kirsty, *Enlarging the EU Eastwards* (London: Royal Institute of International Affairs, 1998).

Grant, Charles, 'The Eleventh of September and Beyond: the Impact on the European Union', in Lawrence Freedman (ed.), *Superterrorism: Policy Responses* (Oxford: Blackwell, 2002), pp. 135–53.

Grieco, Joseph M., 'The Maastricht Treaty, Economic and Monetary Union and the Neorealist Research Programme', *Review of International Studies* 21, 1995: 21–40.

Grieco, Joseph M., *Cooperation Among Nations: Europe, America and Non-Tariff Barriers to Trade* (Ithaca, NY: Cornell University Press, 1990).

Guzzini, Stefano, 'A Reconstruction of Constructivism in International Relations', *European Journal of International Relations* 6/2, 2000: 147–82.

Haas, Ernst, 'Does Constructivism subsume Neo-functionalism?', in Thomas Christiansen, Knud Erik Jørgensesn and Antje Wiener (eds), *The Social Construction of Europe* (London: Sage, 2001).

Haggard, Stephen, M. A. Levy, Andrew Moravcsik, and Kalypso Nicolaidis, 'Integrating the Two Halves of Europe: Theories of Interests, Bargaining and Institutions', in Stanley Hoffmann, Robert O. Keohane and Joseph S. Nye (eds), *After the Cold War: International Institutions and State Strategies in Europe, 1989–1991* (Harvard, MA: Harvard University Press, 1991).

Harris, Geoffrey, 'The Democratic Dimension of EU Enlargement: the Role of Parliament and Public Opinion', in Ronald H. Linden (ed.), *Norms and Nannies: The Impact of International Organizations on the Central and East European States* (Lanham, MD: Rowman & Littlefield, 2002), pp. 33–58.

Hassner, Pierre, 'Fixed Borders or Moving Borderlands: A New Type of Border for a New Type of Entity', in Jan Zielonka (ed.), *Europe Unbound: Enlarging and Reshaping the Boundaries of the European Union* (London: Routledge, 2002), pp. 38–50.

Hayes Renshaw, Fiona, 'The Council of Ministers', in John Peterson and Michael Shackleton (eds), *The Institutions of the European Union* (Oxford: Oxford University Press, 2002), pp. 47–70.

Hayes Renshaw, Fiona, and Wallace, Helen, *The Council of Ministers* (New York: St Martin's Press, 1997).

Hendersen, Karen (ed.), *Back to Europe: Central and Eastern Europe and the European Union* (London: University of London Press, 1999).

Higashino, Atsuko, 'For the Sake of "Peace and Security"? The Role of Security in the European Union Enlargement Eastwards', *Cooperation and Conflict* 39/4, 2004: 347–68.

Hill, Christopher, 'The Geopolitical Implications of Enlargement', in Jan Zielonka (ed.), *Europe Unbound: Enlarging and Reshaping the Boundaries of the European Union* (London: Routledge, 2002), pp. 95–116.

Hix, Simon, Noury, Abdul, and Roland, Gerard, 'Power to the Parties: Competition and Cohesion in the European Parliament, 1979–2001', *British Journal of Political Science* 34/4: 767–93.

Hubel, Herbert, 'The EU's Three-Level Game in Dealing with Neighbours', *European Foreign Affairs Review* 9, 2004: 347–62.

Hughes, James, Sasse, Gwendolyn, and Gordon, Claire, 'Conditionality and Compliance in the EU's Regional Policy and the Reform of Sub-National Government', *Journal of Common Market Studies* 42/3, 2004: 523–51.

Huntington, Samuel P., 'The Clash of Civilizations?', *Foreign Affairs* 72, 1993: 22–49.

Huntington, Samuel P., *The Clash of Civilizations and the Remaking of World Order* (New York: Simon & Schuster, 1996).

Ingham, Hilary, and Ingham, Mike (eds), *EU Expansion to the East: Prospects and Problems* (Cheltenham: Edward Elgar, 2002).

Inotai, Anders, 'The "Eastern Enlargements" of the European Union', in Marise Cremona (ed.), *The Enlargement of the European Union* (Oxford: Oxford University Press, 2003), pp. 79–104.

Jachtenfuchs, Markus, 'Deepening and Widening Integration Theory', *Journal of European Public Policy* 9/4, 2002: 650–57.

Jacobsen, John Kurt, 'Duelling Constructivisms: A Post-mortem on the Ideas Debate in Mainstream IR/IPE', *Review of International Studies* 29/1, 2003: 39–60.

Johansson-Nogués, Elisabeth, 'The Fifteen and the Accession States in the UN General Assembly: What Future for European Foreign Policy in the Coming Together of the "Old" and the "New" Europe?', *European Foreign Affairs Review* 9/1, 2004: 67–92.

Jørgensen, Knud Erik, 'Continental IR Theory: The Best Kept Secret', *European Journal of International Relations* 6/1, 2000: 9–42.

Judge, David, and Earnshaw, Robert, *The European Parliament* (Basingstoke: Palgrave, 2003).

Kagan, Robert, *Paradise and Power: America and Europe in the New World Order* (New York: Knopf, 2003).

Kassim, Hussein, and Menon, Anand, 'European Integration Since the 1990s: Member States and the European Commission', *ARENA Working Papers*, WP 6/04, Oslo: ARENA, 2004.

Keohane, Robert O., 'Theory of World Politics: Structural Realism and Beyond', in Robert Keohane (ed.), *Neorealism and its Critics* (New York: Columbia University Press, 1986).

Kochenov, Dimitry, 'EU Enlargement Law: History and Recent Developments', *European Integration online Papers* 9/6, 2005, http://eiop.or.at/eiop/texte/2005-006a.htm

Kochenov, Dimitry, 'Behind the Copenhagen Façade: The Meaning and Structure of the Copenhagen Political Criteria of Democracy and the Rule of Law', *European Integration online Papers*, 8/10, 2004, http://eiop.or.at/texte/2004-010.htm

Kohl, Helmut, Address by Chancellor Kohl to the Bundestag, *Bulletin*, No. 103, 16 December 1996.

Laffan, Brigid, 'The European Union and its Institutions as "Identity Builders" in R. K. Hermann, Thomas Risse, and Mark Brewer (eds), *Transnational Identities: Becoming European in the EU* (Lanham, MD: Rowman & Littlefield, 2004), pp. 75–96.

Lebow, Richard Ned, 'The Long Peace, the End of the Cold War, and the Failure of Realism', *International Organization*, Volume 48, Number 2, Spring 1994, pp. 249–77.

Leipold, Helmut, 'The Eastwards Enlargement of the European Union: Opportunities and Obstacles', *Aussen Politik* 46/2, 1995: 126–35.

Liebich, Andre, 'Ethnic Minorities and Implications of EU Enlargement', in Jan Zielonka (ed.), *Europe Unbound: Enlarging and Reshaping the Boundaries of the European Union* (London: Routledge, 2002), pp. 117–36.

Linden, Ronald H. (ed.), *Norms and Nannies: The Impact of International Organizations on the Central and East European States* (Lanham, MD: Rowman & Littlefield, 2002).

Lindstrom, Gustav, 'On the Ground: EDSP Operations', in Nicole Gnesotto (ed.), *EU Security and Defence Policy: The First Five Years (1999–2004)* (Paris: EU Institute for Security Studies, 2004).

Ludlow, Peter, *The Making of the New Europe: The European Councils in Brussels and Copenhagen 2002*, European Council Commentary 2/1 (Brussels: EuroComment, 2004).

Lynch, Dov (ed.), *What Russia Sees*, Chaillot Papers, No. 74 (Paris: EU Institute for Security Studies, 2005).

Lynch, Dov, *Russia Faces Europe*, Chaillot Papers, No. 60 (Paris: EU Institute for Security Studies, 2003).

Manners, Ian, 'Normative Power Europe: A Contradiction in Terms?', *Journal of Common Market Studies* 40/2, 2002: 235–58.

Mannin, Mike (ed.), *Pushing Back the Boundaries: The European Union and Central and Eastern Europe* (Manchester: Manchester University Press, 1999).

March, James G., and Olsen, Johan P., 'The Logic of Appropriateness', *ARENA Working Papers*, WP 04/09, Oslo, 2004.

March, James G., and Olsen, Johan P., 'Institutional Perspectives on Governance', *ARENA Working Paper* 94/2, Oslo, 1994.

Maresceau, Marc, 'Pre-accession', in Marise Cremona (ed.), *The Enlargement of the European Union* (Oxford: Oxford University Press, 2003), pp. 9–42.

Maresceau, Marc, 'The EU Pre-Accession Strategies: a Political and Legal Analysis', in Marc Maresceau and Erwan Lannon (eds), *The EU's Enlargement and Mediterranean Strategies: A Comparative Analysis* (Basingstoke: Palgrave, 2001).

Maresceau, Marc, *Enlarging the European Union* (Harlow: Longman, 1997).

Mayhew, Alan, 'The Financial and Budgetary Impact of Enlargement and Accession', *SEI Working Paper* No. 65, Brighton: Sussex European Institute, 2003.

Mayhew, Alan, *Recreating Europe: The European Union's Policy towards Central and Eastern Europe*, 1st edn (Cambridge: Cambridge University Press, 1998).

Mearsheimer, John, *The Tragedy of the Great Powers* (New York: Norton, 2001).

Mearsheimer, John, 'Back to the Future: Instability in Europe After the Cold War', *International Security* 15/4, 1990: 5–56.

Menéndez, Augustin José, 'A Pious Europe? Why Europe Should Not Define Itself as Christian', *ARENA Working Paper*, No. 10/04, Oslo, 2004.

Michalski, Anna, and Wallace, Helen, *The European Community: The Challenge of Enlargement* (London: RIIA, 1992).

Miles, Lee, 'Theoretical Considerations', in Neil Nugent (ed.), *European Union Enlargement* (Basingstoke: Palgrave, 2004), pp. 253–65.

Miles, Lee, 'Enlargement: From the Perspective of Fusion', *Cooperation and Conflict* 37/2, 2002: 190–8.

Missiroli, Antonio, 'EDSP – How it Works', in Nicole Gnesotto (ed.), *EU Security and Defence Policy: The First Five Years (1999–2004)* (Paris: EU Institute for Security Studies, 2004), pp. 55–72.

Missiroli, Antonio (ed.), *Enlargement and European Defence after 11 September*, Chaillot Papers, No. 53 (Paris: EU Institute for Security Studies, 2002).

Morata, Francesc, and Fernandez, Ana-Mar, 'The Spanish Presidencies: 1989, 1995 and 2002', in Ole Elgström (ed.), *European Union Council Presidencies: A Comparative Perspective* (London: Routledge, 2003), pp. 173–90.

Moravcsik, Andrew, 'The European Constitutional Compromise and the Legacy of Neo-functionalism', *Journal of European Public Policy* 12/2, 2005: 1–37.

Moravcsik, Andrew, 'Is Something Rotten in the State of Denmark? – Constructivism and European Integration', *Journal of European Public Policy* 6/4, 1999: 669–81.

Moravcsik, Andrew, 'A New Statecraft? Supranational Entrepreneurs and International Cooperation', *International Organization* 53/2, 1999: 267–306.

Moravcsik, Andrew, *The Choice for Europe: Social Purpose and State Power from Messina to Maastricht* (Ithaca, NY: Cornell University Press, 1998).

Moravcsik, Andrew, 'Studying Europe After the Cold War: A Perspective from International Relations', *TKI Working Papers on European Integration and Regime Formation* (Esbjerg: South Jutland University Press, 1996).

Moravcsik, Andrew, 'Preferences and Power in the European Community: A Liberal Intergovernmentalist Approach', *Journal of Common Market Studies* 31/4, 1993: 473–524.

Moravcsik, Andrew, and Vachudova, Milada Ana, 'National Interests, State Power, and EU Enlargement', *East European Politics and Society* 17/1, 2003: 42–57.

Morgenthau, Hans, *Politics Among the Nations: The Struggle for Power and Peace*, 6th edn (New York: Knopf, 1985).

Mungiu-Pippidi, Alina, 'Facing the "desert of Tartars": The Eastern Border of Europe', in Jan Zielonka (ed.), *Europe Unbound: Enlarging and Reshaping the Boundaries of the European Union* (London: Routledge, 2002), pp. 51–77.

Neumann, Iver B., 'European Identity, EU Expansion, and the Integration/Exclusion Nexus', *Alternatives* 23, 1998: 397–416.

Neumann, Iver B., 'Self and Other in International Relations', *European Journal of International Relations* 2, 1996: 139–74.

Neumann, Iver B., and Welsh, Jennifer, 'The "Other" in European Identity: An Addendum to the Literature on International Societies', *Review of International Studies* 17, 1991: 327–45.

Neunreither, Karlheinz, 'The European Parliament and Enlargement, 1973–2000', in John Redmond and Glenda Rosenthal (eds), *The Expanding European Union: Past, Present and Future,* (Boulder, CO: Lynne Rienner, 1998).

Nicolaides, Phedon, 'Preparing for Accession to the European Union: How to Establish Capacity for Effective and Credible Application of EU Rules', in Marise Cremona (ed.), *The Enlargement of the European Union* (Oxford: Oxford University Press, 2003), pp. 43–78.

Niemann, Arne, 'The PHARE Programme and the Concept of Spillover: Neofunctionalism in the Making', *Journal of European Public Policy* 5/3, 1998: 428–46.

Nugent, Neil (ed.), *European Union Enlargement* (Basingstoke: Palgrave, 2004).

O'Brennan, John, 'Ireland's Return to "Normal" EU Voting Patterns: the 2002 Nice Treaty Referendum', *European Political Science* 2/2, 2003: 5–14.

O'Brennan, John, 'Enlargement as a Factor in the Irish Referendum on the Nice Treaty', *Perceptions: Journal of International Affairs* VII/III, 2002: 78–94.

Onuf, Nicholas, *World of Our Making: Rules and Rule in Social Theory and International Relations* (Columbia: University of South Carolina Press, 1989).

Papadimitriou, Dimitris, and Phinnemore, David, 'Europeanization, Conditionality and Domestic Change: The Twinning Exercise and Administrative Reform in Romania', *Journal of Common Market Studies* 42/3, 2004: 619–39.

Parland, Thomas, *The Extreme Nationalist Threat in Russia* (London: Routledge, 2004).

Peterson, John, and Bomberg, Elisabeth, *Decision-Making in the European Union* (Basingstoke: Macmillan, 1999).

Pettai, Vello, and Zielonka, Jan (eds), *The Road to the European Union, vol. 2: Estonia, Latvia and Lithuania* (Manchester: Manchester University Press, 2003).

Pflueger, Frederik, 'Poland and the European Union', *Aussen Politik* 46/3, 1995: 228–38.

Phinnemore, David, *Association: Stepping-stone or Alternative to EU Membership?* (Sheffield: Sheffield Academic Press, 1999).

Pierson, Paul, 'The Path to European Integration: A Historic-Institutionalist Analysis', in Wayne Sandholtz and Alec Stone Sweet (eds), *European Integration and Supranational Governance* (Oxford: Oxford University Press, 1998), pp. 27–58.

Pinder, John (ed.), *The European Community and Eastern Europe* (London: Pinter/RIIA, 1991).

Pippan, Christian, 'The Rocky Road to Europe: The EU's Stabilisation and Association Process for the Western Balkans and the Principle of Conditionality', *European Foreign Affairs Review* 9, 2004: 219–45.

Politkovskaya, Anna, *Putin's Russia* (London: Harvill Press, 2004).

Pollack, Mark A., *The Engines of European Integration: Delegation, Agency, and Agenda-Setting in the EU* (New York: Oxford University Press, 2002).

Pollack, Mark A. 'Delegation, Agency and Agenda-Setting in the Treaty of Amsterdam', *European Integration online Papers* 3, 1999; http://eiop.or.at/texte/1999–006.htm

Pollack, Mark A., 'Delegation, Agency, and Agenda Setting in the European Community', *International Organization* 51/1, 1997: 99–134.

Preston, Christopher, *Enlargement and Integration* (London and New York: Routledge, 1997).

Prodi, Romano, 'Bringing the Family Together', Speech to the Hungarian Academy of Sciences, Speech/01/158, Budapest, 4 April 2001.

Prodi, Romano, 'Catching the Tide of History: Enlargement and the Future of the Union', Paul Henri Spaak Foundation, Speech/00/374, Brussels, 11 October 2000.

Rasmussen, Anders, 'Institutional Games Rational Actors Play – The Empowering of the European Parliament', *European Integration online Papers* 4/1, 2000; http://eiop.or.at/eiop/texte/2000–001a.htm

Raunio, Tapio, *Party Group Behaviour in the European Parliament: An Analysis of Transnational Political Groups in the 1989–1994 Parliament* (Tampere: University of Tampere Press, 1996).

Redmond, John, and Rosenthal, Glenda (eds), *The Expanding European Union: Past, Present and Future* (Boulder, CO: Lynne Rienner, 1998).

Rein, Martin, and Schön, Martin, 'Frame-reflective Discourse', in Peter Wagner *et al.* (eds), *Social Sciences and Modern States* (Cambridge: Cambridge University Press, 1991).

Risse, Thomas, *et al.*, 'To Euro or Not To Euro? The EMU and Identity Politics in the European Union', *European Journal of International Relations* 5/2, 1999: 147–87.

Risse-Kappen, Thomas, 'Democratic Peace – War-like Democracies? A Social Constructivist Interpretation of the Liberal Argument', *European Journal of International Relations* 1/4, 1995: 491–517.

Robinson, Neil, *Russia: A State of Uncertainty* (London: Routledge, 2002).

Ruggie, John, *Constructing the World Polity: Essays in International Institutionalization* (New York: Routledge, 1998).

Ruggie, John, 'What Makes the World Hang Together? Neo-Utilitarianism and the Social Constructivist Challenge', *International Organization* 52/4, 1998: 855–85.

Rupnik, Jacques, and Zielonka, Jan (eds), *The Road to the European Union, vol. 1: The Czech and Slovak Republics* (Manchester: Manchester University Press, 2003).

Russet, Bruce, 'A Neo-Kantian Perspective: Democracy, Interdependence and International Organizations in Building Security Communities', in Emmanuel Adler and Michael Barnett (eds), *Security Communities* (Cambridge: Cambridge University Press, 1998).

Sakwa, Richard, *Putin: Russia's Choice* (London: Routledge, 2004).

Sakwa, Richard, *Russian Politics and Society* (London: Routledge, 2002).

Sandholtz, Wayne, and Stone Sweet, Alec, *European Integration and Supranational Governance* (Oxford: Oxford University Press, 1998).

Saryusz-Wolski, Jacek, 'Looking to the Future', in Antonio Missiroli (ed.), *Enlargement and European Defence after 11 September*, Chaillot Papers, No. 53 (Paris: EU Institute for Security Studies, 2002), pp. 55–69.

Schimmelfennig, Frank, *The EU, NATO, and the Integration of Europe* (Cambridge: Cambridge University Press, 2003).

Schimmelfennig, Frank, 'The Community Trap: Liberal Norms, Rhetorical Action and the Eastern Enlargement of the European Union', *International Organization* 55/1, 2001: 47–80.

Schimmelfennig, Frank, 'The Double Puzzle of EU Enlargement: Liberal Norms, Rhetorical Action, and the Decision to Expand to the East', *ARENA Working Papers* No. 15, Oslo, 1999.

Schimmelfennig, Frank, and Sedelmeier, Ulrich, *The Europeanization of Central and Eastern Europe* (Ithaca, NY: Cornell University Press, 2005).

Schimmelfennig, Frank, and Sedelmeier, Ulrich, 'Governance by Conditionality: EU Rule Transfer to the Candidate Countries of Central and Eastern Europe', *Journal of European Public Policy* 11/4, 2004: 661–79.

Schimmelfennig, Frank, and Sedelmeier, Ulrich, 'Theorizing EU Enlargement: Research Focus, Hypothesis, and the State of Research', *Journal of European Public Policy* 9/4, 2002: 500–28.

Schimmelfennig, Frank, Engbert, Stefan, and Knobel, Heike, 'The Conditions of Conditionality: The Impact of the EU on Democracy and Human Rights in European Non-Member States', Paper presented at the ECPR Joint Sessions Workshop 'Enlargement and European Governance', Turin, 22–27 March 2002.

Schmitter, Philippe, 'Examining the Present Euro-Polity with the Help of Past Theories', in Gary Marks, Fritz W. Scharpf, Philippe Schmitter, and Wolfgang Streek, *Governance in the European Union* (London: Sage, 1996), pp. 1–14.

Scully, Roger, *Becoming Europeans? Attitudes, Behaviour, and Socialization in the European Parliament* (Oxford: Oxford University Press, 2005).

Sedelmeier, Ulrich, 'Sectoral Dynamics of EU Enlargement: Advocacy, Access, and Alliances in a Composite Polity', *Journal of European Public Policy* 9/4, 2002: 627–49.

Sedelmeier, Ulrich, 'EU Enlargement, Identity and the Analysis of European Foreign Policy: Identity Formation through Policy Practice', *EUI Working Papers*, RSC No. 2003/13, Florence, 2001.

Sedelmeier, Ulrich, 'East of Amsterdam: The Implications of the Amsterdam Treaty for Eastern Enlargement', in Karlheinz Neunreither and Antje Wiener (eds), *European Integration After Amsterdam: Institutional Dynamics and Prospects for Democracy* (Oxford: Oxford University Press, 2000).

Sedelmeier, Ulrich and Wallace, Helen, 'Eastern Enlargement: Strategy or Second Thoughts?', in Helen Wallace and William Wallace, (eds), *Policy-Making in the European Union*, 4th edn (Oxford: Oxford University Press, 2000), pp. 427–60.

Sherrington, Pippa, *The Council of Ministers: Political Authority in the European Union* (London: Pinter, 2000).

Sjursen, Helene, 'Why Expand? The Question of Justification in the EU's Enlargement Policy', *ARENA Working Paper* WP 01/6, Oslo, 2001.

Sjursen, Helene, and Smith, Karen E., 'Justifying EU Foreign Policy: The Logics Underpinning EU Enlargement', *ARENA Working Paper* WP 01/1, Oslo, 2001.

Skjaerseth, Jon Birger, and Wettestad, Jorgen, 'EU Enlargement: Challenges to the Effectiveness of EU Environmental Policy', Paper presented at the ECPR Second Pan-European Conference, Bologna, 24–26 June 2004, http://www.jhubc.it/ecpr-bologna

Smith, Anthony D., *Nations and Nationalism in a Global Era* (Cambridge: Polity Press, 1995).

Smith, Anthony D., 'A Europe of Nations – Or the Nations of Europe? *Journal of Peace Research* 30, 1993: 129–35.

Smith, Anthony D., 'National Identity and the Idea of European Unity', *International Affairs* 68, 1992: 55–76.

Smith, Karen E., 'The Evolution and Application of EU Membership Conditionality' in Marise Cremona (ed.), *The Enlargement of the European Union* (Oxford: Oxford University Press, 2003), pp. 105–40.

Smith, Karen E., *The Making of European Foreign Policy: The Case of Eastern Europe* (Basingstoke: Macmillan, 1999).

Smith, Steve, 'Social Constructivisms and European Studies: A Reflectivist Critique', *Journal of European Public Policy* 6/4, 1999: 682–91.

Sørensen, Georg, *Changes in Statehood: The Transformation of International Relations* (Basingstoke: Palgrave, 2001).

Soveroski, Marie, 'Agenda 2000: A Blueprint for Successful EU Enlargement?', *Eipascope* 1998/1: 1–4.

Stawarska, Renata, 'EU Enlargement from the Polish Perspective', *Journal of European Public Policy* 6/5, 1999: 822–38.

Stone Sweet, Alec, Sandholtz, Wayne, and Fligstein, Neil (eds), *The Institutionalization of Europe* (Oxford: Oxford University Press, 2001).

Szcerbiak, Aleks, and Taggart, Paul (eds), *EU Enlargement and Referendums* (London: Routledge, 2005).

Tallberg, Jonas, 'The Power of the Presidency: Brokerage, Efficiency and Distribution in EU Negotiations', *Journal of Common Market Studies* 42/5, 2004: 999–1022.

Tallberg, Jonas, 'The Agenda-Shaping Powers of the Council Presidency', in Ole Elgström (ed.), *European Union Council Presidencies: A Comparative Perspective* (London: Routledge, 2003), pp. 18–37.

Tewes, Henning, 'Between Deepening and Widening: Role Conflict in Germany's Enlargement Policy', *West European Politics* 21/2, 1998: 117–33.

Tilikainen, Teija, 'The Finnish Presidency of 1999: Pragmatism and Promotion of Finland's Position in Europe', in Ole Elgström (ed.), *European Union Council Presidencies: A Comparative Perspective* (London: Routledge, 2003).

Tremosa, Sonia Piedrafita, 'The EU Eastern Enlargement: Policy Choices of the Spanish Government', *European Integration online Papers* 9/3, 2005, http://eiop.or.at/eiop/texte/2005-003a.htm

Trouille, Jean Marc, 'France, Germany and the Eastwards Expansion of the EU: Towards a Common Ostpolitik', in Hilary Ingham and Mike Ingham (eds), *EU Expansion to the East: Prospects and Problems* (Cheltenham: Edward Elgar, 2002), pp. 50–64.

Ungerer, Werner, 'The Development of the EC and its Relationship with Central and Eastern Europe', *Aussen Politik* 41/3, 1990: 225–35.

Vachudova, Milada Ana, 'The Leverage of International Institutions on Democratising States: Eastern Europe and the European Union', RSC No. 2001/33, Robert Schuman Centre for Advanced Studies, Florence: European University Institute, 2001.

van den Bröek, Hans, Speech to 'Forum 2000' Conference, Speech 98/198, Prague, 13 October 1998.

van den Bröek, Hans, Speech to the EU Enlargement Conference organized by the International Press Institute, Speech 97/264, Brussels, 27 November 1997.

Verheugen, Günter, Speech at the 100th Meeting of the PHARE Management Committee, Brussels, 12 June 2003.

Verheugen, Günter, 'Changing the History, Shaping the Future', Speech at the University of Tartu, Speech 01/215, Tartu, Estonia, 19 April 2001.

Verheugen, Günter 'Enlargement is Irreversible', Speech to the European Parliament, Speech 00/351, Brussels, 3 October 2000.

Verhofsdadt, Guy, 'The Enlargement of the European Union: A Unique Opportunity to Restore the Unity of Europe', Speech to the Hungarian Academy of Sciences, Budapest, 13 March 2001.

Wæver, Ole, 'Insecurity, Security and Asecurity in the West European non-war Community', in Emanuel Adler and Michael Barnett (eds), *Security Communities* (Cambridge: Cambridge University Press, 1998), pp. 69–118.

Wallace, Helen, 'EU Enlargement: A Neglected Subject', in Maria Green Cowles and Mike Smith (eds), *State of the European Union, vol. 5: Risks, Reforms, Resistance and Revival* (Oxford: Oxford University Press, 2000), pp. 149–63.

Wallace, Helen, 'Which Europe Is It Anyway? The 1998 Stein Rokkan Lecture', *European Journal of Political Research* 35, 1998: 287–306.

Wallace, Helen, and Wallace, William (eds), *Policymaking in the European Union*, 4th edn (Oxford: Oxford University Press, 2000).

Wallace, William, 'Where Does Europe End? Dilemmas of Inclusion and Exclusion', in Jan Zielonka (ed.), *Europe Unbound: Enlarging and Reshaping the Boundaries of the European Union* (London: Routledge, 2002), pp. 78–94.

Wallström, Margot, Speech to the Environment Committee of the European Parliament, Speech 00/228, Brussels, 20 June 2000.

Wallström, Margot, Speech to the Polish Parliament, Speech 00/77, Warsaw, 9 March 2000.

Waltz, Kenneth, *Theory of International Politics* (New York: Random House, 1979).

Wendt, Alexander, *Social Theory of International Politics* (Cambridge: Cambridge University Press, 1999).

Wendt, Alexander, 'Anarchy Is What States Make of It: The Social Construction of Power Politics', *International Organization* 46, 1992: 391–407.

Wiener, Antje, 'Contested Compliance: Interventions on the Normative Structure of World Politics', *European Journal of International Relations* 10/2, 2004: 189–234.

Wiener, Antje, 'Constructivism: the Limits of Bridging Gaps', *Journal of International Relations and Development* 6/3, 2003: 252–75.

Wincott, Daniel, 'Institutional Interaction and European Integration: Towards an Everyday Critique of Liberal Intergovernmentalism', *Journal of Common Market Studies* 33/4, 1995: 597–609.

Wind, Marlene, 'Europe Toward A Post-Hobbesian Political Order: Constructivism and European Integration', *EUI Working Paper*, European University Institute, Florence, 1996

Wistrich, Ernst, *The United States of Europe* (London: Routledge, 1994).

Witte, Bruno De, 'Politics vs Law in the EU's Approach to Minorities', in Jan Zielonka (ed.), *Europe Unbound: Enlarging and Reshaping the Boundaries of the European Union* (London: Routledge, 2002), pp. 137–60.

Zaborowski, Marcin, 'Poland, Germany and EU Enlargement: The Rising Prominence of Domestic Politics', *ZEI Discussion Paper* C 51, Centre for European Integration Studies, Bonn, 1999.

Zielonka, Jan (ed.), *Europe Unbound: Enlarging and Reshaping the Boundaries of the European Union* (London: Routledge, 2002).

Zielonka, Jan, 'Ambiguity as a Remedy for the EU's Eastward Enlargement', *Cambridge Review of International Affairs* XII/1, 1998: 14–29.

Index